MORAL MONOPOLY

The Rise and Fall of the Catholic Church in Modern Ireland

For Aileen
and
Luke

Moral Monopoly

The Rise and Fall of the Catholic Church in Modern Ireland

TOM INGLIS

University College Dublin Press

Preas Choláiste Ollscoile Bhaile Átha Cliath

First published 1987 by Gill and Macmillan Ltd
This second edition first published 1998 by University College Dublin Press
Newman House, St Stephen's Green, Dublin 2

ISBN 1 900621 12 6

Cataloguing in Publication data available from the British Library

Typeset in 10/12 Sabon by Seton Music Graphics, Bantry, Co. Cork, Ireland

Index by Helen Litton

Printed in Ireland by Colour Books, Dublin

Contents

Acknowledgements

Much more was involved in producing this second edition than I had originally envisaged. The new chapter 9, which analyses the changes which have taken place in the Irish Catholic Church in the last ten years, is twice as long as I had thought it would be. I also ended up rewriting the introduction and conclusion, and including new sections in many of the other chapters. I hope that I have improved the argument, and made the book more enjoyable.

Eoin O'Mahony assisted me assiduously in this task without great recompense. I am also grateful to Stephen Mennell, who provided the impetus and encouragement to produce this new edition. He also acted as an astute editor, adding to my knowledge of sociology and English grammar. Barbara Mennell, as Executive Editor of UCD Press, was always most supportive. Among the many other people who helped me in my research, I would like to thank, in particular, Ann Hanley of the Episcopal Commission for Research and Development. Much of the original research was completed while I was a doctoral student at Southern Illinois University. I owe a great deal intellectually to the many ideas and insights provided by faculty and colleagues while I was there, especially Tom Burger and Charles Lemert. I thank my colleagues in the Department of Sociology in UCD who in conversations and seminars have helped clarify my thoughts and arguments. Michael Cussen has been a great friend and critic over the years. I am also grateful for the support and encouragement of other friends and members of my family who fortunately are too numerous to mention. My wife Aileen MacKeogh, son Arron and daughter Olwen have borne the greatest burdens. As always, they have been my emotional bedrock during the production of the text. The book is dedicated with love to Aileen, and is in memory of our son Luke.

Tom Inglis
Dublin, December 1997

1
Introduction

When I was about ten years old I had a particular devotion to Our Lady. It came from a deep but simple faith in the Catholic Church. My mother was a devout Catholic. She went to Mass and received Holy Communion every day. She did all the things a good Catholic mother ever did. She made sure that we knew our prayers and that we said them every morning and night. Our lives were rounded by large and small Catholic rituals. We did not talk much about religion; we practised it. There was an emphasis on saying the rosary every night and going to Mass on Sunday. There were special observances such as not eating meat on Fridays, doing penance at Lent (usually giving up sweets or attending Mass every day) and what I liked best, the May and October devotions. As children and not fully fledged devotees, we were not expected to receive Holy Communion every time we went to Mass. But there was a routine, enforced through the school, of going to Confession once a month, and then, as soon as possible afterwards and before committing another mortal sin, to receive Holy Communion. We tried to live in a state of grace, but even then I realised that when it came to being spiritual and moral, others, including my mother, were in a different league.

It was during the May devotions that I got the idea of setting up my own shrine to Our Lady in my bedroom. I already had a beautiful statue of her. It was then a matter of getting a collection of small vases so that I could festoon the top of the dresser with May flowers; just like the altar in the Church. I would kneel in front of the dresser and say the rosary. I had no doubt that I was devotee and there was even talk of me having a vocation. What I remember most from those evenings spent alone in my bedroom was a sense of serenity, peace and consolation. I was able to lose myself in my rhythmic prayers and my unreflected, transcendental gaze upon Our Lady.

But those days were not just filled with innocent bliss. They were filled with fear. I knew I was a sinner and I dreaded the thought of dying with a mortal sin on my soul and being condemned to the fires of hell for all eternity. I also lived in awe and dread of priests. They were dark, distant and unapproachable figures. The figures of power who instilled fear in me were the priests, the De La Salle brothers who educated me and the policemen. But the brothers and police did not have the same awfulness as the priests. Priests would appear on the altar in magnificent vestments. They had direct access to sacredness. They would open the tabernacle and raise the host and I would kneel before them and receive Our Lord. I felt so pure and holy then. It was that sense of moral purity and superiority which enabled me to abide by the strict regulations: never missing Mass on Sundays; fasting from the midnight before receiving Holy Communion; and never receiving it with a mortal sin on my soul.

To understand the power of the Catholic Church in Ireland and how it came to develop a monopoly over morality, it is necessary to understand how being a Catholic occupied the minds and hearts of Irish people. There was a logic and a structure to the way Catholicism organised my life, helped me read and understand the world in which I lived, gave me consolation for the trials, tribulations and sorrows of life, gave me a sense of identity and a meaning in life and, most of all, gave me hope for the world to come and my eternal salvation. Whatever else this life was, it was only a preparation for the next. And so it was crucial to embody the rules of life which emerged from Christ's parables; to trust in God; and to hold on to the belief that the last shall be first and that the poor shall inherit the earth.

The notion that the Irish are almost naturally Catholic has become part of what is sometimes accurately referred to as 'the simple faith'. The criterion of a good Irish Catholic has traditionally been perceived as one who received the sacraments regularly and who followed the rules and regulations of the Church. Innocence was regarded as a virtue. People were not encouraged to question their religion or their priests. The appropriate responses to any questions one might have about religion were learnt off by heart in the catechism. One could be forgiven for breaking the rules of the Church, but questioning them was a different matter. The dominance of 'the simple faith' meant that many Irish Catholics did not develop an intellectual interest in, or critical attitude towards, their religion. This uncritical attitude was also evident in the public sphere. While there were frequent public debates and critical assessments made of the State, political parties, trade unions and other national organisations, the Catholic Church remained above rigorous criticism and public accountability. Irish Catholics secretly bickered and complained about the Church, often in anger and frustration, without being coherent or consistent in their criticisms.

Much of this can be related to the fact that the Church dominated Irish education, and was slow to accept or encourage criticism. The Church demanded reverence and obedience and was inclined to see any public debate about its position as part of what one bishop termed 'a cancer of criticism and dissent' which 'is the result of ignorance' or 'downright antagonism'.[1] Criticism of the Church, particularly if it came from outsiders, was dismissed as being unobjective, unscholarly, and out of keeping with the ethos of Irish society.[2] One can also think of many Irish authors whose literary genius would appear to have been born on the back of a critical reaction to the Church and its influence in their lives. Their literary descriptions provided some good insights into how the Church has operated within Irish society. Yet, in the past, many of these writers were banned and dismissed as disloyal misfits.

But 'the simple faith' and the walls of censorship and silence which in the past protected the Church from criticism are beginning to crumble. The Catholic Church in Ireland is beginning to learn to accept criticism and to defend its position reasonably, rather than by enforcing censorship and appealing to dogma and tradition. One of the major changes which has taken place in Ireland over the past ten years has been the increase in debate in the public sphere, particularly the media, about the role and function of religion and the Catholic Church in Irish society. Much of this debate has been prompted by scandals involving priests and brothers and this has led to a discussion about broader issues such as celibacy, women as priests and the decline in vocations. But a process of critical reflection has also been taking place within the institutional Church about its position and future in Irish society. The scandals and problems facing the Catholic Church are being seen as challenges. There are now regular conferences and public debates about the Church, the faith and Irish culture.[3] These debates represent the reaction of a grassroots social movement within the Church, which is often independent of the Hierarchy. While critical reflection about the Church has always been included in religious journals such as *The Furrow, Doctrine and Life*, and *Studies*, the strength and depth of the questioning have increased significantly. Since the first edition of this book appeared ten years ago, there has been a dramatic increase in the variety and number of writings about the Catholic Church. There has been a radical break in the content and form of such writing, in who is writing it, and in the way in which they are writing. Not only do the authors critically reflect about themselves and the Church in which they have been brought up and lived, but they write in an honest, open and accessible style. They are not writing for an internal, specialised, institutional audience, but for an interested and committed laity. Many of them are critical of the Church and where it is going. Most are pessimistic about its future. One of the most critically reflective publications was Fr Joe Dunn's *No Lions in the Hierarchy*, which remained on the non-fiction bestseller list for many weeks in 1994. It was a commentary on the current state of the Catholic Church around the world, but particularly in Ireland. He discussed many controversial topics, such as the leadership of Pope John Paul II, the making of Irish bishops, celibacy, women in the Church, birth control, war and violence. Many of the stories emanated from the 350 documentaries he made for *Radharc*, a regular series of religious programmes on Irish television over a twenty-five year period. He argued that the decline in the institutional Church was related to a diminished view of the priesthood; a decline in the motive of fear; an insulation from death which was not present in previous generations; the disappearance of family prayer; the dominance of the media; the difficulties with celibacy; diminishing support from within the family; and the lack of interest among existing priests, nuns and brothers in recruiting new members.[4] Another priest, Fr Tony Flannery, has argued that the Catholic Church as it once was in Ireland is dying. The central problem is the dramatic drop in vocations in the last thirty years and that the majority of religious are now over sixty years of age. They were trained in the 1940s and 1950s when the old system was solidly in place. He argues that some religious order priests have adapted to the Church in the modern world, but many have not. There is a generation gap between the old guard and the new recruits. He suggests that while the immediate future for the Catholic Church necessarily involves radical downsizing, this might not necessarily be a bad thing and the future may be brighter elsewhere.[5] Another more radical critique of the Church was by the dissident priest Fr Pat Buckley, who is effectively banned from administering the sacraments – primarily because of his practice of remarrying divorced Catholics.[6] The central argument of these writings is that Irish Catholicism is dying, that nothing new is emerging from within the Church to save it, and that most of the blame lies with the Vatican and, specifically, the present Pope.

However, the role of debate and discussion in a non-democratic institution such as the Church is still a problem. There are still regular instances of priests and bishops being silenced. This was evident in the controversial dismissal in 1994 of Fr Kevin Hegarty as editor of *Intercom* (an internal magazine primarily orientated towards diocesan priests) for provoking what was deemed to be an unbalanced debate on controversial issues within the Church. So while critical reflection within the Church about the power of the Church has grown significantly in the last ten years, there is still a determined effort to guard and defend Roman orthodoxy.[7] Most of what is written about the Catholic Church in Ireland still comes from liturgical, pastoral and theological perspectives. These writings are part of the official, institutional discourse of the Church. They often carry a clearance certificate from the Church censor and an imprimatur or official approval from the local archbishop.

As well as debate within the institution, there has also been a series of critical studies of the Church from lay writers. Perhaps the strongest of these was from the feminist scholar Mary Condren. She wrote a detailed historical analysis of the Church's attempts to suppress women through controlling their bodies and their sexuality. Tracing the history of the Catholic Church from the age of Eve and Brigit through to the present reign of Mary, she argued that the Catholic Church has fully realised itself as a patriarchal institution. This, Condren argued, is evident in the fact that over the centuries the centre of the Church's theological concern, as formulated in its ethical teaching, has been the male seed rather than the community, the family, or the good of the woman.[8] There is, then, according to Condren, no future for the Catholic Church in Ireland, or elsewhere, until women return to the centre of religion – not just through ending celibacy and allowing women to become priests, but by bringing back women as goddesses.[9]

Mary Kenny also has a very pessimistic view of the future of Catholic Ireland. She links the decline in the institutional Church to the decline in the Catholic faith as a central part of Irish culture. She argues that the media have played a central role in its decline. She suggests Catholicism will become like the Irish language: there will be a minority who will hold on passionately to the faith, but for the majority it will be something with which they get involved now and again depending on the moment, mood, occasion, age or crisis.

Although Catholicism has marked certain values, and has deposited its heritage in the culture, it is widely accepted that the Catholic Church means less to young people in Ireland today than it has ever done in the course of Christian history. The young Irish no longer see Catholicity as part of their identity.[10]

Contrary to these pessimistic views, there have been several commentators, particularly social researchers, who have taken a more optimistic view of the present condition and future of the Catholic Church in Ireland. Many of their comments are based on an analysis and reading of findings from social surveys and comparing the results with those obtained from other European countries. They point out that the level of religious belief and practice among Irish Catholics is still the highest in Europe, if not the world. The spiritual life of Irish people is still firmly embedded in the Catholic Church. They agree that there have been changes in the level of adherence to particular Church teachings, especially on issues of sexual morality, but argue that Catholics have never been uniform in their commitment to the Church and have over the centuries regularly distanced themselves from doctrinal teachings which did not suit them. They claim that the old type of traditional, conservative Catholic is giving way to a new Catholic who is certainly different, but not necessarily any less religious, than his or her ancestors. Most of all, they argue that changes in the last thirty years are no indication of long-term trends in the Catholic Church.

For those who are concerned about religious decline in Ireland, the very uncertainty about the causes and direction of religious change might well be taken as a hopeful sign. It means that the falling away from religion which has proceeded a certain distance in Ireland has no well-defined inevitability about it. There is no universal force which has always and everywhere undermined religion and which now, at last, has reached Ireland's shores. Rather, there is a far more complex ebb and flow in religious affairs which means that the way is always open for religion to revive as well as decline. Thus, in turn, in the face of secularising tendencies, when religion is ebbing from people's lives, those with religious commitment always have the possibility and the challenge of finding the key that will unlock the door to a new religious flow in Irish life.[11]

Central to this argument is that there is no necessary connection between industrialisation and modernisation on the one hand and secularisation on the other.[12] In other words, just because Irish society is becoming more urban, educated, industrial, technological, scientific, rational, bureaucratic and complex; just because there has been a dramatic decline in the personnel of the institutional Church; and just because being religious has become more private and separated from other social fields such as politics, education, health, social welfare and the media – Ireland will still not necessarily become less religious.[13] To understand and evaluate this argument it is necessary in the first instance to arrive at a definition of religion or what it means to be religious.

Religion involves belief in God or some kind of supernatural or transcendental reality which has primacy over life in this world.[14] This belief is often associated with religious ceremonies, rites and practices. Finally, we might add that the existence of God or a supernatural reality helps provide an explanation and meaning for this life and that, consequently, most world religions have to do with providing guidance as to how to lead a good life here on earth in order to gain entry to the next life. In other words, religion involves experts, usually priests, setting down ethical rules and regulations for lay people to follow as the means of being saved. Religion is founded on the search for meaning, legitimacy, hope and consolation in face of the certainty of death.

Max Weber saw religion as a universal human interest, found in some shape or form in all societies throughout history.[15] Indeed Greeley claims that to be secular is anathema to being human, as it means having no need for an explanation of human existence and no propensity to hope. He argues that despite various theories and attempts to argue the case, there is no empirical evidence which supports the thesis that systematic secularisation is taking place in the Western world.[16]

Consequently, given that we all die; that the desire to transcend death is a universal human interest; that since the advent of agrarian societies, there have always been religious experts (magicians, priests and prophets) who have tried to dominate or monopolise intercession with the supernatural and who tell stories which provide hope and consolation; it is unlikely that, with the possible exception of former East Germany, there has ever been a truly secular society.[17] But this is not to deny that some societies are more secular than others, or that secularisation is taking place in Ireland. I deal with these issues in chapter 9. The present task, however, is not to discern whether Ireland is becoming more or less Catholic, or more or less religious, but rather to analyse the changes in the religious field in Ireland. In other words, the task is to describe the way religious interests are fulfilled – that is, the way they are constructed and maintained by religious experts and lived out by the laity. We can also describe and analyse how the religious field is moulded by and, at the same time, moulds what goes on in other social fields, for example, the economic, the political, educational, health, social welfare and the media. Accepting that religion has nearly always been with us, the task is to not so much to discover whether society, in terms of the substantive definition of religion previously outlined, is becoming more or less religious, but rather to examine the different ways in which it is religious. Following Weber, we can then study a society like Ireland and try to determine the conditions under which, over the last two hundred years, people were religious, and to establish the effects being religious have had on other aspects of their lives.[18]

One of the great questions in sociology is not so much 'how did I come to be the way I am?', but rather how did *we*, or any society, come to be the way *we* are.[19] This means going back into history. When I was growing up I was led to believe that the Irish have always been a holy and religious people ever since the arrival of St Patrick. Once he converted us, we became fervent Christians – an island of saints and scholars which exported the faith all over the world. Despite various attempts by Vikings, Normans, Danes and, worst of all, the disloyal Protestant English (especially Henry VIII and Cromwell), the Irish have remained devoted to the Catholic Church. However, in answering the question why we became and remained more Catholic than most other Europeans, Irish historians have tended to concentrate on changes which took place in the nineteenth century. Four main reasons have been put forward for what has termed the 'Irish Devotional Revolution'. Emmet Larkin's explanation is that it was a response to a loss of language and cultural identity in the nineteenth century. The Irish, in search of stability in a time of rapid social change, attached themselves to the Church because they feared they were being effectively Anglicised.[20] David Miller has put forward a second type of reason for the devotional revolution. He has argued that before the Famine labourers and cottiers, who formed the majority of the population, were orientated towards magical practices. With the virtual elimination of these classes during the Famine, magical practices declined rapidly and were replaced by institutional church practices favoured by the higher social order of Catholics.[21] This reasoning has been developed by Sean Connolly. He suggests that there was an inherent appeal in the rationalisation of Catholicism 'as a religion, a system of beliefs, values and rules of behaviour supported by an appeal to supernatural realities'. He links this rationalisation to a change in the class structure of the population which brought in a 'new and respectable society in which the Church's discipline was from the start more readily accepted.'[22] This leads to a third type of reasoning put forward by Eugene Hynes. The new and respectable society was created in and through the Church. In other words, the growth in institutional adherence was part of an overall growth in discipline involving the sacrifice of short term goals for long term planning. This moral discipline was exercised through a newly adopted stem family system and was a prerequisite for the modernisation of Irish society.[23] The fourth and final type of explanation for the 'devotional revolution' is a Marxist one, and can be stated as follows: the growth of the institutional Catholic Church and an adherence to its practices were part of an ideological apparatus of the British State, fostered in order to contain the growing class antagonisms which had resulted from divisions that arose with the new mode of agricultural production, the transformation from tillage to pasture farming. Such an explanation argues that popular, essentially class, grievances were sublimated in mass devotionalism, and that repressed sexuality, necessary in the new mode of production and stem family system, found a socially acceptable form of emotional relief in Catholic revival.[24]

Much of the reasoning behind these different types of explanations is, with certain exceptions, incorporated into the present study.

First, although any simplistic notion that the devotional revolution was an ideological apparatus of the British state is rejected, emphasis is given to the role state-financed education played in instilling a new system of discipline, and how the state gradually handed the implementation of this discipline over to the Catholic Church.

Secondly, the growth in institutional adherence was not so much a reaction to becoming Anglicised, but rather part of a modern civilising process that had been spreading throughout Europe since the sixteenth century. This process was imported into Ireland and made acceptable to most Catholics by the Church.

Thirdly, besides being a means of becoming as civil and moral as other Europeans, especially British Protestants, a rigid adherence to the rules and regulations of the Church served to facilitate the adoption of stem-family practices, avoiding the subdivision of already small farms, and improving the standard of living which farming could provide. But because the Catholic Church was the force behind this new system of moral discipline and social control, Irish Catholics became socialised into an ideology of spirituality, frugality and celibacy. This ideology was maintained through practices which centred on individuals surrendering to the interests of Church, family and community, and through an uncritical commitment to traditional rules and regulations. It was partially for these reasons that Ireland did not develop a mature system of capitalist agricultural production and modernise fully until the second half of the twentieth century.

Fourthly, this study seeks to explain how it was, in comparison with other European societies, that a high level of institutional adherence was sustained up to the present day. Emphasis is given to the Church's influence in Irish family life and, in particular, the dependence of mothers on the Church for moral power within the home. It was primarily through this dependence that the Church maintained control of women and sex and was able to develop a rigid adherence to its rules and regulations. Finally, in order to gain an overall understanding of what may be termed 'the long nineteenth century of Irish Catholicism', this study develops a sociological perspective which helps explain how being religious, or ethical, fits into certain aspects of Irish social, political and economic life.

One of the tasks of sociology is to combine an analysis of social structures with an understanding of the lives of people who live within them. Through its beliefs, practices and moral teachings, the Catholic Church has structured the way Irish people have seen, understood and related to each other and the world in which they live.[25] To understand the way the Catholic Church has shaped the lives of Irish people, we need to develop a sensitive eye for seeing how they lived their lives and what Catholic values, beliefs and practices have meant to them. We need to understand how they made the official doctrine and practices of the Church their own; how they lived them out in their everyday lives. But at the same time, we must not lose sight of the fact that the official teachings emerge from within an institutional structure.[26] To understand how the official message gets interpreted and embodied, we need to analyse the structure from which it emerged. To know how the Church has structured the lives of Irish Catholics, we need to have a knowledge and understanding of how it is structured and operates as an institution. Beyond this, we need to know something about the structure of the wider society in which the Church operates. In this respect, we need to analyse how the Catholic Church has operated in other social fields, particularly the economic, political, educational, health, social welfare, media and the family.

The task, then, in sociology is to try to ensure that (*a*) we develop a knowledge and understanding of structures which are linked to everyday life and (*b*) in developing a knowledge and understanding of everyday life, we take into account the language and terms which people use to describe their experiences and thereby try to reveal the logic of their beliefs and practices. The task of sociology is to marry the more personal, subjective understanding of life with a knowledge and explanation of the real, objective structures which exist in our lives. We know that there is an ongoing, deep-down, unquestioned attitude or orientation which characterises being Catholic and, specifically, being an Irish Catholic. It is an intuitive knowledge of what it is to be Catholic: what kind of things need to said and done and when and where it is appropriate or necessary to say and do them.[27] This becomes an in-built, automatic way of relating to situations. Catholics know how to behave in a Catholic manner. There is, then, an inherent, inner logic to the practice of Irish Catholicism which those involved know and understand and enact almost intuitively. Being a Catholic in Irish social life is to know the rules, regulations and permutations of what can and cannot be done. These have been learnt and embodied over the years so that they become almost instinctive. The structure limits, but never dictates, the way religious beliefs and values are lived out. For example, there have been Catholics with a particular devotion to certain saints. But, it is argued, to understand the way Irish people were Catholic, it is necessary to examine the organisational power of the Catholic Church – the number and type of personnel and the physical resources it controlled – and to analyse how the Church operated with the State, political parties, the media and other interest groups.

One of the main contributions Weber made to the sociological understanding of religion was to see it as a separate social field which was characterised by the work of specialist agents or experts. In his historical studies he examined the work of priests, prophets and magicians in meeting the religious interest of the laity and cultivating a following.[28] Although there have been various religious sects and cults in Ireland, very few prophets have mounted a challenge to the Catholic Church's monopoly of the religious field in the last two hundred years. In working to meet the religious interests, priests have to be mindful of the material interests of the laity, particularly their social class. Weber emphasised that the religious interests of the peasantry are more orientated towards magical and legal formulae, while the religious interests of, for example, urban professionals will be more intellectual and based upon principles, duties and rewards.[29] In analysing the religious field, then, it is important to realise that there are different religious interests. I will argue that in Ireland the priests have sought to maintain the following of the laity through magical practices, legalistic regulations and principled ethics; and that while all Catholic beliefs and practices contain elements of these, some are more emphasised than others as the class background of the laity moves from rural farming to urban professional. In this respect, as the class background varies, the religious interests of the laity move from the demand for compensation to the demand for symbolic legitimation.

As Pierre Bourdieu reminds us the religious field is characterised by a competitive struggle among the different religious agents and institutions to establish a '*monopoly of the legitimate exercise to modify, in a deep and lasting fashion, the practice and world-view of lay people,* by imposing on and inculcating in them a particular *religious habitus.*'[30] By habitus, Bourdieu means a lasting, general and adaptable way of thinking and acting in conformity with a systematic view of the world which, in our case, is that produced by the Catholic Church.[31] In other words, the task of the Church has been to get Irish people to read automatically, understand and react to situations in which they find themselves in a way which conforms to Church teaching. It is with the concept of habitus that Bourdieu links structure with agency – that is the free and independent way particular individuals behave. The habitus, embodied in the home, school and church, produces specific Catholic ways of being religious and ethical. Through these practices, people can attain religious capital by being a spiritually and ethically good person. This religious capital then becomes an important source of symbolic capital.[32] Being a good Catholic legitimates whatever economic, political, social and cultural capital already accumulated. But being a good Catholic can also help more directly by enabling people attain these other forms of capital. In other words, being a good Catholic helped get contracts and jobs, be elected, be educated, be well known and liked. It is understanding how this process works which is crucial to fulfilling Weber's command to study the effects of religion in other social fields. But there is a flaw in Bourdieu's method. It does not tell us where to look to see changes occurring. In some respects, change takes place through competition emerging at the level of religious experts. The usual case would be that the laity listen to a new prophet or move over to another sect or denomination. This is not useful in explaining changes in the religious field in Ireland, since the Catholic Church has effectively eliminated all other religious competition. Consequently we have to look elsewhere. In some respects, the media have become a competitor in defining what is morally right and wrong. But the real change has occurred in the religious and moral habitus – in the link between the institutional structure of the Church and the individual. And in the Irish instance it has been a change in the social position of women, particularly mothers, which has been crucial to changing the traditional Catholic way that Irish people used to read, understand and relate to the world.

This is a sociological study which presents an overall understanding of the Catholic Church in modern Ireland. The attempt is to provide a reasonable and coherent explanation of its power. The methodology involves devising general concepts in order to develop some new insights. Reference is made to a wide range of primary and, mainly, secondary sources. There is no attempt or claim to give a complete picture of the Catholic Church in Irish society. The objective is to challenge the received, orthodox view.

The book begins by describing the different ways in which Irish Catholics are religious, and the extent to which the Church exercises control over their ethical behaviour. It is argued that there are three main types of religiosity among Irish Catholics:

(a) magical-devotional which includes traditional spiritual practices of prayer, penance and pilgrimage,

(b) legalist-orthodox which centres on strict adherence to Church rules and regulations and,

(c) individually principled ethics which involve Catholics choosing for themselves the beliefs, practices and ethics to which they adhere.

Over the last hundred years, the power of the Church derived from combining a strong sense of the supernatural through devotional practices with an ability to confine the definition of right and wrong to within its own teachings, rules, and regulations (Chapter 2). The moral power of the Church was created and maintained through the rational, bureaucratic, hierarchical organisation of the Church with its considerable physical and human resources, and the dominant position it held in Irish education, health and social welfare (Chapter 3). But the organisational strength of the Church and its dominance of the religious field is not sufficient to explain its power and influence in Irish society. In the fourth chapter, I examine the influence of the Church in social, political and economic life particularly in terms of Irish people achieving the type of legitimation, honour and respect which were central to attaining and maintaining social, cultural and symbolic capital.

In the second part of the book I examine when and how the Church became so powerful and the mechanisms by which this power was maintained. This involves a structural analysis of shifts which took place in the strength and position of the Catholic Church in the political and religious fields. I argue that the Church first emerged as a power block during the last century when the British State, recognising the failure of political and economic repression, gradually changed its policy and sought to pacify and control the Irish population. After a series of conflicts and compromises with Rome and the Irish hierarchy, it gradually handed this task over to the Church whose organisational strength had increased rapidly during the first half of the nineteenth century (Chapter 5). But the growth of the institutional Church was also based on an interest among Irish Catholics in attaining symbolic as well as cultural capital and in becoming as civil and morally respectable as other modern Europeans. In importing the civilising process into Ireland, the Church gained control of many of the buildings and mechanisms through which modern manners and civility were incorporated and developed among Irish Catholics (Chapter 6).

But the development of the Church's power was also related to changes in the economic field. The widespread adoption of a new sexual morality helped develop and maintain a system of stem-family practices. These new practices helped reduce the strain on economic resources and improve the standard of living of one's family (Chapter 7). As argued previously, besides tracing changes within different fields over time, the task in producing a sociological explanation of the Catholic Church's power in Irish society involves uncovering the link between social structures and individual behaviour. I argue that the link between past and present, and between the institutional Church and the individual, is mothers. Having become dependent on the Church for power in the home, it was the mother who instilled the moral discipline necessary to sustain a new form of family life, who transformed houses into neat, ordered and respectable homes, and who nurtured the vocations on which the Church depended (Chapter 8).

In the final part of the book, I examine the decline of the Church's monopoly over morality during the last thirty years, but particularly since the late 1980s. I argue that there is a steady process of Protestantisation and secularisation taking place among Irish Catholics. The dramatic decline in the numbers of religious personnel and vocations to religious life is matched by a decline in religious belief, practice and adherence to the Church's moral teachings. But the decline of the Church's power is also evident in its having lost its dominance in the politics, education, health, social welfare, the media and the family (Chapter 9). In the final chapter, I argue that it was the power alliance between Church and mother that played a major part in the initial modernisation of Irish society. But once the alliance became established, it helped maintain Ireland as a conservative, rural society and delayed its full modernisation until the second half of the twentieth century. However, despite its recent decline, the Catholic Church still has considerable influence not just in the religious field, but in the character of Irish social life, particularly in terms of defining good and bad social behaviour and people attaining social, cultural and symbolic capital.

PART ONE
The Catholic Church in Contemporary Ireland

2
The Religious Habitus of Irish Catholics

What makes the Republic of Ireland different from other Western European societies, and from all other English speaking countries, is the high level of adherence to the Roman Catholic Church. More than nine in ten of the population identify themselves as Church members, and of these more than six in ten attend Mass at least once a week. The level of Mass attendance has only fallen in recent years. In 1973–74, more than nine in ten Catholics attended weekly. The vast majority of Irish people are born, marry, and die within the Church. They regard their Church membership as important. Religion is not merely a question of accepting certain beliefs and teachings, it is something which is actively practised. Irish Catholics regularly receive the sacraments. They obey Church teachings and many accept its definition of what constitutes good moral conduct. It is for these reasons that being Irish and being Catholic became synonymous. The Irish have often been characterised as a deeply spiritual people, but this does not explain how and why this spirituality is manifested in a strong adherence to institutional Catholicism. The answer to this question lies in events and processes set in train in the last century. However, the reason why the Catholic Church has maintained its dominance of the religious and moral fields, as will be argued in the first part of this book, lies in the organisational manpower and resources of the Church, its dominance in other social fields, and the role being a good Catholic has played in the struggle for symbolic, cultural and social capital – that is having one's wealth and position accepted as legitimate, being seen as a good person, and having good social connections. The task of the present chapter is to describe the religious habitus of Irish Catholics in terms of the different ways they have lived their religion: their beliefs, their practices and, most important in the context of the Church's monopoly over the definition of morality, how they decide what is good or bad, right or wrong. It is important to emphasise that religious habitus refers to the ongoing, flexible and transposable disposition which orients Catholics to recognising, knowing and being religious. It is an inherited disposition which is embodied deep within their social being. The embodied habitus enables them to know what to do to be pious, spiritual and devotional; to accept fully the recognised fundamental beliefs of their faith; and to be aware of what is acceptable and unacceptable moral behaviour. To understand the Church's monopoly over Irish morality, we need to know what it is to be Catholic in Ireland – to know the logic of the practice. But before examining the different dimensions to Catholic religiosity, it is necessary to give a general description of the religious field, particularly of how the island is divided politically and ecclesiastically, and of the high proportion of Roman Catholics that live in the Republic of Ireland.

Irish Catholics

Ireland has been divided politically into the North and South since 1922. The six north-eastern counties of Antrim, Derry, Tyrone, Fermanagh, Armagh and Down comprise Northern Ireland, which is part of the United Kingdom. The remaining twenty-six counties comprise the Republic of Ireland. The Irish Catholic Church extends throughout the whole island, and the ecclesiastical divisions have little or no correspondence with the political divisions. For example, the northern ecclesiastical province of Armagh has two dioceses, Meath and Ardagh, which are completely in the Republic, and four dioceses, Armagh, Clogher, Derry and Kilmore, which are divided by the political boundary. One of the main reasons for the introduction of the boundary in 1922 was to create a political state in which the Protestant minority of the island would be in the majority. The boundary also meant that the southern part of the island soon became almost completely Catholic. The imposition of the border continued to affect the proportion of Catholics in both areas for some time afterwards. In the twenty-five years between 1911 and 1936, the proportion of Catholics in Northern Ireland fell by six per cent, whereas in the Republic it rose by four per cent (see table 1).

The proportion of Catholics in the Republic of Ireland increased steadily throughout the twentieth century until it reached a peak of 95 per cent in 1961. There are four main reasons for this increase:

(1) Soon after its foundation in 1922, thousands of Protestants began to leave the Irish Free State. The main factors were economic uncertainty, loyalty to the English crown, and the incorporation of Catholic teachings in the Free State's constitution and laws. Indeed the population of the Free State would have increased slightly between 1926 and 1946 had it not been for the 24 per cent decline in the number of Protestants.[1]

Table 1.   Roman Catholic population as percentage of Northern Ireland,
The Republic of Ireland, and all Ireland, 1861–1991

	1861 %	1911 %	1936 %	1961 %	1981 %	1991 %
Northern Ireland	41.0	39.5	33.5	34.9	38.0*	38.4
Republic of Ireland	89.4	89.6	93.5	94.9	93.0	91.6
All Ireland	78.1	75.3	75.4	74.7	76.8	75.0
Number in thousands	5,768	4,391	4,248	4,243	4,925	5,123

Adapted from Brendan Walsh, *Religion and Demographic Behaviour in Ireland* (Dublin: Economic and Social Research Institute paper 55, 1970), p.7; and Censuses of Population 1981 & 1991 (Ireland and Northern Ireland).

* Estimated figure.

(2) There was a low rate of disaffiliation from the Catholic Church. Although the actual numbers of Catholics and Protestants who have changed their religion may not differ much, the impact on the Protestant minority has been far greater. Even as late as 1973–74, a national survey of religious practices, attitudes and beliefs showed that 7.5 per cent of Protestants had changed their religious affiliation, compared to only 0.3 per cent of Catholics.[2]

(3) The Catholic Church teaching of *Ne Temere* required that in a mixed marriage involving a Catholic, the children be brought up as Catholics. A mixed marriage in one generation meant, if the regulation was obeyed, an all-Catholic family in the next. An indication of the long-term effect of mixed marriages is that in one year alone (1961), it was estimated that 30 per cent of Other Denomination (mostly Protestant) grooms, and 20 per cent of Other Denomination brides, married Catholics in Catholic ceremonies.[3] As one southern Protestant commentator put it: 'the process of intermarriage continues, and with it the leaching of the Protestant community.'[4]

(4) Another major reason for the increase in the proportion of Catholics in the Republic, and indeed in Northern Ireland, is their higher level of fertility. In the Republic of Ireland between 1960 and 1962, the Catholic birth rate (for married women aged 15–44) was 254.6 per thousand; for Protestants it was 151.3 per thousand. This means that, on average, Catholic families were 50 per cent larger than Protestant families.[5] The differential, as Kennedy shows, was maintained across occupational and social groups. It would seem that regardless of knowledge of or access to

artificial means of birth control, Catholics wanted and had larger families than non-Catholics. It was part of their religious and general social habitus for each new generation of married people to want and to have a large family.[6]

Since 1961, there has been a small decline in the proportion of Catholics in the Republic. This has been due to an increase in the number who have been leaving the Church. They have either not supplied information in their Census returns about their religious denomination, or have declared that they have 'no religion'. An interesting aspect of this process of disaffiliation and of the Catholic Church's monopoly position in the religious field, is that most of those who leave the Church do not join another Christian denomination. Many no longer even regard themselves as Christians. A survey of Irish university students in 1976 showed that one in seven of the students who had been brought up within the Catholic Church no longer identified themselves as members. The majority of these students regarded themselves as agnostics, even though the most frequently mentioned reason for leaving the Church was disagreement with particular teachings.[7] These Catholics were traditionally regarded by the Church as 'lapsed'. They may have claimed to be agnostic, but the depth of their Catholic habitus, the unquestioning nature of the way they were religious and moral, meant that when it came to rearing their own children and send them to school, many were happy to return to the Catholic fold.

A Typology of Irish Religiosity

There are numerous different ways in which Irish Catholics are religious.[8] The most immediate and obvious dimension to being Catholic is belief in God, Christ and Our Lady; that people have souls; that they sin but that their sins are forgiven in Confession; that the Catholic Church is the one true Church; that the Pope teaches infallibly and that if Catholics follow the commandments of God and the teachings of the Church they will gain eternal salvation in heaven and that if they do not they will go to hell. Surveys have shown a deep, unquestioned, orthodox core to Irish Catholic belief. The beliefs which Catholics have most difficulty with are belief in hell, Papal infallibility and that the Catholic Church is the one true church. It is impossible to discern precise causes for the decline in belief in hell. Did the Church stop preaching hell-fire sermons, or did it take the lead from the laity and respond to a new positive, feel-good dimension which emerged in the latter half of this century.[9] At the heart, then, of Irish Catholic belief has been a strong, unquestioned faith in God, Christ and Our Lady. Allied to this high level of religious belief is a high level of religious practice. In 1973–74, not only did nine in ten Catholics go to Mass once a week, but eight in ten received Holy Communion and seven in ten went to Confession six times a year. For a long time the majority of Irish Catholics, without questioning, accepted that they went to Mass on Sunday. They also said their morning and night prayers. But more than that, even if they did not engage in devotional practices such as making novenas and going on pilgrimages, they admired and respected those who did. This was the essence of the simple faith. In the same way that patients handed themselves over to doctors to be cured, the laity handed themselves over to the Church to be saved. The strength of the institutional faith was such that Irish Catholics did not experience, think about or question religion for themselves.[10] There was a close correspondence between the official doctrine of the Church and the way Catholics read, understood and acted in the world religiously. The unquestioning centre of their religious habitus, the orthodoxy, corresponded to the orthodoxy of the institutional Church. With such a monopoly over the way Irish Catholics were religious and moral, the only concerns against which the institutional Church had to guard were Catholics experiencing religion for themselves or making up their own minds in matters of faith and morals. The danger of mysticism is that the mystical experience of the supernatural is so strong that it leads to a schism or break with the institutional Church. The danger of people developing their own individual moral conscience about what is right and wrong is that they increasingly disregard the teachings of the Church, becoming not just *à la carte* Catholics, but effectively Protestants. Given that the orthodoxy of the Irish Catholic habitus was the source of the institutional strength of the Church and its monopoly over morality, it will be useful to analyse the dimensions of Irish religiosity in terms of threats from: (*a*) magical-devotional religion, in which there is an emphasis on personal religious experience and on attempts to secure divine intervention in this life; and (*b*) individually principled ethics in which people make up their own mind as to what is right and wrong.

Christianity is a religion of salvation based on ethics. To be saved in and from this world, and to gain entry to the next, depends upon what one does in this world. There are three main types of ethical behaviour in Christianity: (l) magical-devotional – fulfilling traditional prescriptions and formulas in order to achieve material transformations in this world; (2) legalistic-orthodox – adhering to the institutional rules and regulations of a Church; and (3) individually principled ethics – methodically following an individually reasoned set of ethical guidelines. These types of ethical behaviour are often seen in terms of developmental stages with individually-principled ethics as the most rational. In other words, societies as well as individuals go through stages in which their ethical behaviour develops from being predominantly magical, to being legalistic-orthodox, to finally becoming individually principled. Until the first half of the nineteenth century, unorthodox religious practices, many of which were magical, appear to have been the dominant type of religious behaviour in Ireland.[11] Throughout the next one hundred years a legalistic adherence to the rules and regulations of the Catholic Church became the dominant type. Since the end of the 1960s, religious legalism has begun to be replaced by individually principled ethics in which Catholics develop their own principles about what is morally right and wrong.[12]

The least rationally developed type of religious behaviour is magic. It is based on the correct use of traditional formulas and objects which, if properly enacted, it is believed will bring success or reward. In its most basic form, magic is non-institutionalised. The status of the magician has often depended on the belief in his ability to compel a god or spirit to do his will. In other words, magical behaviour is good if it is believed to work. The practices of prayer and sacrifice have their origins in magic in so far as their ritual fulfilment is associated with attaining material advantage in this world; examples are novenas, or donations to a saint in order to obtain favours. In this way magic can be part of institutional Catholic behaviour. Indeed, as Weber points out, 'magical coercion is universally diffused, and even the Catholic priest continues to practise something of this magical power. . . .'[13]

In contrast to magic, legalist-orthodox behaviour is based on supplication and entreaty to God through adherence to the stable, systematic, consistent doctrine enunciated by a Church. This doctrine may be presented as formal abstract principles, but it is generally translated into specific rules and regulations. Obedience to the law is seen as the distinctive way to win God's favour, and any infraction of the Church's doctrine constitutes a sin. In legalistic religious ethics, behaviour is assessed in terms of the intentions and consequences of numerous individual actions. This is what traditionally occurs in Confession. It is associated with an absolute conviction that the rules and regulations of the Church or sect are divinely ordained and, consequently, are universally binding.

In individually principled ethics, it is the total conduct of the individual and his personality that is evaluated. The assessment is not simply in terms of whether a particular action conforms to the rules and regulations of the Church. The individual makes moral judgments independently of the authority of the priest and the Church. He or she has come to recognise and accept the existence of other ethical principles and the necessity to defend his or her principles through reasoned debate rather than relying solely on the conviction of their sacredness.[14]

Now there are many aspects of modern Irish Catholicism that would link it to individually principled ethics, but ethical principles are rarely incorporated systematically by Catholics. This is due to the dominance of priests and the miracle of sacraments, both of which prevent Catholics from developing a consistent ethical systematisation of conduct and good works and, consequently, becoming autonomous, subjectively responsible individuals. Weber gives a good description of the difference between Catholicism, which still contains many elements of magic, and a highly rationalised religious ethic such as Calvinism:

> The priest was a magician who performed the miracle of transubstantiation, and who held the key to eternal life in his hand. One could turn to him in grief and penitence. He dispensed atonement, hope of grace, certainty of forgiveness, and thereby granted release from that tremendous tension to which the Calvinist was doomed by an inexorable fate, admitting of no mitigation. For him such friendly and human comforts did not exist. He could not hope to atone for hours of weakness or of thoughtlessness by increased good will at other times, as the Catholic or even the Lutheran could. The God of Calvinism demanded of his believers not single good works, but a life of good works combined into a unified system. There was no place for the very human Catholic cycle of sin, repentance, atonement, release, followed by renewed sin.[15]

This is not to say that the Catholic Church is devoid of general ethical principles, but that the Church acts as interpreter and defines explicitly, in terms of laws and regulations, how these principles are to be transformed into practice. It is the Church, rather than the individual, which decides what specific regulations of behaviour follow from general ethical principles. Salvation can be attained through a legalistic, external compliance with the Church's regulations. Consequently, there can often be a compliance with the Church's regulations without an explicit awareness of the ethical principles from which they are derived.

The Catholic Church, then, through its priesthood, establishes a comprehensive ruling and direction of all spheres of behaviour. Everyone who is a member can be saved through adhering to its rules and regulations. Salvation does not depend upon being ethically perfect. Through good works and the miracle of institutional grace, a person who has been perfectly irreligious can become perfectly religious. Members who do more good works than necessary for their own salvation, accumulate grace for the credit of the institution, which distributes it to those in need.[16] Grace, the miracle of the sacraments, and the regulation of ethical behaviour by priests, spare Catholics the necessity of developing an individual pattern of life based on general ethical principles. It is the extent to which Irish Catholics are dispensing with the need for grace, and are making up their own minds about what is good or bad moral behaviour, which indicates that they are moving towards a more Protestant-type faith. However even though there has been a definite shift away from the dominance of legalist-orthodox behaviour towards individually principled ethics, there are still many Irish Catholics who are orientated towards magical practices. Indeed rarely has any modern Irish Catholic adhered specifically to one type of ethical behaviour. Rather, Irish religiosity has been an amalgam of all three types, with one type, an adherence to the rules and regulations of the Church, being dominant over the other two.

Magical-Devotional Practices

The analytical distinction between magical practices and legal religious behaviour is often difficult to distinguish in everyday Catholic life in Ireland. There are many aspects of the Church's rituals which could be seen as magical. Even the most solemn ritual of the transformation of bread and wine into the body and blood of Christ could be interpreted as magical. The more transubstantiation is taken to be an actual, physical rather than symbolic transformation, and the more the transformation is taken to be dependent on the precise repetition of actions and words, the more the sacrament becomes magical. There is one further crucial distinction. The miracles operated by priests are quite different from the magic of a magician in that they are part of an institution of grace founded on the principles of a stable doctrine. In other words, any magical power possessed by the priest comes from the institution rather than from his own personal, charismatic power.

Magical practices are based on the enactment of a formula or ritual which, if followed correctly, will coerce the god into bringing about the desired results. Legalistic religious behaviour is based on winning God's favour by supplication, entreaty and being holy through following the Church's teachings and rituals. It is the priests who interpret God's will and actions, and tell the laity how to be holy and obtain God's favour. Ritual prayer becomes magical when the main interest is in obtaining a temporal favour or the material transformation of existing conditions. Indeed the religious behaviour of Irish Catholics has often been directed as much towards influencing and controlling the irrational forces of nature as it has been to gaining salvation in the next world. It is for this reason that the Catholic Church has institutionalised magical objects and practices, such as relics, medals, holy water, novenas, pilgrimages, and so on. These are what the Church has traditionally called 'sacramentals' and they are used 'in imitation of the sacraments, to obtain from God spiritual favours.'[17] The Catholic Church has allowed these practices to continue even though they may go against the systematic rational control of behaviour. This has been necessary because, until recently, Ireland was a rural society in which the majority of the people came from peasant backgrounds and were bound to traditions based on magic. Indeed, the acceptance and incorporation of magical practices within the institutional Church would seem to have fostered a non-intellectual approach to doctrine and ethical conduct and helped maintain a simple, unquestioning devotion to its rules and regulations.

Two main types of magical practice exist within Irish Catholicism: (1) traditional practices, rituals, and superstitions which are pagan, non-Christian in origin; and (2) sacred objects and practices approved by the Church and used to obtain temporal favours. Again the formal distinction between these two types of magical practice is often blurred in reality. As we shall see, many traditional pagan practices have been successfully incorporated in formal Church rituals.

Irish social life contains myriads of little rituals that are used to avoid bad luck and bring good fortune. Many of these rituals and objects, for example, not killing a house-spider, not walking under a ladder, putting up horseshoes and keeping lucky pennies, may have nothing to do with the Catholic Church, but they are practised by Catholics and they are an aspect of magical religious behaviour. Even if they are done tongue-in-cheek, and 'not really' believed in, they are significant simply because they continue to be practised. There are many Irish Catholics who would not consider themselves to be influenced by magic but who would go to enormous extremes not to walk under a ladder, or to catch sight of a lone magpie. Irish people may scorn the primitive tribesman who chants ditties to make the seeds grow, yet in their everyday life many of them engage in similar practices. They are part of an unreflective disposition or habitus in which it is accepted that people would try to manipulate supernatural forces in their favour. The national survey in 1973–74 found, for example, that one in ten respondents believed that it was bad luck to walk under a ladder (table 2).

Table 2.   Magical Beliefs and Superstitions of the Irish
(National Survey 1973–74).*

Percentage who believed	%
(a) *That it is bad luck to:*	
Walk under a ladder	10.4
Break a chain letter	3.5
Put up an umbrella in the house	8.3
Oppose or contradict a priest	24.9
(b) In lucky numbers/charms/colours	9.4
In fortune telling	6.4

Source: Nic Ghiolla Phádraig, personal communication.

*Based on a national survey of 2,623 respondents of whom 2,499 were Catholic.

It is not that the Irish are more superstitious and magical than people from other Western societies. A survey of Londoners in 1968 found that three-quarters of the respondents touched wood in certain circumstances, while almost half threw salt over their shoulders when some was spilt.[18] These findings give credence to David Martin's claim that Western society, although supposedly secular, remains deeply imbued with every type of superstition.[19] The findings also reveal that even though an individual or society may in most cases adhere to principled ethics, this does not mean that there are not magical aspects to their religious behaviour.

Irish folklore is full of pagan practices and superstitions. The proportion who engage in these practices is generally higher than the proportion who say they really believe in them. In other words, in contrast to other aspects of Irish religiosity, the level of practice is higher than the level of actual belief. People may search desperately for a piece of wood to touch, even though they claim they do not believe in magic or superstition. It has been, and in many respects still is, the ability of the Catholic Church to combine magical practices and superstitions with a predominantly legalist-orthodox type of religious ethic that has aided the growth of the institutional Church both in Ireland and elsewhere. This combination has also helped maintain a rich heritage of folklore. It cannot be denied that fairies, leprechauns, banshees and the like have almost disappeared from the landscape of Irish minds. However, they would seem to have endured for a long time in the face of the onslaught of modern civilisation, science, and technology. This is, it is argued, because they have been compatible with institutional Catholicism. Pagan practices were suppressed only when they posed a direct threat. This is what happened to the wake, which the Church gradually began to change from a festive celebration of death into a ritual occasion of mourning. Instead of a party involving games, some of which were sexually explicit, the wake has become a subdued and decorous occasion where prayers are said for the dead person, and visitors sit talking quietly among themselves.[20]

Another popular magical practice which is still prevalent in Ireland is faith-healing. There are numerous people throughout Ireland who have 'the cure' for specific ailments. The cure is generally performed by rubbing the afflicted spot in a ritualised manner with a sacred object such as a stone. Often the ritual has been Christianised through the recital of a few prayers and the use of a crucifix or medal instead of a stone. Again it is the mixture of object and ritual that creates the cure. There are also those who have the power of healing through touch alone. These faith-healers operate outside the institutional Church. They generally do not claim to derive their powers from Christ and often charge for their services. Some of these faith-healers are the 'seventh son of a seventh son'. In 1972 Logan went so far as to suggest that 'one quarter of the medical practice in Ireland today is done by people who are not on the Medical Register.'[21]

There are many pagan practices which the Catholic Church in Ireland has adopted into its own rituals, for example pilgrimages to holy wells. Wells are essential for survival, and over time some became renowned as having greater properties than others. Consequently many became identified as holy. Over 3,000 holy wells have been catalogued in Ireland, of which more than two hundred are still in use. Logan estimated 'that there are few parishes in which there is not at least one, but in many parishes there are more.'[22] Most of the wells have become associated with particular saints and, although they are undoubtedly pre-Christian in origin, the Church openly encourages pilgrimages to them. But there was a time in the nineteenth century when these pilgrimages were officially discouraged, not so much because they were pagan practices as because, like wakes, they were occasions of passionate, drunken, and often sexually immoral festivities.

Whereas Ireland may not differ from other Western societies in terms of the persistence of practices such as touching wood and believing in lucky numbers, it is different in terms of the variety and frequency with which pagan practices are enacted as part of Catholic religious behaviour. Even the rosary, the most traditional form of common ritual prayer, has many similarities with pagan practices – for example the ritual counting of beads (stones) as one proceeds in a circle. Instead of divine outcomes being derived by the ritualistic enactment of a coercive religious formulae, practices like saying the rosary have become penitential acts of supplication and entreaty. However, very often the ritual is enacted for the purpose of a magical transformation of existing conditions. This is especially the case when a rigid adherence to the details of the ritual are held to be central to achieving the desired result. There is often a thin line between the legalistic enactment of a magical practice and a ritual adherence to the Church's regulations concerning what constitutes good moral conduct.[23] Forming a circle around the fire at home to say the rosary may be done to adore God – that is, with a more spiritual motivation. It may be done to keep the family together. It may also be done for more practical material ends, such as to bring rain or sunshine to help the crops grow.

Pilgrimages to Lough Derg, Croagh Patrick and Knock (where the Blessed Virgin is said to have appeared in 1879 and which, like Lourdes, is associated with miracle cures) are part of a wide range of popular devotional practices that have been enacted for centuries. In the national survey in 1973–74, half of the respondents had made a pilgrimage.[24] Some of the practices involve penitential exercises, for example climbing the rocky slopes of Croagh Patrick in one's bare feet, or going round the 'beds' (of rocks) in Lough Derg in the middle of the night having fasted for two days. Throughout the summer of 1985, there was an upsurge in popular devotion to Our Lady. This manifested itself mainly in outdoor vigils before a small number of the many hundreds of statues to her throughout the country. People gathered, sometimes in their thousands, in front of these statues and sang hymns and said the rosary. Statues were said to have moved, cried and bled.[25] While this outburst of magic-devotional religion was undoubtedly linked to changes in social and economic conditions, it was primarily related to a disenchantment with the failure of the institutional Church to respond to the more emotional, experiential religious needs of the people. This ongoing tension between the institutional Church and a laity who are more devotional and magically-orientated is welldocumented in Taylor's study of a parish in Co. Donegal. One of the main characteristics of the religious field in Donegal was the conflict between those who sought consolation, cures and experiences outside of the orthodox parameters of the institutional Church. In some instances, such as worship at the holy well, the priest engages in the ritual and, as happened in the nineteenth century, makes it Catholic by reciting the rosary. Similarly, the healing Mass was an attempt to keep within the institution tendencies to magical-devotional religion which, if not met within, could end up being fulfilled outside the institution. This was what happened in relation to stories about the curative powers of renegade drunken priests and about miracles performed at a breakaway prayer group meeting.[26]

The nine-day novena has made something of a comeback as a devotional practice. It was very popular during the 1950s and 1960s, but like many other devotional practices it became de-emphasised in the aftermath of Vatican II. However in 1979 it was estimated that up to 40,000 attended a nine day novena to Our Lady of Perpetual Succour in Limerick.[27] Similar levels of attendance have been recorded for other centres in which the novena has been held. A traditional feature of the novena is the petitions for material benefits which, as Kelly pointed out, 'seem to reflect every need of human existence: petitions for positions, for homes, for a good wife or husband, for success in examinations, for advancement in work, for a chance to return to Ireland. . . .'[28]

As well as novenas, there are also various other private, devotional practices associated with the attempt to obtain temporal favours. Nearly every church in Ireland has statues, or a shrine, in front of which are candles. The 'penny candle' is paid for and lit, and a prayer is said, often for a special intention. What makes the practice magical in character is the highly ritual format used to obtain the favour. There are special saints to whom one prays and specific acts are done in order to obtain favours. One prays to Saint Jude for a husband, to Saint Anthony if something is lost, and to Saint Christopher for a safe journey.

The most common sacramental object used in Ireland is holy water. It is generally found outside every church, and inside the door of many homes. It is associated with spiritual protection. Some holy water, for instance from Lourdes or from a holy well, is often used for a cure. Medals are also common. They are used for spiritual as well as physical protection. For example, a St Christopher medal is often hung in a car to protect the travellers against accidents. Relics of saints or holy people are another type of sacred object used to obtain favours, especially cures from illnesses. In the national survey of 1973–74, half of the respondents had worn medals, and three-quarters put up holy pictures or statues.

The devotional piety of Irish Catholics was evidenced by the finding from the 1973–74 survey that 97 per cent of the respondents prayed at least once a day. Almost seven in ten (69 per cent) prayed when things went wrong or when they wanted something. When asked why they prayed, '45 per cent stated that they prayed for material reasons and mentioned such "temporal" favours as protection from illness, comfort, or prosperity.'[29] Examples of thanksgiving for favours obtained from saints through this type of petitionary prayer are found in many newspapers and popular Catholic publications.

There is a similarity between magical practices and legalist-orthodox behaviour. The person who engages in magic believes that unless the formula is followed exactly, the gods will not be coerced and the desired result will not be achieved. The religious legalist holds that, unless there is strict adherence to the letter of the law, there will be no salvation. Consequently, there is often a compatibility in Irish Catholicism, both within the formal structures of the institution and at the level of individual religious behaviour, between a strict adherence to the rules and regulations of the Church and engagement in magically orientated practices. Some of the magical practices described in this section are officially sanctioned by the Church, others are condoned, and some, especially those conducted by individual magicians, are discouraged. In general, as long as the practice is engaged in under the auspices of the Church it is tolerated. Material transformations directly attributed to God and his saints are a major aspect of Irish Catholic behaviour. Indeed some aspects of the sacraments, which are the keystone of the Catholic faith, are quite magical. But the sacraments are not simply received for their magical grace. They are received as part of an adherence to the Church's definition of what it is to be holy. Salvation in the next world is attained by keeping the commandments. But the catechism states that keeping the commandments cannot be done without the grace of God which is obtained through prayer and the sacraments. Receiving the sacraments has become part of adhering to the Church's definition of how to attain salvation. The more one prays, receives the sacraments and follows the teachings of the Church as to how to be holy, the more likely it is that one will be saved. Sacramental practice has less to do with magic than it has to do with the legalistic fulfilment of Catholic teaching which is central to attaining salvation. It is the fear of being denied moral respectability and salvation which is central to the power that bishops and priests have of limiting what the laity do and say.

Legalist-Orthodox Religious Behaviour

The dominant form of religious behaviour in modern Ireland has been, and in many instances still is, an adherence to the rules and regulations of the Catholic Church. The way to be a good moral person and to save one's soul is to accept fully its beliefs and moral teachings and regularly engage in its ritual practices. Moral respectability and salvation are attained through the unquestioning use of rituals, regulations and good works. This is how one becomes holy. Everything religious and moral outside of the Church, whether it is magical-devotional religion or following a personal moral code, becomes incorporated within the Church. Salvation becomes the sole preserve of the Church. It is through a regular and habitual performance of rituals and good works that a state of grace is maintained. Questions of morality and salvation are left in the hands of the experts – bishops and priests. Moral problems for the laity are solved by confessing them to a priest and then, as a penance, actively engaging in good works or traditional, devotional practices. When the legalist-orthodox way of being religious is dominant, the gap between official, institutional discourse – the discourse of the Pope, bishops and priests – and the religious life of ordinary Catholics is small. When magical-devotional religion, or individually principled ethics are dominant, the gap is large. As we shall see, the ability of the institutional Church to keep the gap small depends on the number and commitment of its personnel, its dominance in other fields such as the family, politics, education, health, social welfare and the media. Legalist-orthodox religiosity was maintained through the Church's dominance in these other social fields. Within legalist-orthodox religiosity, there is an emphasis on learning and keeping to the beliefs, practices, rules and regulations of the institutional Church.

Throughout the last hundred years or more in which institutional Catholicism has been dominant in Ireland, the principal form of entry into the rules and regulations of the Church was the Catechism of Catholic Doctrine; the 'penny' catechism or 'little green book'. Although the catechism was used in hedge-schools throughout the eighteenth century, its large-scale use did not begin until the development of confraternities in the first half of the nineteenth century. Its use among the mass of the Catholic population was delayed until the Church gained full control of the national school system during the latter half of the century. The catechism that was used in Catholic schools in Ireland until the end of the 1960s was little different from Dr James Butler's catechism, which was used throughout the nineteenth century, and was itself based on many of the teachings first promulgated at the Council of Trent. It is within the catechism that the general principles of Christian behaviour are given specific interpretations. The importance attached to religious practice as a means of maintaining adherence to its teachings is evident in the Church's commandments:

1. First: To hear Mass on Sundays and holydays of obligation.

2. Second: To fast and abstain on the days appointed.

3. Third: To confess our sins at least once a year.

4. Fourth: To receive worthily the Blessed Eucharist at Easter time.

5. Fifth: To contribute to the support of our pastors.

6. Sixth: To observe the marriage laws of the Church.[30]

In the national survey in 1973–74, respondents were asked questions about some of these Church commandments (table 3).

Table 3. Attitudes of Irish Catholics to Church Commandments
(National Survey 1973–74).

Church Commandment	Always Wrong %	Generally Wrong %	Ambivalent/ Right/Other %
Missing Mass on Sundays*	24.4	61.5	14.1
Failing to do your Easter duty	59.4	19.4	21.2
Not paying dues	47.6	41.6	10.8
Not marrying in church	73.0	11.7	15.3

Source: Research and Development Commission 'Report No. 3, Moral Values',   pp. 2–47.

* Respondents were also asked to agree or disagree, or state if they were undecided about whether 'You can be a good Catholic without going to Mass': 41% agreed, 2.3% were undecided and 56.6% disagreed with the statement.

The vast majority of the respondents considered it wrong to contravene the commandments of the Church. A high percentage took a rigid line regarding failure to do one's Easter Duty and not marrying in church. A less rigid approach was taken regarding missing Mass on Sundays and not paying dues. However the only exception generally mentioned for not obeying these two commandments were 'if ill' and 'if not able to afford it'. What is conspicuous by its absence in these responses is reference to people making up their own mind and making their own choices. Legalist-orthodox religiosity is characterised by a surrender of the self to the institution.

Not only was the gap between institutional discourse and practice and everyday Catholic life narrow, but, as Flannery argues, the teachings on how Catholics should live their lives were a replication of the rules and regulations of the institutional life of religious. He describes the main characteristics of legalist-orthodox religion as the belief that (*a*) this life is not important, but is only a preparation for the next life, (*b*) salvation is attained by avoiding sin, (*c*) being holy involves denying oneself and serving others, and (*d*) there is no salvation outside of the Church. The ideal Catholic was like the ideal religious student who 'obeyed the rule in all areas, did what he or she was told, and generally kept the head down.'[31]

Legalist-orthodox religiosity creates docile, obedient subjects. It instills within them an anxiety and fear about fulfilling duties exactly as they are required to be done. Any infringement is seen as destroying the purpose, meaning and efficacy of the duty, and possibly attracting the negative attention or ridicule of others. Kenny gives some examples of the anxieties Catholics had in the 1950s: women returning from the altar having received Holy Communion wearing a glove on their head (they were required to keep their heads covered in church); or women worrying if they cooked food in beef lard on Fridays (Catholics were required to abstain from meat that day). Kenny gives other examples of the kind of questions which readers used to ask experts in the *Irish Messenger of the Sacred Heart*.

Q. Can a person hear Mass properly without seeing the altar? A. Yes. Q. May one use powder to fix dentures before going to Holy Communion? A. Yes. Q. Is it forbidden to do tailoring on Sunday if it is done for a pious purpose and no payment is received? A. To do tailoring on a Sunday *even* for a pious purpose and without payment is forbidden. Q. Is it sinful to knit or iron clothes on Sunday. A. We are forbidden to do work on Sunday that is both servile and unnecessary. Q. Does a person who says the Rosary wearing gloves gain the indulgences granted for the saying of the Rosary on a blessed beads? A. Yes.[32]

Of all the rules and regulations of the Catholic Church, the one which was central to maintaining the dominance of the institution in the religious field as well as many other fields, was attending Mass on Sundays. Within legalist-orthodox religiosity, it became the litmus test as to whether someone was a practising Catholic. Indeed, as we shall see, it became the criterion for identifying whether a teacher was a good enough Catholic to teach in a Catholic school. In legalistic Catholicism, obeying the rules is essential, and the essential rule is going to Mass. In the national survey in 1973–74,

57 per cent of the respondents disagreed with the proposition that 'you can be a good Catholic without going to Mass on Sundays'.[33] However, within a legalistic interpretation of religious behaviour, it might be also expected that a similar proportion would not be possible to be a good Catholic without getting married in a Catholic Church, having one's children baptised, rearing them as Catholics and sending them to a Catholic school. Within this perspective, loyalty and obedience to the institution are crucial.

Regular religious practice is central to maintaining a legalistic interpretation of what it is to be religious. The level of attendance at Mass by Irish Catholics is almost twice the European average for Catholics.[34] But it is not just the level of Mass attendance which is high in legalist-orthodox forms of religion. Results from the national survey in 1973–74 indicated that nine in ten Irish Catholics adhered to the minimum criterion of a practising Catholic. They attended Mass once a week, and Confession and Holy Communion at least once a year(table 4).

Table 4.   Overall attendance at Mass, Holy Communion and Confession (National Survey 1973–74).

Frequency	Mass Act.	Communion Cum. %		Confession Act. Cum. %			
	Act.	Cum. %	Act. %	Cum. %	Act. %	Cum. %	%
Daily	5.6	5.6	3.6	3.6	–	–	
More than once a week	17.8	23.4	6.1	9.7	–	–	
Once a week	67.5	90.9	18.3	29.0	0.8	0.8	
2 or 3 times a month	2.5	93.4	16.2	44.2	5.3	6.1	
Once a month	0.9	94.3	21.4	65.6	40.4	46.5	
About 6 times a year	0.8	95.1	13.5	79.2	23.3	69.8	
Up to 3 times a year	0.8	95.9	12.7	91.9	20.0	98.8	
Less than once a year	(1.4)	–	(5.1)	–	(6.4)	–	
Never	(2.6)	–	(3.0)	–	(3.7)	–	
no.=	2,499		2,495		2,495		

Act. = Actual
Cum. = Cumulative
Source: Nic Ghiolla Phádraig, 'Religion in Ireland', p. 129.

But it was not just that the vast majority fulfilled the minimal criteria for being a good Catholic; many of them did more than the required minimum. Nearly a quarter (23 per cent) of the 1973–74 survey respondents went to Mass more than once a week; nearly half (47 per cent) attended Confession at least once a month; and two thirds received Holy Communion at least once a month. Regular reception of the sacraments by the majority of Irish Catholics is an indication of their acceptance of the Church's definition of the path to salvation. A prominent conviction among many Irish Catholics would seem to be that as long as one attends Mass every Sunday, confesses any infractions of the Commandments and Church regulations to a priest, and worthily receives Holy Communion, one can be described as a moral person who has a good chance of being saved. However, the more frequently one receives the sacraments the higher one's state of grace becomes and, consequently, the better the possibility of keeping the commandments and being saved. The way to salvation is a complete trust in the Church's definition of moral conduct, and this is maintained by adhering to its minimum standards regarding a practising Catholic.

The level of attendance at Mass, Confession and Holy Communion is lower among certain sub-groups of the Irish population, including the young, males, and those living in cities. A rigid adherence to the Church's definition of sin is generally less likely among the young and better educated. Whereas eight in ten respondents in the university survey in 1976 went to Mass once a week and received Holy Communion once a year, only 65 per cent attended Confession the required once a year. When it is considered that six in ten disagreed with the Church's teaching on contraception, then the indication is that many Catholic university students were following their own definition of sin and were receiving Holy Communion even though the Church may have formally considered them unworthy.[35] It was the movement away from Confession and the Church's definition of what constitutes sin and good moral conduct, to an individual interpretation of morality, which was a sign of the development of individually principled ethics within this subgroup of the population. A further indication of this trend comes from the 1984 update, after ten years, of the national survey. The results indicated that while the proportion attending weekly Mass had not changed dramatically (from 91 per cent in 1973–74, to 87 per cent in 1984), the proportion who did not make their Confession at least once a year had risen from 10 per cent in 1973–74, to 24 per cent in 1984.[36]

That sacramental attendance among Irish Catholics is primarily a legal fulfilment of a Church prescription is demonstated by the facts that not only did the vast majority of respondents in the national survey regard missing Mass on Sundays and failing to do one's Easter Duty as wrong, but when asked why it was wrong, over two-thirds gave the general reason that it was against the law of God or Church, or that it was failing in their duty. Analysing the responses from the 1973–74 survey in more depth, Nic Ghiolla Phádraig found that one in two gave legalistic types of reasons for regarding the following as wrong: missing Mass on Sundays, failing to do one's Easter Duty, not paying dues, not marrying in Church, and not bringing up one's children as Catholics. She also found a positive and linear relationship between levels of religious practice and the likelihood of using legalistic reasoning, e.g. 'against the law of God', 'against Church law', in the assessment of moral conduct. Indeed she found that those who relied on extrinsic legalistic reasoning were, in terms of the indices used, more religious than those who used spiritual reasoning such as 'would lose contact with God', or 'would miss the graces'. She concluded: 'The legalist group, as predicted, were significantly over-represented in traditional categories and had significantly the highest levels of religiosity on most indices. It had been predicted that the spiritual group would be mainly distinguished by high levels of religiosity, but their performance was below average.' However, even the spiritual group were best distinguished by their 'attitudinal and behavioural endorsement of the institutional Church' rather than by their 'beliefs, values, experiences or perceived social support for such endorsement'.[37]

Further evidence that religious legalistic behaviour is a characteristic of Irish Catholic religiosity comes from the survey of university students in 1976, a young, educated sub-group of the population among whom such behaviour might not be expected to be prominent. In fact less than a quarter of the Catholic respondents agreed with any of the three statements that were used to measure religious legalism: 'You cannot be a good Christian without going to church on Sundays', 'It is wrong to work on Sundays if it is not necessary', and 'In order to be saved it is necessary to have been baptised'. In subsequent statistical analysis, these three attitudinal items, along with three other measures ('belief that the Catholic Church is the one true Church', 'belief that the Pope can teach infallibly', and 'frequency of attendance at Confession'), formed a separate dimension to being religious. Again it was only a minority (less than three in ten) of the Catholic students who fully accepted these beliefs and who attended Confession at least once a month. What is important about these findings is that religious legalism was found to be a separate dimension of Irish religiosity, even among university students. Students who were classified as religious legalists were more likely to consider premarital sex, abortion, killing and the use of contraceptives as being wrong primarily because they are contrary to the teachings of the Church.[38]

Attendance at Confession is a major aspect of religious legalistic behaviour, since the individual submits his conduct to the priest for an assessment of its morality in terms of the institution's laws. If Confirmation is the assessment of the individual's knowledge of the rules and regulations by which salvation can be attained, Confession is the continuous assessment of whether or not it is being attained. The rigid legalist does not follow his own conscience. He does not derive his own code of moral behaviour from the principles given to him in the Bible. He follows the norms and regulations which the Church has derived from these principles. It is the legalist who, in the absence of a specific regulation, is often forced to consult with a priest so as to find out what is morally right or wrong.

The Church necessarily advocates a legalistic adherence to its rules and regulations. It discourages following one's own conscience because, as the Irish hierarchy put it, 'it can err, and in fact often does'.[39] Faithful Catholics are expected to accept all of the Church's teachings. As Bishop Newman of Limerick put it, there are 'some Catholics [who] manage to persuade themselves that they are faithful to their Church even though they reject some points of its teaching.'[40] To make a moral decision, according to the Irish hierarchy, the individual conscience must not only be informed, it 'must be guided by Church authority'. In other words, it is permissible for a Catholic to follow his or her conscience as long as it is guided by Church principles and does not contravene any specific regulation. As the Bishops' pastoral put it: 'It is for conscience to consider each new situation in the light of the overall command of love and the relevant moral values, and make the appropriate response. This response must always be in accordance with the specific commandments of God, as authoritatively interpreted by the Church, and must never violate the prohibitions contained in them.'[41]

Individually Principled Ethics

The Catholic Church is founded on a systematic doctrine of ethical principles. It is a complete system within which the morality of any act can be determined. The principles are rationally and logically related to one another. But in the hierarchical organisation of the Church it is not the task of the laity to understand how these principles are logically interrelated. This is the task of the Pope, bishops, and theologians who devise specific rules and regulations for the laity to follow. The 'simple faith' is the embodiment of these rules and regulations without any questioning or individual interpretation. Indeed, as O'Doherty found, there can be a strict adherence to the disciplinary obligations of the Church and an absence of any awareness of general Catholic principles.[42]

There are Catholics who strictly adhere to the regulations of the Church and who are aware of the general principles of their faith. But unless these principles are recognised, internalised, and adopted for their own sake rather than simply because of Church demands, they remain closer to religious legalism than to individually principled behaviour. There are other Catholics who do not have an explicit awareness of general Catholic principles and who appear to follow their own consciences, in that they disobey certain teachings and regulations. They adhere to some regulations, but not to others. But many of these Catholics are closer to religious legalism rather than individually principled ethics in that they continue to interpret their own behaviour, and that of others, as right or wrong in terms of the categories and definitions of the Church. Fully developed principled ethics are based on the ability of an individual to interpret the morality of behaviour in terms of abstract principles, to internalise these principles as his or her own, to adapt them to particular situations, and to explain and justify them to others.

In 1973–74, individually principled ethics did not appear to be very common among Irish Catholics. The majority seemed to follow the Church's interpretation of Christ's teachings. Even though they may have been disobedient, most Irish Catholics rarely seemed to disagree with the Church's teachings. Two-thirds of the respondents said they had no difficulty with any of the Church's teachings.[43] A similar percentage fully accepted the belief in papal infallibility. Such was the acceptance of the Church's interpretation of Christ's teachings, and what constitutes good Christian behaviour, that most Irish Catholics did not bother to read the Bible or gospels.[44]

Approximately one-third of Irish Catholics still identified themselves as Church members but no longer adhered strongly to its teachings. Some of these still assessed what was good moral behaviour in terms of the Church's teachings, even though they may have contravened these themselves. Others adopted their own criteria for deciding whether behaviour was good or bad, and assumed an individual moral responsibility for their own conduct and lifestyle. These Catholics were generally better educated and lived in urban areas. In the 1973–74 survey, six in ten of the respondents who had third-level education said they had difficulty with some aspect of the Church's teaching, whereas only two in ten of those with no more than primary-level education said they had any difficulty.[45] In his survey of Dubliners in 1972, MacGreil found that the level of monthly confession attendance was significantly lower among those with third-level education. Yet they had a significantly higher frequency of receiving Holy Communion.[46] Among Catholic university students, the author found that a majority (57 per cent) disagreed with the Church's teaching on contraceptives and thought that their use was right. Yet this did not make many of them feel immoral or unworthy since more than two-thirds (69 per cent) received Holy Communion up to twice a month.[47]

Conclusion

Three types of ethical religious behaviour which are found in Irish Catholicism have been described in this chapter: magical practices, legalist-orthodox (adherence to the rules and regulations of the Church), and individually principled ethics (individually reasoned principles about moral conduct). This analytical framework helps us to understand the religious behaviour of Irish Catholics. It is not to suggest that Catholics are orientated solely towards one type of behaviour. There are Catholics in Ireland who assess the morality of behaviour in terms of specific Church regulations, but who are also orientated to practices of a magical type such as using relics to produce cures. Equally there are many Catholics who follow a set of individually principled ethics, but who in illness might surrender themselves to a faith-healer. Irish Catholic religious behaviour vacillates between all three different types in much the same way that the Church itself does. There are many institutional Church rituals that are quite magical in their orientation. On the one hand, the Church can advocate that moral behaviour is dependent on a reasonable, informed conscience. On the other, it can foster practices such as the use of relics and holy water which are typically magical. Indeed one of the reasons for the persistence of the Catholic Church in modern Ireland is its ability to reconcile the three types of religious behaviour, and to avoid the rational systematisation of ethics that occurs in certain forms of Protestantism, especially Puritanism. Nevertheless it has been shown that adherence to the rules and regulations of the Church is the dominant form of religious behaviour among Irish Catholics. When, how, and why it came to be – and remain – the dominant form of religiosity will occupy much of the remainder of this study.

What makes Irish Catholics different from Catholics in other Western European societies is the high level of institutional adherence to the Church (especially in terms of sacramental attendance), the persistence of many magical and devotional practices, and the general acceptance of the Church as the legislator and arbiter of morality. In a comparative study of values and practices in different European societies, the weekly attendance at church by the Irish (82 per cent) was found to be three times higher than the general European average (25 per cent), and twice as high as tradition-ally Catholic countries such as Spain (41 per cent) and Italy (36 per cent) where the proportion of Catholics in the population is also nine in ten. The Irish respondents also had a higher level of confidence in their Church, and thought that its answers on individual moral problems were adequate.[48] The power, then, of the Catholic Church in Ireland is essentially a moral one. Instead of a shift towards principled ethics and a more secular ethic of individual responsibility which has taken place in other European societies, there is still in Ireland not only a persistence of magical practices, but also an adherence to the rules and regulations of the Church and a general acceptance of its definition of what is morally right or wrong.

3
Church Organisation
and Control

The high level of adherence to the rules and regulations of the Church among Irish Catholics has been maintained by means of a vast organisation – of both physical capital and personnel – that was developed in the nineteenth century. It was within this institutional network of churches, schools, hospitals, and homes that Irish Catholics became disciplined to the rules and regulations of the Church. It was through the dedicated work of priests, nuns, and brothers that the ability to control the moral discourse and practice of the Irish people was first established. It was they who looked after the health, education, and social welfare of Irish Catholics. It was this care and supervision which laid the basis for, and maintained, institutional adherence. The physical reorganisation of the Irish Church during the last century was part of the extension of bureaucratic control from Rome. A rigorous system of hierarchical discipline was implemented. Bishops and priests were brought into line with Rome. To understand the moral power of the Church in Ireland, then, it is necessary to describe how it has been physically organised and hierarchically structured; the position and role of bishops, priests, nuns, and brothers; the contribution of part-time voluntary workers; and the various strategies and tactics by which this hierocratic power has regulated the laity. It is partly because of its organisational strength that the Church has been able to limit what Irish people did and said. It is through its highly developed bureaucratic apparatus that the Church, like the state in political matters, has been able to maintain control over Irish moral discourse and practice. Other than the state, there has been no institution in Irish society that has had the same level of organisation and depth of resources as the Catholic Church. It has a strict bureaucratic organisation with a hierarchical structure of command from the Pope down to bishops and priests. Its legal system, Canon Law, is as detailed and complex as that of the state. It has enormous economic resources. It owns large areas of valuable land, much of which is located near the centre of towns and cities. Many of the largest buildings that dominate the Irish countryside are owned by the Church. But the source of this material wealth has been the dedicated loyalty of its priests, nuns and brothers. In 1981, it had over 25,000 full-time workers. It had thousands more who worked on a part-time basis. Through its dominance of education, health, and social welfare the Church has been largely responsible for the civilisation, moralisation, discipline, and supervision of Irish people. It was partly because Irish people spend a considerable proportion of their lives in buildings owned and run by the Catholic Church, and under the direct or indirect supervision of priests, nuns, and brothers, that the Church has been able to maintain its moral power. Unless one has an understanding of the size of the material organisation and the way in which it has operated, one cannot appreciate how the Catholic Church has dominated Irish society for so long.

A good deal of the empirical data in this chapter relates to the situation which pertained at the beginning of the 1980s when the Church was still at the height of its power. There have been dramatic changes in the last ten years, and these are detailed and analysed in chapter 9. When relevant new data have been available these have either been included in the tables or referred to in the text.

Physical Organisation

The physical organisation of the Catholic Church in Ireland is based on the twenty-six dioceses within the whole island. The dioceses are subdivided into parishes, of which there were 1,359 in 1997. This is an increase of 37 parishes since 1982. There were just under three thousand Catholic churches in 1997; an increase of 316 since 1982. Each Catholic parish in Ireland in 1997 contained, therefore, on average, 2.2 churches (table 5).

Given a Catholic population of just under 3.2 million in 1991, this means that in 1997 there was approximately one church for every 1,092 Catholics. As well as churches, numerous other buildings belonged to the Church. The number of charitable institutions (hospitals, homes for the deaf, blind, reformatories and so forth) owned by the Church was 667 in 1997 – an increase of 76 since 1982. This increase in the number of charitable institutions is significant because during this period: (a) the economy was going through a recession; (b) there was a dramatic decline in the number of vocations to the orders of religious sisters and brothers who ran these institutions; and (c) there was an ongoing separation between Church and state in other areas of Irish social life. Education was the only area in which the Church showed a decline in physical resources. In 1982 there were 4,754 primary and secondary schools owned by the Church. By

Table 5.   Physical Organisation of the Catholic Church in Ireland,
1982 & 1997

Diocese	Parishes		Churches		Charitable Institutions		Schools (primary & secondary)	
	1982	1997	1982	1997	1982	1997	1982	1997
Armagh	60	61	140	166	11	9	203	201
Ardagh & Clonmacnoise	41	41	78	87	8	11	121	101
Clogher	39	37	87	98	5	6	126	138
Derry	52	52	105	143	11	10	176	165
Down and Connor	81	86	149	202	42	95	227	215
Dromore	20	22	47	66	7	7	66	69
Kilmore	36	36	97	107	3	2	110	94
Meath	68	69	145	132	32	25	221	223
Raphoe	29	31	70	78	9	9	134	122
Dublin	185	198	234	30	186	190	753	719
Ferns	48	49	101	153	9	14	121	116
Kildare & Leighlin	55	56	116	129	8	9	227	199
Ossory	42	42	105	102	36	34	119	108
Cashel	46	46	89	130	8	5	160	151
Cloyne	46	46	105	167	15	20	165	153
Cork & Ross	64	68	121	172	49	49	318	248
Kerry	53	54	110	128	54	56	224	205
Killaloe	58	59	133	137	10	19	188	188**
Limerick	59	60	93*	134	12	15	146	148
Waterford & Lismore	44	45	84	108	14	14	130	130
Tuam	57	56	131	149	10	26	282	282**
Achonry	23	23	47	56	6	3	91	67
Clonfert	24	24	48	60	13	3	77	79
Elphin	33	36	90	89	16	18	168	147
Galway	37	40	66	80	11	8	111	111
Killala	22	22	48	52	6	10	90	79
Total	1,322	1,359	2,639	2,995	591	667	4,754	4,458

* 1980
** 1997 figures not available; 1982 figures taken instead.Source: *Irish Catholic Directory*,
1983, (Dublin: Universe, 1983), p. 349. Annurio Pontificio, 1983, 1991 (Vatican: Libreria
Editrice Vaticana,1983, 1991).

1997, this had fallen to 4,458 – a decrease of 296 schools. Ownership of these schools is crucial to the Church creating and maintaining a commitment, loyalty and obedience to its ethos and teachings. It is within schools that each new generation of Irish Catholics is imbued with the beliefs and practices of the Church. Although adherence to institutional rules and regulations has begun to decline in recent years, it has not been as dramatic as it would have been had there been an end to denominational education. Ownership and control of buildings and land, especially schools, hospitals and charitable institutions, have been an important aspect of the Church's power in Ireland, particularly since the nineteenth century. This power was maintained over many generations because property was held collectively as part of the organisation rather than privately. Indeed Weber argued that the original reason for the emphasis on celibacy was to prevent inheritance rights being claimed by the heirs of priests.[1]

Bureaucratic Organisation

Most churches and religious denominations are seen as voluntary organisations – that is people are free to join and leave them as they please. This is quite different from, for example, a state. However, there are many aspects of the Catholic Church which make it look like a compulsory organisation. It is not something which people often join voluntarily. It has an established order of rules and regulations into which one is born and which are enforced by the threatened denial of salvation. The highly complex legal structure of the Church, which is central to its domination, is administered through the bureaucratic staff of priests, nuns, and brothers. This administrative staff is quite different from that of the state. Its members are generally life-long and often dedicated through vows of obedience, celibacy, and poverty. It is these vows together with their clerical dress which make priests and religious highly distinctive. This cultural distinctiveness, combined with high occupational status, has been central to their power.

Although the Catholic Church often likes to describe itself as the church of the people (*pobal* in Irish has the double meaning of church and people), it is a centralised, multinational organisation which claims a universal legal competence that is exercised by bishops and priests throughout the world. The most important outcome of the Vatican Council of 1870 was not so much the dogma of Papal infallibility as the universal episcopate of the people which, in Weber's words 'created the ecclesiastical bureaucracy (*Kaplanokratie*) and turned the bishop and the parish priest, in contrast to the Middle Ages, into mere officials of the central power, the Roman *Curia*.'[2] The dogma of Papal infallibility and the rationalisation of ecclesiastical bureaucracy were the culmination of a process which had begun in earnest in the eighteenth century, and were in many ways a response to the domination being exercised by the newly centralised power of nation-states. As we shall see in the second part of this study, the growth of the Catholic Church in Ireland was part of this process. From the end of the eighteenth century, but particularly from the granting of Catholic Emancipation in 1829, there was a tightening of administrative control, associated with increased communication between bishops, their priests Rome and London. In 1850, Paul Cullen was appointed Archbishop of Armagh. He had spent twenty years in Rome as head of the Irish College. From then, the entire Irish Church was reshaped in discipline and devotion along Roman lines.

One of the best ways to give an idea of the bureaucratic structure of the Catholic Church in Ireland is to describe how it is hierarchically organised in terms of bishops, priests, brothers, and nuns and what role each of these plays in the day-to-day running of the Church:

Bishops: Since the thirteenth century the Catholic Church in Ireland has been divided into dioceses. Each of these dioceses has at least one bishop. Auxiliary bishops may be appointed. They have the same theological status as the diocesan bishop, but have subordinate administrative functions. For example, Dublin which is the largest diocese with just over a quarter of the island's Catholic population, has a minimum of five auxiliary bishops. There are four ecclesiastical provinces administered by archbishops. There is generally one Cardinal appointed who is the formal head of the Irish Church and who presides over the Conference of bishops. The four arch-bishops have very limited power over the bishops in their archdiocese. It is still the individual bishop in charge of his own diocese who is the crucial link between Rome and the Irish Church.

Each bishop is the authority for matters concerning his own diocese. Matters concerning Ireland as a whole are dealt with in full meetings of the Irish hierarchy which meets three times a year for two days. There are also some extraordinary meetings – for example, to draft joint pastoral state-ments. A Standing Committee of the hierarchy, consisting of the four archbishops and eight other bishops meets about six times a year to deal with current affairs and to draw up the agenda for the full meetings.[3]

Public squabbling between bishops and disregard of directives from Rome, which were quite common in the first half of the nineteenth century, have virtually disappeared. As one bishop described the contemporary scene: 'Each bishop has a responsibility before the Lord for his own dio-cese. . . . But you won't find bishops contradicting one another.'[4] During the 1970s the hierarchy began to issue pastorals and joint statements more frequently. While these are undertaken independently, they rely heavily on papal encyclicals and statements. Individual bishops with special competencies will often issue public statements on contemporary issues – sometimes as individuals, sometimes as spokesmen for the rest of the hierarchy. It is also common for a bishop to issue his own pastoral statement which differs from any joint statement of the Episcopal Conference. This is what happened in 1971 when the hierarchy issued a statement with reference to the proposal to change the legislation on contraception. The statement declared that 'There are many things which the Catholic Church holds to be morally wrong and no one has ever suggested, least of all the Church herself, that they should be prohibited by the State.' However, in his Lenten pastoral the Archbishop of Dublin, Dr McQuaid, went beyond the joint statement, and declared that the proposed legislation offended 'the objective moral law', was a 'curse upon our country', and 'an insult to our Faith'.[5]

Like any other modern bureaucratic organisation, the Conference of Irish Bishops has a number of commissions and advisory bodies, each of which is under the supervision of two or three bishops. These commissions gather and disseminate information and statements concerning various aspects of the Church in Ireland. There are nineteen altogether dealing with: catechetics, clergy (including seminaries and priests), communications, doctrine, ecumenism, education, emigrants, Euopean affairs, finance, justice and peace, the laity, liturgy, missions, pastoral matters, the religious, research and development, social welfare, theology and world development (Trocaire).

Under the hierarchical organisation of the Church, bishops are accountable to Rome, priests are accountable to their bishops, and the laity is accountable to their priests. Canon law obliges bishops to visit their diocese in order to safeguard good customs and rectify evil ones and to promote peace, innocence, piety, and discipline amongst the people and clergy. It is only in exceptional circumstances that a member of the laity makes direct contact with a bishop. Indeed there is something of a tradition of bishops remaining aloof from the ordinary people. This was often due to the fact that many bishops were appointed from the National Seminary in Maynooth, or some other third level institution, and had little or no experience of regular contact with the laity. It would also seem part of a deliberate policy to maintain doctrinal orthodoxy among the bishops: the less contact they have with the theologically illiterate, the less possibility of contamination. This helped maintain the status of bishops. Members of the laity, including the democratically elected leaders of the people, had to come to see them in their palaces if there was reason to meet. For example, during the Mother and Child controversy in 1951, it was the Archbishop of Dublin who summoned the Minister for Health to his residence. In 1963, Blanchard could claim that the bishops of Ireland 'have more power in practice than those of any country in the world', and that 'a member of the congregation listens much more readily to his Bishop than he does, for instance, to his deputy [elected member of political constituency].'⁶ There was a tendency immediately after Vatican II to appoint bishops with pastoral rather than theological experience, but this trend has been reversed in recent years. This is in spite of the fact that in the national survey in 1973–74, two-thirds of the respondents agreed that the leaders of the Catholic Church were out of touch with the real needs of its members, and that half of the respondents felt that lay people should have a say in electing bishops.⁷ In effect, as in any other multinational organisation, bishops are appointed directly by the headquarters in Rome. Other bishops within the archdiocese are consulted, as are priests and some lay leaders within the actual diocese itself. However their choice is often overlooked. Far from being an open democratic process, the appointment of bishops is an autocratic Roman preserve which is kept secret. The internal organisational struggles are probably as great as those concerning the appointment of any politician, but they are clouded by the belief that all the machinations are really an expression of the Holy Spirit.

The methods by which bishops supervise and control their priests are numerous. Most of the formal procedures were set out in the Decrees of the Maynooth Council in 1956. As part of the hierarchical power of the Church, in which the business of bishops and priests is deliberately hidden from the laity, these decrees are written in Latin and are not available to members of the general public. Similarly, members of the laity are denied access to the meetings of the Conference of Irish Bishops, and after the meetings only brief statements are issued about what took place. Blanchard notes that under the Maynooth decrees each parish is formally visited by the bishop every two to three years. The parish priest is required to complete a questionnaire concerning the spiritual welfare of his parish before the visit. Like the Maynooth decrees, neither the details of the questionnaire nor any account of the visit are ever made public. Besides this more formal procedure, bishops can supervise their priests and their conduct, as well as obtain information about their priests' problems, through diocesan chapter meetings, various committee meetings and, perhaps most important of all, during the annual diocesan retreat.⁸

Bishops are also responsible for overseeing the operations of religious orders of priests, brothers and nuns. But here the level of control and supervision is much less – unless, as has been happening in recent years, a religious order of priests is running a parish. A bishop cannot censure a member of a clerical religious order as easily as he can a diocesan priest, and he certainly does not have the same power to say where he or she should go, and what he or she should do.

Diocesan Priests: Although the Catholic Church exercises global control from Rome, and there are regulations under canon law which must be followed, a certain autonomy is nonetheless afforded to bishops and priests in their day-to-day running of the Church. This independence means that bishops in one country can behave quite differently from bishops in another, and yet still be part of the same Church. Similarly, priests can sometimes be quite different from their bishops, and from each other, in the way that they interpret, teach, and enforce the teachings of the Church. Throughout Irish history there have been numerous rebel priests who have disregarded the directives of their bishops especially with regard to political matters, and who have never been censured, let alone excommunicated. In fact it has been one of the organisational strengths of the Catholic Church that the Pope and bishops may state one thing, and that the priests, often reflecting pressure from the laity, may state and do the opposite. It is this gap between formal teaching and its more informal application which is central to the maintenance of the Church's moral power. This gap is formally recognised in Canon Law as the distinction between the External Forum (the official teaching) and the Internal Forum (as it is applied by at local level). In some respects, it is an internal mechanism for dealing with prophecy. In other words, a woman may come to a priest and tell him that she is using contraceptives, and he may say the equivalent of 'it is written, but I say unto you'. The problem, however, also recognised in Canon Law, is that if the gap between the Internal Forum and the External Forum grows too large, the official teaching is undermined and there is the greater danger of schism.[9]

While a bishop may exercise control over his curates by shifting them from one parish to another, he loses this ability once he appoints a Parish Priest. It is often said that if the bishop is master of his diocese, he is not the parish priest of his parishes. It may be because of this relative autonomy possessed by a Parish Priest that, in the 1970s, the appointment to this position was, on average, delayed until he was about 55 years of age.[10]

In 1981, there were 3,653 diocesan clergy of whom almost eight in ten (78.5 per cent) were actively engaged in parish ministry. As we shall see in chapter 9, while there has been a dramatic decline in the number of religious order priests, nuns and brothers over the last fifteen years, the number of diocesan clergy has remained stable. This means that the average parish in Ireland has approximately two priests working in it. The overall ratio of Catholics per priest in 1981 was 978, which was one of the lowest in the world. Other ratios were: England/Wales 989; France 1445; Italy 1398; Portugal 2460; Poland 2200; and the United States 1422. If one expresses the Irish ratio in terms of Catholics to each priest, nun, or brother, it was 174:1.[11]

The task of the diocesan priests is to preach, catechise, and administer the sacraments. They are responsible for the spiritual and often the social welfare of the parishioners. Because they have most contact with the laity, they are at the forefront of the institutional Church's struggle to maintain moral power. It is their task to be familiar with their parishioners' spiritual condition and moral behaviour. They are the day-to-day assessors of what is right and what is wrong. In the heyday of the Church's monopoly over the definition of morality, the priest could be understood as a type of moral policeman whose beat was the schools, homes, halls, and hedges of the parish. He looked after and responded to the spiritual and moral needs of the laity – needs which the discourse of the Church was responsible for creating and maintaining. In other words, the Church and its priests create what is in effect an arbitrary order of symbolic power which it then maintains through various institutional strategies and tactics.[12] The need for salvation can only be met in and through priests. Like the ordinary policeman, the priest was there to respond to the needs of the laity if they, or others close to them, broke the law. But he was also there to enforce the law. It was difficult if not impossible, in many parts of rural Ireland, to maintain one's social prestige if one had been censured or denounced by the priest. This is the reason why many employers traditionally sought a reference from an applicant's parish priest. His status as moral arbiter is dependent on a number of strategies and tactics for maintaining adherence to the institutional Church. Most of these are personal and direct, including home visitation, castigation, denial of absolution, and so on. The ones most feared are public denunciations – informally through the parish grapevine, formally from the pulpit or, rarely though still a possibility, full censure and excommunication.

Just as the state is ultimately founded on a monopoly of the physical means of coercion, such as the army and police, the Church's monopoly over morality was ultimately founded on its means of religious and social coercion: denial of salvation, excommunication, and loss of social prestige. This power was maintained, often in opposition to that exercised by the state, through the services and care that the Church provided especially for the weaker members of society. The exercise of moral power was also dependent upon a detailed knowledge of the behaviour of parishioners. The more a priest knew about their behaviour, the more likely was he to be able to control them. This knowledge was obtained in different ways: as a broker of power, as a social consultant, through house visitation, and in Confession.

At the zenith of its monopoly over morality, the priest in Ireland was not just a spiritual and moral adviser. He was consulted on a wide range of social, political and economic issues. His formal status derived from being the head of the parish, from being the manager of the local school, from being on the management committee of various sports and social organisations, and, at a personal level, being one of the better educated and more refined members of the community. Informally he was often the most respected member of the community. Any outsider or group which became involved in the parish, whether at a social, political or economic level, usually made contact with the parish priest.[13] Rarely was there any social occasion of importance he was not asked to attend. He had most influence as the guardian of virtue and morality, and as the person who symbolically legitimated events and activities in the community. He was the one who supervised access to social and moral respectability.

Visitations to homes were part of the priest's pastoral care of his parishioners. The work of visitations was similar to the labour of love carried out by religious sisters and brothers in their care of the sick, disabled, poor and disadvantaged. The symbolic blessing of the home by his visitation, and the care and concern given to members of the household, were a crucial element in maintaining the Church's monopoly of the religious field. But part of the visitation also concerned an investigation into the spiritual and moral behaviour of parishioners. The friendly and informal parish visits often had a specific purpose. As one priest put it: 'at some stage or stages in the informal chat there must be spiritual welfare business and investigation, for instance "I suppose you have the family rosary" or "I'm sure you have all made the Easter duty". The question about the rosary should be asked only to keep them at it.'[14] In the national survey in 1973–74, nearly half of the homes in the country had been visited by a priest in the six-month period prior to the interview.[15] It was during these visitations that the priest could check up on the signs of moral laxity, lack of discipline in attending Mass or school, or other family problems. The more often the priest visited the home the better the moral supervision. As Abbot pointed out: '[an] advantage of regular, methodical visitation is that "black sheep" will not feel that they are being publicly singled out for visits reserved for backsliders whose names appear on the priest's black list.'[16] The ability of diocesan priests to enter freely the home of Irish Catholics, to know the names of the family members, to remember their cares and concerns and, at the same time, to enquire directly or discreetly whether everyone was adhering to the rules and regulations of the Church, was a strategic element in maintaining a high level of institutional adherence. Most attention focused on the mother, for moral discipline was regarded as her responsibility. In the socio-economic environment of the long nineteenth century of Irish Catholicism, mothers did not go out to work and were confined to rearing and caring for their children. There was a structural similarity between the position and role of priests and the position and role of mothers. The position of priests in relation to the laity was mirrored in the position of the mother in relation to her children.[17] But the mirroring of the external operation of the Church in the parish under the priest and the internal operation of the Church in the home under the mother was also grounded in a material struggle for social and symbolic capital. The mother, as I shall argue in more detail in chapter 8, was generally bereft of economic and political power. She only had access to cultural, social and symbolic power. But access to these forms of power were dependent on the priest. In its heyday it was a symbiotic, dependent alliance, for it was mothers who created the vocations to the priesthood on which the Church depended. It was when a gap arose between priests and, first, young single women, then married women and, finally, mothers, that the Church's monopoly over Irish morality began to decline.

Because the priest is the centre of moral power in the community, he was often used by the laity as a vehicle for attaining symbolic legitimation and social capital. The closer one was to the priest, the arbiter of morality, the more moral one appeared, thereby adding to one's symbolic capital. Having symbolic capital meant that it was easier to gain entry to and stay within the elite social circles of the community. In other words, as much as national politicians were blessed by bishops and archbishops, local politicians were blessed by parish priests. But in the complex web of social relationships, this blessing was given informally in small rather than large gestures and praises. In the search for symbolic legitimation, parishioners often informed the priest of misdemeanours, moral laxity, and blatant defiance of the Catholic moral code in the community. In effect, these informers became the auxiliary force of the priest. Much of the supervision of moral behaviour of Catholics in Ireland was carried out by members of the laity acting as the priest's aides. The more the priest was informed of the misbehaviour of members of the laity, the more he was able to maintain his status as moral arbiter. Abbot described how information should be gathered on a visitation: 'People will certainly from time to time drop useful hints or volunteer information about neighbours. If they do so, the priest need not block his ears. After a short time he should resume the conversation ignoring the hints and the information. These hints, however, may furnish reasons for vigilance and direct enquiries.'[18]

The other method by which the priest traditionally obtained knowledge about his parishioners' behaviour was through the confessional. It was in response to the sins, worries, and concerns being announced to him in Confession that the priest was able to redirect his pastoral care towards the needs of the community. It was when people stopped going to Confession that the priest and the Church began to lose touch with the behaviour and needs of the laity. As mentioned earlier, there is a distinction between the formal teaching of the Church as mediated by the Pope and bishops, and its informal application through the priests in Confession. While the former may demand strict compliance to the Church's teachings, the latter may interpret these more as general rules rather than specific regulations.[19] But when people stop going to Confession, the possibility of a more personal, informal application of the general rule is denied. The formal teaching can then lead to disenchantment with, and alienation from, the Church. This is particularly relevant with regard to the use of contraceptives. In the survey of university students in 1976, six in ten of the Catholic respondents thought that using contraceptives was right, but 35 per cent rarely or never went to Confession. Furthermore, one of the main reasons disaffiliated Catholic students gave for leaving the Church was disagreement with a particular Church teaching.[20] It is precisely because of the absence of frequent personal contact with many young Catholics, either through visitation or Confession, that priests and bishops have had to rely more on the results of social surveys to find out what the laity are doing and thinking. This was one of the reasons the Hierarchy established its own research and development commission.

The power of the diocesan priest in Irish society, was, then, related directly to his level of supervision and knowledge of the moral behaviour of his parishioners. The more he supervised, the more he knew what was going on. But as more people stopped confessing their sins to him, as more people revolted against his supervision, he became more out of touch, and his power diminished. As this process developed, many Irish Catholics first of all no longer interpreted the morality of their actions in terms of what their local priest said, and later distanced themselves from an adherence to the rules and regulations of the Church. There was a gradual progression away from the type of Irish Catholic who believed it was bad luck to oppose or contradict a priest, to the type of Catholic who rarely or never goes to Confession. The more this process continued the more did the status and power of the diocesan priest decline.

Clerical Religious Orders: The organisational strength of the Catholic Church in Ireland can be understood from the fact that in 1995 diocesan priests represented approximately only one in six of the men and women who gave over their lives to working for the Church. No other organisation in Irish society has as many full-time employees who work so long, so hard, for so little. If diocesan priests can be understood as the spiritual and moral carers and policemen of Irish society, religious order priests, brothers and nuns may be seen as exemplary prophets of a life dedicated to the Church. Besides any status which derived from their occupational position as teachers, nurses, and so forth, their power derived mostly from their prestige – from the honour, respect and deference paid to them on account of their vows of celibacy and renunciation of possessions. The dedicated work of priests, nuns, and brothers in providing health, education, and welfare services for Catholics in opposition to those provided by a Protestant English State was crucial to the development of the Church's moral monopoly during the last century. The example they showed of a disciplined, celibate, moral lifestyle dedicated to self-denial and caring for others was crucial to the initial modernisation of Irish rural society, and the successful maintenance of population control mechanisms such as postponed marriage, permanent celibacy, and emigration. The exemplary role of clerical religious orders was also evidenced in the fact that in 1981 there were over six thousand of them doing missionary work abroad (table 6).

Table 6. Religious Personnel of the Catholic Church in Ireland, 1981 & 1995.

		Parish work	Teaching /Medical /Social	Other	Total 1981	Total 1995*
Diocesan Clergy	Ireland	2,869	541	243	3,653	
	Abroad	–	–	109	109	
	Total	2,869	541	352	3,762	3,659
Clerical Religious Orders	Ireland	868	559	2,124	3,551	
	Abroad	2,086	304	770	3,160	
	Total	2,954	863	2,894	6,711	4,564
Sisters	Ireland	–	5,988	6,344	12,332	
	Abroad	–	1,876	670	2,546	
	Total	–	7,864	7,014	14,878	12,104
Brothers	Ireland	–	962	528	1,490	
	Abroad	–	161	68	229	
	Total	–	1,123	596	1,719	1,061
Total	Ireland	3,737	8,050	9,239	21,026	
	Abroad	2,086	2,341	1,617	6,044	
	Total	5,823	10,391	10,856	27,070	21,388

* Details regarding numbers abroad and in different ministries were not available for 1995.

Sources: Research and Development Commission, *Irish Priests & Religious 1970–1975*; Research and Development Commission, *Vocations Returns 1996*.

Half of the Irish religious who were working abroad in 1981 were religious order priests. The majority of missionary priests were in developing countries and were engaged mainly in 'the pastoral care of souls'. Of the religious order priests in Ireland, three in ten were actively engaged in parish work, which included running parishes, running missions and giving retreats. Two in ten were engaged in teaching, mostly in schools of their order. The remainder did a variety of tasks, for example administration, writing, vocation work, and tending to the day-to-day needs of the order.

In 1995, as in 1981, over half of the full-time religious personnel of the Catholic Church in Ireland were nuns. In many ways they have been the silent, solid foundation of modern Irish Catholicism. It was the nuns who disciplined, trained, and educated almost every Irish girl who progressed beyond primary school. They refined and polished these girls into paragons of modern Irish virtue. The occupational choices of these well-educated girls were limited in the past. If they did not become mothers, many became secretaries, teachers, nurses, or nuns themselves. The nuns took over the management of the Irish health system in the nineteenth century, and since then have run many of the hospitals, nursing homes, remedial homes, orphanages, and other charitable institutions of the country. Yet the nuns, like the Irish mother, have been written out of the history of modern Irish Catholicism.[21]

The main work of religious order brothers in Ireland, half of whom are Christian Brothers, has been in teaching. As with the nuns, the contribution of brothers to the maintenance of the power of the Catholic Church in modern Irish society has yet to be fully analysed.[22] It is not that they educated every Irish male. It is rather that they, or the priests, educated and trained nearly every male who attained a high position in Irish society. Moreover it was the brothers who, before the end of the 1960s when the state introduced free secondary education, brought the possibility of post-primary education to the members of the lower socio-economic groups of Irish society.

When the Catholic Church loses control of education, and when priests, nuns, and brothers are no longer responsible for educating, disciplining, moralising, and caring for Irish Catholics, adherence to institutional Catholicism in Ireland will decline. One of the main problems facing the Catholic Church is the dramatic decline in the number of vocations and, consequently, in the number of priests, nuns and brothers. This is dealt with in greater detail in chapter 9, but it is important to draw attention here to two associated problems. The first is that priests, nuns and brothers are no longer significantly better educated than the laity. The symbolic power of priests, nuns and brothers was linked to their having more cultural capital. They were educationally well-qualified. They were also, of course, always well-mannered and refined. The Church used to have the pick of the annual crop of school-leavers. But those entering the religious life from school are no longer top of the class.[23] Another problem brought about by the decline in vocations is an increase in the generation gap between religious personnel and the laity. Priests, nuns, and brothers are all, comparatively, older than the rest of the population. Up-to-date figures are not available, but in 1971 more than six in ten (63 per cent) Irish nuns were over fifty years of age compared to just over four in ten (42 per cent) of the rest of Irish females.[24] Unless there is a dramatic increase in vocations, Irish religious personnel will be mainly involved in caring for their own sick, elderly, and infirm.[25]

Lay Organisations

Lay groups and organisations have always played a significant role in maintaining the position and influence of the Catholic Church in Ireland. However, after Vatican II and the decline in vocations, they began to play an even greater role. Whereas previously they used to be supervised and directed by clergy and religious, they have increasingly become an autonomous social movement operating inside and outside the Church – as loyal followers, but also as loyal critics. Lay people work within a wide variety of voluntary organisations. They have undertaken a number of tasks which used to be the sole preserve of the priest, for example giving sermons and distributing Holy Communion. Lay organisations have also taken over from the hierarchy in putting pressure on the state to amend existing legislation and to bring it into line with the Church's teachings. This has become a major feature of the various referenda on abortion and divorce since 1983. In the national survey in 1973–74, one in seven of the respondents said that they had been involved in some kind of parish work. The activity most frequently mentioned was collecting money.[26]

In 1983, there were twenty-six different Catholic lay organisations affiliated to the hierarchy's Laity Commission. The total membership of these organisations was over 300,000. This list includes many children's organisations, and there is probably a good deal of double counting in that members of one organisation could well be members of another. On the other hand, the list is by no means comprehensive.

It does not include a number of organisations, for example the Catholic Women's Federation, Congress of Catholic Secondary School Parent Associations, Cursillo, Knights of Malta, Irish Guild of SS Luke, Cosmas and Damien, Macra na Tuaithe, Social Study Conference, among others, which have either disbanded, become disaffiliated from the Commission, or whose work is not specifically Catholic. Nor does the list include a wide

Table 7.   Irish Catholic lay organisations: membership and aims (1983)

Organisation	Number of Members	Self-defined Aims
Apostleship of the Sea	150	To show Christian hospitality and concern to merchant seamen and women; to be a home outside of home.
Apostolic Work Society	3,600	To help the Missions by prayer and active work.
Catholic Boy Scouts	35,000	To promote the spiritual, moral, cultural and physical development of its members so that they become mature Catholics, prepared for leadership and service in home and community.
Catholic Girl Guides	13,000	As above
Catholic Marriage Advisory Council	1,809	To help people initiate, sustain and enrich their marriage and family relationships.
*Charismatic Renewal	10,000	The renewal of the individual, the Church and the whole body of Christ through prayer groups.
Christian Family Movement	600	To promote happy family life in accordance with Christ's teaching.
Christian Life Communities	500	Challenges Christians to an awareness of the grave responsibilities involved as Christ's witnesses.
Faith and Light	Not available	To emphasise the contributions that mentally handicapped people have to make to the Christian community.
Focolare	700	To help bring about the fulfilment of the prayer of Jesus 'that all may be one'.

Irish Guild of Catholic Nurses	1,650	To promote the social, educational and professional development of its members, so as to help them work effectively in the service of life.
Knights of St Columbanus	4,500	To promote by personal group action the extension of practical Christianity in all phases of life; to maintain a material order of Catholic lay leadership.
Lay Fraternity of Br Charles of Jesus	150	To achieve the mutual understanding and living unity right and proper for Christians through practising universa charity.
Legion of Mary	10,000	The sanctification of its members by prayer and participation in apostolic works: the provision of a *corps d'élite* at the disposal of ecclesiastical superiors.
Marriage Encounter Ireland	500	To organise weekend retreats for married couples.
Marriage Encounter World Wide	500	The renewal of the sacrament of Matrimony, thereby helping to renew the Church.
*National Federation of Youth Clubs	35,000	The personal development of young people as a process of education through the experience of relationships, through social action as well as ideas and skills.
Opus Dei	700	A personable prelature (*sic*) of the Catholic Church whose members strive to live the fullness of the Christian life, each one in their own state, by sanctifying their daily work and the ordinary circumstances of their family life and social commitments.
Pax Christi	200	To work with all men for peace for all men, always witnessing the peace of Christ.

Pioneer Total Abstinence Society	170,000	The promotion of temperance and sobriety with prayer and self-sacrifice as its principal means.
St Joseph's Young Priests Society	3,500	To promote vocations to the priesthood and to assist selected students financially.
*St Vincent de Paul	9,000	To alleviate need and to discover and redress situations which cause it, mainly through helping people in their homes.
Teams of Our Lady	250	For married couples to help one another live their lives in accordance with their Christian beliefs.
Viatores Christi	135	To encourage Irish people to volunteer for missionary service overseas.
*Volunteer Missionary Movement	230	To spread awareness of the role of the laity at home and abroad and send qualified committed lay people to the third world.
Young Christian Workers	500	To train young people to educate and represent themselves, whether at work or in society, and to see to the neglected needs of young people.

*These organisations are officially non-denominational although the vast majority of their members are Catholic and the organisation is affiliated with the Irish Catholic Episcopal Commission for the Laity, which was the criterion for inclusion in the above table.

variety of lay groups, such as confraternities, peace groups, bible study groups, adult theology groups, and so on, which often operate on a parish level, but which do not have a formal organisation. Nor does it include organisations such as PLAC (Pro-Life Amendment Campaign) and SPUC (Society for the Protection of the Unborn Child) which came together in 1983 to force through the referendum which made abortion unconstitutional.

The contribution of members of these lay organisations to the maintenance of the moral power of the Catholic Church in Irish society is enormous. They have been termed 'the living witnesses of the Catholic faith in Ireland'. They are the apostolic workers who, in their everyday lives and contact with other lay people, put forward the Church's view-point. It is often through their performance of charitable works that the Church is able to look after the sick and poor. For example, the St Vincent de Paul Society is a lay organisation which engages in direct person-to-person contact. In 1983, members visited 10,000 families, 7,000 elderly people, and virtually every hospital and long-stay institution in the country each week. Some of the larger organisations – including the Knights of Columbanus, Legion of Mary and Opus Dei – are secretive about their operations. They meet in private and the minutes of these meetings are not publicly available. Prospective members are instructed on the need to preserve absolute secrecy in regard to any matter discussed at meetings. In some ways these lay organisations resemble the Freemasons. In fact, one of the reasons why the Knights of Columbanus was first established was secretly to promote Catholic social principles and Catholic individuals in the organisations, public and private, in which they were working.[27]

Education

Control of the education system has been fundamental to the Catholic Church maintaining adherence to its rules and regulations. Within the schools young Irish children have been slowly and consistently instructed in and also imbued with the Church's teachings. This instruction takes place through a rigid system of moral discipline, at the centre of which is an inculcation of the Church's doctrine and ritual practices. It has been mainly through these practices, including the rote learning of the cate-chism, that an adherence to the rules and regulations of the Church has been instilled. Furthermore, through the school the Church was able to reach into the home and supervise the mother in her upbringing of her children. As each new generation of Irish parents handed over their chil-dren to Catholic schools – often because of having limited choice – those who had let the reins of the Church's moral discipline slacken were forced to take them up again. The Church's control of Irish education has depended, as Clarke points out, on the state accepting the Church's policy on education: that each child has a right to a Christian education; that parents have a right to educate their children according to their consciences; and that Catholic parents have an obligation to educate their children the way the Church tells them to do so.[28] However, this does not explain why the state pays for and runs the system, and yet allows the Church to con-tinue to control it. Just when, why and how the state handed over control of Irish education to the Churches, and to the Catholic Church in particular, will be dealt with in chapter 6. In this section, the purpose is to document the control that it has exercised in the contemporary education system.

The vast majority of Irish Catholics have been educated by the Catholic Church. The instruction may not have been given by a priest, brother, or nun, but it was generally given by a schoolteacher who was appointed and supervised by a member of the clergy or religious. Within the school – every day, five days a week – children were imbued with the teachings, principles, and ethos of the Catholic Church. Religious instruction is still a major part of the syllabus, and is generally taught for a half hour each day. This is above and beyond any religious practice which occurs during or after school time but which is organised by the school – for example, prayers at the beginning of each day or lesson, sodalities, missions, retreats, and so on. As Murphy points out: 'In National Schools religion is supposed to permeate the whole atmosphere of the class and not to be regarded as just a half hour's instruction.' The Rules for National Schools state clearly that 'Of all the parts of a school curriculum, Religious Instruction is by far the most important. . . .'[29] In primary school, children are prepared for Confession, Holy Communion and Confirmation. They are given a thorough grounding in Catholic doctrine. In the 1960s the Church spent a great deal of time and money devising a new catechetical programme of books and tapes. However, the success of the programme was questionable, especially in terms of instilling a knowledge of the rules and regulations of the Church. Many people, including the former Archbishop of Dublin, Dr Dermot Ryan, called for a return to the 'penny' catechism and rote learning of prayers and doctrine.

The Church has always fought hard to maintain control of education in Ireland. It was treated as a mortal sin for Catholics not to send their children to Catholic schools. The Dublin Diocesan regulations of Dr McQuaid, which were enforced until 1971, stated that:

In the education of Catholics, every branch of human training is subject to the guidance of the Church, and those schools alone which the Church approves are capable of providing a fully Catholic education.

Therefore the Church forbids parents and guardians to send a child to any non-Catholic school, whether primary or secondary or continuation or university. Deliberately to disobey this law is a mortal sin, and they who persist in disobedience are unworthy to receive the sacraments.[30]

It may not still be a mortal sin, but it is nevertheless an unacceptable social practice for Catholics to send their children to Protestant schools. Not only was it regarded as disloyal and conduct unbecoming to an Irish Catholic, but in many circumstances it was an obstacle to social acceptance and being symbolically legitimated by the Church. The insistence on denominational education, both in the North and South of Ireland, is one of the main reasons for the persistence of different cultural practices between Catholics and Protestants. The persistence of segregated schooling is also partly responsible for the maintenance of traditional forms of family life, and of rigidly defined sex roles.

Of the 3,500 National Schools in the Republic of Ireland in 1984, 3,400 were under Catholic management. The remaining 100 were mostly managed by the Protestant Churches – Church of Ireland, Presbyterian, and Methodist. While the number of National Schools has decreased in recent years, the proportion under the patronage of the Catholic Church has remained the same.[31] In the Catholic schools, the land on which the school is built generally belongs to the Church. The State pays for the maintenance cost of the building and the teachers' salaries. There is a management board responsible for each school. Most of these have six members: three are nominated by the local bishop (one of whom is the chairman, usually the local parish priest); two of the members are elected representatives from parents of current school-going children; and the final member is the Principal of the school.[32] In 1985, the Catholic Primary Schools Managers' Association issued a set of guidelines for Management Boards on how to interview and assess candidates for new appointments. The first criterion mentioned for assessing applicants was 'a practising Catholic'.[33] In a subsequent interview, the secretary of the Association, Fr Walsh defined a practising Catholic as someone who attempted honestly to abide by the commandments and who was a very regular attender at Mass.[34]

The National School teachers have been a key element in passing on the Catholic faith in Ireland. For this reason the Church has fought, since the establishment of the system in 1831, for control over their training and appointment. Being a teacher has traditionally been regarded more as a vocation than a job, and although it did not require one to remain celibate, the instruction and discipline within teacher-training colleges was almost as rigorous as that for those training for the priesthood. McCarthy described the background and training of these teachers as follows:

These young men and women were drawn from the most academically able in the country, but certainly in the case of men, from a remarkably limited social group. It appears to me that they came primarily from small farmers and small shopkeepers in the south and west, and in many cases had themselves left home as early as thirteen or fourteen years of age, attending first the preparatory colleges (which now fortunately have been disestablished) and also the diocesan colleges, all residential in character. From there they went to a residential training college which was conducted on remarkably authoritarian lines. No doubt the church authorities were anxious to secure this rigorous training knowing that ninety per cent of Catholic children would receive their education from national teachers. . . .[35]

The Church also exercises considerable control in secondary education. Of the 572 secondary schools in the Republic of Ireland in 1982, forty-six were community schools and fifteen were comprehensive. These schools are formally non-denominational. Of the remaining 516 schools, twenty-five were run by Protestants and two were Jewish. The other 491 schools were Catholic.[36] Nuns are by and large responsible for the education of girls, and administered over half of these schools. In recent years there has been some amalgamation of their schools with those run by brothers, who control about one quarter of the total. However, regardless of any other problems, traditional attitudes towards segregated schooling die hard.

The remainder of the secondary schools are run by diocesan priests, religious order priests, and lay Catholic management boards. Diocesan priests are responsible for running their own colleges which have traditionally been regarded as training grounds either for vocations to the diocesan priesthood, or to the National School teacher-training colleges. Religious order priests are mainly involved in running top quality schools, many of which have expensive fees and boarding facilities and are orientated towards the sons of the upper middle classes.

Not until the 1960s did the state, as part of its programme of investment in education, make a move towards modernising the secondary school system. Many of the schools were in poor condition, and the curriculum was heavily orientated towards classical rather than technical or scientific subjects. The accumulated effect of the classical curriculum was the production of an over-abundance of students who may have known how to decline the Latin word for a table, but had no technical skills as to how to go about constructing one. The influence which the Church's control of education has had in helping to maintain an adherence to its teachings and practices can be seen from the results of the national survey in 1973–74. Those who were educated in vocational schools – which were set up by the State in the 1930s, outside clerical control, and orientated towards practical, manual skills and crafts – were more likely to be underconformers in sacramental participation, less accepting of Church doctrine, and to have a less pronounced general religious outlook than others.[37]

The pervasive influence of the Church in education extends to the third level. As Whyte points out, 'Ireland is the only country . . . where the Catholic Hierarchy has applied the principle of separate education for Catholics at university level.'[38] Until 1971, Dublin diocesan regulations forbade Catholics to attend Trinity College, a Protestant foundation since its beginnings in the sixteenth century. The National University of Ireland, with its three colleges in Dublin, Cork and Galway, and with what was until 1997 its recognised college at Maynooth, although formally nondenominational, is Catholic in its ethos. The NUI was constituted in 1908, after almost a century of agitation by the hierarchy for a Catholic university. It was designed so that the Church would have considerable influence in its governing bodies. This has, until very recent years, had an effect on appointments and the curriculum, especially in those faculties and departments where the knowledge produced was directly related to Church teaching.

The main principle for which the Church has fought, since the beginning of the struggle back in the 1830s, has been control of the type of knowledge that is produced within the educational system. This it has done mainly by censoring the curriculum and controlling appointments. As long as it can confine the knowledge which is produced to that which falls within the limits of its teachings, it does not matter so much whether the state provides the buildings and pays the teachers' salaries. In 1985, a High Court judge implied in his ruling that a Catholic secondary school was permitted to dismiss a teacher whose private life did not conform to the norms and values which the school was attempting to instil.[39]

There have been three main reasons why the Church has placed so much emphasis on maintaining control of the Irish education system. The first, as Titley argues, has been to maintain recruitment to the ranks. The process he describes involves young boys being 'convinced' of their religious calling in primary schools, and then 'fed' into diocesan colleges. He calculates that the influence of four priestly teachers in the period 1956–60 was sufficient to secure three vocations per annum. The second main reason was to maintain an influence and moral control over the future dominant class and political elite. As a Jesuit priest, quoted by Titley, put it in 1915: 'A suitable and thorough education for this body manifestly lies at the very bedrock of Ireland's moral, intellectual and material well-being. If they are sound, the country is safe.'[40] The third reason has been what Titley calls, 'the creation of a loyal Catholic laity', or what Clarke refers to more bluntly as 'indoctrination'.[41] With control of the schools this indoctrination is easily sustained since a lack of genuine alternatives leads each new generation of indoctrinated and unquestioning Catholic parents to go along with the existing system. The schoolchildren reintroduce institutional adherence among the parents who may wish to avoid difficulties by not contradicting what is taught in school. While this argument has validity it does not take into account the crucial role that the family, especially mothers, played in passing on the faith and creating vocations. Nor does it take into account the importance which control of Irish health and social welfare has had in maintaining adherence to Church rules and regulations after education has been completed.

Health

Ever since the nineteenth century in Ireland, but earlier elsewhere in Europe, the Catholic Church has been concerned with the maintenance and care of people, keeping them healthy and free from disease. Health and social welfare became a major point of conflict between the Church and the state, because at issue were spheres of power and, in particular, who was responsible for the care and supervision of people. It was a struggle that was vital to the very survival of the Church. The conflict culminated in the encyclical *Rerum Novarum* (1891) which was as much a dogma against the excessive interference by the state in social welfare as it was against class antagonism. As industrial society developed, the state became interested in creating the conditions of economic growth and political stability and, consequently, in disciplining and controlling people as well as keeping them healthy. It was central to the maintenance and development of the Church's power that social control be considered as a moral issue which came under its jurisdiction. One of the reasons why there is such a high level of adherence to the Catholic Church in Ireland is that the Church gained control of the health, care, and social welfare of the people, as it had done in education. It was mainly nuns, working from the principle that it should be a Catholic doctor and nurse who looked after Catholic patients, who began to build the hospitals and homes in which Catholics were trained, and who eventually took control of what had been until then a state-sponsored Protestant system. As an indication of just how successful this process was, Ryan estimates that by the beginning of the 1970s: 'Religious personnel either owned or had charge of 46 private hospitals, 25 nursing and convalescent homes, 32 geriatric homes, 35 homes for the mentally handicapped, 11 homes for the physically handicapped, 31 orphanages, 29 industrial schools and reformatories, 15 welfare hostels, and 20 student or business.'[42] Within these hospitals and homes, the vast majority of doctors and nurses got their training and practical experience. The medical schools within the universities became dominated by the Catholic code of medical ethics. Religious and medical discourse became interlinked. The physical health and social welfare for the people were not divorced from their spiritual welfare. What life was, when it began and when it ended, was defined within the Church's teaching.[43] Doctors and nurses became obliged to adhere to the Church's code of medical ethics, formally within Church-controlled hospitals, and informally in many State-run hospitals. When a person entered a hospital or institutional home in Ireland it was often assumed that he or she was in need of spiritual as well as physical care. The process of surrendering one's body to the doctors and nurses became allied to the process of surrendering one's soul to the priests and nuns. If anything should happen, the Church was there to save one's soul. Indeed the whole hospitalisation process demanded passivity and surrender. The patient was confined, monitored and supervised. Those who exercised this control over him or her often include priests and nuns as much as doctors and nurses.

Such was the Church's domination of the Irish health system that the medical profession became strongly allied to the Church in order to develop and maintain its own power. Together they developed a virtual monopoly of the knowledge about how the body functions – how it works and should work, especially in terms of sexuality. Not just good health, but to a certain extent the very soul of the modern person, has been founded on a control of bodily functions. At least until the 1960s, the Church and the Irish Medical Association were united in opposition to the state's intervention in their monopoly.[44]

The first major clash between the Church and the new Irish state occurred over health. Although the hierarchy was worried about the possible appropriation of the voluntary hospitals, most of which were run by religious orders, it was really a question of delineation of spheres of power and, in particular, of who had the right to educate and control the health and social welfare of women. It had to do with that section of the 1947 Health Act which required local authorities to make arrangements for safeguarding the health of women in respect of motherhood, and for their education in that whole area. The issue here was the same as the one which was at the heart of the notorious Mother and Child Scheme affair in 1951: 'To claim such powers for the public authority, without qualification, is entirely and directly contrary to Catholic teaching on the rights of the family, the rights of the Church in education, the rights of the medical profession and of voluntary institutions.'[45] It is no coincidence that the issues on which the hierarchy has entered the public arena in Ireland, and which have caused the most division between Church and state, have been those that deal with the control of women's bodies in general, and motherhood, divorce, contraception, abortion, and legitimacy in particular. In terms of maintaining its power, the problem for the Catholic Church was that once women began to gain control of their bodies, primarily through diffused medical knowledge and technology, the bonds that tied them to the home and rearing children gradually loosened. As that happened, the consolation and compensatory power which the Church in Ireland provided for women over the last hundred years was no longer as necessary because they were able to gain entry to the positions, resources and prestige to which they have previously been denied access.

Conclusion

In this chapter it has been argued that the high level of adherence to the rules and regulations of the Catholic Church, which was the main type of religious behaviour in Ireland during its monopoly over morality, was maintained through the rational bureaucratic organisation that the Church developed in Ireland from the middle of the last century. The Catholic Church was able to dominate the religious and moral fields of Irish society because it developed large numbers of dedicated personnel and an organisational network which was second only to that of the state. Religious tradition is not simply a set of beliefs and values which are held within the mind and passed on from generation to generation. It involves a physical and political control of social structures. The power of the Catholic Church in Ireland was not just ideological. Its ability to limit what people did and said; to imbue the Irish habitus with its moral ethos and sensibilities; and to form good Catholic personalities, was founded on an ownership and control of physical resources which were operated by a well-trained, disciplined and devoted team of priests, nuns and brothers. This is not to argue that the Catholic Church is an elitist, hierarchical organisation in which power resides only in full-time clerical members. There are thousands of voluntary, part-time workers who are equally responsible for maintaining an adherence to the Catholic Church's teachings. It is rather to argue that the Catholic Church in Ireland is a diffused, pluralist organisation of power in which those at the centre, especially the bishops, are able to limit what those at the periphery, and even those outside the institution, do and say. It is also to argue that the way in which the teachings, beliefs, and values of the Church have been maintained among the Irish has not depended simply on historical loyalty or some innate spirituality, but rather on a systematic process of socialisation exercised in churches, schools, hospitals, and homes. It is within these buildings that Irish people have been instructed, supervised, and disciplined to the ritual practices and teachings of the Catholic Church.

4

Power and the Catholic Church in Irish Social, Political and Economic Life

Theoretical Framework

A key issue in developing a sociological explanation for the monopoly which the Catholic Church developed on morality in Ireland is to link an explanation of the institutional structure of the Church with the everyday needs, concerns and interests of Irish Catholics. The power of the Catholic Church in Irish society, its monopoly over morality, was founded on its influence in Irish social, political and economic life. Such was the dominance of the Church in other social fields, besides the religious, that it was able to limit and control what people did and said when they met socially, engaged in politics and dealt in the marketplace. The Catholic Church had considerable influence in the way people viewed and understood their world and was able to set parameters for how people behaved socially; for the type of people who got jobs and became leaders; for the kind of laws that were passed; and for the type of economy that was developed and the way business was conducted. In other words, the Church constructed an orientation to life that defined the way they behaved in different social fields and the strategies and tactics people used as they engaged in the daily struggle to attain power.

Following Bourdieu, the argument in this chapter is that capital attained in the religious field was important when it came to people struggling to attain other forms of capital, particularly social, cultural, political, economic and symbolic capital.[1] To help understand this process, it is necessary to remember that capital accumulated in one social field is often used to attain capital in another field, and that one form of capital can be traded for another. For example, educational qualifications are an important form of cultural capital. In Irish society, being well-educated has become central to attaining economic and political capital. Similarly, being civilised and well-mannered, and knowing what to say and do in different social situations is also an important form of cultural capital. Being socially acceptable and respected is important when it comes to attaining political and economic capital. In Irish social life, religious capital was attained by being spiritual and moral in ways set out by the Catholic Church. But, in Ireland, unlike in other European societies, religious capital remained an important form of cultural capital which could be traded for other forms of capital.

Before analysing how this has operated in Irish society, it is important to explain in a little more detail what is meant by these different forms of capital and the role they play in social life. We are all engaged in a wide variety of social fields throughout our lives. Some of these are small and narrow, for example the field of sociology. Others are large and broad, encompassing a wide range of people and activities – for example, the fields of politics, economics, religion and education. Through engaging in these fields people acquire different forms of capital. A person's overall social position in society depends on the volume and structure of the different forms of capital they have accumulated. People accumulate cultural capital in a similar way to accumulating economic capital. They have some resources; they know the way the market operates; they have engaged in the game of buying and selling before; they have a feel for what is a good and bad strategy; and they make their investments accordingly. Similarly, for example, in the religious field; people already have some religious capital; they know how being religious operates; they have a feel for what is a good thing to do and say spiritually and morally; they engage in practices; and they make their investment accordingly. All of this takes place within the religious field. The Catholic Church and its experts, that is its bishops, priests and theologians, have dominated the way Irish people think and act religiously. Only those with good Catholic religious capital were able to contribute to the institutional discourse which structured the religious habitus. This is the link between the institutional structure of the Church, whose teachings helped define the way Irish people read, interpreted and acted in the social world in which they lived, and the capacity of individuals to contribute to and change that structure. To have what one said or wrote accepted by the institution necessitated having the right mix, among other things, of religious and cultural capital – that is being spiritual and moral in a way that the Church recognised and accepted, as well as having the right kind of education.

But the acquisition of religious capital was also important in everyday life. During the long nineteenth century of Irish Catholicism, when the Church held a moral monopoly, religious capital was an important component in the structure and volume of a person's capital and, therefore, in defining their overall social position in society.[2] It is argued, then, that in this century in Ireland religious capital remained more significant as a component of cultural capital and, therefore, in defining a person's social position than it did in other modern European societies. This is not to deny that there were other ways of attaining cultural capital which were also important to defining a person's overall social position. Following Bourdieu, we can identify three different forms of cultural capital. In its most basic form, cultural capital derives from embodying the different ways people develop of saying and doing things, that is, for example, the peculiar Irish way of social interaction and communication – the idioms, folkways and mores of Irish culture. This embodied form of cultural capital is essential to acquiring other forms of capital. It is knowing what to say and do, with whom, when and where. It is fundamental to being socially acceptable and respected. Now, in a society like Ireland, where the Catholic Church developed a monopoly on morality, religious capital and, in particular embodying the Church's definition of what was a good person, became important in being socially accepted and gaining respect.

Social prestige, or embodied cultural capital, is only one form of cultural capital. There are two other forms. Cultural capital can be objectified and possessed. This is often in the form of cultural artifacts such as books, paintings, music recordings, ornaments and furniture. In many Irish houses, the most significant cultural artifacts are still crucifixes and religious pictures and statues. However, these are increasingly being replaced by secular cultural artifacts, for example, domestic and landscape paintings, posters of film, sport and pop music stars. Lastly, cultural capital exists in an institutionalised state in the form recognised social awards of which the primary form has become educational qualifications.[3]

Social capital derives from being a member of different groups and being known and accepted in different institutionalised networks of family, friends and colleagues. Within these networks favours are granted and allegiances honoured. Being well-connected is central to acquiring political and economic capital, but it can also be important in acquiring cultural capital through, for example, gaining entry to clubs, associations, trade unions and schools.[4] The acquisition of social capital, and the strategies and tactics by which it is attained, is often dependent on previously acquired cultural capital, particularly being socially acceptable and educated. In Ireland, attending Mass on Sundays was a key strategy in maintaining social capital.

The next stage in this analytic model is to see cultural and social capital as being important assets in attaining and maintaining political capital.[5] Political capital enables someone to be a leader; to have followers; to give commands and be obeyed; to make important decisions regarding other people; and to be able to mould their behaviour. It can derive from professional status, hierarchical position in an organisation or personal charm. For a long time in Ireland, being a good Catholic was crucial to getting a job or being elected or chosen as a leader. Although less significant, religious and cultural capital were also important in being successful in the economic field. The influence here was in the way business was done, as well as in what was sold and bought in the marketplace. The acquisition of wealth never operates on pure economic behaviour. Doing business in Ireland, as it is elsewhere, is heavily influenced by cultural practices and, consequently, by cultural capital. Consequently, what needs to be investigated is what role religious capital has had in the struggle to attain economic capital in Ireland.

There is, finally, one last connection or capital conversion which needs to be addressed, that is how religious capital can be traded for symbolic capital. Symbolic power functions to legitimate and disguise other forms of capital. In its simplest form, symbolic capital legitimates the wealthy and politically powerful. They are seen as good people. In the heyday of the Catholic Church's power in Ireland, the blessing (often given discreetly and indirectly) of bishops, priests, nuns and brothers, functioned to legitimate what we deemed to be economic and political leaders. For example, the Church symbolically legitimated the proposition – and the businessmen and politicians who advanced it – that 'a rising tide (of capitalist economic growth) lifts all boats'. Religious capital enabled people to attain the symbolic power of the Church, to be seen as just, moral and good Catholics and, consequently, to be perceived as rightful inheritors and possessors of economic and political capital and of their position in society.[6]

The Social Grounding of Loyalty to the Catholic Church

Irish Catholics rarely adhered to the Church for purely religious reasons. Being spiritual and moral and following the teachings and practices of the Church were not simply ends in themselves; they were also means of attaining and maintaining power. The implications of religious activity reached beyond the religious field into other social fields. Being Catholic was as much a public as it was a private affair. Believing in and practising the Catholic faith had as much to do with being rewarded in this life as being saved in the next. Irish Catholics were brought up to believe that there is an eternal life after death and that the way to be saved is through following the Church's rules and regulations. But if Irish people followed the rules and regulations of the Church purely in order to avoid damnation and attain salvation, then one would expect, for example, that the level of belief in hell and heaven would be at least as high as the proportion, for example, going to Sunday Mass and fulfilling their Easter Duty. This is not the case. Whereas nine in ten Irish Catholic respondents in the 1973–1974 national survey went to Mass once a week and fulfilled their Easter Duty, only half fully accepted belief in hell.[7] Among Catholic university students in 1976, eight in ten respondents went to Sunday Mass, yet only 57 per cent fully accepted belief in heaven, and only 21 per cent fully believed in hell.[8] So it would appear that there were social reasons, besides the religious motive of being saved, for Irish Catholics maintaining their religious practice and allegiance to the Church. This chapter identifies and describes some of these reasons. It is argued that adherence to the Church in Ireland was not purely a religious matter, but was tied in with the acquisition of cutural, social, political and economic capital. It was because being a good Catholic was tied in with the individual struggle to attain power that the Church was able to limit not just what individual Catholics did and said, but also what the state, political parties, and other national organisations and associations did and said. As well as the interest in being spiritual and moral, the reason why Irish people adhered to the Catholic Church – as they did to any other power bloc or alliance – was in the more immediate, material interest of attaining different forms of capital. The task, then, in this chapter is to outline the transfers and conversions between religious capital and other forms of capital.

Cultural Capital

There is a form of cultural capital which is embodied through socialisation and which enables people to behave and be regarded as the same as everyone else. This capital comes from basic social know-how which has been embodied in the practices, rules, regulations, traditions and customs by which one becomes regarded as socially acceptable, polite, civil, and moral. At the most basic level, these practices centre on not behaving like an animal. They are rigorously enforced and are a minimum requirement for attaining social acceptance and respect. The practices by which embodied cultural capital is attained become more numerous and varied as society becomes more complex.[9] But there are societies in which these practices are closely allied with religious practices. Given that Ireland is almost homogeneously Catholic and that the Church acquired control of education, health and social welfare, there has been a close link between religious capital and social acceptance and respect. In other words, the practices by which one attained religious capital became part of the practices by which one came to be regarded as the same as everyone else. To be accepted and regarded as a civil member of society, it was expected if not required to engage in the rites, rituals and morally approved practices of the Church.

Social respect is also attained by people engaging in practices which mark them out as being different. Engaging in different lifestyles and tastes give people distinction and can mark them out as morally superior. Art, music, food, dress, and certain types of religious rituals are examples of cultural practices which bring social honour and respect. But it is important to remember that such practices only accumulate cultural capital if the person embodies the basic social practices which, so to speak, mark the society as a whole as different. Thus, for example, someone might be brilliant at art or music, but if he is a drunken, violent lecher, it is doubtful that he would be an esteemed and respected member of the community. If, on the other hand, one is self-disciplined, peaceful, sober, and moral, and also engages in cultural practices such as painting or playing the violin, then one is likely to have a high level of embodied cultural capital within Irish society.

Such was the power of the Catholic Church in Ireland that it was, and in many places still is, difficult for a Catholic to be regarded as the same as everyone else and to attain and maintain the basic respect of others without going to Mass on Sundays. Going to Mass established someone as part of the community and, consequently, bestowed a basic minimum of cultural capital on the individual and the family. Sunday Mass was a very prestigious occasion, a major public event. It was a time when people were on their best behaviour. They wore their best clothes, made sure their children were well-behaved, and greeted and talked to each other politely. In other words, within the overall pattern of sameness there were certain practices which distinguished people. A religious practice which marked people out as morally superior was receiving Holy Communion. Receiving Holy Communion was also a form of symbolic legitimation. In the 1973–74 national survey, Catholic respondents with white collar jobs received Holy Communion more frequently than those employed with blue collar occupations, even though there was no significant difference in their level of attendance at Confession.[10] Being well-groomed, wearing a white collar and receiving Holy Communion indicated that a person was purer and, thereby, closer to God. These practices provided crucial religious capital and symbolically legitimated the person's social position in society.

As part of the strategy for attaining distinction – as well as educational qualifications – children were sent to schools run by priests, nuns, and brothers. As Bourdieu has pointed out, these schools were primary mechanisms for solidifying and augmenting the cultural capital already attained in the family.[11] The religious provided a stricter training in manners and discipline, which marked the children as superior civil and moral human beings. In the national survey in 1973–74, nearly six in ten respondents preferred religious-run schools for both girls and boys at primary and secondary level. The most frequently mentioned reason for sending children to these schools was not that they provided a better education, but that they provided a better training in terms of discipline and manners.[12]

There is a further, more fundamental, link between social acceptance and loyalty to the Church and adherence to its practices. The whole ethos of the Catholic Church is one of surrender to the institution and its rules and regulations. The basis of social acceptance is engagement in practices which constitute and identify someone the same as everyone else. Surrender to the institution is at the heart of Catholic morality; and surrendering to the interests and needs of others is key strategy in attaining social acceptance. Salvation in the Catholic Church necessitates doing good works and caring for others. This becomes translated into the definition of a good person. Social respect comes from doing good works and surrendering economic and political interests to those of family and community. In concluding his review of the moral values of Irish religious tales, O'Healai states that: 'The stories show a fundamental respect for things holy and above all a practical application of the Golden Rule. Any form of behaviour which is helpful to others and which leads to harmony in the community is commended, while that which is unmindful of the neighbour's needs and disruptive of peace is condemned.'[13] Cultural capital is attained by surrendering oneself to the needs of others and being uncontentious. Leyton notes that:

To be a 'decent' man is to carry out one's obligations to society in a style characterized by cheerfulness and friendliness, to pause willingly for a chat and, most importantly, to refrain – regardless of provocation – from any display of overt hostility. Esteem is reserved for those who succeed in maintaining cordial relations with everyone in the village; and the greatest contempt is reserved for those quarrelsome individuals who are frequently involved in disputes.[14]

We can see here how the struggle to be accepted and respected is different from the struggle to attain economic and political capital. McNabb gives a similar description of 'good-stock' and the 'decent' man, and notes that neither is dependent on economic or political capital.

The people of 'good-stock' can transcend the class barriers, and labourers' families who have been in the community for many generations, who are known to be respectable and whose children are well cared for and neatly dressed, will be spoken of as 'good-stock'. The 'decent man' does not depend for his status on his family background. People describe him as a person who is straight-dealing and honest, who does not talk too much and who is always willing to help a neighbour. He has a reputation for sober judgement and people tend to ask him for his advice and use him as an intermediary in settling community conflicts.[15]

Attainment of social acceptance and respect in Ireland involves avoiding conflict, especially through argument, and surrendering individual interests by engaging in practices which help others. The person who openly seeks to increase his/her own political and economic capital and who does not engage in the basic social and cultural practices which maintain attachment to the community, is criticised and censured. The 'gombeen man', for example, is a caricature for someone who is selfish and greedy; putting his own interests before those of the community. The conception of a good man as someone who surrenders himself to the community can be linked to the moral teachings and practices of the Church. But it is more than being a good Christian. Just as the Catholic Church has fought against any notion of individual faith and discouraged the individual from using his uninformed private conscience, so too does the family and community tend to reject self-promotion, assertion, or ambition.

The value placed on social prestige and participating and contributing to the needs of others, rather than attaining possessions or striving for political position, was reflected in traditional Irish farming practices. As in many other peasant societies, mutual aid or 'cooring' was a traditional aspect of Irish rural life. In their study of rural Irish families at the beginning of the 1970s, Hannan and Katsiaouni found that mutual aid was still common. Thirty-eight per cent of the husbands they interviewed said it would be very difficult to manage the farm without the help of their neighbours. The type of help generally mentioned was labour; five per cent mentioned the loan of farm equipment and only one per cent the loan of money. One third of the respondents mentioned labour exchanges of a habitual nature, while just over half (51 per cent) mentioned labour in an emergency situation.[16]

The importance of an adherence to the teachings and practices of the Catholic Church as a means of attaining social prestige has been maintained within families through the mother. Once a woman got married and gave up her dowry (economic capital) and her occupation (political capital), her ability to attain other forms of capital became dependent on being well-respected, civil, and moral. This was one of the reasons why Irish mothers allied themselves with the Catholic Church. In almost every aspect of religiosity, that is in relation to religious practice, religious belief, religious experiences, and the general importance of religion in their lives, Irish women tend to be more religious than Irish men. Children growing up tended to perceive their mother as the primary religious figure in the home.[17] In the same way that the Church developed a monopoly of religion and morality in the wider society, so too did the mother in the home. She created and maintained the supervision and discipline of the Church within the family. It is the mother who brought the family together to say the rosary and night prayers. It is she who washed, clothed and ushered the family out to Sunday Mass. It is she who struggled to confine what her family did and said to within the rules and regulations of the Church. In this respect the mother played a central role in the maintenance of the power of the Catholic Church in Ireland. But her moral power, like that of priests, nuns, and brothers, was maintained through caring for the sick, poor and underprivileged. It was through doing the dirty, menial, and economically unrewarding tasks of caring for the less powerful that she gained the honour and respect of others and, consequently, attained religious as well as cultural capital. It is through the civility and morality of her children and husband that she maintained her cultural capital within the community. As Viney pointed out, 'It is the women in most rural families that influence the education of their children and so improve the standing of the family by rearing a priest or a doctor.'[18] This is echoed by McNabb:

People who neglect their children are looked down on. It is noticeable that this community judges the character of a family by the dress and general health of the children. One constantly hears some such expression as 'Mrs X is a good class of person, her children are always well fed and well dressed.' It is not incumbent on adults to be well dressed except on Sundays, but it is unusual to see a child in poor or ragged clothes. The blame for neglect falls on the mother, and it is generally held that the standing of individual families in the community is due to the work and influence of the mother. 'A good mother is everything'.[19]

Traditionally, then, the Irish mother was responsible for the moral training and discipline of children within the home. She was the last but vital link in the Catholic formation of each new generation. It was often because of her, and an interest in maintaining the solidarity and prestige of the family, that children maintained their adherence to the Church in later life. Children who did not behave in a disciplined, moral manner and obey the teachings of the Catholic Church could bring disgrace to themselves, their mother, and their families. It should be remembered that in Ireland the mother was held responsible for the behaviour of her children, regardless of their age, as long as they were living at home. Consequently, she often treated her sons and daughters as children until they left home. It was the mother, then, who emphasised the importance of social prestige to the individual and family, and an adherence to the teachings of the Church as the primary means towards attaining it.[20]

Political Capital

As well as trying to be accepted and attain social prestige, people are also involved in a struggle to attain political capital, particularly power of command over others. The higher your position in society the more likely it is that you will be able to persuade if not tell others what to do and say. Positions of command, as held for example by employers, managers, professionally qualified people and so forth, often involve some power of direction, supervision and control over others. While someone's status is generally derived from their occupation, it is also derived from all the different, often informal, positions which he or she may hold. Thus, for example, one's overall status and power of command may be derived from being a manager in a factory, a secretary in a local residents' association, and a member of a political party.

Part of the argument of this study that when the Church had a monopoly on morality, it was in the interest of those who held positions of command over others to adhere to the moral ethos and teachings of the Church. It was not so much that the Church directly interfered in political or occupational appointments; it was more that it was often easier for people with religious capital to accumulate political capital. Public adherence to the Church was especially important for those who were directly or indirectly employed by the Church such as doctors, teachers, and nurses. Blanshard noted an example of this in his study on the power of the Catholic Church in the 1950s:

Dr X and his wife, both baptised Catholics, have long ceased to believe in the major Catholic doctrines. In private conversation they express strong criticism of priestly policy. When Dr X started to drift away from the Church openly by failing to attend Mass, he was warned by his priest. Now he attends conspicuously with his wife. 'I must live, you know,' he says. My practice would disappear if I were branded as a lapsed Catholic.'[21]

Protestants have religious and political freedom in the Republic of Ireland. Nevertheless, in the past they have been prevented from obtaining public positions which involved moral supervision of Catholics.[22] But it was the Catholic dissenter, especially when employed in health or education, who was often under the greatest threat not to go against the teachings of the Church. Religion and morality were public matters in Ireland. Teachers, nurses, and doctors were under an obligation to behave in a manner deemed moral by the Church. If they did not, they might have been regarded as a potential traitor who could undermine the loyalty of others. As an editorial in *The Irish Rosary* put it: 'We allow no claim to good will come from those who have been brought up in the Catholic faith if they abandon it, but we can admire the good faith of those born outside the Church, even while we detest their errors.'[23]

It was also in the interest of those whose positions depended on public support, or which had a high public profile, to be openly loyal to the Church. Amongst these occupations were traders, journalists, politicians and other elected public representatives. In the past, it did not pay to oppose publicly the moral dictates of the Church. Censorship was often self-imposed; anything which was offensive or critical of the Church was hidden away. Booksellers, chemists, and other traders often ran an economic risk in selling goods which went against the dominant Catholic morality. Writers and journalists were also forced to abstain from any serious criticism of the Church and its teachings. An employee of the supposedly secular *The Irish Times* noted that in the 1950s, journalists in that newspaper 'had to avoid writing about any subject in which criticism, even if justified, could be construed as criticism of the Church.'[24]

The pressures on politicians to remain loyal to the Church were perhaps strongest of all. Whyte noted that 'two ex-ministers whom I have met told me that they are no longer believing Catholics. Neither of them ever avowed this in public.' Even self-confessed Catholic politicians were afraid to criticise the Church in public. Whyte quoted a long letter from a TD to *The Irish Times* in 1955 which was critical of a speech made by a bishop. The TD did not sign the letter 'because I do not want to finish my political career before it starts.'[25] The power of the Church in the political field survived more on the threat of censure rather than its actual implementation. Nevertheless it produced very real consequences. It may have been that a shopkeeper did not stock a particular magazine or book, or that a chemist did not consider it 'worth his while' to stock contraceptives. It may be that a doctor decided that it would be best not to do a certain operation which was contrary to Church teaching. It may be that a teacher did not say what he or she would like to say at a meeting because the parish priest was there. The power of the Catholic Church in Ireland was perhaps most evident when people were disgusted by what the Church and its representatives did and said, but did and said nothing themselves, partly because, as one fearful dissenter put it, 'you'd be destroyed – you'd be ostracised . . .' if you questioned the authority of the priest.[26]

Economic Capital

Loyal adherence to the Catholic Church played a major part in maintaining Ireland as a conservative, rural society in which people were encouraged to live in frugal comfort, and not to attach importance to material possessions. The good life was defined as a commitment and surrender to the spiritual things above oneself. The good life was always in opposition to the materialism associated with industrial, consumer society. This was religious rhetoric which was embodied into political ideology. Being non-materialistic became part of Irish Catholic identity. These ideals, as Daly points out, had very real consquences.[27] They became part of the Irish Catholic habitus and become embodied in social policies as well as everyday practices. An emphasis on frugal comfort and a suppression of individual interests in favour of those of Church, family, and community, were associated with an absence of a rugged, ambitious individualism and purely economic rational choices which were features of more mature capitalist societies. The traditional absence of entrepreneurs and people taking risks with capital in Ireland may be linked to the practices described above and a morality propagated by the Church, in which individual satisfaction and pleasure were subdued through an inculcation of humility, shame and guilt.

Through its control of education the Church also limited the production of the type of scientific and technical knowledge which could have produced a more modernised, industrial society earlier in Ireland. But it would be wrong to think that the Catholic Church has had only a negative impact on economic life in modern Ireland. As we shall see in later chapters, it provided the basic moral discipline which was associated with the initial modernisation of Irish society in the last century. But once this basic minimum of modernisation was attained, a high level of adherence to the Church's rules and regulations prevented the type of individualism necessary for further modernisation and industrialisation. It may be more than a coincidence that the decline in the institutional power of the Church in the 1990s has been associated not only with the emergence of a new individualism, but with rapid economic growth.

Beyond the limitation of economic life within certain Catholic parameters, the Church also contributed to the way in which economic capital was unevenly distributed. This was done through symbolically legitimating the people who had accumulated economic capital and the means by which it had been accumulated. So although the Church was actively involved in redistribution through its many social welfare agencies and programmes, at the same time it justified and legitimated the unequal distribution of economic capital. This was been done mainly through its teachings on vocationalism which were promulgated in two important papal encyclicals *Rerum Novarum* (1891), and *Quadragesimo Anno* (1931). These legitimated the positions of individuals as members of different occupational groups, and vindicated their right to fight for their own interests. It could, then, be implied that those with high positions, and as a result more economic capital, had them because they were fulfilling their vocational duty. On the other hand, the Church provided consolation and compensation for the poor and underprivileged; first by providing a wide variety of charitable services, especially in health and education; secondly by telling them that in the next world 'the last shall be first'; and thirdly by providing magical, devotional practices such as novenas which, if engaged in, supposedly brought about material transformations in this world such as getting money, jobs, or marriage partners. The Church in Ireland, like churches elsewhere, consistently played down the importance of material benefits in this world, and suggested that people should accept their God-given position, and follow Christ's example in their suffering. In this respect Catholicism was the opium of the Irish working class in that it maintained the status quo, and did little to reduce the economic divisions in society.

Church and State as Power Blocs

A power bloc such as the Catholic Church in Ireland primarily exists through its ability to limit the practice and discourse of a large number of people. The manifestation of Church power is when Catholics limit what they and others do and say to what falls within its moral teachings. This limitation is most effective when Catholics did not have to be told or persuaded to do it. When Irish politicians did not enact legislation which was contrary to Church teaching, this should be seen less as coincidence and more as an indication of the power of the Church. This is not to say that there were no instances of the state proposing or passing social legislation which was opposed collectively by the hierarchy or by individual bishops. But the power which the Catholic Church has had over the state in modern Ireland cannot be reduced simply to the occasions when bishops have made a direct contribution to the formation of state law. This is the type of definition which Whyte used in his analysis of the relation between Church and state in modern Ireland. He reduced Church power to occasions when social legislation was affected by a direct input from the hierarchy.[28]

What Irish people do and say is limited by numerous power blocs and alliances, based inside and outside the country, whose influence spreads across various social fields. The two major power blocs in Irish society since 1922 have been the state and the Catholic Church. The state exercises its power through laws enforced by such apparatuses as the courts, police, army and through policies implemented within institutions such as the civil service, schools, health and social welfare agencies. The Church maintained its power through its moral teachings being inculcated by priests, nuns and brothers, as well as by committed members of the laity. However, whereas the state exercises its power in a wide number of social fields, the Church has exercised its power mainly in those social fields relating to education, care and morality. It has been on moral issues, particularly in relation to health, education and the family that most struggles between these two power blocs have taken place. But the history of the relationship between Church and state in modern Ireland has been characterised not by struggle but rather by peaceful coexistence, each maintaining the power of the other. The vast majority of Irish politicians and civil servants were socialised within and educated by the Catholic Church and, sometimes unwillingly and sometimes unconsciously, limited legislation and policies to within the general ethos of the Church's teachings.[29] On the other hand, the Church was a major source of political stability in modern Irish society. Not only did it regularly preach submission to the power of the state, it continually condemned all forms of political violence. The first fifty years of the modern Irish state may be seen in terms of a happy marriage between it and the Catholic Church; and despite the odd row, each partner respected and symbolically legitimated the other.[30] It was not until the 1960s, when the state began to pursue rigorously a policy of industrialisation and modernisation, that the marriage began to break down. It was only in the 1970s that a formal separation was openly discussed for the first time.[31]

This is not to say that there have not been occasions when Church and state have clashed, and when the Church has become directly involved in state matters. Confining himself to legislation which was formally enacted between 1923 and 1970, Whyte compiled the following list of occasions in which there was a direct input from one or more bishops:

Censorship of Films Act 1923
Censorship of Publications Act 1929
Legitimacy Act 1930
Vocational Education Act 1930
The Constitution of Ireland 1937
Public Health Bill 1945
Health Act 1947
Intoxicating Liquor (Amendment) Bill 1948
Adoption Act 1952
Vital Statistics and Registration of Births, Marriages and Deaths Act 1952
Health Act 1953
Agriculture Act 1958
Intoxicating Liquor Act 1960
Charities Act 1961
Adoption Act 1964
Succession Act 1965.[32]

It is obvious from this list that any direct input from the bishops in terms of law creation was confined to moral conduct in general, and family, education, and health in particular. Besides the general reasons mentioned above, this list is unrepresentative of Church power because, as Whyte admitted, it does not take into account 'important policy decisions in which the bishops took an interest, but which were not embodied in statute'. Whyte mentioned as examples the educational changes in the 1960s, and the Mother and Child Scheme (1951) which provoked the first extended debate on Church and state relations to take place in Ireland. If one includes these policy decisions, and a number of other measures where consultation between the government and the hierarchy would appear to have been probable, then there were about three or four dozen items of legislation or other questions on which state and Church were in formal consultation. Given that about 2,000 statutes were enacted between 1923–1980, this suggests that the impact of the Church on the state has been slight. Chubb does not agree and argues that 'the political effects of the dominant position of the Catholic Church have been immense.'[33] The reason the effects were immense was that in maintaining its institutional monopoly of morality, the Catholic Church was able to inoculate Irish minds against the introduction of any legislation which was contrary to its interests. It was this institutional monopoly which inhibited a rational differentiation between religion and politics which, in turn, had a limiting effect on social, political, and economic development in Ireland.

The amendments to the social legislation to which Whyte refers were not so much the result of pressure by the hierarchy as independent initiatives of successive governments to maintain state power by appeasing the Church and entering into a grand alliance with it. This alliance was partly founded on the recognition that the state could not govern successfully if it were strongly opposed by the Church. The way for a political party to obtain and maintain state power became related to how it dealt with the interests of the Church. As Whyte points out, the first Cumann na nGaedhel government needed support from whatever quarter it came and, consequently, 'proved willing to use the power of the state to protect Catholic moral values'. Not to be outdone, its main opponent Fianna Fáil seized any chance to appear more zealously Catholic.[34] The situation has not changed dramatically in the last sixty years.

The process of incorporating Catholic teaching in Irish legislation, which began shortly after the foundation of the Free State, reached a peak with the passing of the Irish Constitution of 1937. The Constitution strongly represents Catholic moral teaching, especially with regard to family, private property, and education.[35] The original Constitution contained an article which recognised 'the special position of the Holy Catholic Apostolic and Roman Church as the guardian of the faith professed by the great majority of the Citizens'. This article was deleted in a referendum held in 1972. However the Preamble to the Constitution still reads: 'In the Name of the Most Holy Trinity, from Whom is all authority and to Whom, as our final end, all actions both of men and States must be referred, we, the people of Éire. Humbly acknowledging all our obligations to our Divine Lord, Jesus Christ, Who sustained our fathers through centuries. . . .'[36] The social legislation of the 1920s and 1930s, followed by the Constitution, set a precedent by which the hierarchy seemed to have the right and duty to limit the state when it came to legislation involving moral issues. But there were many pieces of legislation which involved moral issues of some kind and, at the height of their power in the 1950s, some bishops came close to advocating a theocratic state. This is best illustrated by a statement from the Bishop of Cork, Dr Lucey. Referring to the Health Bill of 1953, he noted that 'their [the bishops] position was that they were the final arbiters of right and wrong even in political matters'. Two years later Bishop Lucey amended his position and stated that 'their [the bishops'] power extends only to the religious and moral implications of what goes on – the Church has no competence to control public affairs itself or indicate the practical ways and means of dealing with current public problems.'[37] Since the 1950s, the Church's interpretation of its relation with the State has varied enormously. Some bishops have taken a rigid line and have suggested that, especially in moral matters, the state is subservient to the Church. Collectively, the hierarchy has tended towards a more liberal distinction between public and private morality. Liam Ryan argued that in the period 1955–80, there were four distinct viewpoints:

(1) That the state cannot enact something contrary to moral law: this was the viewpoint of the late Archbishop of Dublin, Dr McQuaid, when in a pastoral in 1971, he spoke of the proposed legislation on contraception as 'offending the objective moral law'.

(2) That state laws must reflect majority opinion: this was the position of the late Bishop Newman of Limerick, that the Catholic majority have a political right to the provision of a social framework that supports their moral and religious principles.

(3) That an appeal be made to the loyalty of the people: the position of the former Archbishop of Dublin, Dr Ryan, which was to advise Catholics that as Catholics they could not accept legislation contrary to the Church's teaching.

(4) That a question of public morality must be decided by the people, which Liam Ryan argued was the clear and consistent position of the hierarchy as a whole from 1973.[38]

In defence of his claim that the fourth viewpoint represented the hierarchy's position in general, Ryan quotes their 1973 statement: 'There are many things which the Catholic Church holds to be morally wrong and no one has ever suggested, least of all the Church herself, that they should be prohibited by the state.' This was, Ryan argued, the formal position of the Church throughout the 1970s and 1980s, which was outlined in greater detail during its submission to the all-party Forum on Northern Ireland in 1984. The main issue, however, has been whether Catholics are free to go against the teachings of the Church in making political decisions about moral issues. In light of a pastoral letter from the hierarchy in 1980, the answer is not certain since Catholic response to the moral issues of social legislation 'must always be in accordance with the specific commandments of God, as authoritatively interpreted by the Church'. In other words, while the bishops have moved away from the extreme viewpoints adopted by Archbishop McQuaid and Bishop Newman, they strategically vacillate between the requirement that Catholics adhere to the Church's teaching, and that it is a matter which each individual Catholic decides, being fully informed by the Church's teaching and in full consideration of the issues and their implications. During the Family Planning Amendment Bill (1985), Bishop Newman, who became a prominent spokesman within the hierarchy following the appointment of Dr Kevin McNamara as Archbishop of Dublin, reminded 'all politicians who profess to be Catholic that they have a duty to follow the guidance of their Church in areas where the interests of the Church and State overlap'. Although Liam Ryan argued that the hierarchy had a clear, consistent position, there were regular dissenting voices. Bishop Newman, for example, complained of 'the way in which some Catholics manage to persuade themselves that they are faithful to their Church even though they reject some points of its teaching.'[39]

The distinction between having to adhere to the Church's teaching, and being able to assume individual moral responsibility for political decisions, is important since Ireland is a homogeneously Catholic country, and because the Church has had such enormous institutional power. It was this power over people's consciences, instilled in churches, schools, hospitals, and homes which made the Church unlike any other power bloc in Irish society. It was a power which, as every politician knew, could be exercised at any time with devastating consequences. It is for this reason that the main political parties were so cautious when dealing with moral matters. It is no coincidence that in describing the relation between Church and state in Ireland up until 1970, Whyte quoted O'Faolain twice:

The Maynooth Parliament (i.e. the hierarchy) holds a weapon which none of the other institutions mentioned holds: the weapon of the sacraments. The Church of England cannot wield the power of the Catholic Church because it does not hold this weapon. If a prime minister in England were informed by the Archbishop of Canterbury that a proposed law would be condemned by the Church of England, he would deplore it, but he would not be afraid of any effects other than political effects. If our Taoiseach were informed thus by the Protestant Archbishop of Dublin he would measure the effects in the same way. And likewise with most other institutions, religious or secular. But when the Catholic Church, through its representatives speaks, he realises, and the Roman Catholic public realises, that if they disobey they may draw on themselves this weapon whose touch means death.[40]

But O'Faolain was writing in the early 1950s and while there may have been some fear that ecclesiastical censure might have damaged their chances of salvation, the main fear of politicians would have been the Church turning voters against them. Moreover, as Keogh points out, there are many examples of the two main political parties and their leaders standing up to the Church.[41] What was true about O'Faolain's description, however, was that the majority of Catholic politicians accepted that the Church had power over Irish people's consciences. And so the distinction, once again, returns to the issue as to whether Irish Catholics and especially politicians were operating in a compulsory rather than a voluntary organisation. In particular, on what occasions were voters and politicians able to follow their individual conscience even when it went against Church teaching. The Church has vacillated on this issue. In some of their formal statements the hierarchy admitted to there being a rational differentiation between politics and religion; between what politicians did, and what they as bishops did. But in other statements members of the hierarchy called on individual Catholics not to make this rational differentiation between their work and their religion. As the late Archbishop of Dublin, Dr Kevin McNamara put it: 'For the Church a major challenge today is to help people make a closer connection between their religious practice and their daily lives; between worshipping God in church and serving Him in the world of work, recreation and culture.'[42] This applied to politicians as much as it did to any other Irish Catholic. One of the main reasons why the Catholic Church remained so powerful in Irish society was that it was able to dissuade people from limiting religious practice and discourse to specific times and places. In the national survey in 1973–74, more than six in ten (64 per cent) of the Catholic respondents said that their religious principles always guided their behaviour with regard to their occupation. Moreover, seven in ten said that they would always choose their religion if its demands conflicted with their occupational demands.[43] The Catholic Church remained a power bloc in Irish society as long as people adhered to its teachings and did not make a distinction between their work, whether as politicians or otherwise, and their religion.

The Constitutional Referendum on Abortion (1983)

Weber once remarked that the power of hierocratic or priestly religion was dependent on its ability to get people to maintain their allegiance despite the often opposite pull or attraction of family and kinship.[44] In the modern era we could extend this to other interest groups. In other words, modern civil society is made up of a number of interest groups to which people give allegiance. These may be political parties, professional associations (of, for example, barristers, doctors and teachers), trade unions, farming organisations and so forth. There are hundreds of such groups in Irish society representing interests as diverse as adult education and zoological gardens. Following Weber, we can say that the strength of the Catholic Church in Ireland is indicated in its ability to get people to rank their allegiance to the Church primary to, for example, their allegiance to a political party, professional association, voluntary association, community or family to which they belong. This power was evident throughout the 1983 Constitutional referendum on abortion. In other words, it is not just that the Catholic Church was, for example, a major player in the health field in that it was able to structure the immediate, ongoing, predisposition as to what constituted good medical practice. It was that when it came to an issue such as abortion, the Church was able to push through a referendum that led to debate on a moral issue which caused divisions in professional associations of consultants and doctors. A description of that referendum will provide an example of how the Church exercised its power, not just over the state but over political parties and other interest groups.

Abortion is contrary to the teaching of the Catholic Church and has regularly been the subject of statements from the Irish hierarchy. In September 1983, a referendum was held in the Republic of Ireland to decide whether to amend the Constitution by including a statement which acknowledged the right to life of the unborn. The background to the referendum lay in the rapidly increasing availability of abortion in many Western societies. Whereas abortion services had been legally available in countries such as the United States, England, France and Germany for a long time, it had only been a few years since traditionally Catholic countries such as Italy and Spain had made new legal provisions for abortion. The Pro-Life Amendment Campaign (PLAC) did not formally come into existence until April 1981. The seeds of the campaign had been sown in the previous summer during a meeting of the Irish Catholic Doctors Guild and a conference of the World Federation of Doctors who Respect Human Life. The campaign was hastened into existence by the growing awareness that over 3,500 Irish women had had abortions in England the previous year and that the Woman's Right to Choose Group had begun to press for the legalisation of some kind of abortion in Ireland.

The initial aim of PLAC was to pressurise the government into holding a referendum which would not only make abortion illegal, as it was under the Offenses Against the Person Act (1861), but unconstitutional, and therefore irreversible by any act of parliament or decision by the Supreme Court. Within two weeks of its formation PLAC had gained commitments from the leaders of the two main political parties to hold such a referendum. The reason for the rapid success of PLAC was it exerted its pressure in the weeks prior to the General Election of June 1981. It may not have been political suicide for the main political parties to say that they were against holding such a referendum, but once Fine Gael had committed itself, Irish history has shown that Fianna Fáil was bound to follow.

After a long and heated campaign which drew thousands of letters to the national newspapers, the amendment was voted on in September 1983. Two thirds of the 55 per cent of the electorate who voted accepted that the

Constitution should be amended to make abortion unconstitutional. The proportion of these 'yes' voters varied throughout the country. It was highest in rural constituencies, especially in the West. For example, Mayo and Donegal voted four to one in favour of the amendment. It was lowest in urban constituencies, especially in those with an identifiable 'middle-class' population.

The success of PLAC was that it was able to make use of the thousands of committed Catholics already involved in lay organisations and parish work to do its canvassing. This enormous physical organisation through-out the country, which had existed for many years but which had never previously been mobilised as a unified force, was central to PLAC's victory. It brought Catholic moral principles to the front door of Irish homes. As one of their spokespersons stated: 'It's the ordinary people of Ireland coming out to canvass their neighbours and friends'. It was only towards the end of the campaign that the clerical resources of the Church began to be used fully. The anti-amendment campaign group had tried to argue that the decision to make something which was already illegal, unconstitutional, was strictly a political one. It complained about priests giving partisan sermons and inviting pro-life movement speakers to give their views in church. But it was obvious that advice in favour of the amendment would come from church pulpits. As a priest from Kerry put it: 'Country people need to have quite a lot of things explained to them. They are too busy and do not have the time to read the newspapers carefully.' While the bishops were careful not to instruct the laity directly as to how to vote, they were equally careful to remind politicians that morality was their sphere of jurisdiction. The then auxiliary Bishop of Dublin, Dr Comiskey, stated that 'when politicians concern themselves with values they are engaging not merely in stagecraft, but in soulcraft.' In certain dioceses, bishops requested that either their own letters be read out, or sermons be given, urging a 'yes' vote. In Dublin, the largest diocese in the country containing nearly one-third of the electorate, the Archbishop, Dr Ryan, had a pastoral read at all Masses in the diocese on the Sunday prior to polling day, urging support of the amendment. This was above and beyond the collective statement already issued by the hierarchy. The collective statement had begun assert-ing that, according to the moral law, abortion was wrong in all circum-stances. It noted that 'on an issue of such fundamental importance . . . everyone has a clear responsibility to vote', but it recognised 'the right of each person to vote according to conscience'. The statement concluded by urging a decisive 'yes' vote to the amendment, and by linking an anti-amendment stance to a pro-abortion stance, that is, 'defeat of the amend-ment could well be represented as a victory for the abortion cause.'[45]

The Effects of the Campaign

The main effect of the campaign was that it demonstrated the power of the Catholic Church in the Irish political field. It showed the ability of the Church to limit political practice and discourse, and what was to be regarded as legal and unconstitutional, to what falls within its teachings. This power was dependent on its ability to divide members of other interest groups and alliances in terms of their allegiance to its teachings. What maintained the power of the Church was its ability to get members of political parties, national organisations, professional associations and other interest groups to ally themselves first and foremost with the Church, especially when there was, as in the case of the abortion referendum, a clash of interests.

The division in Fine Gael, which was the major party in the Coalition government during the campaign, was slow to materialise. From the outset the Fine Gael parliamentary party had decided that the proposed wording of the amendment, put forward by Fianna Fáil, was ambiguous and could lead to unforeseen and undesirable changes in medical practice. It decided that it would not support the amendment, and that its members would remain silent except for a statement to be issued by the Taoiseach, Dr FitzGerald. However, like most other politicians, the majority of the Fine Gael TDs were committed Catholics. Even if they were not fully committed, many of their constituents were, and without their support the chances of re-election would be diminished. Again this reminds us that many TDs, especially those living in rural areas, were dependent on the Church for the symbolic capital which legitimated their political capital or standing.

By the second week of the campaign the number of Fine Gael TDs who disregarded their collective parliamentary party decision and openly supported the amendment, had risen to eleven, and it was estimated it could rise to fourteen. Even the Cabinet became divided and members spoke openly about how they would vote. The chairman of the parliamentary party issued a public statement in which he criticised the Minister for Finance Alan Dukes, and the Minister for Education, Gemma Hussey, for not keeping their views on the referendum to themselves. He stated categorically that 'if members of the Cabinet are not prepared to accept and abide by decisions of the party they should cease to be members of the Cabinet.'[46]

The medical profession also became bitterly divided during the campaign. The whole idea of the amendment was fostered originally by a group of committed Catholic doctors. The chairperson of PLAC was Dr Julia Vaughan. The professors of obstetrics and gynaecology in the country's four main universities were original supporters of the amendment. One of these, Professor O'Dwyer of University College Galway, insisted that the amendment would make no difference to current legal or medical practice. Two days later, twelve of the country's leading gynaecologists condemned the proposed amendment, and urged people to vote against it. Three of these gynaecologists were lecturers in the same institution as Dr O'Dwyer. At a press conference organised by the doctors against the amendment, the claim was made, supported by a statement from the Government Information Service, that if the amendment were passed several contraceptive methods could be outlawed. This was counteracted by the chairman of the Irish Medical Association. He stated that he intended to vote 'yes' and that '60 per cent of the doctors in the country had signed a statement to the effect that passage of the amendment would not alter current medical practice'. Nevertheless doctors throughout the country continued to sign petitions against the amendment and to urge a 'no' vote.[47]

The legal profession became divided on the same issues as the medical profession: would certain forms of contraception become unconstitutional; would the treatment of the mother during pregnancy be affected; and would there be a threat to the mother's life? It was a member of the legal profession who was responsible for the actual wording of the amendment. The chairman of the anti-amendment campaign, Adrian Hardiman, was also a lawyer. He claimed that there were over 100 barristers in Dublin who had come out against the amendment. About the same time the Irish Association of Lawyers for the Defence of the Unborn was formally launched. The division within the legal profession continued to grow, and just over a week before polling day a press conference was called at which it was announced that 600 lawyers, including 22 Senior Counsels were opposed to the amendment.[48]

The referendum also caused open dissension within the Irish Farmers Association, the largest farming organisation within the country, with over 130,000 members. Shortly after the beginning of the campaign there was report of a newly formed 'Farmers Against the Amendment Group' of which Donal Cashman, the President of the IFA, was a member. A few days later, in an attempt to prevent an open rift, seven members of the executive committee who had been linked to the anti-amendment group, issued a statement saying that they would have no involvement publicly or privately in an organised effort to influence voting in the referendum. But the damage had already been done and when the IFA council met shortly afterwards, Cashman and eleven other members of the executive were suspended from their posts for two months for attempting to set up an anti-amendment group.[49]

It would be facile to argue that the divisions that occurred in Fine Gael, the medical profession, the legal profession, and the IFA were simply a consequence of disagreement with the actual amendment. The amendment was from the beginning an initiative of a lay Catholic social movement which attained the full support of the Church. The issue which mainly divided these power blocs and alliances was whether the Constitution should be changed to reflect the interests of this lay Catholic pressure group and the Church as a whole. The referendum became a test of the loyalty and respect of the Irish people for the bishops, Pope John Paul II, and the teachings of the Catholic Church.

The result of the referendum may be taken as a victory for the Catholic Church in that the majority of those who voted did what the bishops had urged and voted 'yes'. However, the result may be interpreted differently. If it is accepted that the statement of the hierarchy was an appeal to the loyalty of the people and that it was, as they stated, 'an issue of such fundamental importance' on which 'everyone has a clear responsibility to vote', then the proportion of the Catholic electorate who complied with their advice and voted 'yes' was only 37.5 per cent. This is an extreme interpretation since the bishops did recognise the right of each person to vote according to conscience. The reaction of many Catholics, confused by the divisions in the medical and legal professions, might have been not to bother their conscience, especially since an opinion poll published two days before indicated that there would be a 2:1 majority in favour.[50]

Whichever way the results of the referendum are interpreted, an analysis of the campaign in terms of the power of the Catholic Church in Irish society indicates that:

(1) Having lost its ability to influence the social legislation passed by the Dáil, the Church moved back to the Constitution as a means of safeguarding Catholic moral principles.

(2) The way the Church operated in the political field was to accept formally the principle of the rational separation of the religious from the political sphere in modern social life and that Catholics were not bound by the teachings of their Church in making political decisions. But at the same time, for the Church to urge members of the laity to lead a holistic lifestyle and not to segregate religious practice and belief from the rest of their lives. While acting as 'the conscience of society' the hierarchy used the full organisation of the Church to urge the laity to remain loyal to its teachings and to incorporate these into the political framework of the country.

(3) The rational separation of the religious from the political was in practice loosely interpreted by clergy and religious who were likely to give more direct advice in their moral direction of the laity.

(4) The task of maintaining loyalty to the teachings of the Church and, where possible, incorporating these within the political framework of the country had by the middle of the 1980s moved away from the bishops to lay Catholic organisations. This was a significant shift in the power structure

of the Church in Ireland. While the referendum represented a victory for Catholic moral principles and was a demonstration of the loyalty of the people to the teachings of their bishops, it also represented a victory for lay organisations within the Church, and the increasing role which they had begun to play in Irish Catholicism since Vatican II. This is not to suggest that lay organisations had not previously played a role in the formation of social legislation, but that this was the first time that they openly initiated and directed such a campaign. It was the first time that the laity were the vanguard, while the bishops played a more covert role. Thus, the full potential of a resource and strength of the Church which had previously operated quietly in the background, was shown for the first time. It was this force of committed Catholics, for a long time the pawns of the Church, who entered the centre stage of the battle for Catholic moral principles in the 1980s and 1990s.

(5) Because of the loyalty of these Catholics, the membership of every major interest group and alliance in Irish society, which itself sought to create and maintain its power in civil society and which endeavoured to develop cohesion and maintain control over what its members did, were easily divided in terms of its members' loyalty to the Church.

The Divorce Referendum (1986)

In June 1986, a further referendum was held to decide whether the article in the Constitution prohibiting divorce should be removed. The coalition government of Fine Gael and Labour proposed that the original article, *viz.*, 'No law shall be enacted providing for the grant of dissolution of marriage,' should be replaced with a new article which would allow a court of law to grant a dissolution in certain circumstances, that is where the marriage had failed for a period of at least five years, where there was no possibility of reconciliation, and where adequate provision was made for any dependent spouse or child. To counteract the government proposals, the hierarchy issued a series of statements and a fifteen-page pastoral letter 'Marriage, the Family and Divorce' of which one million copies were distributed nationwide. In their final statement two weeks before the referendum, the hierarchy said that the granting of divorce on the basis of 'failure of marriage' was a 'concept of the broadest and vaguest kind', and that in country after country such 'abstractness and vagueness' had led to divorce becoming 'more and more easily available'. They were 'convinced that the proposed amendment would weaken rather than strengthen marriage and the family'. They were emphatic that the provision of civil divorce was a moral issue.

The questions raised in this debate are not simply political. They are also moral. Each legislator and each voter is faced with a moral decision. Changes in civil law can influence moral attitudes and affect the whole moral atmosphere of society. They can make it more difficult for people to walk in the path of God's commandments.[51]

However, they concluded that 'the ultimate decision rests with the people' and they exhorted that 'each individual make a reflective, prayerful, conscientious decision'.

In a press conference at the time the statement was issued, the official spokesman for the hierarchy, Bishop Cassidy of Clonfert, insisted that 'We're not telling them [the people] how to vote on this matter'. He emphasised that 'conscience is the final arbiter', and intimated that a Catholic could vote in favour of the removal of the ban on divorce without incurring guilt.[52] This announcement, that it was permissible for a Catholic to vote in a civil referendum for something which was contrary to Church teaching, represented an interpretation of informed conscience which had not been declared during the abortion referendum. But individual bishops again interpreted their collective statement differently. Less than a week before polling day, the Archbishop of Dublin, Dr McNamara, stated that the view of some Catholics that the introduction of divorce into our society would be morally good and in conformity with God's intentions 'finds no warrant, no justification in the teaching we have given. It finds no basis in Catholic social and moral doctrine.'[53]

Up to a week before the referendum, the government remained confident that the amendment to the Constitution would be carried. Opinion polls over the previous three years had shown a steady increase in the proportion who thought that divorce should be permitted in certain circumstances. This proportion reached 77 per cent in February, 1986. As late as April of the same year, 57 per cent of those interviewed had said that they would actually vote to remove the ban. However, an opinion poll conducted a week before the referendum and published the day before polling, showed that the proportion who would vote to remove the ban had declined sharply to 40 per cent and indicated that there was now a majority against removing the ban.

This dramatic shift in public opinion was reflected in the actual results. Nearly two out of three voters (63 per cent) rejected the government's proposal to remove the ban on divorce. In fact, the results of the divorce referendum were almost an exact replica of the abortion referendum, even though the turnout this time was substantially higher (63 per cent). While Dublin constituencies voted very narrowly in favour of divorce, other urban areas such as Cork, Limerick, Galway and Waterford voted against it, and in the majority of rural constituencies more than seven in ten voted against the amendment.[54]

Given the accuracy of the opinion polls prior to the referendum, the questions which arise are how and why there was such a dramatic shift in attitudes away from removing the ban in the weeks before polling. Initial consideration would suggest four main reasons:

(1) Whereas the pro-divorce lobby had been active since the 1970s and had attained widespread coverage in the media of its position and objectives, the anti-divorce lobby, although formally organised since 1983, had remained virtually silent until the referendum was announced.

(2) The anti-divorce lobby proved to be very well organised and to have access to considerable funding and a large network of canvassers.

(3) The anti-divorce lobby, although not formally linked to the Church, closely followed its teachings and helped transform the central issue from one of minority 'civil' rights for non-Catholics to an issue about the common good of Irish society. It was argued that the removal of the ban would be a threat to every marriage and family in Ireland, particularly in relation to inheritance and social welfare rights.

(4) In the confusion of issues, most voters seem to have been swayed by the statement from the hierarchy, and the 'personal' position of most Fianna Fáil and many Fine Gael TDs.

The referendum demonstrated the continuing ability of the hierarchy to set limits to the political field of Irish society. Their argument that the referendum was not simply a political matter but also a moral one was effectively followed by Fianna Fáil who held that the referendum was not a party political issue, but rather a matter to be decided by each individual legislator and voter. Their tactics were also similar to those of the bishops; they would not advise the electorate how to vote, but all their leading spokespersons were against removing the constitutional ban. The official position of Fine Gael was in favour of the amendment but, as in the abortion referendum, members became divided on the issue. The Minister for Education, Mr Cooney, as well as prominent backbenchers, spoke frequently against their own government's proposed divorce measures. In other words, as had happened in the abortion referendum, adherence to the teaching of the Church came before their membership of their political party. It was the ability of the Church to divide the membership of organisations and groups in terms of commitment to its teachings which demonstrated its continued powerful position in Irish society.

The results of the divorce referendum indicated that the separation between Church and State in modern Ireland was still far from being completed in the 1980s. The homology between Church and state was maintained because Irish politicians, especially those in Fianna Fáil, regarded many social issues, particularly those pertaining to sex and the family, as essentially religious and moral issues which belong to the sphere of religion and should be decided by each legislator's and voter's conscience. When political issues were left to individual moral consciences, most Irish legislators and voters still made decisions in accordance with the advice given by the Catholic Church. As we shall see in Chapter 9, this was no longer the case in the 1995 referendum on divorce.

The Media

The reason why the Catholic Church was able to maintain its monopoly over morality until the end of the twentieth century was because of its ability to limit what people did and said to within the ethos of its teachings in most fields of Irish social life. At the height of the Church's power, this limitation became a form of self-restraint which was instilled during social-isation within the home and cemented within the Church's control of education, health, social welfare and, as we have seen in this chapter, its dominance of social, economic and political life and, within this, the struggle by people to attain and maintain power. When it was most effec-tive, this limitation was not even felt or noticed as a form of self-restraint. Being Catholic and adhering to the moral ethos and teaching of the Church was natural, immediate and obvious. It was part of what people considered themselves to be, in the same way they considered themselves to be male or Irish. It was part and parcel of what one was, an unquestioned orthodox at the heart of the Irish social habitus. But there was also a need for external restraint, ostensibly for the minority of Catholic dissidents who could not abide by this orthodoxy or, more likely, for those who did not have the faith.

The Censorship of Films Act (1923) was one of the first acts passed by the new Dáil. It was a Catholic law for a new Catholic people and there was no dissent from within the media.[55] There are no overall figures for the number of films which were cut or banned during the next sixty years. However, of the 1,587 films submitted to the Censor in 1935, 258 were passed with cuts and 58 were totally rejected.[56] There was an equally rigorous censorship of books. Adams examined the list of books censored between the first (1929) and second Act (1946). Of the 1,700 books which were banned, he identified 153 which he deemed to be serious literature.[57] These acts were rigorously enforced up to the 1960s by a Censorship Board which was vigilantly supervised by Catholic lay organisations such as the Knights of Columbanus. Bolster indicates that on many occasions the Knights dominated the actual membership of the Board.[58] There was little need for radio censorship since it was under state control. Indeed such was the symbiotic relationship between Catholicism and nationalism, that when de Valera was opening the first high-powered radio broadcasting station in 1932, he saw the station as helping to fulfil the Irish mission of saving Western civilisation from materialism. Ireland, he claimed, 'can do the world a service as great as that which she rendered in the time of Columcille and Columbanus . . . that, true to her holiest traditions, she should humbly serve the truth, and help by the truth to save the world.'[59] When the strict censorship of films and books was introduced it was, as Woodman argues, part of a symbiotic process between Church and state of establishing on the one hand civil order and, on the other, the moral monopoly of the Church.[60] Censorship was a fundamental aspect to the construction of a Catholic nation whose two leaders, Church and state, spoke with one voice. Anything which posed a threat to the new moral order, whether it was materialism, individualism, socialism or sexuality was to be silenced. Moreover, as Murphy suggests, 'official censorship created layers of unofficial, self-righteous, busybody censorship in many a local community. In turn, this provoked evasion, and thus contributed further to the superficially conforming, furtive, under-the-counter mentality which is one of the more unlovely facets of the Irish heritage.'[61]

Television changed the face of Catholic Ireland because the practice and discourse of imported programmes was at variance with traditional Catholic principles. They portrayed life-styles in which religion had little or no importance. The concentration was on urban individuals rather than on rural family life. This was quite different from home produced programmes in which family life and the priest always played a significant role. A way of life was brought into Irish homes in which people were not limited in what they did and said by mothers and priests, but by police, doctors, and lawyers. Television brought the sophisticated glossy image of urban life into the heartland of rural Ireland. It provided a constant reminder of what most Irish people were not. The demand for a modern Western lifestyle did not lag far behind the advent of television. Indeed television played a crucial role in developing and maintaining consumer demand, and this stimulated increased production. Television, then, was an important factor in the second stage of Irish modernisation which brought an end to the dominance of rural life centred on small-scale agricultural production, and its replacement by industry, urbanity and individuality, all of which added to the decline of the power of the Catholic Church.

The development of the media and the decline of censorship also brought an end to the tradition that bishops and priests were above public criticism. From the middle of the last century a halo of sanctity had hung over the heads of Irish clergy and religious. People may have disobeyed them and muttered criticisms in private, but it was rare for any detailed, systematic critique of the Church and its clergy and religious to be voiced in public. 'Respect for the cloth' made almost any public criticism about the Church and its teachings appear as antagonistic. Even as late as 1984, Bishop Newman could argue that:

There is frequently to be found a lukewarm practice which is no real faith at all. And there is certainly to be found, far too often I am afraid, a cancer of criticism and dissent, a cynicism about the faith. Sometimes it starts from the media, sometimes from elsewhere. At times it is the result of ignorance, and other times it is the result of downright antagonism.[62]

It was the media that broke the tradition of not criticising the Church and its teachings in public. It was the media that forced the Church into giving a public account of itself. It was the media, and in particular television, which brought an end to the long nineteenth century of Irish Catholicism. The social process where moral discourse was limited to what was taught in the school, read in the occasional newspaper, heard on the radio and from the pulpit every Sunday, was changed by the little box which appeared in the corner of Irish homes. It was then, for the first time since the middle of the nineteenth century, when the process began in earnest, that many Irish Catholics stopped being limited by the moral discourse and practice of the Church.

Conclusion

Adherence to the rules and regulations of the Catholic Church was maintained, since being a good Catholic was central to the attainment and maintenance of power, especially the honour and respect of others. Through its institutional monopoly of morality, operated through churches, schools, hospitals and homes, being a good Catholic became central to being regarded as a decent moral person, the same as everyone else. For many Irish people, but in particular mothers, being able to limit the discourse and practice of others depended not on economic or political power, but on maintaining a moral superiority by over-conforming to the rules and regulations of the Church. For others, conforming to the Church's teachings and ritual practices was part of attaining and maintaining status within the community. This was especially true of doctors, nurses, and others who supervised or dealt with the public. Adherence to the Church also legitimated the rich and compensated the poor. It maintained the status quo. It inculcated conformity to family and community, and stifled individualism, creativity and ambition. With its monopoly over the definition of morality, the Church became a power bloc that was able to limit the practice and discourse not just of the state but other interest groups and alliances in Irish society.

Although formally removed from political life, the Church was powerful because of its ability to divide the members of these interest groups in terms of their commitment to its teachings and practices. The Church's monopoly on morality was dependent on the laity maintaining a holistic lifestyle in which their religious beliefs and practices were not compartmentalised from the rest of their daily lives. To understand how the Church gained such control over the state, education, health and social welfare and came to dominate not just the family but social, political and economic life, it is necessary to retrace some of the major social transformations in Irish society in the last two hundred years. And, as we shall see in Part Two, it was within the nexus of the power struggle between power blocs and alliances, and in particular the British state and Rome, that the institutional power of the Irish Catholic Church was first established.

PART TWO

Origins of the Power of the Catholic Church in Ireland

Part Two
Introduction

One of the tasks of sociology is to explain long-term social change.[1] How has social life in Western society become the way it is and why is it not different? Has social life in Ireland become more capitalistic, civilised, rational, bureaucratic and secular?[2] In the second part of the book, I develop a sociological explanation for the changes which have taken place in social and cultural life in Ireland over the past two hundred years. By piecing together changes at the macro level – that is in the Irish Catholic Church's relation with the British state and Rome and in the development of the civilising process throughout Western society – and then linking these changes to micro-level changes in the way people behaved, particularly in churches, schools, homes and pubs, I hope to develop a general understanding of how the Catholic Church became so powerful in Irish society.

This sociological analysis is different from the traditional method of doing history. The emphasis is on changes in institutional relations and social and cultural processes. It is about identifying radical shifts and discontinuities in the way Irish people viewed and understood the world in which they lived and the way they related, communicated and behaved with each other.[3] Depending on one's interest or theoretical framework, there are different ways of interpreting the history of Irish Catholicism. There are historians who, although recognising various ups and downs in the history of the Church, emphasise a linear development from the time of Saint Patrick.[4] On the other hand, we can look at the history of the Catholic Church in terms of ruptures and discontinuities. In other words, the Church in which St Brigid operated bears little resemblance to that of modern Ireland.[5] The argument which I develop is that there was a radical rupture in the institutional Church in Ireland and in religious belief and practice during the nineteenth century. A new morality, discipline and civilised way of behaving had become predominant by the end of the nineteenth century which was not there at the beginning. In the religious field there was, as already indicated, a partial shift from more pagan, magical religious beliefs and practices towards more institutionalised forms of piety, rules and regulations. This fundamental shift in religious values, beliefs and behaviour was to last until the latter part of the twentieth century, and it was to dominate Irish social and cultural life. The period from 1850 to 1970 represented the long nineteenth century of Irish Catholicism. Although the official teachings of the Catholic Church may not have changed dramatically during the century, there were dramatic changes in the lives of Irish Catholics and in the way they related to the Church and each other. In effect what happened was that in the second half of the nineteenth century, there was a narrowing of the gap between the official discourse of the Church and the way Irish Catholics lived and viewed their lives.[6] There came to be a close correspondence between formal declarations by bishops, priests, nuns and brothers as to how people should live their lives and the way they actually did. It was not until the 1970s that the gap began to widen again.

But to understand the radical shift in nineteenth-century Irish Catholicism, we need to focus on broader, macro-structural changes in the triangular relationship between Rome, the Catholic Church in Ireland and the British state. We can then see the origins of the power of the Catholic Church in Ireland in terms of the failed attempts of the British state symbolically to dominate the Irish through legislation (the Penal Laws), religion (Protestant proselytism) and education (state-run schools), and the state's gradual acceptance of and surrender to the symbolic legitimation of the Church.[7] In other words, to understand the shifts which took place in Irish Catholic life in the nineteenth century we need to focus on shifts in the relations of the cultural producers of symbolic power and, in particular, in the shift within the British state away from the perceived necessity of Ireland becoming Protestant to a gradual appreciation and acceptance of the symbolic legitimacy of the Roman Catholic Church.

It would be wrong, however, to think that the origins of the power of the Catholic Church was located simply in shifts in institutional power. It was also located in changes in the hearts, minds and everyday lives of Irish Catholics. In some respects there was something deeply abhorrent to many Irish Catholics in the attempt to colonise them symbolically. The campaign led by Daniel O'Connell was for civil religious rights and freedom. It was a struggle for meaning and identity, and for the freedom to worship and preach. The willingness to adhere closely to the Catholic Church was located in a desire to be and be perceived as morally equal, if not superior, to their colonisers. In other words, it is important to see the change in Irish Catholic religiosity – that is people becoming more ethical, spiritual and closely allied to the institutional Church – not just as an end in itself, not just as the fulfilment of some inherent natural allegiance to the Church, but as part of a struggle to attain religious, cultural and symbolic power. The symbolic struggle for moral and spiritual equality became tied into a strict ethical life, a rigid adherence to the rules and regulations of the Church. This rigorous orthodoxy was to equal if not surpass anything produced by the most conservative of British Victorians; it was to outlast them by well over fifty years.

Closely allied with the struggle for symbolic legitimacy was the growing interest Irish people had in becoming as polite, well-mannered and civil as their Protestant ascendancy colonisers. Again, it is important to place the changes in Irish social and cultural life in the context of changes taking place elsewhere in Europe. A number of gradual changes which grew from the sixteenth century, had reached Ireland in different shapes and forms. There was, for example, the growth of the capitalist world system. In the political field, there was the emergence of nation states. In the cultural field, as well as ongoing symbolic struggles between Catholics and Protestants, there was the Enlightenment and a growing emphasis on reason and rationality. Whatever else was happening, there was a growth in the complexity of society, in the number and variety of social interactions and, consequently, in the need for social integration. This centred on people behaving in a way which was reliable, predictable and inoffensive. Elsewhere in Europe, this movement towards civility – this civilising process – although it was initially operated in and through religious institutions, became an essentially secular movement. Ireland was an exception, in that most people learnt to become polite, well-mannered and civil through the Catholic Church. What is important to emphasise here is that this sociological approach to Irish history is not only long-term, but places the changes which took place in a wider European context.

Another important element in a sociological understanding of history is to recognise that the interest in and struggle to be more ethical, spiritual and civil – that is to attain religious and symbolic power – were not ends in themselves. They were closely tied in with the struggle for political freedom and more important perhaps, the struggle for economic survival and to increase and maintain standards of living. In other words, the task of a sociological explanation of Irish Catholic history is to link changes in religious life not only to changes emerging in Europe as a whole, but to the fulfilment of other needs and interests, particularly the ownership, control and efficient use of the means of production – for the most part farms – and the attainment of home rule and the creation of an independent nation state. Given the wealth of detailed research on the latter, I concentrate in this study on the links between becoming devout, orthodox Catholics and

– particularly for those living on farms – attaining and maintaining an increased standard of living.[8] It was soon realised that living a good Catholic life and following the rules and regulations of the Church, besides bringing symbolic power, were also means to regulating marriage and thereby gradually improving the standard of living which could be derived from small holdings.

Another crucial element in a sociological interpretation of Irish Catholic history is to identify and describe the links between institutional changes, for example the growth in the organisational strength of the Church, and the actions and behaviour of individuals.[9] I will argue that the Irish mother had a pivotal role in Irish Catholic history, acting as the link between the institutional Church and ordinary everyday life. It was mothers who created and maintained a rigorous, legalistic and, at the same time, devout adherence to the Church which, in turn created the vocations to become priests, nuns and brothers on which the Church depended. At the same time, it was the bishops, priests, nuns and brothers who dominated, supervised and regulated the lives of Catholic men and women, particularly mothers. Through focusing on the role of the mother we can understand the relation between the institutional structure and the actions of individuals and, consequently, how the moral monopoly of the Church was maintained from one generation to the next in the long nineteenth century of Irish Catholicism.

Finally, it is necessary to say something about the way my sociological approach to the history of Irish Catholicism differs from that of more traditional historians. The most important difference relates to the role of theory. Constructing a history of Irish Catholicism necessarily involves a detailed accumulation of what happened, what was said and done. This is extremely important work and is central to our knowledge and understanding of the history of Irish Catholic life. But it is important to realise three things. First, the process by which events, texts and people are selected for study is crucial. Why, out of the myriad of acts, events and people which make up the Irish Catholic history, are some chosen and others omitted? It is not a coincidence that in the traditional approach the emphasis was on great men who made the Catholic Church in Ireland, with little attention being given to the contribution of women. Irish history is now undergoing a revision which details, in particular, the contribution of nuns. In many respects, this revised emphasis is due to the emancipatory struggle of women in the last thirty years. But selecting what events and people to study is not only related to political interests, it is also dependent on the theoretical framework which one brings to bear. For example, the events which a feminist or Marxist historian selects to study might be very different from those chosen by a traditional Church historian. Second, even if there is agreement about what events or people were important, there will always be different perspectives on what happened and different statements which can be made. It is undoubtedly an historical fact that Pope John Paul II came to Ireland in 1979. But the meaning of this 'fact' changes if I say 'the Pope decided to come/was invited/was brought to Ireland in 1979'. The statement made, the choice of words, depends on the theoretical framework and political interest of the author.[10] It is important then, in a study such as this, that my theoretical framework and political interest be made clear at the outset. Third, historians as well as sociologists make use of theoretical concepts in their writing. There is no readily identifiable entity such as 'the nation', 'the state', or indeed 'the Church'. These are analytical devices used to unify a vast array of people, practices and events. For example, when an historian such as Connolly writes 'Pre-famine Ireland was a violent society in which public order was often precarious and sometimes non-existent' it is necessary to realise that pre-famine is a generalisation for an indefinite period of years up to say 1845.[11] The concept of 'society' is another generalisation which is used to cover all the people and the families, groups, organisations to which they belong. The concept of violence covers a multitude of actions from insults to murder. In a way, the task of the historian is to elucidate the extent to which this generalisation corresponds to empirical events in the real world. On the other hand, the task of the sociologist is to produce a more highly generalised and summary account of history. In the sense that sociological theory tries to devise more precise, consistent concepts of what, for example, constitutes a religion, church, society or state and then makes use of these concepts in historical investigations, it may be deemed an auxiliary science to, or 'handmaiden' of, history.[12]

The Growth in Power of the Institutional Church in Nineteenth-Century Ireland

The common Irish will never become Protestant or well affected to the crown while they are supplied with Priests, Friars, etc., who are the fomenters and disturbers here. So that some more effectual remedy to prevent Priests and Friars coming into this kingdom is perfectly necessary. The Commons proposed the marking of every priest who shall be convicted of being an unregistered Priest, Friar, etc., and of remaining in this kingdom after the 1st May, 1720 with a large P. to be made with a red hot Iron on the cheek. The council generally disliked that punishment, and have altered it into that of castration which they are persuaded will be the most effectual remedy that can be found out to clear this nation of the disturbers of the peace and quiet of the kingdom, and would have been very well pleased to have been able to have found out any other punishment which might in their opinion have remedied the evil.[1]

Within less than eighty years of that draconian proposal the relationship between Church and state in Ireland was to change dramatically. In 1795, the state introduced subsidised education for Catholic priests. Maynooth College, the National Seminary, opened its doors. On the evening of the official opening, instead of being branded or castrated, the Catholic Archbishop of Dublin, Dr Troy, went to dinner in Dublin Castle.

To quote a Catholic pamphlet of that year: 'This was the first time since the Reformation that a Catholic Bishop was permitted to dine or sit in the company with a Lord Lieutenant of Ireland.' Four years later, ten of these 'Castle' bishops – as they were to become known – took the idea of state support for the Irish Catholic Church to its logical conclusion and made a detailed submission to the government favouring a state subsidy for the whole of the Irish Catholic clergy.[2]

The proposed power alliance between Church and state that was discussed openly at the beginning of the century was to be thwarted by Rome and by the newly emergent Catholic bourgeoisie. By 1845, the Irish Catholic Church had become an independent power bloc to which the

British state had decided to bequeath the task of civilising and socially controlling the Irish people.

The Penal Laws

The proposed bill of 1719 to castrate Irish priests was rejected by the English House of Lords. The bill represented the climax of a whole series of Penal Laws which were directed not so much at the Catholic religion and its priests, as against Catholics. The laws were an attempt by the Protestant Ascendancy to maintain its position by making the Catholics a servile caste. The strategy would seem to have been to reduce the Catholic Irish to ignorant savages, and by maintaining them in that state, deprive them of all civil life. The Lord Chancellor and the Chief Justice both ruled that 'the law does not suppose any such person to exist as an Irish Roman Catholic.' The Penal Laws were a crude and brutal attempt by a Protestant state to secure permanently the Ascendancy of a dominant class whose interests they solely represented. They were basically class laws directed at denying Catholics ownership of the basic means of production. Lecky summarises their economic content:

No Catholic was suffered to buy land, or inherit or receive it as a gift from Protestants, or to hold life annuities, or mortgages on land, or leases for more than thirty-one years, or any lease on such terms that the profits of the land exceeded one-third of the rent. If a Catholic leaseholder, by his skill or industry, so increased his profits that they exceeded this proportion, and did not immediately make a corresponding increase in his rent, his farms passed to the first Protestant who made the discovery.[3]

This law against production was in addition to the confiscations of land in the previous century. These had resulted in the Catholic share of Irish land falling from 59 per cent in 1641 to 14 per cent in 1703.[4]

The laws restricting education and religion can be understood as part of the strategy to demean and demoralise. Without knowledge and discipline there was every chance the Irish Catholic would remain ignorant. As an uneducated, uncivil, disorganised alliance, Catholics might occasionally burst out in open rebellion, as they had done in the past, but at least they would not be able to engage in any organised political revolution. Bishops and priests – both diocesan and members of religious orders – were the means towards the goal of a civilised, moralised and disciplined Catholic population; this was a further reason for the expulsion of bishops and priests belonging to religious orders, and for the reduction of diocesan clergy to the role of merely saying Mass. If after 1698 any priests other than diocesan clergy were found, they were to be imprisoned and transported out of the country, and if they returned, were liable to be hung, drawn and quartered.[5] Under a further Act of 1703 diocesan clergy were required to register with the state. If they did not they were to be banished. One thousand and eighty nine did register, some of whom belonged to religious orders. They were free to say Mass, to administer the sacraments and carry out all the functions of a parish priest. However, since priests could not be trained in Ireland, and since there was no provision for any further registration or replacement of existing priests, the notion was that they would quietly die out within a generation. The purpose behind the proposed branding or castrating of registered priests was that they could not be secretly replaced by transferring names from one to another. By this time, the vast majority of priests had become technically outlaws since they had refused to take the Oath of Abjuration (1708) which denied any Catholic the right to the English throne.[6] 'Magistrates were empowered to summon any papist over the age of sixteen and require him, under oath, to reveal when and where he had heard Mass, who celebrated the Mass, and who were present. . . .'[7]

The extent to which the laws were enforced varied enormously throughout the country. The absence of chapels and the outlaw status of priests meant that in many areas Mass attendance was literally carried out openly, often at what became known as 'Mass-rocks'. In the north of the country these were the most common place of worship until the end of the eighteenth century. In urban areas, the more well-to-do Catholic merchants had sufficient wealth and status to confront the law, and practise their religion publicly in the back-streets. Burke notes that 'Catholic chapels usually had neither street-frontage nor adjacent graveyard and their sites were usually small. They were approached by narrow lanes for they were usually at the rear of houses, occupying sites of former stables and warehouses.'[8]

The open-air or back-street religion of Catholics was to persist in many areas well into the nineteenth century, and stood in stark contrast to the substantial brick and stone buildings of the established Protestant Church. As late as 1845, an English commentator described the poverty of the Irish Catholic Church as follows: 'They worship in hovels, or in the open air, from the want of any place of worship. Their religion is the religion of three fourths of the population. Not far off, in a well-windowed and well-roofed house, is a well-paid Protestant clergyman . . . crying in the wilderness . . . furious against the errors of Popery.'[9] It is only when one understands the enormous demoralisation which took place under these Penal Laws that one can comprehend why it was that Catholics of later generations gave so much of their time, money and effort to constructing the large number of church buildings that became monuments to their faith and respectability.

Penal Education

A central aspect of the demoralising process was to see that the Irish Catholic was and remained ignorant and uncouth. Again Lecky summarises the main effects of the laws: 'The Catholic was excluded from the university. He was not permitted to be the guardian of a child. It was made penal for him to keep a school, to act as usher or private tutor, or to send his children to be educated abroad; and a reward of £10 was offered for the discovery of a Popish schoolmaster.'[10]

It was at this time that the famous 'hedge-schools' came into existence. These were to dominate the field of Irish education until the establishment of the National School system in the 1830s. Although there was a hedge-school in every parish in the country, they varied enormously in quality. Much depended on the individual teacher. The curriculum was inconsistent and relied heavily on Latin and Greek classics handed down over the years. They were attended by an elite who could afford the few pence necessary to pay the teacher. Their success rate, even in basic literacy, was highly uneven. The buildings, if any, were rough-and-tumble places. The absence of confined and defined space militated against supervision and the inculcation of discipline and civility. It was this educational system which gave rise to the classical contradiction of the uncivil, ill-mannered Irish peasant being well-versed in Homer and Virgil.[11]

The Penal Laws had the unintended consequence in establishing an alliance between schoolteachers and priests.[12] Although the priest was strictly responsible for catechising the people, Corish claims that a share of this work had already devolved onto the schoolmaster in the first half of the eighteenth century. He cites three instances where it was explicitly stated that school was held in the Masshouse, and claims that 'the archbishop regarded the schoolmaster as an object of his visitation equally with the parish priest.'[13]

It was the persistence and prevalence of illegal Popish schools – a survey in 1731 had revealed at least 549 – which led to the state's strategy of establishing subsidised schools to Protestantise the Irish. The Charter Schools were based on the principle of the state intervening and detaching children from their ignorant, uncivil and immoral parents so that they 'may be instructed in the English tongue and in the principles of true religion and loyalty in all succeeding generations'. As opposed to the more classical orientation of the hedge-schools, the Charter Schools aimed to train children in 'labour and industry in order to cure that habitual laziness and idleness which is too common among the poor of this country.'[14] But the whole attempt to Protestantise the Irish could only be successful if the children were detached from the bad habits of their parents. Consequently, admission to the schools depended upon Catholic parents handing over all rights to the bodies and souls of their children who, once they had entered the schools, were apprenticed out to Protestant families and were forbidden to communicate with their parents. The schools were intended, in the words of their programme, 'to rescue the souls of thousands of poor children from the dangers of Popish superstition and idolatry, and their bodies from the miseries of idleness and beggary.'[15] Nurseries were set up in the schools in an attempt to persuade mothers to abandon their children in early infancy. This practice of state-subsidised, Protestant societies detaching children from what were deemed to be their uncivil and immoral parents, was also perpetuated in Foundling Hospitals.[16]

The schools were a failure. They became the object of scorn and ridicule and, Lecky claims, even in bad times when they were used most, 'it is doubtful that they had more than 2,000 pupils.'[17] The Royal Commission on Irish Education (1825) stated that in the ninety years the schools were in operation a total of only 12,745 children had been apprenticed.[18] However, the social and political interest of the Protestant Ascendancy in moralising and controlling the Irish population continued. Following the Act of Union (1801) which brought Ireland under direct British control, it constantly pressurised the state to do something. As the Association for Discountenancing Vice and Promoting Knowledge and Practice of the Christian Religion noted:

It is a melancholy truth that the Irish vulgar are in too many instances bloody and ferocious, retaining the habits and feelings of Savages, devoid of lasting gratitude, and ready at the impulse of any groundless resentment, to exercise the most unrelenting cruelty where shortly before they had professed the most affectionate attachment. . . . Should not every expedient that either honest Policy or pure Religion can furnish, be instantly resorted to, in order if possible to introduce among them the habits and principles of rational beings, and of Christians? The change from Savageness to Civilization has been too often realised to be any where despaired of. But it must begin somewhere.[19]

In other words while the Charter School system had failed, it was still felt that the best way to achieve social and political stability was through education and moral discipline, especially since the Irish were making such strenuous efforts to educate themselves. But at this stage it was still seen as essential that the education be Protestant and carried out through state-subsidised, Protestant societies. Otherwise, the Association claimed, 'the pernicious doctrines of treason and rebellion' would continue to be disseminated among the lower classes by hedge-schoolmasters. 'The necessity of providing some remedy for an evil of such magnitude, must be as obvious in a political as in a moral view.'[20] This pressure had results. The state, through various reports from its commissioners, began to accept the need for uniform instruction and supervision in order to control the Irish population. The commissioners contended that it was necessary 'to substitute for the ill-taught and ill-regulated Schools which we have been describing, a systematic and uniform plan of instruction, such as should gratify the desire for information, which manifests itself among the lower classes of the people of Ireland, and at the same time form those habits of regularity and discipline which are yet more valuable than mere learning. . . .'[21]

The British state's interest in providing a national school system of education which would standardise, regulate and supervise the morality and discipline of the Irish was fostered and cultivated by various Protestant societies throughout the first thirty years of the nineteenth century. With state support these societies felt that they could quickly civilise and moralise the Irish into the true Christian religion. The interest of these societies was essentially a missionary religious one, quite similar to that which later led thousands of Irish priests, brothers and nuns to the four corners of the earth. However, the social interest of the state in civilising the Irish cannot be separated from its political interest in disciplining and controlling the population. To answer the question, which Akenson raises, as to why a state system of mass education was introduced in Ireland four decades before it was introduced in England or Scotland, it is necessary to understand the background to the British interest in Ireland, and its wider policy of policing and controlling the Irish people.[22]

State Mechanisms of Political and Social Control

Throughout its history Ireland had been like no other British colony, being right next door and yet separated by a stretch of sea. It was the sea which made Ireland easily accessible to France and Spain, and its insular proximity which made Britain feel militarily vulnerable. It was mainly this military vulnerability which made Ireland of unique colonial interest. It was a country with no obvious natural resources, other than some reasonably good land. The British were forced to try various methods to pacify and subdue the natives and sustain a permanent colonial presence. The confiscation of lands and the experimental plantation system of the sixteenth and seventeenth centuries had largely failed, except in the North. The attempted 'legal' subjugation of Irish Catholics through systematic penal legislation had also failed. By the 1820s, the state had begun to show visible signs of concern, if not outright worry, about the Irish problem. The first detailed census, carried out in 1821, had shown that the Irish population had grown to 6.8 million – more than half the population of England, and one third of the British Isles altogether. To have so many traditionally rebellious people living 'next door', who to all intents and purposes were regarded as savages, posed a threat to the peaceful industrial order of Britain. Within the wider context of previous failures at political and social control, the British state became willing to experiment with a number of strategies and tactics in order to subdue and pacify the Irish.

The Policing of the Irish Body: Because Irish Catholics were successfully educating themselves – and, according to many accounts, in seditious and rebellious literature – and because agrarian outrages, organised by secret societies such as the Whiteboys, were becoming more common, the British state was forced into trying alternative methods to subdue them. One of these methods was the expansion of the existing constabulary, which in the seventeenth century had acted more as watchmen than as a custodial and investigative force. The Police Acts of 1786 (for Dublin) and 1787 (for the rest of the country) were an attempt to specify how a new police force should operate. The Dublin Act brought in paid constables endowed with wide new powers who, operated under the orders of three Commissioners of Police.[23] These acts represented a further experiment in the British state control of the Irish. As Maitland pointed out, 'down to 1856 there was no law for the whole of England requiring that there should be paid police-men.'[24] These acts were also the beginning of the modern concept of a civil police force that was to be widely imitated in many Western societies.

The early Police Acts were revised and updated in 1814 by Sir Robert Peel, the Under-Secretary for Ireland. His new act established the Peace Preservation Force (which became known as 'Peelers'). This Act gave greater control of police activities to the centralised state. Breathnach notes that 'the Lord Lieutenant was empowered to proclaim any county or city or portion of any country to be in a "state of disturbance", in which case he could appoint a chief magistrate, a chief constable and fifty sub-constables to such an area. . . .'[25] The constitution of the police as a specific apparatus of the state was treated with suspicion by the Protestant Ascendancy. The state may have been representing their interests, but according to McDowell they abhorred 'the arbitrary tendencies inherent in centralisation almost as much as they disliked the destruction of local patronage.'[26] Indeed it was partly because the state made the decision which area should be policed, but yet required each area to pay for the force as long as it remained there, that the alliance between itself and this ruling class started to deteriorate.[27] This was all part of a new period of Irish history in which the policies of the British state became distanced from the interests of the Protestant Ascendancy. The concentration was on establishing peace and order in the colony, partly as an end in itself, partly as another experimental attempt at civilisation, and partly out of fear that 'savage' Irish practices and customs might spread to British cities.

By 1820, there were at least five police forces in existence in Ireland. In 1822, a further police Act was passed establishing a new force under a provincial and county organisation. This was a paramilitary force, uniformed and armed. Soon after its establishment there were 5,008 such constables, operating under 313 chief constables. As Brady notes:

It throws an interesting sidelight on the nature of British administration in Ireland in the years immediately after the union that two entirely different police systems should be developed for a supposedly 'united' kingdom. Britain got an unarmed policeman, answerable not to central government but to a Watch Committee and depending in the last analysis on the moral support of the community to enforce the law. Ireland, by contrast, got an armed garrison, rigidly disciplined and directly controlled by Dublin Castle, operating with the backing of the Martini-Carbine, the bayonet and the sword rather than the support of the community.[28]

The principal reorganisation of the Irish police came with the Constabulary Act (1836). The Peace Preservation Force was scrapped and a new hierarchical system of inspectors and sub-inspectors established. The key difference in this reorganisation was the emphasis on surveillance and intelligence, and the structures instituted to develop state knowledge and power. Breathnach describes the growth in the new state apparatus:

Every conceivable part of the country came within the Castle's intelligence. Baronies, which hitherto occupied 16 constables, were divided into sub-districts and as many men stationed in them. Stations were made as central as possible and took the name of their respective townlands. Even to the present day . . . these areas, including districts, sub-districts and stations, are the same as they were almost a century and a half ago, the older stations still containing their lonely, hideous and formidable appearance.[29]

These new organisational structures did not, as was hoped, provide for the permanent civilisation of Ireland. They were rejected by the Irish peasant, the emerging Catholic bourgeoisie, and the state's own arm of enforcement – the magistrates – who still rejected state centralisation and interference.[30] The early experimental Police Acts did not even have the short-term effect of curtailing agrarian outrage. In effect, the peasants were shut off from the most effective means of civilisation – the Catholic clergy and bourgeoisie. It was only when these forces could gain prominence in Irish society, with or without state approval, that the mass of the Irish population could become civil in a modern European manner.

State Care and Maintenance of the Irish Body: A central aspect of the growth of state power from the mid-eighteenth to the mid-nineteenth century was the growth in the number of institutions (in the beginning mostly charitable) which cared for, maintained and incarcerated the Irish people. Although workhouses and foundling hospitals date from the beginning of the eighteenth century, the rapid growth in total – that is life-encompassing – institutions which gained complete control of those who entered them, did not begin until the first half of the nineteenth century. The failure of the early institutions, e.g. Charter schools and foundling hospitals, was not so much because they were proselytising agencies, but that they did not really care for the inmates. Robins points out that:

The enquiry of the Commissioners of Irish Education revealed not only that the governors had failed in their efforts to fashion the children into upright, moral citizens, but that the death rate amongst the foundlings was still of huge proportions. Statistics included in the report of the enquiry disclosed that of approximately 52,000 infants reared during the period 1796 to 1826, 32,000 had definitely perished either as infants in the institution or after being sent to the country; about 9,600 others who could not be ascertained for were also thought to have died.[31]

In 1828, John Douglas made a forceful argument as to why the state should begin to develop a welfare system for the Irish poor and, in particular, extend the poor laws to Ireland. 'The necessity of protecting all classes in Britain from the degrading competition of Irish pauper labour, and the consequent augmentation of the pressure of pauperism on the British soil and capital, have become too urgent to be trifled with.'[32] The movement from a direct policing of the Irish, which was obviously ineffective, to more indirect, softer forms of social and political control, had obvious advantages.

Such a grateful common object of universal concern, as the comfortable maintenance of the poor – the substitution of industry, morals and order, for the idleness, dishonesty, profligacy and audacity of daily public begging and midnight marauding – could not but tend greatly to soothe the asperity of political and religious rancour – to calm the agitation of the public mind – to render government more easy and mild – to reconcile and restore the absentees to their pacified country, excite and reward local industry by local expenditure of the revenues of the land and the church, and gradually invite capital to establish manufacturers, by the cheapness of labour and food among a happily tranquilised population.[33]

The growth in private and state-funded health services was spectacular. By 1836, there were 36 infirmaries and almost 500 dispensaries. At the beginning of the century there were only eleven hospitals in Dublin, by 1845 there were thirty. On the basis of this phenomenal growth McDowell concludes that 'the Irish poor enjoyed better medical services than their fellows in wealthier and healthier countries.'[34] The other system of general care and maintenance which the state introduced was the workhouse. During the first half of the 1840s, 118 workhouses were built throughout Ireland. They were exact models of those already established in Britain under the 1834 Poor Law. They were total institutions founded on the famous principle of 'less eligibility' – that is to say, the relief to be provided was not to be made 'really or apparently so eligible [i.e. desirable] as the situation of the independent labourer of the lowest class.'[35]

The main buildings used for politically controlling the Irish were prisons and gaols. In 1839, there were 148 official prisons of which 39 were long-term county gaols. The county gaols had 2,957 cells which in that year held up to 6,117 prisoners. Of the 8,729 prisoners sent to gaol in 1839, 7,726 were sent for less than six months; 874 for 6–12 months; and 128 for 1–3 years.[36] It was also during the first half of the nineteenth century that long-term institutions, other than gaols, began to be built. Houses of Industry, originally established for the destitute poor and which later in the eighteenth century began to be used as asylums, became total institutions for young criminals – that is they were locked up and shut off from the outside world. However it was almost another sixty years before a full system of reformatories was established throughout the country. But by that time the Catholic Church, through its orders of nuns and brothers, was beginning to establish its right to the moral jurisdiction and guardianship of all young Catholics.[37]

Emigration

The British state's policy of incarcerating the totally destitute in Britain and Ireland can be seen as part of an overall strategy of maintaining the environmental conditions for industrial order and the exploitation of the labour power of the working classes, which constituted the wealth of Britain. It is difficult to separate the political interest in peace, order and stability from the genuine, humanitarian, social interest which existed at the time. Politicians had been long aware of the dangers of a mass invasion of cheap Irish labour to the industrialised cities. In his evidence to the Select Committee on the State of Ireland (1825) Mr McCulloch stated that the 25,000 natives of Ireland operated injuriously upon the British labourers in two ways: '*first*, they operate to reduce their wages by the increased number of labourers brought into the market, and by the greater competition there is for employment; and *second*, they operate in another way, by the example they set to the English and Scottish labourers. . . .'[38] These opinions were echoed by Malthus two years later, when he gave evidence to the Select Committee on Emigration.

Are you able to give the Committee any information with respect to the effects already produced by an increased number of Irish coming over to England?
— I have only understood it generally, that in western parts of England, in the manufacturing districts, in Manchester and in Glasgow particularly, the wages of labour have been lowered essentially by the coming over of the Irish labourers.
In your opinion, might this emigration of Irish contribute to alter materially the habits of the labouring class in England?
— I should think it might, and that it might have the pernicious effect of introducing the habit of living almost entirely upon potatoes.

What general consequences would you suppose would be the result of that change in the habits of the people in England with regard to their subsistence?
— That they would be very much worse off in every respect.
In their manners and conduct?
— Yes in every respect, moral and physical.[39]

Between 1815 and 1826, the state had conducted six separate experiments in state-aided emigration. One of these experiments was carried out in Ireland in the spring of 1822 when, following a bad harvest, it was estimated that half the population of half of Ireland was destitute. Sir Robert Peel hesitated to supply food and instead decided that 'this was the proper moment for the government to offer to remove surplus population. . . .' He made two specifications: 'first the emigrants should be recruited in southern Ireland; second, the measure should be financed entirely by the government with no expectation of reimbursement from local assessment.'[40] The experiment in getting potentially rebellious Irish peasants to settle in Canada produced more reports than success. Emigration was to become a private rather than a state-subsidised practice. Although most of the pre-Famine emigration was to the United States and Canada, up to half of it was to the cities of Great Britain. Politicians continued to be suspicious that the arrival of so many poor, ignorant, uncivil Irish natives was having a bad effect on the good habits of the indigenous working class. In 1833, Cornwall Lewis was directed to inquire into the state of Irish labourers in Great Britain because there was a fear that: 'the Irish immigrants have exercised a pernicious influence on the English and Scottish working classes, by lowering their wages and debasing their moral character, and that certain measures ought to be introduced in Ireland with a view to preventing the emigration of the poor to Great Britain.' The testimonies given to Cornwall Lewis suggested that the Irish were 'the first to commence riots'; were 'more drunken and idle'; and tended to 'live in squalid filth in cellars'. A Liverpool priest testified that 'an Englishman who earns 18s a week is found to have his children neatly clad and his house comfortable: whereas an Irishman on the same wages has his children ill-clad, and his room and cellar filthy'. The pragmatic Cornwall Lewis warned, however, that it would be unwise to overlook the advantages which a reserve army of Irish labour supplied at such cheap rates and short notice. 'Their irregular habits and low standard of comfort may be regretted; but it is to be remembered that the Irish have been and are, most efficient workmen: that they come in the hour of need, and that they afforded the chief part of the animal strength by which the great works of our manufacturing districts have been executed.' While many of the witnesses argued that the irregular and bad habits of the Irish injured the superior character of the Scottish and English poor, Cornwall Lewis argued that 'because the Irish lived in ghettoes and did not mix with the natives' they would not endanger 'in any material degree, the moral habits of the latter.'[41]

Cornwall Lewis's report, which was over 300 pages long, was only an appendix to one of the numerous volumes which the Poor Law Commissioners produced on Ireland. These, in turn, were only a small fraction of the total number of reports produced by other commissions, select committees, and so on, during the first half of the nineteenth century. Through these reports, documentations, statistics and censuses the state accumulated an enormous body of knowledge about how the Irish people behaved, and about the environmental conditions which produced their behaviour. This knowledge became the basis of state policy in Ireland.

Unfortunately no systematic analysis has been made of the overall content of these reports and the role they played in state policy formation. However, an indication of the primary importance given to producing knowledge about Ireland can be gauged from the fact that in the *General Index to the House of Commons Accounts and Papers* there are 462 references to reports on Ireland, compared to only 210 on Scotland.[42]

The State/Church Alliance

By the middle of the eighteenth century British politicians had begun to realise that the attempt to abolish Catholicism in Ireland through persecution had failed. Nevertheless the Protestant Ascendancy still feared for their possessions and position. Any sign of 'native unrest', or indeed any large gathering of Catholics, even if for a pattern or pilgrimage, 'struck terror into the hearts of Protestants.'[43] But it was soon realised that, as Lecky puts it, 'the higher Catholic clergy, if left in peace, were able and willing to render inestimable services to the Government in suppressing sedition and crime, and as it was quite evident that the bulk of the Irish Catholics would not become Protestants, they could not, in the mere interests of order, be left wholly without religious ministration.'[44]

It was at this stage that a tentative power alliance began to be formed between the British state and the Catholic Church. As long as the Irish could be dissuaded from bloody rebellion and became civil and disciplined, it did not matter so much who produced the results. The Protestant Ascendancy continued to press for a return to the penal code. Throughout the first half of the nineteenth century, members of this class argued and wrote at length about the necessity of expelling all forms of popery from Ireland.[45] In contrast, many British politicians, responding perhaps to pressure from the British bourgeoisie, began to realise what a powerful ally the Church could be in the pacification of the Irish masses. The constant exhortations by Catholic bishops and clergy for law and order provided continuing evidence of their good intentions.[46]

But whatever role the Church might have played in bringing modern civilisation to the Irish population, it was hampered by a lack of manpower. Towards the end of the century the population was rising rapidly, but, following the French Revolution and the closure of Catholic seminaries, the supply of Irish priests was stopped. The medium for putting across the message of civility, law and order was in danger of being cut off. In advocating the unprecedented notion that the state should initiate and support a college for the training of Catholic priests in Ireland, the Archbishop of Dublin, Dr Troy, coyly pointed out to the Lord Lieutenant that the moral instruction of the people 'may appear to his Majesty's Ministers a subject not unworthy of his Royal consideration and Bounty.'[47] Another consideration in favour of supporting a national seminary was that once the Catholic seminaries on the Continent were reopened, young trainee Irish priests might be imbued with the revolutionary spirit which had swept France. Indeed that revolutionary spirit had already reached Ireland. Some of the more enlightened members of the Irish Protestant bourgeoisie had begun to argue for Catholic emancipation because they associated the rapidly increasing prosperity which had occurred since the middle of the eighteenth century with the greater freedom of Catholics. If economic prosperity were to continue, they felt it was essential that an alliance be made with the new wealthy Catholic bourgeoisie. In fact, the idea had been current for a long time that persecuting the Irish Catholic was of little use and, as a strategy, decidedly ineffective. As Wolfe Tone, the Protestant leader of the unsuccessful rebellion in 1798 argued, it made matters worse:

Persecution will keep alive the foolish bigotry and superstition of any sect, as the experience of five thousand years have demonstrated. Persecution bound the Irish Catholic to his Priest, and the Priest to the Pope; the bond of union is drawn tighter by oppression, relaxation will undo it. The emancipated and liberal Irishman, like the emancipated and liberal Frenchman, may go to mass, and tell his beads; but neither the one nor the other will attend to the rusty and extinguished thunderbolts of the Vatican. . . .[48]

Along with the general increase in economic prosperity which was spreading throughout Europe, and the enlightened civilised approach to religious adversaries which accompanied it, there were other factors associated with the new approach by the state to the Catholic Church in Ireland. These had to do with the rational differentiation that was taking place in European civilisation between the religious and political spheres.[49] As part of this process, Rome began to curtail the political activities of the regular clergy in Ireland. In 1751, Pope Benedict XIV issued a decree confining them to living in their community houses, and putting them under the supervision and control of the local bishop.[50] In the past it had been the regular clergy who operated closest with the ordinary people and who were most feared by the Protestant Ascendancy. Within twenty years the number of regular clergy had been halved. In 1757, the bishops circulated a document to the whole of the clergy requesting that it be read at the first Sunday of every quarter. The document emphasised that 'it is not and never was a doctrine or tenet of the Roman Catholic Church that the Pope or general councils have power to depose kings, or absolve subjects from their allegiance', or that Catholics 'may break faith with, murder, or plunder, or defraud those of a different communion or religion.'[51] Furthermore, because most of its priests had been trained on the Continent, the Irish Catholic Church had for a long time been tainted with Gallicanism, a central tenet of which was that the Pope received only spiritual authority from God.[52] The more the bishops and clergy formally denied any temporal power of the Pope and any Catholic right to the English throne, and continued to denounce riots and rebellions, the more British politicians and the Protestant Ascendancy became reassured of their loyalty. Catholic Relief Acts were passed in 1762, 1774, 1778, and 1782, and Emancipation Acts in 1792 and 1793.[53]

Having gone so far as to subsidise the education and training of priests in Maynooth in 1795, the state was urged to consider providing for all the bishops and clergy. In terms of attaining civil and moral order this was desirable because the Protestant Church did not have the necessary allegiance, and the Protestant Ascendancy was too small and scattered to be effective civilising agencies. However, such a consideration would only be possible if the state had a veto over the nomination of bishops. (In effect, such a veto was part of the ongoing process of the rational differentiation of the religious from the secular sphere since its purpose was to avoid the appointment of seditious and treasonable bishops. In other words, a state subsidy for the clergy would be appropriate as long as priests stuck purely to moral matters.) Such veto powers were in fact part of a state-subsidised clergy proposal put forward by the trustees of Maynooth in 1799. Rome was consulted and, as Gwynn puts it, 'declared emphatically against any proposal of paying state salaries to bishops, [and] asserted that no Protestant sovereign could be allowed the power of nominating Catholic bishops. . . .'[54] This opposition can be understood as an attempt to maintain its own centralised power and to avoid any alliance between the Irish Church and the British state. But six years later Rome changed its ruling when the Congregation of Propaganda admitted that a veto might be accepted as part of a bill emancipating Catholics.[55] It was at this stage that O'Connell, the leader of the Catholic Association, who had already criticised the bishops for supporting the Union, denounced any links either between the bishops and the state through a subsidy, or between the state and Rome through a veto. Soon afterwards the bishops expressed their opposition to both a state subsidy and a veto. This was the beginning of a shift away from any possible alliance between the bishops and the state, and a move towards a new and eventually permanent alliance with the emerging Catholic bourgeoisie.

Even before Catholic Emancipation (1829) there was a hardening attitude among Catholic bishops and clergy against the idea of a state provision, and a conviction that 'the voluntary system was an essential part of the bond between them and the people.'[56] Although the Church never became a subsidised apparatus of the state, many of the bishops favoured strengthening any power alliance that existed. Others, led by Archbishop MacHale of Tuam, were adamant that any alliance must be with the laity, led by the emergent Catholic bourgeoisie and Daniel O'Connell.

When the state failed to get the hierarchy to enter into an alliance with it, it did its best to ensure that there was no alliance between the Church and the Catholic bourgeoisie. In their anxiety to control Irish Catholics, especially in their movement towards repeal of the Act of Union, British politicians attempted to counteract any unified Catholic alliance. This they did by sending an agent to Rome and offering appeasements to the hierarchy. This caused a split among the bishops and clergy, and a split between the Catholic Association and the Church. The state, in fact, was attempting to exercise power by dividing the hierarchy, setting its members against each other, the diocesan clergy and religious order priests against the bishops, and the laity against the clergy and hierarchy. When Peel appointed Heytesbury as Lord Lieutenant, he told him about 'the absolute necessity . . . of disuniting, by the fair legitimate means of a just, kind and conciliatory policy, the Roman Catholic body and thus breaking up a sullen and formidable *confederacy* against the British connection.'[57] However, what was really happening was that despite the efforts of the state, the Irish hierarchy was emerging as a major, organised power bloc in Irish society.

Although the bishops may have been divided they were, unlike at any other time in their history, communicating and regularly meeting each other. With constant advice from Rome, especially from Cullen, the then Rector of the Irish College, and his vice-president Tobias Kirby, the hierarchy was being moulded into a body which was increasingly able to limit successfully the actions of the state, especially in matters of morality. It was a constant fear of many members of the hierarchy, clergy and laity that not only was their destiny being moulded by Rome, but that this was being done in and through a concordat with the British state.[58] Moreover, insofar as it was primarily interested in gaining moral control of Irish Catholics and remained unsupportive of their economic and political struggles, Rome operated in the political interests of the British state. From the time of his appointment as Rector of the Irish College in Rome, and later becoming the official representative of the Irish bishops, Cullen was groomed to the main task of bringing the Irish Church under Roman control. This he was able to do, first by building up a detailed knowledge of the situation in Ireland and then, secondly, by granting favours and fixing episcopal appointments. An effective tactic was to get the new nationalist Gallicans to supplant the old state-supportive Gallicans, and then to supplant the new Gallicans with his own Ultramontane appointees. Cullen promoted the cause of Rome first and foremost. According to Bowen he was against the nationalist struggle because it promoted religious indifference. Indeed Bowen goes so far as to argue that Cullen was so intent upon rectifying the religious malaise of the Irish Church that 'he showed little interest in the temporal needs of the people.'[59] What the strategies and tactics employed by Cullen and the other Ultramontanes achieved, was to reconstitute the Irish Church slowly as a united body directly accountable to and regulated by Rome. What it did not achieve was to stem the involvement, particularly of priests, in the economic and political struggles of the new class of substantial Catholic tenant farmers. But, as we shall see, the growth in the organisation and size of the Church can be linked to a gradual shift away from open rebellion to democratic parliamentary procedures as a means of gaining both control of the land and Home Rule. It was within a complex web of relations between London, Rome, and mainly Dublin that the Catholic Church in Ireland began to emerge as a power bloc. The end result, which was of most interest to the administrators in Rome and London, was that a civilising and moralising force was being exercised over the Irish.

The Growth of the Institutional Church 1750–1850

The attempt to eliminate Catholicism through the repression of the institutional Church was a failure. Instead of detaching the people from the bishops and clergy it had the opposite effect of uniting them in a struggle against the state. The penal laws failed because they did not stop the formation of a Catholic urban bourgeoisie which, in its search for civility, morality and legitimated status, allied itself closely with the Catholic Church. The new urban merchant class was to become a social model for the tenant farmers of the nineteenth century. When the British state attempted to control the Catholic bourgeoisie and the Church, it was too late. This formidable alliance was already well established and would be fully cemented after 1922 in the new Irish state. Moreover the fight for a

Church independent of the state had been encouraged and partially directed by Rome as part of its own multinational power consolidation process. Such a process was not new and had been rigorously pursued in Ireland throughout the seventeenth century, even though the Church and Catholic population were often in the depths of religious persecution. The Tridentine reforms which Rome sought to introduce involved the establishment of a parish system of pastoral care operated in and through the Church rather than the home; the pursuance of a catechetical programme to produce a uniform, orthodox doctrine; and the constitution of the priest as a man of Roman precept and morality rather than a mere religious functionary. The Penal Laws brought a temporary halt to this process of Tridentine reform. Nevertheless even in the period of active enforcement of the laws, Rome continued to exert considerable power over the Irish Catholic Church.[60]

The growth in the discipline and bureaucratic organisation of the Church can also be linked to a general explosion of Catholic discourse in Irish society which was made possible by the physical development of the infrastructure of communications, including printing, roads, and the postal service. The growth in the popular press, for example, was associated with an increase in the actual reporting of the activities of the Catholic Church.[61] This, together with the fact that much of the reporting was of a favourable nature, did much to give the Church a legitimate position, especially among the more literate Protestant community. It was not that Church organisation and discipline were new. Instructions regarding clerical discipline had been laid down since at least the eleventh century. What was new was the extent to which bishops began to communicate with each other and reform their dioceses. Much of the discourse and practice of bishops in the first half of the nineteenth century was taken up with tightening clerical discipline. There was a general clamp down on public disorders and scandal-giving practices of the clergy, especially insolence, drinking and cavorting with undesirables. Larkin concludes that 'what happened between 1800 and 1845 is that the character and conduct of the clergy, which certainly left a great deal to be desired at the beginning of the period, was gradually and uniformly improved. By 1830, the worst was over since the Irish bishops with the help of Rome finally secured the upper hand over their priests.'[62] He notes that the improvement was greatest in the east, especially in the Archdiocese of Dublin, and in the towns where better mannered, better informed priests were generally placed. Throughout the rest of the century, this growth in manners, discipline and civility was to spread westwards, being instilled into the homes and bodies of most Irish Catholics through the organisations and buildings supervised by priests and religious.

But the creation of the Catholic Church as a power bloc in Irish society did not occur simply through increased communication and the greater exercise of Roman bureaucracy, discipline and control. It was also rooted in changes in Irish economic and social conditions which, in turn, cannot be divorced from the general increase in prosperity and civility spreading throughout Europe at the time. Greater economic prosperity had its particular translation in Ireland. For the Catholic Church it meant a large increase in the size of its flock without a concomitant increase in the number of priests to minister to them – a situation which only the Famine was to rectify. In 1731, the ratio of diocesan priests to Catholics was 1:1587, which is not very different from the present-day European average.[63] However, the ratio deteriorated rapidly, not because of a decline in vocations but because of a rapid rise in the population. Among the lower classes, where the population increase was concentrated, the effects of greater economic prosperity resulted in more births, more marriages, and a greater subdivision of already small holdings. The moral discipline that was needed to forgo gratification in order to accumulate and reproduce wealth did not exist. Priests, nuns and brothers, and the institutions of discipline that were to become the principal means towards such ends, were not yet ubiquitous. The temporary closure of the continental seminaries had not helped the situation. Even if these colleges had remained open, it is difficult to imagine that the vocation rate would have been much higher. Sending one's son to be trained as a priest in a continental seminary, or indeed to Maynooth, was an expensive practice which could only be supported by the better-off.

Once Maynooth opened, and the new class of tenant farmers became established, the number of vocations to the priesthood began to rise. This should not be taken to mean cottiers, landless labourers, or small tenant farmers on holdings of less than five acres – all of whom made up seven-tenths of the rural population – but rather the large Catholic tenant farmers. It was only they who could actively seek the social prestige to be gained from having a son a priest, and who could afford to send him to be educated in Maynooth. The cost of sending a son to Maynooth for the first year was £40–£50.[64] Given that the average agricultural wage was not much more than 1s. a day, this would mean that the cost of educating a son to be a priest was more than double the annual income of most people at the time.[65] In 1808, of the 205 students in Maynooth, 159 (78 per cent) were the sons of farmers.[66] From the beginning of the nineteenth century, the heart of Irish Catholicism shifted gradually from an urban merchant class to a rural tenant farmer class.

Catholic priests may have worked among the poor laity but they were always from a different economic class. Indeed, given the low earnings of the majority of the laity it was quite an exploitative relationship. The average income of a parish priest in 1750 was about £30 to £35. By 1801, this had increased to £65. In the next twenty-five years it doubled and continued to improve.[67] The main cause for this rise in income had less to do with increased contributions from the successful bourgeoisie – which may have been directed more towards funds for church building – and more to do with the greater number of fees and dues received for services rendered.

The rise in population meant more marriages and births, which necessitated employing the services of a priest. These services were not cheap, and all the evidence goes to show that the money received for them, especially marriage offerings, was among the principal resources of the clergy, particularly in the southern half of the country.[68] Although the fees charged for marriages, baptisms, etc., were in theory 'offerings', they were socially obligatory, with standard rates charged. The amount charged depended upon the service rendered, whether it was a rural or urban parish, and the economic class of those receiving the service. To be married in 1825 could cost as little as five shillings, but the general figure was from half a guinea to a guinea. In the Dublin province in 1831, the bishops jointly fixed the fees as follows: 'Five shillings to be paid after the celebration of baptism, forty shillings after the celebration of marriage: ten shillings for letters of freedom to marry, two shillings for private masses.'[69] Given an average agricultural wage of not much more than 1s. a day, the cost of the services of the priest was very high by present-day standards. It is no wonder that many couples resorted to clandestine marriages performed by 'couple-beggars' (mostly ex-priests) in the cities.[70] Voluntary offerings were also expected for funerals. The amount given ranged from five to fifteen shillings depending on how many priests assisted. Offerings might also be expected for visiting the sick, usually from the better-off parishioners, and for churching – the readmission of a woman to the Church after the birth of a child.[71] The other main source of income of the clergy was dues. Dues were defined by a priest in 1806 as: 'a certain sum paid by the head of every family to the parish priest for his support and in consideration of his trouble in catechising, instructing and hearing confessions of his family. The sum is greater or smaller in proportion to the circumstances of the parishioner. In the country parishes it is generally a shilling at Easter and a shilling at Christmas: some give half-a-crown, some a crown and some few a guinea a year.'[72]

Religious dues and services were one of the main items of expenditure for the lower classes in the first half of the nineteenth century. But the services of the priest were matters of 'life and death', and of all things, including food, an absolute necessity. Because of the high prices for their services, especially for the cottiers and landless labourers who so rarely dealt with actual money, it is not surprising that there were often rebellions against them.[73] All of the agitation was local and often depended on the character and charges of the particular priest, and whether or not he had been denouncing his parishioners for their involvement in secret agrarian societies. However, besides occasional conflicts most accounts indicate a general reverence and affection for the priest, and an eager willingness to hand over their hard-earned cash to support him in a life-style which, Connolly claims, was 'somewhere, but not very much, above that of the more prosperous members of their congregations.'[74] As Murphy points out: 'It was part of a resurgent Catholicism that the priest should be seen to have a social position and residence which would compare favourably with that of his Protestant counterpart.'[75] If having a son who was a priest gave moral legitimation to the new class of tenant farmers, having a well-housed, well-heeled, and well-mannered priest as their representative, raised the prestige of the whole Catholic community.

The general increase in the support of the Church was also reflected in a substantial growth in capital. The days of inconspicuous mass-houses down back-alleys were superseded by the building of new monumental, if not ostentatious, stone churches. Much of this building took place after Emancipation (1829) and was, at first, confined to the east and to the towns where the wealthier Catholic merchants, traders and farmers were able to afford monuments to their respectability. Between 1823 and 1852, during the time Daniel Murray was Archbishop of Dublin, ninety-seven new churches were built.[76] The buildings were large and costly, but eagerly subscribed to. They were featured on the front covers of popular Catholic magazines, such as *The Catholic Penny Magazine*, which went into great detail about the opulence and ornateness of their interiors. The German traveller Kohl remarked in 1844: 'In many parts of Ireland the Catholic churches are now beginning to tower over those of "the establishment" . . . and all over the country the Irish Catholics are vying with the English Protestant in the zeal with which they build new churches and repair old ones.'[77] In reviewing the progress of Catholicism in the nineteenth century, O'Reilly estimated that:

In twenty-five of the twenty-eight dioceses of Ireland, embracing 944 out of the 1,085 parishes into which Ireland is divided, there have been built in the sixty-three years since 1800:

1. 1805 Churches which have cost	£3,061,527
2. 217 Convents	£1,058,415
3. 40 Colleges or Seminaries	£308,918
4. 44 Hospitals, or Asylums, or Orphanages	£147,135
making a total expenditure of	£4,575,995[78]

If the Catholic church was the largest building to be built in the towns of Ireland in the first half of the nineteenth century, the convent was often the second largest. Not only were the nuns responsible for one-third of capital expenditure in the first sixty-three years of the century, they were also responsible for diversifying the institutional Church into hospitals, asylums, and orphanages. The above figures do not take into account the other significant growth in Church organisation, which was much less costly but of lasting importance: the development of schools. O'Reilly estimated that between 1800 and 1863, 2,990 National Schools were erected 'without any government aid, and under Catholic management.'[79] This does not include the many schools such as those of Christian Brothers which O'Reilly estimated at being sixty-eight for the period, or the number of schools established by nuns, which Fahey claims to have been the same as the number of convents.[80]

Education

One of the important aspects in the emergence of the Catholic Church as a power bloc in Irish society was the control it gained of the education and discipline of Irish children from 1750. By 1846, the Church had won decisive battles which made it clear that it, rather than the British state or the established Protestant Church of Ireland, had moral jurisdiction over Catholic children and how they were to be educated. It had begun to exercise control in the state-subsidised, and supposedly non-denominational, national school system. It had vetoed state proposals to establish 'godless colleges', and was preparing to establish its own voluntary Catholic university. At the second level of education, orders of nuns and brothers, especially the Sisters of Mercy and Christian Brothers, had already built a reputation as the providers of a relatively cheap, well-disciplined, moral education which was to become all-important in the creation of a new rural Catholic middle class. By the middle of the last century, state supervision of education had given way to a situation in which the Church was about to take control of Irish education – and without much disapproval from the state. The main transformation in education in the last century was not just the dramatic expansion in the number of well-built schoolhouses, but that the state paid for them and, by and large, handed its supervision and control over to the Church.

The origins of the Church's domination of Irish education can be traced back to the Penal Laws. The number of hedge-schools had increased rapidly in the latter half of the eighteenth century. The Relief Act of 1782 restored to Catholics the right to teach in schools. From then on, most of the hedge-schools became known as pay schools and were linked into the parish system. The school was either set up and run by a priest who appointed a teacher, or, if set up by a private teacher it was under the priest's authority and supervision.[81] It is difficult to estimate how quickly the pay schools proliferated. However, by 1807, it appears that a Catholic system of education was fully established, even though it may have been under the roughest conditions. In that year, the Bishop of Cloyne and Ross reported that there were 316 schools in the diocese with a total of 21,892 pupils attending them.[82] In 1824, official returns estimated that there were 10,453 schools with a total of 522,016 pupils, 397,212 of whom were Roman Catholics.[83] Dowling estimates that the total number of schools under Catholic teachers was over 8,000, and of these no fewer than 7,600 were independent pay schools under lay teachers.[84]

It was the growing success of the pay schools which brought evangelical Protestant agencies and societies into the field of Irish education. Their aim was to spread Protestantism throughout Ireland by disseminating Bibles into every Irish cottage, and by eliminating 'poisonous hedge-schools' which, they constantly reminded the state, were hotbeds of sedition and treason.[85] These Protestant societies were the forerunners of the Society for Promoting the Education of the Poor in Ireland. From 1812, their Kildare Place Schools were part of a new state policy aimed at controlling hedge-schools. They were based on standardised buildings, school-rooms and fittings, as well as standardised timetables and curricula. These models of time and space were intended to be the institutions in which Protestant practices and doctrines were to be inculcated into Irish children. But the Kildare Place Schools were based on the principle of teaching scripture without note or comment. It was this insistence which led O'Connell to break with them.[86] He was the first snowball in an eventual avalanche of Catholic opposition. By 1824, the Society had become, in Akenson's terms, 'just another Protestant agency'.[87]

The following year, a Royal Commission recognised that the Kildare Place system had failed because the religious and moral instruction was not compatible with the principles and discipline of the Catholic Church. Nevertheless the Commission came out against denominational education because it felt that many of the evil habits and ideas which divided Catholics from Protestants would continue. It was then that the Catholic Church made its boldest move. In 1826, the bishops issued a unanimous declaration which stated that while they accepted the principle of a National School system, they insisted that: 'in order to secure sufficient protection to the religion of the Roman Catholic children . . . we deem it necessary that the master of each school, in which the majority of pupils profess the Roman Catholic faith, be a Roman Catholic.'[88] The bishops also demanded that the masters who taught Roman Catholic children should be trained and supervised by people of the same faith, and that they (the bishops) should select and approve of the books to be used. What was remarkable about this declaration by the bishops was that it was unanimous. Secondly, it challenged the system advocated by the Established Church and the state's own commission. Thirdly, it occurred before Catholic Emancipation, and at a time when the Catholic bishops were not legally recognised as holders of their sees. The declaration indicated clearly, for the first time, that the Catholic Church had emerged as a power bloc in Irish society, and was willing to define and defend its sphere of power over and against all others. Most remarkable of all was that within the next twenty-five years many of their demands had been granted.

When it came to the actual formation of the National School system in 1831, the state recognised that the principles of the Kildare Place Society were totally at variance with those of the Roman Catholic Church and that: 'the indiscriminate reading of the holy scriptures without note or comment, by children, must be peculiarly obnoxious to a Church which denies, even to adults, the right of unaided private interpretation of the Sacred Volume with respect to articles of religious belief.'[89] Their solution was a formally non-denominational system with religious instruction one or two days a week, either before or after ordinary school hours. What made the system denominational in practice was, firstly, that individual managers were not strictly controlled and, secondly, that because the vast majority of the school population was Catholic, the manager generally turned out to be the local parish priest. Akenson lists three main effects of the national school system on the Irish religious situation.

1. The Church was saved – in comparison, for example, with America – an enormous amount of money.

2. It placed control of a considerable amount of money in the hands of the local clergy. It provided financial patronage for clerical use, and brought control over valuable local preferments, such as the positions of principal, assistant, and monitor in national schools.

3. It reinforced the walls between the denominations.[90]

The National School system was a major blow against the Established Church from which it never recovered. It heralded the decisive and last battle with the Catholic Church for moral control of the Irish population. It was a battle that the Catholic Church won easily. In effect, the state deserted the cause of Protestantism in Ireland. Political and social control was of primary importance. It did not matter who did the moral training as long as it was done effectively. Even if the growing alliance between the Church and bourgeois nationalism became increasingly obvious, the state through various political strategies such as appeasement, threats and sanctions was at least able to stem the tide of change for many decades, and most of all, to shift the political struggle in Ireland from bloody rebellion to rational discourse.

Indeed it was partly because the Catholic Church proved so capable of educating and caring for the poor that British politicians became more willing to hand over social control of the Irish people to it. Caring for the sick, poor, and uneducated has always been a major source of the Church's moral power. In the nineteenth century it was the zealous efforts of priests, who came increasingly from the expanding middle classes, as well as the dedicated and materially unrewarded work of nuns and brothers, which was to prove crucial in the struggle to establish moral control. By the middle of the century, glowing reports were coming of the civil and moral revolution being achieved among the Irish by the Catholic Church. Fahey quotes many reports from those of school inspectors to that of a House of Commons Committee (1864). One of these concerned a school run by nuns in Enniskillen:

The nuns belong to the order of the Sisters of Mercy in which capacity they frequently visit the sick and dying belonging to the most destitute classes. During these visits they turn to good advantage the opportunities which occur of inducing parents, hitherto careless about the education of their children, to send the latter to school. But these poor children must generally be supplied with some articles of clothing before they can attend school, this the nuns accomplish by means of their industrial school.[91]

As well as their important contribution to education, the nuns also played a crucial role for the Church in gaining control of the health and social welfare of Irish Catholics.

Health

Institutional health care of the Irish population was not to become a central practice of the Irish Catholic Church until the latter half of the nineteenth century. When it did, it was mainly operated by nuns. It was their pioneering work in caring for and nursing the sick poor which was to become the basis of the medico-religious jurisdiction of the Church over the Irish population. It was orders such as the Irish Sisters of Charity and the Sisters of Mercy who, from the 1830s, began to establish hospitals and other institutions. The system of health care extended into areas such as special schools for the deaf and blind, asylums and industrial schools. Their efforts were emulated by various religious orders of brothers, such as the Brothers of Charity, and St John of God.

There had existed in Ireland at the beginning of the nineteenth century a number of charitable institutions and hospitals.[92] The charitable institutions were small in number and predominantly Protestant. The hospitals, of which there was a large number, were mainly for those who could afford them. There were no institutions which provided systematic health care for the Catholic lower classes, and which attended to their spiritual as well as health needs. The 1838 Poor Law established a tightly organised administration for the relief of the poor, and subsequently became responsible for the development of a number of health services. The workhouses established under this act could not be described as hospitals in the ordinary present-day meaning of the term but, as time went by, hospital services were developed in them. There was, then, no general health, nursing and medical care for poor Catholics unless they committed themselves to the workhouse. This gap was filled by the Sisters of Charity who, under Mother Mary Aikenhead, opened St Vincent's Hospital in Dublin in 1834. One could be sick and in need of medical care and nursing without formally having to declare oneself destitute, or committing oneself to a Protestant hospital. The prospectus of St Vincent's stated: 'They [the Sisters of Charity] have been, in fact, for nineteen years, visiting a class of sick persons who will not go to common hospitals; and they have constantly had the painful trial of witnessing their best exertions, though aided by occasional advice from medical gentlemen, defeated by the unpropitious circumstances of the patients, the want of wholesome air, and of those comforts and accommodations which are strangers to the abodes of the poor.'[93] Although the hospital was formally for every sect and every creed, Mother Aikenhead was fully aware that in the public hospitals many poor Catholics were dying without the help of the last sacraments. She had in fact founded the first Catholic hospital run by Catholic nuns, staffed by Catholic doctors, and with Catholic priests in regular attendance. In other words, it was a specifically Catholic institution although, as was made clear to one nun, 'prayer and little practices of piety were to be interwoven with the day's routine, the patients were on no account to be fatigued or harassed with too many devotions.'[94]

St Vincent's filled a gap, but long into the nineteenth century Irish hospitals continued to be dominated by Protestants. In many of the hospitals, positions were filled by friendship or the highest bidder rather than by merit; both of which militated against Catholics. Even when Catholics were trained as doctors, they were trained by Protestants in Protestant establishments. As one of the few well-known Catholic doctors at the time testified: 'There is no use in Roman-Catholics in Dublin pursuing the [medical] profession, unless they have a chance of getting those situations [medical officers], because if they do not hold hospitals in a large city, they have no chance of acquiring character; and, therefore, as long as such a system of exclusion exists, you keep Catholics from entering the profession.'[95] This was one of the reasons why Newman's Catholic University concentrated on opening a medical school, and why the urge to have a specifically

Catholic system of health care persisted even though Dublin was already well endowed with public hospitals.

In 1861, the Sisters of Mercy opened the Mater Misericordiae Hospital in Dublin which in its accommodation and design was one of the most modern in Europe at the time. The nuns, through their dedicated and economically unrewarding work, provided institutions for the care of the Catholic poor in a Catholic manner, as well as places where Catholic doctors could be trained. The health and care of Irish people was to become a thoroughly denominational practice, and it was St Vincent's and the Mater which struck the first blow against the Protestant domination of the medical profession. The domination was to last a long time. The Dublin Hospitals Commission (1867) concluded that:

In the hospitals which we have mentioned, with again the exception of Jervis Street, the medical staff are, we believe entirely of one creed, Protestant, and this is so, not because there is anything in their constitutions which requires that the medical officers should profess that religion, but because having been founded in the days when it was the dominant creed, the traditional practice was always in favour of selecting Protestants, while it must be admitted that until lately Roman Catholics did not possess the educational advantages enjoyed by the Protestants, it is not surprising that such institutions as the Mater Misericordiae and St Vincent's should have sprung into existence, for although the influence of religious zeal must not be overlooked in accounting for their origin, it is almost certain that the need for such institutions, as places where Roman Catholic medical men might look for the means of acquiring professional reputation, lent an impetus to the movement in favour of starting them which would have been weaker, if not ineffectual, without this propelling cause.[96]

The care of the nuns did not extend merely to hospitals. In 1819, the Sisters of Charity had opened a house for the training of girls for domestic service and an industrial school for wayward girls. The same order had an asylum in Donnybrook, Dublin and in 1866 they opened a home for the blind. In 1856, the Sisters of Mercy began a refuge for female prisoners of Mountjoy Jail, Dublin to conclude the last part of their sentence. At the same time, the Sisters of St Vincent de Paul opened an orphanage and a lunatic asylum in Dublin. Orders of Brothers also expanded their sociomedical activities. The Carmelite Brothers started a blind asylum for boys in Dublin, while the Christian Brothers opened a home for the deaf and dumb.[97] Robins indicates that by 1864, in the Dublin area alone, there were twenty-four Catholic lay bodies or religious communities operating orphanages or boarding-out arrangements and that similar arrangements were being made throughout the rest of the country.[98] In 1877, Frederick Falkiner, Recorder of Dublin, described the scene at Artane, the largest industrial school being run by the Christian brothers:

Seven hundred children, happy, healthy and busy as the bees: with its dozen trades taught in the best methods by the best practical farmers: its youthful brass band playing national and imperial airs in a fashion which would be creditable in a regiment: its one hundred or two hundred tiny knitters making socks for the large household instead of festering in the slums: its groups of glee singers chanting the national anthem . . . instead of listening to ribald howlings in the Liberties–before such scenes political economy stands touched and silent, if not convinced.[99]

Conclusion

In this chapter I have begun to trace the origins of the institutional power of the Catholic Church in modern Irish society. This power developed as the result of the conjuncture of numerous processes and events of which, at the level of power blocs and alliances, the most important was the struggle for control of the Irish population by the British state, Rome, and the newly emergent Catholic bourgeoisie led by O'Connell. The Penal Laws can be seen as an unsuccessful attempt at the subjugation of Irish Catholics through state legislation. It was their failure that led the British state to attempt various experimental strategies to pacify and control the Irish population. A rigorous form of policing, state-subsidised emigration, and a decent system of Protestant education had all failed before the state realised, mainly through knowledge produced by various parliamentary commissions and committees, that neither it, nor the established Protestant Church, could ever carry through successfully the pacification and civilisa-tion of the Irish people. It attempted to come to an agreement with the Irish Church to extend the newly introduced system of state-subsidised educa-tion for Catholic priests to a fully subsidised clergy. It was thwarted in this strategy, first by Rome which was extending its multinational control throughout various European states, and then by the emergent Catholic bourgeoisie, and finally by the Irish Church itself as it began to realise its new power. This meant that when the state came to implement its most successful system of pacification and civilisation, the national schools, it was persuaded to hand over much of its operational control to the Church. Although the institutional power of the Church had been growing since the end of the previous century, partly as an equal and opposite reaction to the degradation and demoralisation caused by the Penal Laws, and although the Church gradually began to gain control of the systems of health and social welfare, it was the fact that the state gradually conceded control of education to the Church which was to prove decisive in the moralisation of the Irish population. It would be wrong, however, to consider that Irish population as a mere pawn which the state handed over to the Catholic Church. The interest in modern civility was part of a much wider process that had been spreading across Europe since the sixteenth century. It was because an adherence to the Catholic Church became the means towards modern civility that the Irish became and remained legalistically religious rather than secularly civil for more than a century afterwards.

6
The Irish Civilising Process

Early Beginnings

It is necessary at this stage of the argument to move outside Ireland and locate the change in what Irish people began to do and say within the wider history and geography of modern Western civilisation. Being an island off the north-western mainland of Europe, Ireland has been slow to incorporate many social and economic changes. St Patrick did not arrive until AD 432. However, he made an immediate impact; and not only did Ireland become a major centre of the Christian movement in the sixth and seventh centuries, but it sent out missionaries to reform continental Europe. More important, it became a centre for the development of penitential practices. It was through these practices of private bodily mortification that guilt, conscience and the soul of the modern ascetic Christian were slowly defined. The penitentials introduced three processes which were much later, in nineteenth-century Ireland, to attain major significance:

(1) A scaled system of penance which, as Spear points out, became the basis of a legalistic mentality which later dominated Western moral practice.[1]

(2) A shift from canonical, or public confession and penance, to a private relationship between confessor and penitent which increased the power of the priest, and inculcated individual shame and guilt.

(3) An emphasis on celibacy and virginity that made second-class citizens of married people who pursued the ordinary way of life, because they did not have a higher calling.[2]

Controlling sex was not just another problem with which the Church had to deal. Its regulation was central to the Church maintaining its power. The penitentials were an attempt to regulate sexual activity among lay persons and to eliminate it from the lives of clerics, monks and nuns. This regulation was enforced through the systematic classification of sins in the course of private confessions. The basis of the penitentials was the devising of concrete rules for actions and a suitable punishment for each moral offence. Although the penitentials were placed in the hands of clerics rather than the laity they became, through the ministry of confessors, general guides for Christian behaviour. But it would be wrong to assume that penitential practices and sexual morality were imposed upon an unwilling pagan people. Engagement in these practices was undoubtedly part of the overall struggle to attain social prestige by appearing to be morally superior. Chastity was a means of controlling animal passion, and as Spear states 'a dynamic way of separating oneself from the surrounding pagans and proclaiming the superior character of Christianity.'[3]

Penitentials were to play a crucial role in the civilisation of Western society. It was in and through penitential exercises, among which the confessional was to achieve the greatest importance, that the Christian's soul and conscience were developed. It was through a systematic classification and analysis of bodily, especially sexual, functions and activities, as well as traditional penitential practices such as praying, kneeling and fasting, that sexual instincts were controlled and regulated. The penitentials of Irish monks made a major contribution to the Christian Church. With them the Church was able to combat the magical, pagan practices which dominated Europe. But because the Irish monks' effort was a missionary one, orientated to an export rather than a home market, and because the Church lacked any rationally developed organisation, penitential practices became intermingled with the pagan practices which pre-existed them. This compatible mixture of penitential practices and more traditional pagan ones survived in Ireland until the last century when the Catholic Church, as part of a rigorous process of moralisation, set about controlling the practice and discourse of sex, and eliminating everything that was instinctive and pagan. In the intervening centuries, the Irish penitentials had been transformed and developed in continental Europe from a specifically religious practice into a more general, secular civilising process.

The Western Civilising Process

The Western civilising process was not simply some cultural movement in which people became more refined and behaved less like animals. It had to do with changes in the way people adapted to living in more complex, centralised and regulated communities and societies. As cities and states grew, there was an increasing expectation and demand that people be less emotional, violent and unpredictable and more peaceful, considerate and self-reflective. It had to do with the end of the Middle Ages in which warriors and knights were the real rulers. From the thirteenth century onwards there was a centralisation of power all over the Western world and the gradual formation of states. Instead of battles between warriors, there were now long drawn out wars between these states. But internally these states became pacified. They developed a monopoly over the means of violence and taxation. Instead of power being a monopoly of the aristocracy and the Church, it became diffused among the lower orders. Through the growth in trade, the use of money, the division of labour and the development of administrative apparatuses, states were able to 'play off' relatively equally balanced interest groups against each other.[4] The improvement in communications, especially the invention of printing, allowed the bourgeoisie, and later other classes, to behave in a civilised manner, very similar to that of the higher classes. The internal pacification of states, then, came about through a new, differentiated, well-ordered struggle for power that was based on being civil as much as physically powerful. Being civilised and mannerly became associated with a disciplined control of the body. For a long time in human history this control was attained through external mechanisms based on physical punishment. Western civilisation and manners were developed when mechanisms of control became internalised, and physical control became based on self-discipline. This self-discipline was mainly attained through a supervision of the body similar to that developed by Irish monks in their penitentials.[5]

The modern civilising process was essentially a secular movement which began when chivalrous society and the unity of the Christian Church began to disintegrate. It was associated with the growth of cities, the taming of warriors, the reorganisation of the upper class and the development of an urban bourgeoisie who imitated aristocratic courtly behaviour. This not only helped to legitimate and maintain their own power, but also to regulate commerce. As towns and commercial life expanded, the need for civilised, regulated and disciplined behaviour extended first beyond the aristocratic court, and then beyond the confines of bourgeois family networks. With the differentiation of the work and domestic spheres, trust – the yeast of capitalist development – became dependent not merely on who one was, but on a series of practices and conventions which convinced the people with whom one was dealing that one was a trustworthy person. A manifestation of this was the extent to which one was able to regulate and internally control irrational, animalistic drives and behaviour. To sell anything in the open market, even one's labour, began to necessitate a civilised demeanour. The structure of power began to expand beyond a traditional dependence on land and position and involve a new element, the prestige that came from well-mannered behaviour. It was through social prestige that possessions and positions could be maintained and augmented. But social prestige was also a powerful end in itself, because it allowed the possibility of limiting what others did and said. Elias describes the process as follows:

People, forced to live with one another in a new way, become more sensitive to the impulses of others. Not abruptly, but very gradually the code of behaviour becomes stricter and the degree of consideration expected of others becomes greater. The sense of what to do and what not to do in order not to offend or shock others becomes subtler, and in conjunction with the new power relationships the social imperative not to offend others becomes more binding, as compared to the preceding phase.[6]

With the acceleration of the modern civilising process in the sixteenth century, and the increasing centralisation of state power, there was a gradual but relentless shift from direct, external forms of body control such as slavery, execution, torture and beating, to softer indirect forms centred on a control and confinement of the body in schools, asylums, and prisons.[7] Within the Catholic Church there was also a shift from more extreme forms of physical penance such as flagellation, to softer forms such as prayer and charitable works. Nevertheless in the same way that magical practices have persisted within the Church, so too have direct assaults on the body as a form of penitential practice. Wearing hair shirts and body chains as still practised in Ireland until quite recently. (Blessed Matt Talbot who lived in Dublin at the beginning of the century was renowned for engaging in these practices. He was found dead on the street wearing a hair shirt. Body chains were found in his room.) Irish penitential practices still contain a high level of self-imposed pain. Every year pilgrims climb Croagh Patrick and walk through the rock beds of Lough Derg in their bare feet.

The modern civilising process was not merely a change in the way in which power blocs such as the state and the Church exercised control. It was an extensive diffusion of power and a diversification of the strategies and tactics by which it was attained. Once the bourgeoisie began to imitate the behaviour of the aristocracy, as a means of socially differentiating themselves from the lower classes and morally legitimating their possessions and position in society, there was a great elaboration of etiquette and manners. First the aristocracy sought new means to differentiate themselves socially from the bourgeoisie, and then the lower classes began to imitate the behaviour of both of these classes. In Western societies today this process of imitation has been accelerated, and mass production, communications and education have made it very difficult for the upper classes to maintain a different type of language, dress and manners from the lower classes.

There are three aspects of the modern civilising process which are important in understanding how it spread throughout Europe and the Western world and how, and in what form, it reached Ireland in the nineteenth century. Firstly, because modern civilised behaviour was essentially a new type of behaviour based on increased internal control and an inculcation of shame and guilt about the body, it never lost its religious associations. Secondly, there arose a socio-religious interest, as well as a political interest in disseminating it as widely as possible. Not only did the upper and middle classes of society, as in England, want to civilise other nations such as Ireland, they also wanted to disseminate civilised behaviour to the lower classes of their own society. Thirdly, the Catholic Church played a major role in popularising and disseminating civilised behaviour throughout Europe and the rest of the world. The Catholic Church proved to be what Elias calls 'one of the most important organs of downward diffusion of behaviour models'.[8] Restraint of the emotions and disciplined behaviour, which were a major characteristic of the civilising process, have always been a major characteristic of ecclesiastical institutions.

The French Connection

It is at this point that the French connection with Ireland becomes important. Although there can be little doubt that modern Western civilisation came into Ireland on the back of Catholic morality, an innocent reading of Irish history would suggest that this morality was Jansenistic and came via France. In fact the situation was a little more complicated.

In the eighteenth century, a good deal of the education of French children was carried out by nuns, brothers and priests. Civil and religious training were seen as synonymous. What had started out as a secular movement was reintegrated into Catholic life in eighteenth-century France. Numerous books on civility and morality were written during this time, and were printed and distributed together with first instructions on reading and writing. Many of these books were translated and disseminated throughout Ireland in the nineteenth and twentieth centuries. One of the main guides for the civil and religious behaviour of Irish priests in everyday life was a translation from a book by a Frenchman, Benedict Valvy. The Christian Brothers translated De La Salle's *Christian Civility* for use in their schools. Finally, and most important, most of the philosophy and theology books used in the national seminary in Maynooth were French. But the French connection extended beyond the dissemination of moral and civil literature for, as we saw in the previous chapter, during the seventeenth and eighteenth centuries, the majority of Irish priests were trained in French seminaries. Many of the orders of nuns who came to Ireland in the late eighteenth and nineteenth centuries, for example, the Presentation Sisters and the Sisters of Charity, were of French origin. Moreover, when Maynooth College was founded there was a strong French influence in its teaching and administrative staff. All but three of the founding professors were either French or else had been educated in France, and French became the customary language of the professors' dining-table.[9]

The important question for understanding modern Irish Catholicism is whether the French connection involved the import of Jansenism along with the personnel and the literature. There is little doubt that Gallicanism, both in its old and new Irish nationalist variety, dominated Maynooth until 1850 when Cullen arrived from Rome to pursue his Ultramontane campaign. But was Gallicanism associated with Jansenism? This question has beset modern Irish historiography. Connolly argues that the historical evidence shows clearly that the theory that Irish Catholicism had come under the influence of the Jansenist movement is without foundation.[10] Clark insists that at no time, beyond a few isolated incidents, were Irish clerics influenced by Jansenism.[11] Keenan states emphatically that there were no Jansenists in Ireland.[12] Healy, the official historian of Maynooth, concludes that,

although so many of our Irish ecclesiastics were educated in France during the eighteenth century, none of these who came to Ireland ever showed the slightest traces of Jansenistic influence, either in their writings or sermons. Nor has any respectable authority asserted, as far as we know, that the French professors of Maynooth were in any way tinged with the spirit of Jansenism.[13]

With such clear enunciations about the course of Irish history one might wonder why anyone ever thought that Jansenism had been imported into Ireland. There are two reasons. First, there is a confusion of Jansenism with Gallicanism and, second, a confusion of Jansenism with rigorism or Augustinianism. Bowen states that Cardinal Paul Cullen, the man who dominated Irish Catholic church affairs in the nineteenth century, used the labels Gallican and Jansenist as almost interchangeable terms. Other bishops at the time also made this association. What emerges from Bowen's research is that the Ultramontane Cullen, along with his newly recruited allies such as Slattery – either unconsciously or as a deliberate strategy – lumped together all deviations from Roman orthodoxy. Cullen regarded Gallicanism and Jansenism as equally heretical because they were anti-Roman. Bowen explains further:

The French Jansenists of the eighteenth century had long abandoned their early theological speculations, and from the standpoint of Rome their concerns were increasingly political. Like the Gallicans, they believed that bishops should have immediate jurisdiction independent of the papacy, that spiritual authority rested with the whole body of the faithful and not merely with the hierarchy, and that temporal governments should have complete authority in their own domain.[14]

Besides the confusion on a more political level with Gallicanism, there is still, nevertheless, confusion as to whether the moral spirit of Jansenism was imported into Ireland. Keenan claims that there was a Jansenistic ethos within nineteenth-century Irish religious practice.[15] Turner, however, argues that it is essential to differentiate between rigorism and the Jansenism which has been associated with Maynooth.[16] Healy admits that the tendency of the early moral teaching in Maynooth was towards rigorism. He describes rigorism as 'the moral system of those who draw too tightly the reins of law in restraining man's liberty of action: those who are inclined to make precepts out of counsels and mortal sins out of venial sins.'[17] Turner argues that this rigorism was not specifically related to France but was part of Roman orthodoxy. In 1796, the Congregation for the Propagation of the Faith warned Maynooth against 'the excessive and wanton liberalism of some in laying down rules of morals. . .'. On the other hand, Aidan Devereux, an Irish priest trained in Rome, wrote to Cullen in Rome and referred to a 'spirit of rigorism which has been introduced into the national seminaries by French Professors and their disciples.'[18] Larkin follows yet another line, and argues that rigorism was something instigated by the Irish bishops themselves.

The rigorism that pervaded the teaching at Maynooth was also the result of the growing awareness on the part of the bishops of the need to meet the requirements of the Irish mission. The geometrical increase in the population after 1800 obviously required more priests, but given the arithmetical nature of the supply they must be better disciplined and more attentive in their pastoral duties. Given the launching in 1820, moreover, of the New Reformation in Ireland by the Protestant evangelicals or Biblicals, a more learned and articulate clergy was also required. Maynooth responded to the challenge, and the result of providing a better-educated, disciplined, and pastorally attentive clergy was to produce a morally rigorous one as well.[19]

On the other hand, Connolly argues that the severe discipline and rigorist doctrines imposed in Maynooth were not radically different from those which had shaped priests educated elsewhere.[20]

Accepting the theological and historical confusions and distinctions that exist between rigorism and Jansenism, it nevertheless seems reasonable to conclude that the former was an institutional adaptation to the latter. Connolly and Turner are both in agreement that the discipline and doctrines taught at Maynooth were, in Connolly's words, 'of a kind calculated to foster the most severe moral attitudes and a puritanical outlook on life in general.'[21] Turner notes that 'the priests who emerged from Maynooth, especially in the first half of the 1800s, are credited with inducing an ascetic chill on the previously uninhibited and often Rabelaisian ardours of the Irish peasants.'[22] Connolly agrees with Humphreys that the Augustinianism – the religious outlook laying stress on such themes as the sinfulness of man and the innate corruption of human nature – can be detected in the religious attitudes of both clergy and laity in the nineteenth century. The whole debate regarding rigorism, Jansenism and Augustinianism comes full circle when Connolly insists that practices associated with these intellectual movements were to be found at a much earlier time in Ireland and in places beyond where the movements reached. He links the popular tradition of extreme asceticism to the penitential tradition. It was this tradition, he argues, which made the Irish priests particularly receptive to rigorist influences from England or the Continent.[23]

The rigorism which, with the new physical growth and discipline of the institutional Church, began to be disseminated throughout Ireland in the nineteenth century, was based on a far more rational and complete system of practices than that found in the early Irish penitentials. Regardless of its theological background, rigorism was constituted by a systematic discipline, surveillance and sexualisation of the body.[24] It was these practices which transformed the Irish into a modern civilised people. The majority of the practices were instituted in and through the Catholic Church. Many of them were similar to the Puritan ones which achieved prominence in other Western societies in the nineteenth century. In 1849, Sir William Wilde wrote that 'the tone of society in Ireland is becoming more *Protestant* each year; the literature is a Protestant one, and even the priests are becoming more Protestant in their conversation and manners.'[25] This is a confusion of Protestantism with the modern Western civilising process. It was peculiar to Ireland, and it was to have a lasting effect, that the whole civilising process took place in and through the Catholic Church. Owing to the absence of a native rural bourgeoisie, the priests and later the nuns and brothers were the most accessible and acceptable models of modern civilised behaviour. Catholic tenant farmers wanted to be as civilised and well-mannered as the Protestant Ascendancy which had dominated them for so long. But from an inherited hatred, they were loth to be deemed Protestant by imitating their behaviour. McRedmond makes the same mistake as Wilde: he conflates the modern Irish civilising process, which was essentially European in origin, with an embodiment of British Protestant Puritanism.

The God of the latter-day Irish was not in fact the God of Catholic tradition in Ireland or anywhere else. He was the God of Victorian puritanism, a British and Protestant God most unnaturally superimposed upon a Latin Church which, while unIrish in its externals, was unquestionably Catholic. In straight historical terms what happened . . . was that the stringent social norms of nineteenth-century Britain became entangled with a fervent and essentially non-intellectual form of Catholicism.[26]

The Irish may have wanted to be as moral and civil as the English; they may have wanted to speak, dress, eat, and generally live as they did; but they firmly rejected the latter as a means towards that end. This is the dialectical process within the civilising process: by using different means to become civilised, the Irish avoided becoming Protestant and fully Anglicised.

The civilising process was delayed in coming to Ireland not merely because of its insular position on the north-west coast of Europe, but also for a number of economic, political and social reasons. Chief among these was the absence of any security of tenure for the majority of Irish farmers. It was only from the beginning of the nineteenth century that a substantial body of settled tenant farmers (that is, holders of 31-year leases), began to emerge in Ireland. Although these farmers gained greater control of the means of production, it was the absence of a sense of security that prevented them from becoming disciplined and industrious. Another reason was the absence, due to the Penal Laws, of decent schools to which farmers could send their children. Finally, there was the Church's lack of human and physical resources, together with a lack of discipline and organisation among its own members. Once these inhibiting factors began to be removed and, in particular, once the British state developed a social and political interest in civilising the Irish, the process developed rapidly throughout the nineteenth century.

Civil Order and Social Control

The modern civilising process was a transformation in what people did and said. It was a transformation of lifestyle, customs and manners. It was a transformation of the body in terms of the mechanisms by which it was controlled. It involved changes in the space in which the body operated; from one-roomed mud cabins to multi-roomed brick houses, from sleeping with animals to sleeping only with humans – first with the whole family, later with one's brothers and sisters and, finally, on one's own. It involved a change in the manner of eating – from wooden bowls on the floor to pottery, knives and forks on the table; and in diet – from one consisting mainly of cereals, milk and potatoes to a more varied one including bread, meat and other vegetables. It involved a transformation of space – from open fields to the confined spaces of school-desks and from mass rocks and houses to ornate churches with pews. It involved changes in dress and language – from coarse woollen garments to manufactured clothes and shoes. And it involved a change in language – from Irish to English. It was above all a transformation from open, passionate bodies to closed, restrained bodies. In Ireland, priests, nuns and brothers were the main agents responsible for bringing about these transformations.

In summarising the decades before the Famine, Connolly describes it as a period in which a clear conflict arose between the code of conduct which the authorities of the Catholic Church were seeking to impose, and the attitudes and standards of behaviour of their congregations. Connolly sees three main areas in which the Church sought to impose changes: (1) traditional practices of the pattern and wake, (2) marriage and sexual behaviour, and (3) the problem of public order, particularly in relation to the activities of secret societies and local feuding factions. In effect, the three areas were closely interlinked, and involved a new supervision and control of instincts and passion. Wakes and patterns began to be supervised because they involved submission to passion: the former to sexual passion, the latter to aggressive passions, in fighting (usually after drinking). The changes which the Church sought to impose on marriage and sexual practices were prompted not by high levels of adultery and illegitimacy, but rather by an interest in instilling shame and guilt about the body. Not only was this a means towards the discovery of the soul, as the early Irish monks had discovered, but it led to internally controlled bodies which, in terms of public morality, were highly desirable. Connolly notes that Irish rural society in the early nineteenth century placed little emphasis on physical modesty or on verbal reticence. There was an unambiguous sexual symbolism in wake games and May Day festivals. However this openly ribald sexuality was accompanied by a remarkably high level of chastity. Connolly estimates, from a sample analysis of parish records between 1759 and 1860, that the proportion of Irish brides who were pregnant at the time of their marriage was about one in ten. In rural England in the eighteenth and early nineteenth centuries the proportion was four out of every ten marriages. Official statistics became available from 1864. These show that the proportion of illegitimate to total births was 3.2 per cent, which was less than half the European average.[27] But although the level of chastity in Ireland may not have changed greatly from the eighteenth to the twentieth century, this does not mean that shame and guilt about sex were not becoming inculcated during that time.

Ariès gives an example of the transformation from what he calls immodesty to innocence. 'One of the unwritten laws of contemporary modesty, the strictest and best respected of all, requires adults to avoid any reference, above all any humorous reference, to sexual matters in the presence of children. This notion was entirely foreign to the society of old.'[28] Elias gives a further description:

In the civilising process, sexuality too is increasingly removed behind the scenes of social life and enclosed in a particular enclave, the nuclear family. Likewise, the relations between the sexes are isolated, placed behind walls in consciousness. An aura of embarrassment, the expression of sociogenetic fear, surrounds this sphere of life. Even among adults it is referred to officially only with caution and circumlocutions. And with children, particularly girls, such things are, as far as possible, not referred to at all.[29]

In nineteenth-century Ireland sexual transgressions were reduced from the physical to a verbal level. Sex became a serious subject and the Church developed a monopoly of knowledge about it. Shame and guilt about sexual practices were instilled in each individual, privately, in a hushed manner, in the dark isolated space of the confessional. Sexual morality became a major issue, but it was wrapped up in a veil of silence. When it was talked or written about, it was in a vague abstract formal language which prevented the laity from developing any communicative competence about it. The control of sexual knowledge was crucial to the maintenance of the Church's power. The humorous references and asides about sex and breeding may be understood as unconscious relief mechanisms from a rigid system of sexual supervision and control. Sexual ribaldry, like some of the pagan practices, is a cultural residue of past practices. It appears, like many other aspects of Irish life, as ambivalent, and yet relieves tension from rigid norms of social conduct which regulate the relations between men and women.

The other area in which the Church sought to impose changes was in terms of what Connolly calls 'vile and wicked conspiracies'. It was not that the Church was uninvolved in political matters. As Nowlan points out: 'Politics remained sectarian and the chances of the clergy withdrawing from politics remained rather theoretical.'[30] The Church was, however, against the passionate, violent rebellious activities of secret societies such as the Whiteboys and Ribbonmen. The activities of these societies were an attack on its own political strategies and tactics, which were essentially populist and democratic. Ever since 1825, when the Catholic Association had become a mass movement, the clergy had proved to be of enormous importance in the hard, slogging work of organising the people, collecting funds, arranging meetings, and acting as the literate interpreters to O'Connell's mass following. This was when the new Gallican nationalism began in earnest. There was a notable change in doctrinal emphasis: the sinfulness of particular crimes replaced the duty of unqualified obedience to temporal authority.[31] These particular crimes had often been directed as much against the Church as against the forces of the State. Attacks on priests were related to denunciations by them of the secret societies, as well as to the high prices which they charged for their services.[32] Garvin notes that the Defenders, another secret society, 'had a noticeable anticlerical tinge and was receptive to the ideas of the French Revolution. . . .'[33]

Secret societies such as the Ribbonmen were the violent tip of an iceberg of class, nationalist and sectarian sentiment which was floating in an ocean of Irish discontent. The struggle between the Church and the Ribbonmen, who were the forerunners of the Fenians, was a struggle over obtaining control of the form and content of political activity. Even though there may have been class solidarity between the leaders of the Church and the secret societies, many bishops were opposed to the societies not just because of their violent tactics, but also because they were not sectarian enough.[34] This is the reason Bowen gives for Cullen's opposition to Fenianism. 'Religiously it promoted indifferentism, tolerating the faith of a Thomas Davis or a Charles Gavan Duffy, while it deplored the kind of sectarian division between Catholic and Protestant which Cullen so assiduously tried to foster.'[35] The Church, like the state, wanted to shift the struggle for the land and Home Rule away from passionate, violent rebellion to orderly, peaceful, legal and parliamentary means. The suppression of vile and wicked conspiracies was only part of a much wider effort to civilise the Irish. This gap between savagery and civility was clearly described by Dr Kinsella, Catholic Bishop of Ossory, in 1835:

I must admit that it is in part true. . . . The people has some of the characteristics and, unfortunately, some of the defects of savage people. This people has all the virtues dear to God: it has faith: there is no better Christian than the Irishman. Their morals are pure: premeditated crime is very rare. But they basically lack the civil virtues. They have no foresight or prudence. Their courage is instinctive: they throw themselves at an obstacle with extraordinary violence and if they do not succeed at the first attempt, give it up.[36]

Mechanisms of Social Control

There were three methods by which the priest acted as a civilising agent in Irish society. The first was his mere physical presence as a civilised, disciplined and well-mannered Catholic man. He was a model of morality and civility, a shining example of what could be produced from a tenant farmer background. He interacted with the poorest of people, bringing civility and morality into their humble homes. The second method had to do with the transformation of the priest from a religious functionary who officiated at major rites of passage – birth, marriage and death – into a rigorous disciplinarian who, through pastoral visitation and confession, began to supervise and control all aspects of social life. The third method was the dissemination of a detailed body of Catholic doctrine and practice, first through confraternities and book societies, and later through schools, hospitals and homes.

The Church also had formal mechanisms which it employed to moralise and civilise the Irish body. The main one, in terms of the ultimate threat (in the same way that execution was the ultimate threat of the state), was denial of the sacraments and excommunication.[37] Excommunication as the ultimate penalty was effective in two ways. It made the victim into a social outcast which could have disastrous effects on a person's social and economic life. Secondly, it was a threat held over people which could be enacted at any time. To understand the power of this threat, which may have been as much feared as that of execution itself, it is necessary to appreciate the faith of the Irish as it was expressed in their acceptance of the priest as the mediator between God and the individual. As God's delegate, the priest could practically ensure eternal damnation. Congregations were reminded of the pains of hell. Liguori provides an example of a hell-fire sermon:

This fire shall torment the damned, not only externally but also internally. It will burn the bowels, the heart, the brains, the blood within the veins, and the marrow within the bones. They are tormented not only by the stench of their companions, but also by their shrieks and lamentations. . . . The damned must remain for ever in a pit of fire, always in torture always weeping without ever enjoying a moment's repose.[38]

We do not know how often these hell-fire sermons were given. However, Turner states that the moral theology textbooks used to train priests in Maynooth were those of Scarini which were modelled on the works of Ligouri.[39]

The method by which the Catholic Church in Ireland helped people develop a new morality and civility was to foster a formal, rigid adherence to its rules and regulations. This had the effect of delaying internalised self-restraint becoming the basis for civilised behaviour. Priestly censure was to be avoided by a strict adherence to Church rules. It was these rules, and the legalist manner in which they were complied with, that became the foundation of priestly power. Garvin points out that various ploys were used by members of secret societies such as the Ribbonmen to avoid being excommunicated. One was to attend the sacraments of Communion and Confession after the passwords had lapsed at the end of a quarter and before accepting the passwords for the subsequent quarter.[40] Such strict adherence to the letter of the law was reflected in other cultural practices. Mr and Mrs Hall in their literary description of Ireland recollected:

A man swearing he would not drink for a month – he soaked bread in spirits and ate it; another, who swore he would not touch liquor while he stood on earth, got drunk amid the branches of a tree; another, who vowed not to touch a drop indoors or out, strode across his threshold, placing one leg inside and the other outside – and so, persuading himself he did not break his oath, drank until he fell.[41]

While these anecdotes should not be taken as depicting common practice, they do indicate that aspects of legalism are closely allied to a ritual fulfilment of magical formula, in which intentions and consequences play no part in the evaluation of conduct.

To constitute itself as a power to be obeyed, the Church had to break away from all informalities with the laity. This depended on preventing the priest from mixing religious ceremonies with social occasions held in the homes of his parishioners. From the beginning of the nineteenth century in Ireland there was a general differentiation of space, and of power exercised within spaces. As part of this process, there was a differentiation of the religious from the domestic space. The ability of the priest to limit what his parishioners did and said came to depend upon him operating in and through his church rather than their homes. When Dr Walsh of the Cork diocese, writing in 1806, discussed the disadvantages arising from the custom of having stations in private houses, one of the objections, which in his view was of no small weight, was that the clergyman, 'by his uninterrupted intercourse with the lower orders of the community, may lose that polish which by education or observation he may have attained, and be by degrees totally unfitted for more select society.'[42] House visitations were to become a formal practice rather than a social occasion. The obedience of the laity to the priest came to depend on him getting them to come to his church once a week, and to confess their sins to him in church at least once a year. The transformation of space, from the home to the church, was a crucial feature in the new exercise of clerical discipline. This may be one of the reasons why so much emphasis was given to church building in the first half of the nineteenth century. But it must always be remembered that it was the laity who built the churches, and it was ultimately they who wanted to go to church and to be disciplined. The civilising process was carried through not simply because of the new rigorous discipline which began to emanate from Maynooth, but because of the construction of churches and schools which provided the space in which moral discipline could be exercised. There is, in other words, a very close link between the construction of churches, schools, and houses, and the moralisation of Irish society through promoting adherence to the church's rules and regulations. It was in church that most Irish people first learnt to control their bodies, and to behave in a civil as well as a legalistically moral manner. Etiquette and good manners became associated with going to church and fulfilling rules and regulations. There were strict regulations as to how people were to behave when in church:

1st. Persons whilst in the Church should as much as possible avoid coughing, spitting and all manners of noise.
2nd. Should be remarkably clean in their dress and person and avoid the slightest appearance of foppery and indiscretion.
3rd. They should look only at the altar or on the priest and recollect that it is to speak to God and not to man that they appear there.
4th. Whilst they appear in a respectful posture they should avoid any ridiculous gestures or forms.
5th. All who can read should use prayer books, unless when meditation may be preferable.

6th. Mothers should take care not to disturb the congregation by bringing children under the age required.

7th. On Ash Wednesday each should approach the priest in a respectful manner to receive ashes, and on Palm Sunday act in a similar manner to receive palm.

8th. Catholics should take care never to turn their backs to the altar when the Blessed Sacrament is exposed, but kneel in a respectful posture.

9th. Children serving at Mass should not be allowed to answer the priest in a hurried manner, but in an edifying way.

10th. Communicants should approach to and proceed from the altar, in the most recollected manner and also to and from the confessional in a similar way.

11th. It is an edifying sight to see all stand when gospel and creed are read and kneel together at the same time when they come to the words, 'And God was made man, etc.'

12th. Communicants should take care to hold the communion cloth in a proper manner and on no account run out of the church in haste after approaching the holy altar.[43]

Miller has shown that the overall attendance at Sunday Mass in 1834 was about 40 per cent, but that this varied enormously, from as low as 20 per cent in rural areas (especially Irish speaking ones in the West) to near 100 per cent in some towns (especially in the East). He argues that the low attendance had partly to do with a moral laxity, and says that in the West of Ireland there were obviously enough priests to say Masses if there had been sufficient demand.[44] Larkin, on the other hand, has argued that the reason why the attendance was so low was because there were not enough churches to accommodate those who might be inclined to attend to their religious duties.[45] However, these two explanations for low Mass attendance are not contradictory. Even if there were sufficient priests to say Masses, a regular, disciplined adherence to the rules and regulations of the Church depended on the availability of a church. The devotional revolution, and the development of a legalistic adherence to the Church cannot be divorced from the building revolution which preceded them. It is no coincidence that weekly Mass attendance in 1834 was lower in rural areas, especially in the poorer Western region, where there were fewer churches. It was only when the churches were built that the process of getting the people into them on a regular basis could be achieved. In this respect the devotional revolution, as described by Larkin, could only have been consolidated in the decades after the Famine when the building revolution had reached its peak. Once the churches were built, the people began to flock to them, not just for Mass, Communion and Confession, but for a whole host of devotional activities.

To encourage the laity, missions were held in nearly every parish in Ireland in the decade of the fifties. Pastoral gains thus made were consolidated by the introduction of a whole series of devotional exercises designed not only to encourage more frequent participation in the sacraments but to instil veneration by an appreciation of their ritual beauty and intrinsic mystery. The spiritual rewards, of course, for these devotional exercises were the various indulgences, which short-ened either the sinner's or the sinner's loved one's time of torment in purgatory. The new devotions were mainly of Roman origin and included the rosary, forty hours, perpetual adoration, novenas, blessed altars, *Via Crucis*, benediction, vespers, devotion to the Sacred Heart and the Immaculate Conception, jubilees, triduums, pilgrimages, shrines, processions and retreats. These devotional exercises, moreover, were organized in order to communalize and regularize practice under a spiritual director and included sodalities, confraternities such as the various purgatorian societies, the Society of St Vincent de Paul, and Peter's Pence as well as temperance and altar societies. These public exercises were also reinforced by the use of devo-tional tools and aids; beads, scapulars, medals, missals, prayer books, catechisms, holy pictures, and *Agnus Dei,* all blessed by priests who had recently acquired that privilege from Rome through the intercession of their bishops.[46]

Larkin's argument that (*a*) these devotions were only introduced after 1850, (*b*) they were Roman, and (*c*) they were introduced mainly by Cullen and the other bishops, has been criticised by Keenan. He provides contrary evi-dence to show that many of these devotions were in existence long before the Famine, that they were French in origin, and that they were introduced not by bishops, but by the individual efforts of priests and nuns.[47]

The successful fostering of an adherence to the rules and regulations of the Church depended a great deal on regular attendance at Confession. The evidence suggests that there was a continual improvement in confessional attendance throughout the nineteenth century. Connolly cites examples of neglect to complete the Easter Duty and attend Confession at least once a year.[48] However, evidence from Dublin Diocesan Archives suggests that by the 1830s, at least in the Eastern region, this neglect had begun to decline. Parish visitation records for Arklow in 1837 indicate that in an adult population of 5,000 probably 100 missed their Easter Duty, and most of these, according to the report, 'have since contritely applied to be admitted to Penance'. Similarly, in a rural parish such as Ballymore Eustace with a population of about 4,000, there were about 10 persons who did not comply with their Easter Duty in the previous year.[49]

Connolly emphasises the central importance which Confession had in maintaining discipline and control of the laity in pre-Famine Ireland.

It provided both for a regular and thorough scrutiny by the parish clergy of the behaviour of individual members of their congregations and for an important per-sonal confrontation between priest and parishioner, with the former in a position of unquestioned authority, able to interrogate, exhort or reprimand the penitent as he saw fit. To conceal an offence in the confessional invalidated the whole process, while a person who had not received absolution could not receive the other sacra-ments without committing sacrilege and risked damnation in the case of sudden death.[50]

Confession played a crucial role in sexualising the body. The confessional was where the activities of the body were examined and suitable penances distributed. The modern Irish Catholic soul became constituted through a discipline of the body created and maintained by a rigorous system of examination, supervision and punishment. The body was seen as a major source of evil. Under examination in the confessional, it was confined in a dark space, hidden from public view, from the confessor, and from the penitent himself. Sex became problematical and privatised. A sense of private guilt and public shame was inculcated through a thorough investigation of the penitent's sexual practices. It was through such an examination procedure that 'ignorant savages' were made to feel self-conscious about their bodies and, thereby, became constituted as moral human beings. Alexander Irwin provides a translation of the instructions issued to priests regarding Confession in the *Treatise on the Decalogue,* a textbook used in Maynooth in the first half of the nineteenth century.

Since the confessor acts the part both of judge and a physician, he ought to become acquainted with the diseases and the offences of the penitent, in order that he may be able to apply suitable remedies, and impose due penance, and lest a sin that is mortal should be accounted as venial, or the foul viper lurking in the deep recesses of the heart should not venture to put itself forth to view, he ought to therefore sometimes to question the penitents on the subject of the 6th (7th) commandment, where he suspects that they are not altogether pure, especially if they be rude, ignorant, bashful or agitated. . . . A prudent confessor will, as far as in his power, advance from more general statements to more particular: from the less shameful to those which are more so; nor will he take his commencement from the external acts, but from the thoughts. Has not the penitent revolved some improper ones in his or her mind? Was this done advertently? What kind of desire was it? Has he or she felt unlawful passions? But if the penitent shall declare that he, or she, has not felt them, the confessor ought usually to stop there, unless the penitent be very ignorant and dull. But if the penitent shall answer that he, or she, has had improper thoughts or irregular desires, the confessor shall ask whether any improper actions followed. But if the penitent shall confess this, the confessor shall ask again, what were these actions. If the penitent be a girl, she should be asked whether she has adorned herself in order to please the men? Whether for this purpose she has used paint, or stript her arms, shoulders or neck? Whether she has spoken, or read, or sung anything immodest? Whether she is not attached to somebody with a more peculiar affection? Whether she has not allowed herself to be kissed?[51]

We can see here how sexual shame and guilt, which were to become the basis of the modern Irish Catholic soul and the mainstay of the civil and moral revolution of the last century, were dependent on the construction of churches, and within those large, awesome buildings the construction of small dark spaces in which the penitent was confined and interrogated. But, as can be seen from the above quotation, the sexual moralisation process became centred on gaining control of women's sex. Sex was portrayed as a disease which lurked deep within the recesses of women's bodies. Unless it was controlled, it would awaken the most grotesque animal passions. It was only when it was controlled that the refined, delicate nature of women could be revealed. If the sexual vipers within women were awakened, then all delicacy and civility would be lost. The Church was presented as the only means by which women could be saved from themselves. Sex was a sickness that could never be cured. It could only be monitored and controlled by the priest. It was such a dreadful disease that the penitent, like the modern patient under a doctor, could only be told about it in vague terms. Any detailed knowledge of the condition would destroy an innocence which held the disease at bay. It was through this detailed knowledge of sex, and the means by which it could be controlled, that the priest maintained his power, especially over women.

There were other methods besides Confession by which the priest helped instil a new morality and civility in the Irish Catholic. Sermons were an important method. The priest was one of the most literate people in the parish. Newspapers, while more prevalent from the beginning of the nineteenth century, only found their way into the better-off households. Consequently, the priest's sermon, which was usually given in English, would have been one of the main talking points in the local community. The priest talked about the meaning of life and its obligations. He developed a monopoly of ethical ideals. Through the sermon he transferred these ideals into rules and regulations.[52] Liguori wrote sermons which, in terms of civilisation and sexualisation, are indicative of the new discipline and sexual morality which priests began to demand in Ireland at this time. In *The Education of Children*, he gave a long and detailed account of the obligations of a father in raising his children. He ended with some disciplinary practices for removing the occasion of sin from the children:

Fifthly, a father should remove from his house romances, which pervert young persons, and all bad books, which contain pernicious maxims, tales of obscenity, or of profane love. . . . Sixthly, he ought not allow his children to sleep in his own bed, nor the females and males to sleep together. Seventhly, he should not permit his daughter to be alone with men, whether young or old. . . . Eighthly, if he has daughters he should not permit young men to frequent his house. . . .[53]

It may be noticed that the moral education of children in this sermon is taken to be the responsibility of the father. This was to change. By the end of the nineteenth century, and throughout the twentieth century in Ireland, the moral supervision of children became the sole preserve of the mother.

Sermons could also be used in a more direct manner to attain adherence to church rules and regulations. A strong sermon could be a public warning against an individual or group. It might take the form of a public damnation or make an indirect reference such as 'there are some here among us'. But the priest did not always have to enforce discipline and morality. During the nineteenth century in Ireland, priests – who increasingly came from tenant farmer backgrounds – were sent back to their dioceses as exemplars of civility and morality, after a strict and rigorous training in Maynooth. A priest may not have had the same manners as those to be seen at the top of the scale among the Protestant Ascendancy, but he had by the beginning of the last century reached a level not far removed from that of the petty gentry, among whom he generally found acceptance.[54]

Besides the actual training received in Maynooth, manuals were written for priests which served as reminders of the duties of the religious life. One of the manuals was a translation of Valvy's, *A Guide for Priests*. This contained sections dealing with the priest's private life, and offered guidelines for: Care of the body, Rising, Retiring to Rest, Dress, Deportment, Meals, Recreation and Travelling. On deportment, Valvy noted: 'the Priest, if anyone, should be a person welcome to all good society: but to be faultlessly correct in matters of politeness before the public, he must put constraint upon himself to be so when not in company. Without noticing, we carry with us into society all the defects which blemish our private life.' Valvy strongly advocated that priests should have one or two books which dealt with the rules of manners, that they should consult these regularly, and that they should pay attention to the language and manners of those priests who passed for models of politeness and good breeding. However, the translator of his work was obviously so sure that Irish priests would not have any books on manners that he felt it necessary to include a long and detailed section at the end of the manual entitled 'Hints on Etiquette'. This contained subsections on etiquette at home, visiting, dining out, and correspondence. Attention is paid to the minutest detail.

> When conversing with others, care should be taken not to address the conversation to one only, and each one should be looked at in turn. But if one of the company be of much higher position than the rest, the eye may be fixed upon him more than upon the others.
> Politeness requires that, when visitors of either sex enter the room, we should arise from the chair and welcome them. It is still more polite to advance and meet them, and the compliment is greater in proportion to the distance travelled.
> When walking up and down with a companion in any confined space, so as to be obliged to turn every now and then, each should avoid turning the back to the other.[55]

Once these rules of etiquette are practised sufficiently, they become almost automatic actions. Indeed it is how automatically one acts out rules of etiquette that indicates the degree of one's civility. In Ireland, as in most other Western societies, rules of etiquette have been learnt in the home. But mothers and fathers must have learnt them somewhere other than from their own mothers and fathers. Going back to the nineteenth century we can see that a certain amount was copied from the Protestant gentry, especially by those who acted as servants in their households. Many rules of etiquette were also learnt in schools. But long before then, and long after, the priest was an exemplar of good manners and etiquette for Irish Catholics. An exemplar of morality and civility who rose up from among themselves and with whom they identified and regularly interacted.

Good manners were essential for the priest in the nineteenth century if he was able to maintain respect from the lower orders and if he was to socialise with the established Catholic bourgeoisie. He had to maintain his status in society, and since he may not have had many personal possessions (excluding knowledge), he had to rely on social prestige, on being a paragon of civility and morality. It was only then that he would be able successfully to limit what his parishioners did and said. As the translator of Valvy pointed out:

The great majority of our Clerics come from families more or less straitened in circumstances, and if the contempt with which poverty and obscure birth inspire the higher circles of society be not compensated by observance of the laws of good breeding, and by a noble and faultless demeanour, what can we expect from a coarse and boorish ecclesiastic save that he will be a dishonour to the Church and an object of disdain to seculars? And, to tell the plain truth, how can a Priest command respect, who, even when in Church, cannot speak without shouting: who, by his ungainly postures, whether seated or standing, resembles a field labourer more than a cleric . . . who is untidy, grotesque in his dress, unshaven, with his hair all in disorder? Who is there but has a repugnance for such a person, and who can doubt that such a one would repel the very people whom he ought to draw to him in order to gain them to God.[56]

By entering the houses of even the most humble people, sometimes to visit the sick or aid the dying, sometimes on parish visitation, or sometimes on social occasions such as stations and marriages, the priest acted as an exemplar of civility and morality who drew out the best manners in the people. Parish visitation became a central aspect of the civilisation process in Ireland. It was through regular visitation that the priest attained a detailed knowledge of the moral behaviour and habits of his parishioners. Such knowledge was, and still is, central to the maintenance of priestly power. Valvy describes how the priest should proceed to record and organise knowledge gained from parish visitations.

Throughout the period that you are employed in visiting the parish, take notes every evening on matters which have attracted your attention. Make a list of the ill-taught who have to be instructed, the poor who must be relieved, the afflicted to be consoled, the families to be reconciled, etc. . . . There are priests who have a complete classified catalogue of their whole flock, and who examine themselves every month as to their obligations to each of these different classes.[57]

A detailed knowledge of the behaviour of his parishioners became the mark of a priest who had organisational control over his parish. The modern morality and civility of the Irish people grew alongside the moral supervision which priests began to exercise over their parishes. Dr Murray, the Archbishop of Dublin, required before his visit to a parish that the parish priest 'deliver in writing . . . the names of the most obstinate Absenters – of Public Sinners in the Parish, with some account of their crimes respectively, and of Public Abuses, such as illegal combinations, drunkenness, violation of the Lord's day, Night-Wakes, or Public Dances.'[58]

The moralisation of Catholics, simply in terms of instilling knowledge of the rules and regulations of the Church, was too much for the priests, especially in a rapidly expanding population. The response to their need was the creation of a number of lay organisations to help the priest in this task. The schedules from Archbishop Murray's parish visitations give detailed information on the activities of Confraternities of Christian Doctrine in pre-Famine Irish society.

Confraternities, in the words of Dr Doyle in 1825: 'consist of young men and young females of a religious character, who assemble at an early hour on Sundays, and dispose the children in classes and teach them the rudiments of the Christian religion. . . .'[59] Besides their crucial role in moral instruction, members of confraternities also helped in assisting the dying and reading the office of the dead. Nearly all the parish returns for the early 1830s in the Dublin Diocesan Archives show at least one active confraternity, and usually two.[60] Connolly notes that the Irish Education Inquiry had found that even by 1824 confraternities existed in many of the towns and most populous parishes of the south and west of Ireland. There were strict rules laid down for the running of confraternities. Teachers had to confine themselves to the instructions contained in the approved catechisms and books, and were forbidden to give any explanations other than what were contained in them.[61]

Another method which the Church used in the moralisation of Irish Catholics was the dissemination of a wide range of Catholic literature. In 1827, Dr Doyle, Bishop of Kildare and Leighlin, established the Irish Catholic Society for the Diffusion of Useful Knowledge. It later became known as the Catholic Book Society. The objects of the Catholic Book Society were:

First—To furnish the People of Ireland, in the most cheap and convenient manner, useful information on the truths and duties of the Christian Religion. Secondly—To supply to all classes of person, satisfactory Refutations of the prevailing errors of the present age. Thirdly—To assist in supplying to Schools throughout Ireland, the most approved Books of elementary Instruction.[62]

In its first year, the Society printed and distributed 43,000 catechisms, and a similar number of doctrinal manuals. The general agent of the Book Society, W.G. Battersby, established the *Irish Catholic Penny Magazine* in 1834. This was followed in 1836 by the *Irish Catholic Magazine of Entertaining Knowledge*. In 1836, Battersby published the first of what was his most successful venture, *The Irish Catholic Directory*, which has appeared every year since then.[63] The Catholic Book Society and the *Catholic Penny Magazine* were mainly a response to the increasing number of publications on civility and morality many of which were objectionable because they were Protestant, and derived from England, for example, *The Accomplished Youth: Containing A Familiar View of the True Principles of Morality and Politeness, Moral Essays in Praise of Virtue,* and *A Catechism of Morality*.[64] In effect, most of the civil instructions contained in the tracts were quite secular and were to find their way into the lesson books used in the national school system.

The final and most important mechanism by which the Catholic Church civilised the Irish was through gaining control of the education system. From its first gaining momentum in the sixteenth century, the modern civilising process became centred on the education of children. The very early texts on manners, written in the thirteenth century, were addressed to adults. However, later treatises such as Erasmus's *On Civility in Boys* (1530) were specifically addressed to children and youth. Elias notes:

The standard which is emerging in our phase of civilisation is characterized by a profound discrepancy between the behaviour of so-called adults and children. The children have in the space of a few years to attain the advanced level of shame and revulsion that has developed over many centuries. Their instinctual life must be rapidly subjected to the strict control and specific moulding that gives our societies their stamp, and which developed very slowly over centuries.[65]

In modern Western societies in which the bourgeoisie have become the dominant class, the family has become the main agent for instilling moral discipline and self-control. In nineteenth-century Ireland, the Church played a major part in the constitution and formation of a class of Catholic tenant farmers which became the dominant class in Irish society during the next hundred years. A major part of the formation of that class took place in schools where rude, ignorant, and what many English commentators considered to be 'savage', children learned to be civil and moral. In subsequent generations, when the initial phase of civil and moral conditioning had been completed in the school, the family, or specifically the mother, became the prime agent of Irish civilisation and moralisation. It was not until the 1960s, and the new dominance of a commercial and industrial bourgeoisie in Irish society, that the Church's control of sexual morality and discipline began to weaken, and the family, especially mothers, became increasingly autonomous vis-à-vis the Church and assumed greater responsibility for instilling morality and civility.

The Influence of Schools

The mass civilisation of the Irish people began in earnest with the development of the National School system in 1831. Although there were Catholic pay schools in every parish at this time, they were gradually supplanted by National Schools. The pay schools were uneven institutions. Much depended on the individual qualities of the teacher. There were few official school buildings; a lack of organised space; few desks, tables and chairs; little or no equipment; no standard texts; and no rigorous timetable. Most of these defects were due to a lack of finance. When introduced, the National Schools were, in theory, non-denominational. Catholic opposition to them always remained strong, but because they were managed mostly by priests, who selected and supervised the teachers, the schools soon became to all intents and purposes denominational – even if Catholic practices and doctrine were not officially permitted. This was recognised by someone like Cardinal Cullen who remained a fervent critic of the system throughout his life. In 1869, he wrote: 'In the greater part of the country the schools are in the hands of Catholics, under Catholic managers, under Catholic teachers and conducted in such a way that they cannot do much positive evil.'[66] What was important was that the Catholic Church operated and controlled the civil and moral education of Irish Catholics. It was the priests, nuns and brothers, and the teachers under their supervision, who instilled into the uncouth, boorish Irish children of the nineteenth century all the manners and habits which we today regard as standard social practices. It was they who took over the task of making the Irish into a clean-living, orderly, well-managed, self-controlled, literate people. They were the forces which girded the bent and unruly bodies of the Irish and fashioned them into fine, upstanding, moral citizens.

Many of the original plans and objectives of the Kildare Place Schools were incorporated into the national school system. The object of the Kildare Place Society, founded in 1812, had been 'to diffuse throughout the country a well-ordered system of Education of the Poor, which shall combine economy of time and money, and bestow due attention on cleanliness and discipline.'[67] The Schoolmaster's Manual, used by the Kildare Place Society, noted that in order to preserve public order it was necessary

to establish those habits of thoughtfulness and foresight, which would enable the poor to add to their comforts, and thereby produce content; – to confirm habits of self- control and rational obedience, and thereby produce good order and subordination; – and by early inculcating the principles of honesty and truth, to prepare the mind to resist those vices to which they are exposed; and, in particular, to supplant that tendency to drunkenness, which is the dreadful but natural resource of unoccupied minds in the intervals of hard labour.[68]

The most important transformation which schools brought to Irish life was an organised sense of time and space. All over Ireland, these nurseries of the body began to control undisciplined children. They taught them how to operate when it was necessary to share confined spaces with others. It was that discipline and control of the body whose importance underlay anything else to be learnt, and still does to this day. The schools of the national system were of a standard design.

A more particular description . . . of the school room may be useful. . . . It was a room twenty-five by sixteen, and along the front were three latticed windows, about four feet and a half from the ground: the sashes of these turned on pivots fixed in the centre, so that they could be opened for the purpose of ventilating the room. . . . The desks and forms were each fourteen feet long, which accommodated ten children, sitting at their ease; the breadth of the desk was twelve inches – of the form, six inches; distance between plumb of desk and form was three inches; and breadth of passage behind form fifteen inches, making the whole three feet for desk, interval, form and passage. Five of them were placed so as to front the mistress's seat; besides which were two small tables with drawers, each seven feet long, where the children who worked at the needle sat; and there was also a space, seven feet wide, between the end of the desks and the wall, where the children could form in classes. All round the school room there were racks, for hanging the spelling and reading tablets. . . . In short, there was a place for everything and everything in its place.[69]

The main social transformation which was ushered in with the school system was the creation of these highly specified spaces in which young children were confined. Central to the moral and civil revolution of the last century was that at the same time each day, and in the same type of regulated space, children gradually became disciplined by learning, saying and doing the same things. It was crucial to produce a similarity of behaviour throughout the country. This was the essence of education as mass civilisation. It was a transformation, by way of confinement, of the space in which children operated. Given the space, the next requirement was to issue a set of regulations which governed behaviour in that space. These regulations were centred on the timetable and regular supervision:

The hours of school attendance are from ten o'clock till three, except on Saturday, when the school breaks at one o'clock.

The entrance doors are to be closed each morning at half past ten o'clock, after which no child shall be admitted.

The children are to come with hands and face washed, hair cut short and combed, and clean apparel: those who neglect this rule to be sent home and marked absent on that day.

The monitors are required to be at school a quarter of an hour before the others, to prepare their classes. They are to examine their children to see if they are clean: they are to see that they do not idle, and to instruct them to the best of their knowledge. They are never to sit apart from their class, nor to leave it unless permitted by the mistress, and they are to be accountable for all books, slates, pencils, etc., given out for the use of their class.

All play things brought to school shall be forfeited.

As the improvement of the child must depend on the regularity of their attendance, those who are absent three times in one month without leave, shall be struck off the roll of admission.

When any child has been admonished for bad conduct, the parents or guardians shall be made acquainted with the circumstance: if warned a third time, the child shall be publicly reprimanded, and, if incorrigible, shall be expelled from the school.

Every child who is considered able to assist in cleaning the school-room desks, etc., must remain when required.

The mistress is to furnish the parents of the children with these regulations, and it is expected that this paper be pasted in every room in which there are children who receive instruction in the schools, in order that these rules be duly observed.[70]

The systematic regulation of time and space was the principal feature of all schools introduced into Ireland in the nineteenth century. Schools reached out and brought the family into their system of rules and regulations. The school required a transformation of the family. Indeed the transformation in terms of simply getting children out to school every day was an enormous task and, regardless of the above rule, regular attendance was not something attained by the majority of school-going children until the end of the century. But it was not simply a case of getting them ready for school. There was no let up from the rigid system of supervision and discipline exercised in the school. Once children entered the grounds, they came under the eye of monitors, pupil-teachers, masters and managers. Their whole character came in for assessment. Supervision and assessment extended into play. It was in play that a teacher could establish to what extent moral instruction had been successful in controlling wild, uncouth behaviour.

It is scarcely necessary to add, that all the educationalists of the present day consider the play-ground as essentially necessary for moral training. It is, in short, the best place for discovering the dispositions, developing the character, and forming the habits of the children.

The children, while in the playground, therefore, are never left to themselves. They are always under the superintendence of the teachers, and paid monitors; who, without controlling or embarrassing them by their presence, keep a strict watch over their words, actions and general demeanour.

Of all the regulations this is the most important. The playground is not intended as a place in which the children may riot uncontrolled. It is the school for moral instruction: and inasmuch as moral improvement is of more importance than mere literary information, there is even greater necessity for the master's presence in the play-ground than in the schoolroom itself.[71]

In effect, this strict supervision of the playground eventually brought an end to play, and the rules and regulations by which modern games are constituted were gradually introduced. How to play the game became, and remains to this day a vertebra, if not the backbone, of most methods of schooling. The inculcation of morality did, in fact, extend beyond the playground into the schoolroom. Indeed it was the central focus of the learning process. The whole curriculum of the school was centred on moral instruction. The Commissioners of National Education were delighted with the standard set of lesson books which they had ordered to be written and used in every school throughout the system.

Every page of them is replete with the best and fittest instruction for those whose use they are designed. They teach children their duty to their parents, to their masters, to each other, and to their fellow-creatures generally. They teach them that they must control their angry passions, be kind to the defenceless, attentive to the aged, respectful to females, obliging to one another, and merciful to animals. They teach them that it is the will of God, that they should be temperate in eating and drinking, should avoid indecent language, and be modest in all their deportment. They teach them to be industrious in order to maintain themselves and aid their parents; to be frugal, in order that they may give to those who want, and that they may not come to want themselves. They show them that, if God has ordained they should labour, labour will make them vigorous both in mind and body: that if He sends them sickness it is intended to make them patient and pious: if He allows them to wrestle with difficulties, it is to improve their tempers and hearts: and that in all emergencies they should depend for their happiness first on God, and, subordinately to Him, on their own industry intelligence, good character, resolution and fortitude.[72]

The Christian Brothers introduced a text into their schools which was specifically designed to produce and maintain civility and morality. *Christian Politeness* was mainly a translation of De La Salle's *Civilité Chrétienne* which was one of the most extensively used textbooks on civility found in France, both at home and in schools, throughout the eighteenth and nineteenth centuries. By 1857, *Christian Politeness* was in its third edition. The book is divided into two parts. The first part deals with 'modesty in the exterior' and contains chapters on deportment, control of the head, countenance, eyes and looks, and the body. The second part deals with 'decorum of ordinary actions'. It has chapters on rising and going to rest, dressing and undressing, table manners, visiting, recreation and conversation.[73]

There is a sharp contrast between *Christian Politeness* and the book on civility written for priests. When dealing with etiquette for priests, attention was paid to the finer points of body control. It was assumed that the priest had basic control over his passions and body, but that there were social conventions which applied to higher society of which he should be aware. In *Christian Politeness,* which is for use among school-children, nothing is assumed and everything is discussed in detail. The detail has primarily to do with the body. This subject takes up the whole of the first part of the book. The layout of the book implies, as does the text itself, that it is only when the body is controlled that issues such as what is said, and how it is said, come into play. In other words, in social interaction what we do with our bodies takes precedence over what we say. Practice comes before speech in establishing a person's civility. This is the fundamental characteristic of good manners. For example, as *Christian Politeness* points out, 'the head should be kept erect, it should not be turned giddily from side to side. . . . Putting the hand to the head, or touching the hair, particularly at the table, should be avoided. The ears should be kept very clean: but they should never be cleaned in the presence of others.'[74]

Of the first twenty pages of *Christian Politeness,* which deal with Modesty in the Exterior, twelve have to do with the head and the countenance. The soul is seen as constituted in and through the body as regulated by the head. A regulated head indicates a regulated body. The heart is seen as the centre of the body. A regulated heart is not controlled by passion but by the community. The soul is constituted in and through a sacred heart. 'The source of true politeness is the heart, in which there must exist a great degree of good will to men and a sincere desire to promote their happiness.'[75] Community and civil life are seen as founded on a non-rational commitment which comes from the heart. But the heart must be regulated in and through shared conventions of civility, otherwise it will be dictated by passion. In small isolated communities, these conventions are few and simple. In modern Western society, with enormous centres of population and increased geographical and social mobility, they have increased in number and complexity. The essence of modern civility is that the body be controlled by the heart which has been cleansed of its individual passion. This control comes from the head. Communication depends on facial expression, especially eye and head movement. It is in this sense that a civilised, controlled body reveals itself in the face which becomes the main sign of civility, above and beyond anything that is actually said.

The countenance must, and indeed will, give expression to different sensations of the soul; but the man of sense and virtue possesses sufficient self command to observe due moderation in any manifestation of his sorrow or joyous feelings.

In Holy writ, the eyes are called *the windows of the soul,* because its various feelings and emotions are easily discernible through them. Their movements should, therefore, be regulated with special care. . . . To turn the eyes lightly from side to side, without fixing them on anything, is a sign of a giddy and unstable character.[76]

The body without a soul is an uncontrollable mass of passions and instincts. Through the modern civilising process it became an object of private guilt and public shame. It was to be hidden. Only the face, which is the mirror of the body, was to be revealed. Particular attention had to be paid to going to bed at night and rising in the morning for that was when the mind was dull and the body revealed. It is for this reason that morning and night prayers were necessary. One of the changes which has occurred in Ireland since the 1960s has been the control of passion in the face of a greater revelation of the body. Indeed the most modern form of self-discipline within Western civilisation involves a delicate balance between continually exciting the passions and yet, at the same time, exercising a rigid control over them.[77]

It should be remembered that all the instructions contained in *Christian Politeness* derive from De La Salle's book which had been first published in France in 1729, over a hundred years previously. The obsession with modesty and the inculcation of shame and guilt both played a central part in the manuals on good manners.[78] However, given the more explicit instructions which were contained in De la Salle's original French edition, one wonders if, by the time *Christian Politeness* came to be written, Irish sex had already been shrouded in a veil of silence and consequently, the more explicit sections in De La Salle's work were deleted. In the original work, De La Salle refers openly to how one should behave when sharing the same room or bed with a member of the opposite sex. However, as the civilising process developed it became difficult even for educators to discuss such things without shame and embarrassment. In time this led to the practice of moralists not referring to the subject directly. Writing on chastity in 1815, Henry Tuke stated: 'I wish to say as little as possible on this subject, remembering that the vices alluded to are such as the Apostle says, should "not be once named among Christians".'[79] Children were instructed about sex in an indirect and veiled manner. Soon a new generation of parents emerged who although subjected to the forces of sexualisation could not discuss sex since they had no communicative competence in the subject. Elias notes that

As in the course of the civilizing process the sexual drive, like many others, is subjected to even stricter control and transformation, the problem it poses changes. The pressure placed on adults to privatise all their impulses (particularly sexual ones), the 'conspiracy of silence', the socially generated restrictions on speech, the emotionally charged character of most words relating to sexual urges all this builds a thick wall of secrecy around the adolescent.[80]

This is not to say that sex was not discussed at all. In fact, there was an enormous expansion of sexual discourse throughout the nineteenth century in Ireland. What emerged was a science of sex which became the sole domain of the Church. Controlling sex, as a practice and a discourse, became one of the main strategies by which the Catholic Church maintained its power. Not until the 1960s did a whole new public awareness, expression and discourse of sexuality began to emerge. The discourse and practice of sexual arousal contained by strict body discipline, which is at the centre of Western civilised behaviour, was mainly developed in Ireland through the media. The bonds of censorship which the Church had tied around sex were shattered, thereby allowing it to enter the market place of everyday life. However although there was a new sexualisation of the Irish body from the end of the 1960s, the communicative competence to discuss these changes in social and cultural practices did not come until the 1980s. Since then the Church's monopoly on discourse about sex has been broken; shame and embarrassment have wilted away, and many Irish Catholics are now able to discuss subjects like masturbation and orgasms, even on radio and television.

Conclusion

What priests, nuns, brothers and teachers began to instil into Irish Catholics was not much different from what had been happening to other people throughout Europe since the sixteenth century. The civilising process may have taken many different paths, and it may have changed greatly in the interim, but nevertheless one of its consequences was that eventually, even after almost three hundred years, farmers in the remotest part of Ireland – which was one of the remotest parts of Europe – began to behave in ways similar in some respects to the aristocracy of the sixteenth century. What was different about Ireland was that the civilisation of the Irish body was a state-sponsored project, operated by the Church through schools. It was not so much that there was a body of prosperous native tenant farmers in Ireland at the beginning of the nineteenth century waiting to be civilised, but rather there was a network of small tenant farmers who became bourgeois through a civility and morality fostered by priests, other religious, and teachers. It was through the schools that bodily discipline, shame, guilt and modesty were instilled into the Irish Catholic. Through such discipline and control, successive generations of farmers were able to embody practices which were central to the modernisation of Irish agriculture, including postponed marriage, permanent celibacy and emigration as well as a routine, regulated life-style which was central to maintaining production. However, because it was the Church which was the civilising force behind the embourgeoisement of the Irish farmer, and because it gained a monopoly of control over their bodies, secular civility became almost synonymous with Catholic morality. The Church, family, and community, with the priest at the head, became major power blocs and alliances in Irish society. Attaining social prestige in Ireland became reliant not so much on being secularly civil as being a good Catholic – that is adhering to the Church's rules and regulations. This was the foundation of the legalism which, as was seen in chapter two, is still a significant, though diminishing, aspect of present-day Irish Catholicism.

7
The Transformation of
Irish Society

The civilising process was delayed in coming to Ireland not merely because of its insular position but because the British state, in order to maintain political control, had attempted to convert the Irish to Protestantism and, where that failed, to keep Catholics from religion and civil society, that is decivilised and demoralised. It was not until the beginning of the nineteenth century, by which time the attempts to penalise and convert Irish Catholics had obviously failed, that the state gradually changed its policy and began to foster their education, moralisation and civilisation. One of the reasons the state was so willing to hand this task over to Catholic Church was the enormous growth in the Irish population. Having a population of almost seven million uncouth peasants living nearby, who had traditionally exhibited a violent and passionate hatred of the British, became a major concern of a state which was supervising the development of Britain as the core area of world capitalism. It was for this reason that so many censuses, so many parliamentary committees of enquiry, so many commissions, and so many detailed reports were produced on Ireland. It was for this reason that the state tried experiments such as subsidised emigration and a national system of education, and gradually handed the job of civilising and moralising the Irish over to the Catholic Church, as soon as it was feasible to do so without raising too much opposition from Protestants, especially evangelicals in Britain.

But the civilising process was not something which was planned or forced upon unwilling bodies. Regardless of the Protestant Evangelical crusade which continued in Ireland until the 1860s, and regardless of the fears which such crusades caused within the Catholic Church, the fact of the matter was that the majority of the Irish people steadfastly refused to be the same as the English Protestant.[1] Although one of the reasons why Cullen was sent from Rome was to stem the tide of English Protestant proselytisers, and although there were constant reports of souperism and mass defection, when the census of 1861 was published it showed no marked increase in the number of Protestants, even in Connaught where the crusade had been waged the hardest. As Bowen notes: 'If any simple answer can be given to the question of why the ICM (Irish Church Mission) crusade failed, it is that the movement was English, in origin, in design, and in the goals it sought to achieve.'[2] But the Irish did want to be civilised, not merely to show that they were as moral and civil as the English Protestants who had dominated them for so long, but as a means towards improving their standard of living. To understand why the Irish were so willing to accept the rigorous discipline of the Catholic Church, it is necessary to understand the social and economic conditions which prevailed in Ireland before the Famine and, in particular, the enormous growth in population from 1750 onwards.

In brief, through adhering to the rules and regulations of the Church, Irish Catholics were better able to introduce the type of stem-family practices which, intentionally or not, helped improve their standard of living. If tenant farmers were to prevent subdivision and consolidate the already meagre size of their holdings, they had to ensure that their sons and daughters adhered to the disciplined, celibate lifestyle advocated by the Church. An improvement in their standard of living became dependent on encouraging practices such as postponed marriage, permanent celibacy and emigration. This form of population control had been practised throughout Europe since the sixteenth century but, mainly due to the Penal Laws, the interest and means to embody them had been absent in Ireland. It was the rapid growth of the Irish population which led to the adoption of these practices and the formation of stem families in which generally one son inherited the land and, as a consequence, three generations sometimes lived in the same household. Coincidentally, the general abandonment of these practices of population control was one of the causes of the growth in the rest of Europe's population.

The Growth in European Population

World population rose from an estimated 545m. in 1650, to 750m. in 1750, to 1,000m. in 1830.[3] In Western Europe there were three major periods of population growth: between 1100 and 1350, between 1450 and 1650 and from 1750 onwards.[4] In some countries the rise in population after 1750 was faster than in others. In England and Wales, for example, the population rose from 5.895m. in 1750, to 17.719m. in 1851, an increase of 200 per cent.[5] This was higher than the growth rate in Sweden and France, but lower than that of Ireland. The Irish population increased from 1.690m. to 2.274m. between 1687 and 1754, but between then and

1841 it rose spectacularly to 8.18m: an increase of 260 per cent.[6] When, how and why European population rose so quickly has been the subject of major debate ever since Malthus wrote his seminal essay at the beginning of the last century. To understand the power which the Catholic Church attained in modern Irish society, it is necessary to understand some of the causes of the enormous increase in population that took place in the century before the Famine, and the role the Church played in ensuring that such population growth did not occur again.

Two major explanations have been offered for the growth in Western European population from 1750 onwards. The first emphasises the fall in the death rate which, while related to socio-economic development, was more directly linked to improvement in medical knowledge and public health.[7] On the other hand, it has been argued that the growth in population was caused by an increase in the fertility rate which was linked to an improvement in economic conditions. Habakkuk, for example, links the rise in Western European population to a dramatic shift in marriage patterns, away from the traditional one of postponed marriage and permanent celibacy, to earlier marriages and unregulated fertility.[8] This was associated with the break-up of households and the type of traditional society in which families and the Church exercised moral control. This transformation has been summarised by Peterson, who identifies three main types of family in Western European history:

In the *traditional family* typical of the pre-industrial period, the postponement of marriage plus the non-marriage of a portion of the population, constituted an onerous but efficient means of holding fertility in check. In the *proletarian family* typical of the mass of either rural or urban workers released from the prior institutional and normative restrictions, there was no effective ban either to early marriage or to procreation. Indeed, social control was often barely strong enough to compel marriage once a child had been conceived. In the *rational family* type, which arose among the middle classes during the nineteenth century and then gradually spread to the rest of society, a sense of parental responsibility reappeared, and with it a limitation of family size. The average age at marriage rose again, and later the same end was achieved with less privation by the use of contraceptives.[9]

The rise in European population from 1750 may be attributed to a decline in the rate of mortality, and a shift from 'traditional' to 'proletarian' type families in which people married earlier and did not regulate the number of children they had. Shorter claims that increased fertility was part of a wider sexual revolution which took place in the eighteenth and nineteenth centuries. This revolution was directly associated with female emancipation but had different effects among different social classes.[10] For the lower orders of society the break-up of the traditional family system led to an isolation which became associated with romantic love and, assuming that romantic love is directly linked to more sexual intercourse, this led to higher fertility. Among the higher orders of society, female emancipation became associated with women being less willing to succumb to the sexual bidding of their men.[11] Towards the end of the nineteenth century, this rise of a new order of middle-class women began to be combined with a decline in marital fertility which was associated with such factors as the increased cost of rearing children, the weakening of religious beliefs, the cult of hedonism and the spread of contraceptive technology. However, as Borrie points out, restraint from marriage continued to be a Western European phenomenon right up to the present day.[12] The question is to what extent did these transformations take place in Irish society?

The Growth and Curtailment of Irish Population

The increase in Irish population which occurred from 1750 corresponded with a general increase in trade and prices throughout Europe from that time. The years from 1793 to 1815 were the culminating phase of a long wave of expansion going back to the 1740s.[13] Connell's explanation for the sudden rise in population is that the general, increasing prosperity led to a desire to marry early which, in turn, led to an increase in the birth rate.

At the close of the eighteenth century, and early in the nineteenth, it was the practice for the farm to be subdivided, and for cultivation to be pressed higher up the mountain-side, and farther in the bog, so that children for whom neither Irish towns, nor overseas countries, had adequate opportunities, might settle near home. The son did not need to delay marriage until his father was disposed to relinquish ownership and control of his land, he did not need to accept his father's choice of bride as the condition for acquiring the means of livelihood that made marriage possible. If his father should refuse to give him a part of the family's land this was no insuperable obstacle to marriage: he could rent a scrap from a neighbour, and marry whom he pleased when he pleased.[14]

The desire to marry early arose, according to Connell, because there was an increased demand on the world market for grains. Landlords, in order to increase rents and profits, actively encouraged subdivision of farms, and a shift from pasture to arable farming. This increased the amount of labour required in farming and, by producing a greater yield, allowed larger families to survive.[15] The potato could be cultivated easily in lazy beds in poor quality soil, and since a pig or grain could be raised to pay the rent, cultivation began to be extended into wasteland with peasants content to live in mud-cabins which were easily constructed in a matter of days. As Clarkson describes it: 'so enduring was poverty in pre-Famine Ireland, and so hopeless the future, there was little point in postponing marriage to more propitious times: two could live as miserably as one and children were both a comfort to ageing parents and labour for tilling the potato patch.'[16]

This explanation for the growth of Irish population based on a decrease in the age of marriage would appear to fit in with the general Western European model. Cullen, however, argues that there was no dramatic shift from late to early marriage in Ireland in the eighteenth century. Ireland, he claims, was unaffected by the demographic revolution which had affected Western Europe in or before 1500, in which the marriage age rose progressively to around twenty-seven for males and twenty-five for females.[17] He argues that the Irish marriage age had been around twenty-one years since the early seventeenth century. Ó Gráda has found supporting evidence from literary sources which indicates that a relatively early age of marriage was common in Ireland from the seventeenth century on.[18]

This is where the potato enters the scene. Even if the switch from pasture to arable farming, along with the greater subdivision of holdings and the adoption of the potato, did not lead to any dramatic increase in early marriages, eating potatoes did mean that the Irish were not only better fed but healthier.[19] Drake argues that a highly nutritious and regular diet of potatoes so improved the health of Irish women that their fecundity increased markedly. Moreover the dramatic increase in the use of the potato between 1740 and 1780 led, according to Drake, to a once and for all drop in the level of mortality.[20] Cullen, on the other hand, has argued that the potato was not used extensively in Ireland until after 1780 and that, consequently, its adoption did not lead to the growth in population, but that rather its use was a response to population increase. In Cullen's perspective, the growth in population from the mid-eighteenth century was due to an expansion in domestic industry and trade which helped to maintain a high birth rate. It was this expansion, combined with a decrease in mortality, which caused the population to grow.[21] Mokyr, in a more detailed survey of available data, argues that large amounts of potatoes were cultivated even before the 1740s, and that while population growth would probably have occurred in the absence of potatoes, they nevertheless allowed the Irish to marry younger and have more children.[22] However, a decline in the death rate is the key factor. Regardless of whether the Irish started to marry younger, if the reduction in the death rate were concentrated on the young (0–5 years), then a sharp rise in the number of marriages would have followed some twenty years later.[23]

In broad terms it may be said that up to 1750 the Irish married comparatively early and had a high level of fertility. Population was regulated more by famine and disease than by postponed marriage, permanent celibacy, or emigration.[24] When economic conditions began to improve, there was an increase in the birth rate. People, especially labourers and cottiers, continued to marry at a comparatively young age. They began to cultivate the potato more and rely on it as a staple food. The change in diet was associated with a decline in mortality and an increase in fertility. There was a decline both in major famines and in outbreaks of disease.[25] This situation continued among the majority of the population until the Famine which, in three years, eliminated more than one and a half million people through death and emigration.[26] Most of these were from the labourer and cottier classes. The devastating effects of the Famine brought about harsh changes. The potato could no longer be relied upon. Landlords who had been trying to push through consolidation of farm holdings prior to the Famine now found that the small tenant farmer was himself reluctant to subdivide. Commercially viable farms on compact holdings were the only hope of survival, let alone a decent standard of living. There was a growing tendency to pass the farm on to just one son. His marriage was delayed until the father died, or was ready to surrender possession of the farm. The dowry obtained from the incoming bride allowed one daughter to marry. The remainder of the brothers and sisters had the choice of remaining single or leaving the land.

This general description of Irish demographic history hides a number of sub-currents which are crucial to an understanding of the transformations in Irish society in the nineteenth century. The population did grow until 1841, but the rate of growth had been declining for some time. In the period 1753–91, the rate of growth of population was between 1.6 and 1.9 per cent per annum which, as Clarkson indicates, is very high and unmatched elsewhere in Europe.[27] Between 1791 and 1821, the overall growth rate had declined to between 1.3 and 1.6 per cent; between 1821 and 1831 it was 1.4 per cent; and, finally, between 1831 and 1841 it had dropped dramatically to 0.63 per cent.[28] There is even some evidence to suggest that the population had actually begun to decline in the 1840s before the Famine struck. From his analysis of the population changes in the Trinity College Estates 1841–1843, Carney concludes that the population slightly decreased in absolute terms before the onset of the Famine.[29] If the rate of population growth declined between 1821 and 1841 and, possibly, actual numbers declined in the years immediately before the Famine, this indicates that, notwithstanding minor outbreaks of famine and disease, some measures of population control began to be exercised in Ireland from 1820 on. I will now examine how those practices of population control, traditionally associated with the stem-family system, came to be embodied and maintained within the Irish population.[30]

Emigration

The Battle of Waterloo (1815) and the end of the Napoleonic wars were the whip which forced many Irish into changing their habits. The decline in economic prosperity, associated with the end of a war economy and the inability of a cottage-based industry to compete with the factories of Britain, prompted many Irish people to do what the British state had tried to force them to do – to emigrate *en masse*. More than one and a half million people emigrated from Ireland before the Famine.[31] During the Famine 801,000 emigrants were reported, and over a million in the five years following it.[32] Emigration continued to be Ireland's main form of population control right up to the 1960s. In the 120 years from 1841 Ireland had the highest rate of emigration in Western Europe. Without emigration there would have been a natural increase in the population during this time, when in fact it was declining rapidly. Between 1871 and 1901, 1.5m. people left Ireland, and a similar number (1.6m.) left between 1901 and 1966.[33]

Kennedy has made some important points concerning the pattern of emigration. Overall, but especially from 1885, there were more female emigrants than male. Female emigration occurred in a steady stream, mainly to urban areas in America in the nineteenth century, and to Britain in the twentieth century. There were greater fluctuations in male emigration which increased when the switch from tillage to pasture farming gathered momentum, when labour-saving devices such as the horse and the tractor were introduced, and when there were no wars to be fought. In other words, it was a more common and expected practice for females to emigrate. Males were inclined to wait around more. This was linked to the practice of the father not naming the inheriting son until quite near the end of his life. Consequently, because emigration among females was higher, permanent celibacy was more common among Irish males. Both of these trends are the reverse of the general Western European pattern.[34]

While this interpretation of the emigration data for Ireland is acceptable, Kennedy assumes that all those who emigrated did so voluntarily as a means of raising their standard of living. This is an over-simplified explanation. It was in the economic interests of those who were to remain on the farm that all unnecessary labour, especially daughters, emigrate if they did not intend to remain single.[35] This was crucial both for those smaller farmers who wanted to sell up, and the bigger farmers who wanted to raise their standard of living by introducing labour-saving techniques. This is not to suggest that sons and daughters were thrown out. It is to argue that emigration did not always occur spontaneously, and that in many cases those who did go had to be persuaded or coaxed into doing so. As we shall see in the next chapter, present ethnographic evidence suggests that mothers raised many of their children, especially daughters, in the expectation that they would emigrate. In this respect, the traditional notion of Irish mothers raising their children for emigration is correct. It could be that the objective was to obtain emigrant remittances – the money sent home by sons, daughters and relatives who had emigrated. However, the question that Irish historiography has yet to answer is not only why mothers continued to engage in the practice of rearing children for export but also how, when necessary, they managed to persuade their children to emigrate or, if they stayed at home, to delay marriage or not to marry at all.

Even if sons and daughters decided not to emigrate but to stay on the farm, the interest in raising the general standard of living and developing the practices associated with the stem-family system meant that the inheriting son, and the daughter who was to receive a dowry, would have at least to postpone marriage, while the others who resisted emigration could not marry at all. Again it should not be assumed that postponed marriage and permanent celibacy were practices which were chosen voluntarily. It would be naïve to think that the urge to marry early, so common among the Irish in previous generations, was suddenly and easily transformed into an urge not to marry. The successful acceptance of postponed marriage and permanent celibacy were dependent on the new discipline and sexual morality which were brought to bear on the body externally through surveillance and schooling, and internally through the creation of shame and guilt about sex. Without the new rigorism of the Catholic Church, imported by the priests into schools and homes, there could not have been the successful embodiment of postponed marriage and permanent celibacy which characterised social life in Ireland in the generations after the Famine.

Postponed Marriage and Permanent Celibacy

It was not until after the Famine that delaying marriage and remaining single became common practices among the Irish. However, this does not mean that such practices, as well as stem families, did not exist prior to 1845. They clearly did. The overall or 'crude' marriage rate fell from 6.0 per thousand in 1830, to 3.8 per thousand in 1844. This is the opposite to what one would expect, for as Crotty notes: 'In a population growing younger with a large number of people in the marrying age group, it is to be expected that the crude marriage rate would be increasing, and that possibly the average age at marriage would be falling.'[36] Drake claims from an analysis of 1830 marriage statistics that the age of marriage in the generation preceding the Famine was much higher than previously supposed.[37] Lee points out that it is a mistake to generalise from a particular class to the whole of pre-Famine Irish society, and that the age of marriage among cottiers and labourers continued to be low right up to, and even after the Famine.[38] In other words, from a couple of decades before the Famine, although there may have been a shift to postponed marriage among a new middle class of tenant farmers, nevertheless labourers and cottiers, who formed the majority of the population, continued to marry early as they had always done.

By 1841, the level of postponed marriage among males in Ireland was 43 per cent, which was 6 per cent higher than it was in England and Wales in 1851. The level among Irish females in 1841 was 28 per cent, which was 5 per cent higher than it was in England and Wales in 1851. Although the Irish were new to the practices of postponing marriage or not marrying at all, they became so good at them that within the space of a hundred years they had become the most extreme example of the general European pattern. In 1936, 74 per cent of males and 55 per cent of females aged 25–34 years were single. In the same year, 29 per cent of males and 24 per cent of females aged 45 years and over were single. This compares, for example, with a postponed marriage rate (for 1936) of 17 per cent for French males and 15 per cent for French females; and a permanent celibacy rate of 8 per cent (males) and 10 per cent (females).[39]

In his explanation of why the Irish delayed marriage, or did not marry at all, Kennedy rejects the notion, which he associates with Connell, that rigorous Catholic practices and beliefs instilled a fear of sex and degraded the status of marriage compared to celibacy. He argues that the Church never condemned sex as immoral and that during the nineteenth century early marriage was encouraged by the Church as a deterrent to immorality. Moreover, he argues, history shows permanent celibacy to be equally prevalent among non-Catholics.[40] His own thesis is that postponed marriage and permanent celibacy were the means which individuals, mainly men, chose to raise their standard of living. 'These persons did not marry because they could not support a family *at the same level of living* which they shared as a member of a landholding family.'[41] He points out that the Catholic Church was strongly opposed to married women working, and since there was a permissive attitude to single working women, marriage often meant two adults living together on one income where, previously, two had been living separately on two incomes.[42] When Kennedy tries to explain why the Irish disregarded the Church's teaching on early marriage and yet adhered to its teaching about married women working, he points to dominant cultural beliefs, for example that a working wife is an indication of the failure of the husband, and available jobs should go to married men first.[43] This is where Kennedy's argument, that the special character of present-day Irish Catholicism is the result and not the cause of a high proportion of single persons in the Irish population, breaks down. It is not a question of whether one caused the other, but rather, in a reproductive process, how one maintained the other. The family is at the heart of Irish social reproduction. If mothers had not stayed at home and had gone out to work, the very means by which postponed marriage and permanent celibacy were maintained would have been threatened. The mother staying at home was central to ensuring that her sons and daughters adhered to the rules and regulations of the Church, and at the same time preventing them from getting into situations in which they may have had to marry.[44] For, as Kennedy himself notes: 'if one of the unmarried relatives married and set up a second household on the same farm, he would be in effect reducing the standard of living of the other persons dependent on the holding to a level below the acceptable minimum.' The Catholic Church's teachings, especially those on sexual morality, were the means by which the emergent stem family kept its sons and daughters from marrying, and thereby increased its standard of living. The Protestant Church provided similar means for Protestants.[45]

Finally, Kennedy's claim that the Church encouraged early marriage throughout the nineteenth century needs investigation. The only primary source which he cites for this claim is the statement by a twentieth-century bishop of Cork, Dr Lucey, that 'late marriage, particularly if so late as to entail a small family or none at all, is undesirable and in a very real sense unnatural as a population practice.'[46] There is some evidence that indicates that up to 1825 the clergy might have encouraged marriage since it was among their principal sources of income.[47] However, since the number of priests from a tenant farmer background increased, it is more than likely that they too recognised the detrimental effect that early and prolific marriage was having on Irish rural life. Connell suggests that 'many a priest's attitude to marriage, whatever its veneer of learning, was that of the peasant society from which he sprang.' He goes on to argue, from a survey of late nineteenth-century literary sources, that for most priests' parents, the purpose of marriage was seen mainly in terms of ensuring labour for the land and an heir for the family. Thus 'barring a parent's premature death or incapacity, every child was wise to postpone it [marriage] and not a few to forgo it altogether.'[48] The moral rigorism which the Church brought to bear on nineteenth-century Ireland was the most persuasive and the most pervasive of the agencies which stemmed the passions of the Irish and reconciled the young to non-marriage. It is important in this respect to realise that, contrary to what Kennedy suggests, Connell did not see the Church as the *cause* of delayed marriage and non-marriage, but rather as a *means to the end* of consolidating the size of the farm and improving the standard of living.

The question still remains as to how postponed marriage and permanent celibacy were maintained in everyday life. It is too simple to think that a new economic man or woman rose automatically like an invisible hand within Irish families, and was maintained by adopting existing

Catholic practices and beliefs. Postponed marriage and permanent celibacy involved dramatic changes in lifestyle which were unlikely to have come easily. These practices required a whole new discipline of the body which began to be learnt among Catholics from the beginning of the nineteenth century. It was first introduced in the Catholic pay schools and confraternities, but these were ineffective because they had no systematic organisation and regulation of time and space. It was more successfully inculcated in the thousands of schools which sprang up around the country during the rest of the century. It was maintained through a system of surveillance which extended beyond the school, into the family, and, finally, into the wider community. The school, the family, and the community began to supervise the activities of girls and boys.

Even allowing for the possibility that the Church and school did an excellent job in instilling sexual morality and discipline into Irish bodies, and that the process spread slowly throughout the country, there is still the problem of how conformity was ensured in everyday life. It was not that the Church just poured beliefs and practices into the minds and bodies of Irish children and that they were then set on the right path for life. The shame and guilt about the body, created through confession, sermons, and in the schools, needed to be maintained in everyday social relations. The primary mechanisms undoubtedly operated within the family. But if these strategies of power which limited what boys and girls did and said were to be maintained successfully, there needed to be mechanisms of control within the wider community. Young men and women had to be discouraged from marrying. Marriage had to be portrayed as something to be avoided. Just how successful the community became in fostering such a perspective is difficult to assess. However, some insight can be gauged from McNabb's description of Limerick in the 1950s and 1960s:

> The consensus of opinion seems to be that in the course of time one marries, just as in the course of time one grows old, and that as old age is a limitation of life, a narrowing of one's sphere of activity, so marriage is also an inevitable limitation. The community is not opposed to marriage . . . but each individual avoids it as long as possible, just as one tries to avoid old age. Where such an attitude to marriage reigns, the institution has low status. It may be a personal necessity but it is not a social ideal, nor is it a positive goal for the majority of the community.[49]

This indicates how successful the community became in reinforcing a negative perspective on marriage among young people, but it still does not tell us anything about the practices or mechanisms by which this perspective was maintained. While this area of Irish social history has yet to be investigated, there is some evidence about one of the major mechanisms – the bachelor drinking group.

The Bachelor Drinking Group

It is not certain when the bachelor drinking group first emerged in Ireland. Stivers, who has given a detailed account of the group, suggests that it arose between 1840 and 1870. The male drinking group is not peculiar to Ireland. It has a long history and is strongly linked to traditional European marriage patterns and the stem-family system. However, like permanent celibacy itself, once it took root, the Irish became the most extreme example in Western Europe.[50]

The bachelor drinking group was a power alliance which grew up among Irish males as a means of maintaining their independence of marriage and women. It was an alliance often founded on the relationship between sons and their maternal uncles, and equally often fostered if not directed by the mother. Since, from 1840 on, more and more males had to postpone or delay marriage, it was in their interests, as well as the interests of their family, that they ally themselves with this group. Consequently, the all-male group, in Stivers's terms, 'functioned to make palatable the system of single inheritance, few and late marriages, and chastity to young males not naturally inclined toward delayed gratification. Older males socialised younger males into the bachelor group traditions, attitudes and norms that served to elevate the unmarried state at the expense of the married.'[51]

As much as the Church and school served to develop a rigid system of sexual morality, the pub, in later life, served to maintain this morality, albeit in a more convivial but nevertheless highly ritualistic and disciplined manner. The pub became the place where men displaced their sexual frustration through a repetitive compulsive pattern of drinking. If the school was the penitential house which characterised the transformation of Irish society in the first half of the nineteenth century, the pub became a type of perpetual secondary school for males. Even to this day, Irish towns are characterised by the number of small pubs dotted along their main streets. Pubs were traditionally male sanctuaries. It was not until the 1970s, with the spread of the sexual revolution and female liberation, that women were seen in these dark holes. Throughout the last century, as the differentiation of the work and domestic spheres took place, and as women through their alliance with priests took control of the home, men – not just bachelors – began to congregate in pubs. Stivers argues that this was crucial to maintaining the religiously inspired segregation of men and women which even marriage did not break down. Moreover, to make the celibate state attractive it was necessary that married men continue their bachelor group activities. It is important to realise that the male drinking group was not some spontaneous functional response to new needs. It arose in and through a struggle for power. Inasmuch as the home became the space in which women exercised control, the fields and the pub became the spaces in which males exercised their power. As much as there was, in the increasing rationalisation and differentiation of the spheres of Irish social life, a time and place for everything, there was a time and place for males in the pub.[52]

As Irish life became routinised and disciplined, it also became ritualistic and legalistic. The shift to institutional religious behaviour was a major characteristic of the nineteenth century. This was reflected in other aspects of social and cultural life. Drinking in the pubs became not so much a festive event as a ritualistic, almost dutiful activity. It came to involve a type of ethical behaviour in which there are general rules which may vary from group to group and which are open to interpretation – for example, whether or not singing or card-playing is allowed. But there are also specific regulations to which everyone is expected to conform. Irish pub life has been traditionally associated with the rounds system of drinking. There is a highly complicated but unwritten code of regulations pertaining to this system.

Drinking became a ritual practice that many males embraced in order to be considered and treated the same as other males. Buying a round of drinks, in the order of one's turn, was the social practice by which the male drinking group was established and maintained. Buying out of turn, whether it was to get home, to go to work, or because one had a higher position or class, was unacceptable. Once a drink was offered, there was an obligation to accept it.[53]

Now while much of the rounds system corresponds to the intricate rules and regulations which pertain to all gift relationships, a full understanding of the system can only be attained by placing it within the overall Irish social context. The bachelor drinking group is not constituted solely in and through a social exchange of drinks.[54] It is developed within a much wider network of social relations, not simply in terms of women and the home, but also in terms of the Church – since, while in the pub, men escaped from the moral supervision of priests and women. Moreover, even within the group, social exchange is not so much an end in itself as a means by which individuals can attain social prestige and, thereby, limit what other members do and say.

It is only by fully accepting the social and cultural practices associated with drinking that a member can attain social prestige within the group. This prestige is quite independent of a member's formal position or occupation (political capital) in the outside society, or his possessions (ecomonic capital). Male prestige is often attained by what a man does and says within the legalistic confines of the round system. There is, for example, the need for self-control. A man who cannot hold his drink, in terms of either being physically sick, or losing control of his passions, will rarely attain social prestige within the group. As Stivers points out, prestige accrues with the ability to consume alcoholic beverages frequently, for extended periods of time and with little outward display of intoxication.[55] Peillon has remarked that the highly legalistic pattern of Irish drinking, in which extreme control is exercised over the body and the passions, is in contrast to the general European pattern in which drinking is associated with festivity and letting go with mocking and breaking the rules by which people are limited and controlled.[56]

But although this analysis helps to explain how a male power alliance was maintained within the pub, it does not explain how the alliance limited the practices of its members outside the pub. This is particularly important in maintaining its members as desexualised beings, both inside and outside of marriage. This process of desexualisation was linked not just to a surrender to the group, but to the establishment and maintenance of an inhibition of creativity and achievement. Just as the group depended on its members staying together and not going off with women, it also depended on its members not getting high-and-mighty notions that they were above the group, or capable of being independent of it. Such notions would be a threat to the survival of the alliance. One of the mechanisms by which they were suppressed was through a ritual put-down of those members who were perceived as being above and beyond the group. McNabb refers to this practice. He notes that when men drink heavily and their tongues loosen, they engage in an unfortunate habit of taking a rise out of some person. In this way, 'a group of men when over-confident by drink may chafe one of the company on his shortcomings'. But what McNabb refers to as 'an unfortunate habit' is not so much a social problem but rather a practice by which the drinking group is maintained. The ritual put-down through 'taking the mickey', slagging, and teasing, and so on, is a strategy by which members strengthen the alliance. Again it is important to remember that these shame-producing practices did not arise spontaneously within the home. Another more direct strategy by which the alliance is maintained is overt criticism of its members. But this overt criticism takes a particular form which can be linked to other more general religious social practices, that is, silence and excommunication. One of the mechanisms by which shame is inculcated is to make out that the subject is too grave to be discussed – this, as we saw above, is a major practice in reproducing sexual morality. The offender is excluded through silence. McNabb describes the process:

The groups in bars have developed an interesting method of community criticism and ostracism. The offending party is allowed to sit on his own. The men are polite but restrained. On such occasions there is always an air of tension in the public-house. Later in the night, a group of men will begin to talk in stage whispers (loud enough to be heard by the offender), in general terms and in a derogatory manner about people who commit offences similar to the one which he has committed. The offender may choose to ignore the indirect criticism. If so, he loses face. It is more common for the offender to challenge the group to say what's in their minds. Here we have the very essence of expression in this community: the fear of giving direct offence even to one who by his actions has merited exclusion, and the inability to step outside accustomed behaviour without the support of the group.[57]

As already noted, the drinking group is constituted as a power alliance in and through a wider network of power which is centred on the family and the Church. It is no coincidence that the strategies by which the group is maintained are similar to those by which the family and the Church maintain their power over the individual. Stivers has given a plausible explanation of the relationship between the drinking group and the family. He argues that in Ireland the father-son and husband-wife relationships have tended to be cold and formal, while the maternal uncle-nephew and brother-sister relationships have tended to be warm. This has been crucial, he claims, because it has often been the maternal uncle who has tied each new generation of males to the bachelor drinking group. Unfortunately while there is some ethnographic evidence to support the claim that the relationships between fathers and sons, and husbands and wives, have tended to be cold and formal – although the relationship between brothers and sisters has tended to be warm and strong – there is little or no evidence about the uncle-nephew relationship.[58]

There is much that is appealing and reasonable about Stivers's structuralist analysis, but it does not explain why the father-son and the husband-wife relationships came to be cold and formal. Moreover, it does not describe the conditions and mechanisms which prevented the relationships from becoming warm and informal. In fact, the cold relationship between father and son can be linked with the rise in the new stem-family practices whereby sons were prevented from marrying by being denied plots of land subdivided from the family holding. The farm began to be handed over intact to just one son. But which son that would be was not made clear for years. This was a strategy by which postponed marriage and permanent celibacy were maintained. While none of the sons knew which one would inherit, there was little point in courting women. When the father eventually made the announcement, the inheriting son was usually in his thirties or forties and had little or no experience with women other than his mother. If he decided to get married, which his widowed mother may often have actively discouraged because of her reluctance to hand over the home and her son to another woman, he arranged through a matchmaker to get a wife in the same way that he might arrange to buy a cow.[59] This helps to explain why the initial relationship between newly married couples would be cold and formal; above and beyond members of one's own immediate family, there was simply no experience or competence in relating to the opposite sex. But how was this cold relationship maintained in everyday life? One might argue that a man not able to interact freely and competently with his wife sought refuge in the drinking group. But not even Irishmen could spend all their time in the pub. It is here that the Church, and in particular the priest, enters the network of power relations.

For a number of reasons, some of which are dealt with in the next chapter, the priest came between the husband and wife, and formed a power alliance with the woman. It was through this power alliance that the mother gained moral power in the home, not merely over her children but also over her husband. It is this moral power, and the ensuing control that the Church gained over women, which helps explain why, from the end of the nineteenth century, Ireland developed a higher level of marital fertility than any other country in the Western world. In 1960–64, Ireland had an annual married fertility rate of 195.5 legitimate births per 1,000 married women aged 10–49 years. This was higher than other traditionally Catholic countries such as Portugal (148.9), Spain (142.1) and Poland (130.1). In 1871, the Irish rate had not been significantly different from that of England and Wales. However, whereas the latter's rate dropped to 111 by 1935, Ireland's rate was 248 in 1950.[60] Efforts to control Irish fertility not only appear later than in other European countries, but until recently they were still either less extensive or ineffective.

In trying to explain why so many Catholic women accepted the Church's teaching on a large ideal family size, Kennedy is forced, in the absence of a general theoretical model, to suppose that the women who remained in Ireland and married young were more conservative and willing to accept Catholic Church teaching. He argues that those who postponed marriage to a late age, or who remained permanently single, were less influenced by the Church.[61] Even if this were true – which appears unlikely since single middle-aged women have often had the highest levels of religiosity in Ireland – it does not explain why women who married late had a high level of marital fertility. In effect, why Irish women had so many children, no matter at what age they married, was because not only did the Church demand such behaviour but their mothers and other married women also demanded it. Just as hard drinking was the ritual practice by which men allied themselves with the bachelor group, bearing numerous children was the ritual practice by which mothers became allied to each other and the Church. To understand why and how this occurred it is necessary to understand some of the changes that occurred in Irish rural life in the first half of the nineteenth century, including the end of home employment for married women, the rational differentiation of the domestic (women's) sphere from the work (men's) sphere, the growth of a substantial class of tenant farmers, the constitution of modern motherhood and its responsibilities in and through churches and schools, and the mother's dependence on the Church, through which she would attain moral power in the domestic sphere.

A New Class

A central part of the argument of this chapter has been that the adoption of the rigorous moral discipline of the Catholic Church – the shift from a magical-legal to a more institutional-legal type of religiosity – had an impact not only in the religious field, but in the economic field. One could make at least four different types of arguments about the relationship between the new adherence to the institutional Church and the modernisation of Irish agriculture. The first would be to deny the relationship. In other words, the transformation in ownership and control of property had little or nothing to do with what was happening in the religious field. The changes in Irish agriculture had less to do with changes in religious and moral behaviour and more to do with changes in politics, technology and the world capitalist system. The second type of argument would be that the strict discipline and civilised behaviour inculcated in churches and schools led to a greater control of sex and marriage, the unintended consequence of which was regulation and control of property, leading in turn to increases in the standard of living.[62] A third argument would be that it was the new class of farmers which were in ascendancy and – given that priests, nuns and brothers derived from this class – the ideology of the Church, its teachings and practices, reflected the needs and interests of this new class. The best argument is that there was a compatibility or affinity between the new message of the Catholic Church and the religious, social and political as well as the economic needs and interests of the emerging class of farmers.[63] In the religious field, the rationalisation of religious ethics away from magic towards institutional rules and regulations was not something imposed by authoritarian priests on an unwilling new class of laity. It was something worked out with them.[64] Within the religious field, priests produced a new form of piety and ethics through which the new class could attain religious power. They became symbolically legitimated. But, as we have seen, this religious power became an essential ingredient in their upward social mobility.[65] It was the key to being civilised and attaining social honour and respect. In this chapter, I have argued that religious power was also the key to attaining economic power.

But there is one affinity which I have not discussed and which was to have enormous consequences for the modernisation of Irish society and the subsequent strong relationship between Church and State. This was the importance of having religious capital in order to attain political power. While there have been numerous analyses of the relationship between religion and politics in Ireland in the last two centuries, there has been a dearth of analysis of the relationship between being a good Catholic and becoming a political ruler.[66] What was the mentality, the habitus, the on-the-ground practice and process through which being a good Catholic became an essential ingredient in being politically acceptable – not just in the field of politics, but in law, education, medicine and practically every other social field, including the arts. Murphy argues that if we examine the short stories of Carleton we can see that the give-and-take relationship between priest and peasant in the first half of the nineteenth century became replaced 'by the dominance of the new gombeen ethic of respectability and propriety.' He continues:

In small town and countryside the priests were then powerful members of a social order of merchants, professional men and strong farmers. Robust criticism of the clergy was replaced by private grumblings, respect became confused with obsequious-ness and the situation did not change with the advent of political independence.[67]

The picture which O'Shea paints of priests in post-Famine County Tipperary is that they were involved with everything which was political.[68] Religious and political interests operated side-by-side, sometimes in conflict, sometimes in tandem. As he suggests, the preference for political candidates may have been that they were wealthy, good Catholics who supported the nationalist struggle. But this did not prevent priests and bishops from initially supporting someone like Parnell, even against the directions of the Vatican.[69] From the nineteenth century, the struggle for ownership and control of the land, the struggle for political independence and, later, the struggle to establish a new State, were always part and parcel of a struggle for the religious freedom of Irish Roman Catholics.[70] However, the problem with historical research to date is that it has not dealt adequately with the extent to which politicians strenuously stove to avoid the fate of Parnell. Nor has historical research dealt with the extent to which politicians saw it necessary to have their political capital symbolically legitimated by the Church. Keogh has rightly described the relationship between Church and State during the period 1922–1972 as one of 'informal consensus'.[71] However, what we need to know is how this informal consensus was produced and reproduced on the social stage of Irish life. If the close relationship between Church and State in modern Ireland was founded on a similarity of class and habitus between priests and politicians, what needs to be investigated is not so much for example the relation between governments, political parties, national politicians and leading civil servants and the Vatican and the Catholic Church in Ireland, but the allegiance and deference given to priests and the Church by local politicians and prominent people.

Conclusion

The growth of the Catholic Church in nineteenth-century Ireland cannot be divorced from the growth in population which began towards the end of the eighteenth century and the means that were employed to stem that growth. As the Church grew in strength, many Irish Catholics – in particular a new middle class of substantial tenant farmers – began to adopt population control practices which had become common in many parts of Europe in the two previous centuries. Postponed marriage, permanent celibacy and emigration were central features of the stem-family system in which one son inherits all the land. It was the Church which provided the moral discipline and supervision necessary to incorporate this new system. To some extent the breakdown of the stem-family system in Europe, and the growing inability of institutions such as the Catholic Church to control sexual behaviour, were associated with a growth in population. That growth in population was checked not so much by redeploying stem-family practices, but by wives saying no to their husbands and, later, using contraceptive devices. What makes Irish demographic history interesting is not that the Western European stem family and its associated practices were embodied by the majority of the population after the Famine, but that marital fertility grew to be the highest in Western Europe. The reason for this is that adherence to the Catholic Church, which had helped bring about the moral discipline necessary to introduce and maintain the new stem-family system, prevented the adoption of strategies and practices which might have reduced marital fertility. The development of the Catholic Church in modern Ireland went hand in hand with the attempt to control the growth in population and improve the standard of living. But as the power of the Church grew, especially over women, there was little or no attempt to control fertility once they did marry. This maintained the need for postponed marriage, permanent celibacy and emigration and, in turn, the need to adhere to the Church's rules and regulations, especially on sexual morality. It also institutionalised patterns of emotional relationships within families, especially between husbands and wives, and mechanisms of control within the wider community such as the bachelor drinking group.

8

The Irish Mother

I see that little mother, and hear her as she pleads.
Now it's getting on to bedtime, all you children get your beads.
And she lit our drab existence with her simple faith and love.
And I know the angels lingered near, to hear her prayers above.
For her children trod the paths she trod, nor did they later spurn
To impress her wholesome precepts on their children in their turn.
Ah those little Irish mothers, passing from us one by one.
Who will write the noble story of the good that they have done?[1]

Women have been written out of Irish history. It is men, we are told, who have shaped the course of Ireland's development. O'Connell, Parnell, Pearse, Collins and de Valera are put forward as the heroes who took Ireland by the scruff of the neck and led it reluctantly into the twentieth century. Great men, it would seem, make great history; women make only beds and dinners. — *and war*

There are three main reasons why women, and in particular mothers, have yet to gain the recognition they deserve in Irish history. First, men have written most of the history. Second, Irish historiography has concentrated on politics and personalities as the causal factors in Ireland's development. Third, because they had no jobs or incomes of their own, women were considered to be powerless. Since the 1960s, historians have begun to rewrite Irish history and to take into account the position and role of women. There has been a concomitant shift away from politics and personalities as the key explanation of historical change, and a greater emphasis has been placed on economic and social factors. The social history of Irish women has only begun to be written.[2] Nevertheless the crucial role of the mother in passing on the Catholic faith from one generation to the next and instilling a devotion and loyalty to the institutional Church is only beginning to be recognised.[3]

A central argument of this study is that, far from being a nonentity, the Irish mother has played a crucial part in the social and economic development of Ireland. It was the mother who, from the middle of the nineteenth century, became the organisational link between the Catholic Church and the individual. It was she who carried through the new moral and civil code from the church and school into the home. It was she who, through a variety of social and cultural practices which were handed down through generations from mother to daughter with the support of the priest and Church, produced the Catholics of modern Ireland. Indeed it was the continuous bearing of children, once she got married, that necessitated the inculcation of strict discipline and sexual morality.

It was this rigorous moral training which helped in the subordination of individual interests to those of family and community. But it was the mother who enforced the necessary moral discipline. It was she who, through a variety of subtle strategies and practices, persuaded her children to emigrate, postpone marriage, or not to marry at all. It was she who, through inculcating these practices and a rational regulation of life in her family, provided the vital force necessary for the restructuring of Irish rural life in the late nineteenth and early twentieth centuries. It was she who, through the changes she helped introduce in Irish lifestyles, became the impetus behind the creation of homes, the consolidation of Irish farms, and the general social maintenance of a class of tenant farmers which was at the centre of the initial modernisation of Irish society. Whatever power an Irish mother had was mainly a moral power which was derived from and maintained through the Church. Her ability to rule morally over her husband and children, to get them to do what she said, depended heavily on the support she received from the priest and Church teaching. The effect of this powerful alliance between priests and mothers was that once the initial modernisation had been attained, Ireland became a highly conservative society in which the Church's definition of the good life held sway. It was through this alliance, and the practices by which it was maintained, that the Church became a dominant force in economic and social life. For it is argued that it was through a continual demand for self-surrender to the family, and its ally the Church, that inhibition and shame were nurtured, and ambition and creativity – necessary ingredients for a fully mature capitalist society – were impeded.

Women and Change in Nineteenth-Century Ireland

To understand the role which the mother has played in modern Irish society, it is necessary to appreciate the transformation that took place in agriculture and, consequently, in the position and occupation of women in

Ireland from the beginning of the nineteenth century. Unfortunately, compared with other European countries and regions, very little is known about the Irish family and in particular the role of wives and mothers in social and economic life in previous centuries. Nevertheless it would appear that the institution of motherhood – that is the specific occupational position of women, whose sole task it was not just to feed and clothe their husbands and children, but to instruct and supervise them morally – did not flourish until the beginning of the last century. Modern Irish mother-hood developed in association with the differentiation between the work and domestic spheres of life. Until the beginning of the nineteenth century, home employment, especially the manufacture of wool and linen, was a regular feature of tenant farm production. This went into decline with the arrival of steam-driven machines in the new industrial cities of Britain, and the flooding of the Irish market with cheaply manufactured yarn and cloth. This transition mainly affected married women who did much of the spinning and weaving. It was also associated with a change in marriage formation patterns away from a free and easy system to the deployment of the matchmaking system. Hynes has described the change as follows:

At an earlier stage the domestic textile industry provided widespread spinning employment for women, and a wife brought her labour power to her husband at marriage. As this industry declined and agriculture began to shift from tillage to livestock (both processes accelerating after the economic depression following Waterloo in 1815) the value of a woman's labour declined and, increasingly, dowries in the form of capital rather than labour skills were required.[4]

There is considerable debate as to when and where the shift from tillage to livestock, mentioned by Hynes, took place. This is important as such a shift may be associated not just with the advent of dowries and match-making, which were major characteristics of stem-family life, but also with the institution of practices such as postponed marriage, permanent celibacy and emigration. Crotty, in his seminal work *Irish Agricultural Production,* argues that the shift from tillage to livestock occurred in the second quarter of the nineteenth century.

The years 1820 to 1850 span the period during which Irish agriculture and the Irish people struggled to adjust to the new conditions created by the market changes which were initiated in the years immediately following the Battle of Waterloo. Essentially the changes necessary, given the economic and institutional conditions of the time, were twofold: first to halt and then reverse the population growth and second, to halt the fragmentation of farms and to consolidate and to reorganise them on a pastoral, livestock basis.[5]

Crotty goes on to argue that under the new market conditions, capital in the form of livestock once again became a factor of major importance in agri-cultural production. People without capital could not compete successfully for land and, therefore, could not marry and have families. (In fact this only pertained to a small but historically significant section of tenant farmers. In the poorer regions of the West small farmers continued to marry early, without capital, and settled on subdivided, reclaimed or rented land for some time after the Famine.) Lee, on the other hand, insists that the Famine was the watershed in Irish history, and that none of these social and economic changes, which Crotty associates with the Battle of Waterloo (1815), were established until after mid-century. Nevertheless the trend he outlines is similar, especially the decline in women's economic power.

Before the Famine women's economic contribution was so essential to the family economy that they enjoyed considerable independence. Growing factory competition was, it is true, sapping the strength of domestic industry, but as late as 1841 women accounted for more than half of the non-agricultural labour force.

The Famine helped change this situation in three main ways. First, it delivered a crippling blow to domestic industry. The numbers of spinners of wool, cotton and linen fell about 75% between 1841 and 1851. . . . Secondly, the Famine permitted a marked shift from tillage to livestock, and agriculture became less labour intensive. Women were now less necessary about the farm. . . . Thirdly, the proportion of agricultural labourers to farmers, and of smaller farmers to strong farmers, fell sharply. As women had probably enjoyed greater economic equality among the poorer orders than among the wealthier, this in itself sufficed to tilt the balance of economic power within the family in the male direction.[6]

There is, then, agreement about the nature of the social and economic transformation that took place in Irish society in the last century and how it affected women. The only question is when did it begin. There is evidence which supports the timing put forward by both Crotty and Lee. An examination of export figures indicates that in the decades coming up to the Famine, Irish farmers were already switching from tillage to livestock farming. Up to the mid-1830s, there was an expansion in the export of oats, wheat and barley, but from then on these went into decline and were replaced gradually by the export of cattle. On the other hand, Ó Gráda has quantified agricultural output in the period 1840–44 without referring to export figures. He comes to the conclusion that potatoes and all other crops formed 63 per cent of production in this period, and that cattle, sheep and wool output was only 13 per cent. Furthermore he contends that tillage farming increased right up to the Famine.[7] This question about the shift from tillage to pasture farming brings in a whole series of questions which have obsessed Irish demography and historiography, and which have yet to be resolved: When did the subdivision of farms end? When did farm consolidation begin? When did postponement of marriage begin? In other words, when, where, and among whom did population growth begin to decline? Did these changes occur before or after the Famine and, consequently, what role if any did the Famine play in Irish social history?

There are too many issues involved in these questions to deal with here. However, the major point that has confused the debate is that of economic class. As mentioned in the previous chapter, it makes a great difference whether or not one is talking about Irish population as a whole, or a particular economic class in the society, which adapted more quickly to the changing social and economic conditions. In effect, the shift from tillage to livestock, from free and easy marriage to postponed marriage and permanent celibacy, from subdivision to consolidation, and from the production of a bare minimum for survival to economic security and comfort, were changes which had been embodied for some decades before the Famine by a small, but significant, proportion of the rural Irish population, namely the medium-to-large Irish tenant farmer.

Connell, the doyen of Irish demographers, failed to distinguish between the various economic classes in pre-Famine Irish society, and to recognise the sharp divisions in the social and cultural practices by which these classes were established and maintained. In Connell's perspective, there were just peasants and landlords (of whom middlemen were a sub-category). The absence of a satisfactory class model led him into making three erroneous conclusions about pre-Famine Ireland:

(1) Society was stagnant due to landlord exploitation and the absence of a middle class.

(2) The absence of a middle class was associated with the absence of a family system which could impose the practices necessary to consolidate the farm holding and improve the standard of living.

(3) Consequently, 'the desire to postpone marriage until the accumulation of capital, or the acquisition of a better farm which would allow a higher standard of living could seldom, it is clear, have influenced action in Ireland in the period under review [i.e. pre-Famine].'[8]

It was not until Crotty pointed out that there had been a class of substantial tenant farmers in Ireland prior to 1760, which had gone into decline because of a switch to tillage farming, that a new generation of scholars began to investigate the class structure in Ireland in the decades immediately prior to the Famine.[9] Clark has argued that besides landlords and middlemen, there were basically two other classes: large landholders who after the Napoleonic wars preferred grazing livestock, and small tenant farmers, cottiers and landless labourers who preferred tillage. Taking twenty acres as a rough division between the large farmer class and the rural poor, Clark estimates that, in 1841, 25 per cent belonged to this farmer class.[10] Connolly, in a more thorough working of the figures, estimates that between 1841 and 1845, only 277,000 (18 per cent) belonged to the category of having over 15 acres.[11] This still leaves us in a quandary as to what proportion of these were Catholic. If we use Larkin's arbitrary figure of 70 per cent, which is based on the fact that 80 per cent of the population at the time was Catholic and that there would be an over-representation of Protestants in the large land-holding class, then there were approximately 194,000 Catholic farmers in 1845 with more than 15 acres.[12] Regardless of the exact size of this Catholic tenant farmer class, Clark, Larkin and Connolly are in agreement that it was largely untouched by the Famine. In effect, the Famine decimated the rural poor. Clark estimates that 'the percentage of the adult male agricultural labour force comprised by labourers fell from 56 per cent in 1841 to 38 per cent in 1881, while the percentage composed by farmers and farmers' sons rose from 42 per cent in 1841 to 60 per cent in 1881.' In other words, the tenant farmers became the largest group in the class structure of post-Famine Ireland. There was a definite shift in the type of agricultural production. Between 1847 and 1876 the cattle population rose by almost 60 per cent, while the sheep population rose by more than 80 per cent.[13]

What these researchers have shown is that, contrary to what Connell argued, there was a small, but vibrant, class of substantial Catholic tenant farmers in Ireland before the Famine, who comprised up to one-seventh of the total agricultural labour force. These farmers were employers both of labourers and servants. They were the mainstay of the Catholic Church in terms of providing money and manpower. It was mainly they who had the necessary capital for church building, and who could afford to educate their sons and daughters for the religious life. It was they who united with the urban bourgeoisie to form the Catholic Association and push through Emancipation and other reforms. It was they who, in Larkin's terms, 'have not only remained economically viable and maintained their numbers, but . . . have also emerged as the dominant political class in modern Ireland.'[14] But how did they do it? They did it in and through a power alliance with the Catholic Church. For just as the Church was reconstituted as a power bloc in and through the new tenant farmers, these farmers were constituted as the dominant economic class in modern Irish society in and through the Church. The Church offered these farmers the means of becoming civil and moral. Through an adherence to the Church's new moral discipline, these farmers could not only attain the same social prestige as the Protestant gentry who had dominated their lives but also, hopefully, the same economic class. Through the Church they were to become more Puritan than the Protestants themselves. But it was because these farmers became a power bloc in and through the Church that, once they had consolidated their holdings and the struggle for ownership of the land had ended, they became a highly conservative force. They were limited by the rules and regulations which had made them civil and moral. It was this limitation which inhibited the economic individualism central to the development of a fully mature capitalist agricultural mode of production. On St Patrick's Day 1943, that 'great man' of twentieth-century Irish history, Eamon de Valera, who himself came from a small farming background, defined what has come to be recognised as the classical vision of Catholic Ireland:

That Ireland which we dreamed of would be the home of a people who valued material wealth only as the basis of right living, of a people who were satisfied with frugal comfort and devoted their leisure to the things of the spirit – a land whose countryside would be bright with cosy homesteads, whose fields and villages would be joyous with the sounds of industry, with the romping of sturdy children, the contests of athletic youths and the laughter of comely maidens, whose firesides would be forums for the wisdom of serene old age. It would, in a word, be the home of a people living the life that God desires that man should live.[15]

But what were the mechanisms by which this power alliance between the new rural bourgeoisie and the Church was constituted? How did it work out in everyday life? How was the new moral discipline established? What were the micro-structures of power by which this grand alliance was maintained? In effect, it was not so much the Church's relationship with the farmer that was to turn out to be crucial, but the relationship with his wife. It was the mother who became the organisational link between the newly institutionalised power of the Roman Catholic Church and the individual farming family. It was she who instilled and maintained in her husband and children all that was disciplined, moral and civil. Within the rational differentiation of the work from the domestic sphere, the home became the space within which the mother began to fulfil herself in carrying out her new specialised tasks, and to wield her new power. The home became central to the moralisation and civilisation of Irish tenant farmers and, consequently, to the consolidation of their holdings and the reproduction of their standard of living. The importance given to the home can be gauged from the fact that in the years following the Famine, while there was no great change in the size of farm holdings, there was a considerable change in the type of houses in which people lived.

The main change in the size of holdings in the nineteenth century came with the Famine. Between 1841 and 1851 the proportion of farms over 15 acres increased from 18 per cent to 51 per cent (table 8). However, in the next forty years there were few changes in the size of farms. By 1901, the proportion of farms over 15 acres had increased to only 58 per cent. The decades after the Famine were a period of consolidation, of holding onto and perhaps improving what had been already gained. Farms were no longer subdivided, but there was a dramatic change in the size and quality of houses.

In 1841, the Census Commissioners undertook an assessment of housing conditions in Ireland. This assessment was repeated in subsequent

Table 8.   Percentage of Distribution of Holdings Above One Acre, Ireland
(32 Counties), 1841–1901

| Year | Size of Holding in Acres | | | | | Number of Holdings (Thousands) |
	1–5 %	5–15 %	15–30 %	30 and over %	Total %	
1841	45	37	11	7	100	691
1851	15	34	25	26	100	570
1861	15	32	25	28	100	568
1871	14	31	26	29	100	544
1881	13	31	26	30	100	527
1891	12	30	26	32	100	517
1901	12	30	26	32	100	516

Source: Kennedy, *The Irish*, 89.

censuses. It was based on three criteria; the extent of the house (number of rooms); the quality (number of windows); and its stability (material of walls and roof). They then composed a scale compounded from these criteria: 'in the lowest, or fourth class, were comprised all mud cabins having only one room – in the third class, a better description of cottage, still built in mud, but varying from 2 to 4 rooms and windows – in the second, a good farm house, or in towns, a house in a small street, having from 5 to 9 rooms and windows – and in the first, all houses of a better description than the preceding classes.' This classification changed slightly over the years. In 1871, third-class houses of brick and stone (which formed approximately one third of the total), were classified separately from those of mud. By 1891, the classification of the two lower classes had become as follows: 'In the lowest of the four classes are comprised houses built of mud or perishable material having only one room and window: in the third a better description house, varying from one to four rooms and windows. . . .'[16]

As the Famine brought a dramatic change in the size of farms, it also brought a dramatic change in housing conditions. In 1841, 37 per cent of Irish houses consisted of one-roomed mud cabins many of which were made in a matter of hours with sods of soil stacked up on top of each other, often allowing no space for a window or chimney (table 9). By 1851, these mud cabins formed only 13 per cent of Irish houses. The majority of the population then lived in a more defined, permanent space which may have been made of mud and other materials, but which contained separate rooms and windows. It was in these newly defined spaces that the civilisation and moralisation of the Irish people began to reach down to the lowest

common denominator – the individual. In the next forty years there was
an even greater revolution in the size and quality of houses. In 1851,
almost two thirds of Irish houses were still in the third or fourth class. By
the turn of the century (1901), 70 per cent of the population were in the
second or first class, that is they were living in 'good farm houses' or better.

The transformation of Irish society in the last century was essentially
based on a transformation of space and time.[17] In pre-Famine Ireland, there
was the impressive programme of building churches and schools. Within
these large, ordered spaces, priests and teachers began to define and
regulate time. In the decades after the Famine, this civilising and moralising
process reached down to the smaller ordered spaces of houses, and within
these to the even smaller spaces of rooms.

Table 9.   Percentage Distribution of Class of Houses, Ireland (32 Counties)
1841–1901.

| Year | Class of House | | | | | Number of Houses (Thousands) |
	1st Class %	2nd Class %	3rd Class %	4th Class %	Total %	
1841	3	20	40	37	100	1,329
1851	5	30	52	13	100	1,046
1861	6	36	49	9	100	995
1871	6	40	50	4	100	961
1881	7	46	42	2	100	914
1891	8	54	36	2	100	871
1901	9	61	29	1	100	858

Source: Census of Population 1901, General Report, Table 49.
Census of Population 1851, General Report, xxiii.

It was in these new houses and rooms that behaviour became regulated
and supervised by mothers. It may have been the men of Ireland who built
these new houses, but it was the women of Ireland who transformed them
into homes. It was by making the space in which they lived a home rather
than an unregulated, undefined, badly constructed living space, that Irish
mothers were able to establish and maintain the practices associated with
the new stem-family system. Through the moral and civil instruction
received from Church and school, Irish women began to transform the
confined space in which they operated from what would now be seen as an
outhouse for animals into a modern, civilised home. It is crucial to realise
that a major aspect of the Irish civilising process was the expectation, if not

the demand, which was reflected in their new training and education, that Irish women become good mothers. It was the confinement of women to the house which led it to be turned into a home. It was from within the home that the practices central to the modernisation of Irish agriculture – postponed marriage, permanent celibacy, and emigration – were developed. In this respect mothers became a major power behind the modernisation of Irish society, and not mere servants of their menfolk. This is the mistake Lee makes, for although he recognises the important transformation from houses to homes, and the central position of the kitchen within the home, he reduces the role of mother to that of a slave:

Before the Famine women did not have to know much about cooking. The potato pot demanded no great culinary pretensions. The spread of stoves and ranges, and the greater variety of diet, meant that women had to spend far more time cooking after the Famine than before. As the clothes and utensils the family possessed increased, the wife had to spend more time cleaning and scouring. Making the bed and washing the sheets was a simple matter in many cases before the Famine, when the bed was often a pile of straw on the floor. Pre-Famine women did not spend most of their day isolated in the kitchen, if only because more than half the houses had no separate kitchen.[18]

Lee's argument is that after the Famine, with declining marriage prospects in an increasingly male-dominated society, women were reduced to a subservient, if technologically transformed, role in the home. Women may have been servants, but like many other Irish servants, civil or otherwise, they nevertheless wielded considerable power. Unless the nature and extent of this power, how it was established and maintained, and its consequences for everyday social and economic life are understood, there can never be a full comprehension of the power of the Catholic Church in modern Irish society.

The Constitution of Irish Motherhood

Towards the middle of the nineteenth century, reports from various parliamentary commissions began to indicate that the civilising of Irish society depended not just on giving more power to the Catholic Church, but on the transformation of Irish women into good mothers. The Poor Law Commissioners, for example, drew an unfavourable and unfamiliar portrait of Irish mothers:

Another circumstance, which has a powerful influence in retarding the improvement of the Irish settlers in Great Britain, is the unthrifty and dissolute character of the women as it is on the wife that the care of the house, and on the mother that the training of the children, chiefly depend among the poor. The Irishwomen are likewise, for the most part, not only wasteful and averse to labour, but also ignorant of the arts of domestic economy, such as sewing and cooking. Hence they are unable to make the best of the plain food which they purchase, or to keep their own and their husband's clothes in order, even when they only require mending.[19]

This was one of the reasons why, when the National School system was set up, such a heavy emphasis was given to the training of girls to be good mothers. However, it was not simply a case of teaching girls the skills of household care and management which, once learnt, would never be forgotten. They had to be monitored and supervised within the house. This became the task of the Church. It was mainly priests and nuns who from the middle of the nineteenth century began to define the tasks of mothers, and supervise them in their new roles. As we saw earlier, one of the main ways in which priests gained control of women was by gaining control of their sexual life. This they did by portraying women as weak, fragile beings who must be protected (by the priest) from the sexual viper which lurked within them. This was not just a strategy of the Catholic Church but was, as Taylor points out, part of a wider Puritan strategy by which 'women are forced into an exaggerated femininity, magnifying their relative weakness into complete helplessness, their emotionality into hysteria and their sensitivity into a delicacy which must be protected from all contact with the world.'[20] In Ireland, it was the knowledge and control that priests and nuns had over sex which helped maintain their power and control over women. Women especially were made to feel ashamed of their bodies. They were interrogated about their sexual feelings, desires and activities in the confessional. Outside the confessional there was a deafening silence. Sex became the most abhorrent sin. It was through the control of sex that the modern Irish mother and family were first established. The Church's strategy of keeping women ignorant about sex and their bodies was later maintained in and through the control of medical science and practice in Ireland. Just how successful this control of knowledge became over the years can be gauged from the comments of a married woman in Humphreys's study of Dubliners in the 1950s:

I think it is really sinful that I was allowed to marry as ignorant and as innocent as I was about the whole matter. At the time the only way you learned was from the girls you worked with, but I did not work in a factory and I knew nothing. Honestly, I could surprise you with what I did not know. I used to think of marriage as a mere matter of companionship. I thought the children just came somehow I knew not how. It never occurred to me that children or the purpose of marriage had anything to do with sex.[21]

One of the best-known descriptions of how priests gained control of women was given by Michelet. He argued that the priest, like any other man, is born strong and virile, but is trained into being weak and resembling women. This androgynous being interposes in marriage between the husband and wife. Michelet argued that as an unwitting instrument of

Jansenist repression, the priest through confession gains control of the woman, and in the process attains a knowledge about her sexual feelings far greater than that of her husband who, consequently, feels alienated from his wife and becomes submissive to the moral power of both wife and priest. Estranged from her husband, the wife confides in and associates with her daughters. On the priest's advice, she sends them to the nuns, and brings up her sons like priests.[22] Michelet was writing about France, but Stivers comes to a similar conclusion about Ireland. 'No wonder then that the Irish priest was sometimes referred to as "she". The priest sometimes acted just like one's mother in the rigid enforcement of the moral code. The Irish mother often desired that at least one son become a priest. The priest was the mother's ideal of manhood for her sons.'[23]

Where Michelet and others have gone astray is in describing the mother as a helpless, powerless, and isolated being. It was not simply that the Church gained control of women but that, because of their isolation within the domestic sphere, women and especially mothers were forced in their struggle for power to surrender to the control of the priest and ally themselves with the Church. For women to attain and maintain moral power, it was necessary that they retain their virtue and chastity. This was the message which mothers began to pass on to their daughters. Within the rational differentiation of spheres of moral responsibility, chastity and modesty became the specific goals for women. Temperance became the goal for men. Referring to the reform of abuses in female manners, an editorial in the *Catholic Penny Magazine* asked:

Is it not possible that a Christian company cannot exercise themselves, or take a few hours of agreeable relaxation, without having their shoulders bare, or their bosoms uncovered? Do they ever think upon the tremendous consequences of their subjecting themselves or others to gross temptations? But it is not merely the dress, but the manners of females, that we condemn. Can a lady of the least virtue, or modesty, behold, much less take part in some of these scandalous dances, called Waltzes, in which common decency is set at defiance? . . . Every lady then, of virtue, and of decency, who wishes to preserve her character pure should utterly discountenance such an invasion on the pleasures of private and public life. There is no charm in the female sex which can supply the place of modesty. . . . The best preservative of female honour is female delicacy – we mean a delicacy not assumed or affected, but the delicacy of a modest mind, and a pure heart. This is the visible angel guardian of the female sex, which even the ruffian will respect – it is the handmaid of virtue which attends her coming in and going forth: without it no female is safe or beautiful.[24]

What happened, then, during the nineteenth century was that a Puritan sexual morality, which maintained women as fragile, delicate creatures whose nature had to be protected, began to be instilled among Irish women, first by the Catholic Church and later by women, as mothers themselves. It was the creation and maintenance of such women which was the mainstay of bourgeois Catholic morality, and the basis of the initial phase of the modernisation of Irish society.[25]

Motherhood as Learnt in the School

A major aspect of the civilising process was the segregation of the sexes, first into separate beds, then into separate bedrooms and finally into separate lifestyles. Such an historical pattern of events is not easily discernible in Ireland, but there is evidence of segregation being an integral part of the modern schooling process. Nano Nagle, who started convent schools in Ireland, not only had separate schools but also separate curricula for boys and girls. 'I have two schools for boys, and five for girls. The former learn to read, and when they have the Douay catechism by heart, they learn to write and cypher. There are three schools where the girls learn to read, and when they have the catechism by heart, they learn to work.'[26] An examination of the texts used in National Schools shows that segregated education was a key component of the system. Boys were instructed on how to run a successful small farm. *The Agricultural Class Book* which was introduced in 1850 tells in story form how a peasant transforms his land through drainage, does mixed farming, rotates crops, keeps fowl, keeps his accounts, and so on. The story goes on to relate that while the man is busy outside tending his fields, his wife is inside preparing a varied diet of bread, meat and soup, keeping her house clean and repairing clothes.[27] Needlework was made out to be the essential skill for any woman to acquire. Indeed, as an instructional manual for teachers indicated, the development of a sense of decency and industry often depended upon it. 'To needlework she [the teacher] must be particularly attentive, for on her instructions (of course assisted by their own exertions) may depend whether many a poor, friendless girl shall or shall not have the means of supporting herself, and, if she becomes a mother, whether her children are to be in dirty rags or decent clothes, or brought up in idle or industrious habits.'[28]

The whole structure of a girl's education was towards the development of modesty and virtue and the practice of being industrious. Idleness was portrayed as the vehicle which passions used to express themselves. Consequently, if a mother was not cooking, tending her garden, cleaning the house, or mending clothes, she should be praying. These tales of domestic economy and housekeeping were also set out in the *Reading Book for the Use of Female Schools* which had been brought out five years earlier.[29] The book is best summed up by its table of contents which shows that most of the essays, borrowed mainly from the writings of contemporary moralists, were concerned with housekeeping and child-rearing practices. In 1853, the Commissioners described the lessons as forming 'a complete manual of the moral and domestic duties of females, whether in single or married life, and cannot be read frequently and attentively without producing the most beneficial results.'[30]

After the Famine, nuns began to have a major influence on the education of Irish Catholic girls. This occurred at two levels. First, the nuns went out and brought into their schools children of the destitute classes who would otherwise probably not have attended school. Second, and this was of importance to the constitution of a new bourgeois farming class, the nuns came from good backgrounds and were, in Fahey's terms, 'solid examples of middle class respectability.'[31] Not only did they teach all that was contained in the National School syllabus, but they often had knowledge of foreign languages, art and music which were essential for the constitution of good mothers and fair ladies. Tynan, writing towards the end of the nineteenth century, had little doubt that the transformation she witnessed in Irish homes was largely due to nuns: 'Housecraft is seen in its perfection in a convent. What was it that made the girls who would have been slovenly at home, fit in with the life so exquisitely neat and feat? Perhaps those who went back leavened the lump of indifference and unthrift. Certainly, coming back to Ireland after twenty years absence, I find in the Irish households an order and efficiency which were rare in my young days.'[32]

The school was more than just a place of education. It introduced a whole cycle of discipline into the family. Children had to be got up and out to school. Family life began to revolve around the school timetable. Throughout the nineteenth century the number of children attending school increased rapidly. In 1833, there were 107,042 children on the rolls. Even after the ravages of the Famine, the number continued to rise, although the population was declining rapidly. In 1852, there were 544,604 children on the rolls. However daily attendance was another matter. From 1875, when figures first became available, to 1900, the average daily attendance did not increase much beyond 60 per cent.[33]

It was through the school that priests, nuns and brothers reached out into the home. The child became the link between the moralising forces of the Church and the isolated homes of Ireland. The forces of discipline which were applied in the school began to be extended to the home. Parents, but especially the mother, began to be held responsible for the conduct of their children in school. Children were inspected for cleanliness. If they were dirty, or misbehaved, they were sent home. Throughout the nineteenth century the control of instincts, passions and emotions shifted gradually from the school to the home, where such control became the specialised task of the mother.

It is important to realise that the disciplines and control which began to be exercised over mothers and their children was not something which was inflicted by the Church and State on an unwilling people. Reluctant, lazy and uncivilised as many might have been in the beginning, it did not need much insight to realise that control of the instincts and passions through moral discipline was the key to modernisation and an improvement in the standard of living. More important, it was the care and dedication which especially the nuns and brothers brought to their work, that allowed the Church to instil into the lower orders an interest in being civil and moral. It was that care and dedication, something that the State could never attain, which was central to the ability of priests, nuns and brothers to limit what Irish Catholics did and said. A report of the National Commission on Education (1864) described this relationship:

When the nuns find that anyone of their pupils has been from school for some days, they enquire into the cause of the absence, and generally employ the monitresses, or some of the more grown girls, to ascertain the facts. Parents, more specifically those belonging to the humbler classes, are pleased to find that persons filling a high and respected position take a deep and sincere interest in the well-being of their children. They are consequently forced, as it were by feelings of thankfulness and gratitude, to see that their children attend school as regularly as their circumstances will permit.[34]

It was in and through the National School system that Irish females were taught the basic practices of housekeeping and the moral upbringing of children. It was in the school-room that the specific tasks of motherhood were systematically defined and explained. The system was slow to get started and depended on a feedback mechanism. In the beginning not everyone got the message because going to school depended largely on the existence of a 'yet to be constituted' good mother. It would follow that it was those farmers who already had substantial holdings of fifteen or more acres, who were more successful in getting their children to school. Once mothers began to send their children to school, they and their children became more and more disciplined, regulated people, and their daughters learnt the skills and tasks of housekeeping and mothering more diligently.

Priests, Mothers and the Moralisation of Irish Children

Deprived of possessions, unable to contribute to the income of the household, and having no formal occupational status, the already negligible power of women went into decline during the first half of the nineteenth century. It was the priest, and later the nuns, who were the only light at the end of this dark tunnel of powerlessness. They were the only people with power who regularly visited women in their homes and took an interest in what they were doing. Priests and nuns did not have personal wealth. Their ability to limit what others did and said depended on the services which they rendered, often free of charge, and on their being more moral and civil than those with whom they interacted. The same means became those by which mothers created and maintained their own power.

The ability of the Church to limit what its members did and said, depended on the indoctrination of children into its rules and regulations. This was originally carried out through the confraternities of Christian doctrine and, later, through the schools. But the success of the indoctrination process depended upon its being followed up within the home. The home became the object of supervision and surveillance by the Church. This was part of an overall differentiation of space between the home and the church. Whereas previously the home had been the place of socio-religious practice, such as house stations, marriages and wakes – as well as a good place for priests to eat and drink, it now became primarily a private space. There was a differentiation between private and public religious practices which mainly took place within the Church. The way for the mother to obtain the priest's blessing and approval was to bring up her children within the limits that he laid down. In doing so she was able to call upon him as an ally in her attempts to limit what her husband and children did and said. Moreover, through engaging in the same humble tasks of moralising children and looking after the sick, elderly and dying, mothers began to attain a similar perspective on the world to that of priests and religious. This was a crucial aspect of the alliance with the Church, for it was through this similarity of practices and perspective that mothers fostered the vocations among their children on which the Church depended. Equally important, it was through an imitation of their celibate lifestyle, their body discipline and morality, that the mother inculcated a sexual and emotional repression which was crucial to the attainment of postponed marriages, permanent celibacy and emigration. Even when they emigrated, Irish women gained a reputation as self-sacrificing, noble mothers. Diner states that women in Irish-American communities were noted not only for holding the family together but for propelling it 'out of poverty and into the respectability of the middle class'. Irish women were regarded as 'civilisers', especially in their attempts to stop men from drinking, and in this activity, Diner notes, 'wives operated in league with the priests.'[35]

We have seen how, within the new discipline and organisation of the Catholic Church in Ireland, priests and religious brought a new Puritanical sexual rigour to Irish social life. What is of concern in this chapter is how this was imparted to children. In other words, what were the practices by which first the priest and later, through imitation, the mother instilled in children not merely a sense of modesty, but an emotional and physical segregation of the sexes that resulted in an uneasy and awkward communication between them and which became the backbone of virtuous, moral and civil behaviour in Ireland? Unfortunately historical sources which would provide an insight into how such practices were first established are few and far between. This is related to the fact that one of the chief strategies in this moralisation and socialisation process was the institution of silence about such matters. Connell has reviewed Irish literary sources that deal with the sexual supervision of young people by priests. We are told of priests separating courting couples, of a priest who every night used to walk through all the lonely lanes and by-ways, threatening the lovers with his big stick; of others bursting in upon private social parties; and of how generally they brought an end to traditional courtship practices.[37] The image of what Murphy calls the blackthorn stick of the prowling priest is a popular one in Irish folklore, but it is one which seems only to have come to the fore towards the end of the nineteenth century.[38] This was the priest at the zenith of his power which was to last, especially in rural areas, well into the 1960s. But when and where he began to exercise such power, and how frequently he did so, is something that Irish historiography has yet to answer.

The model of modesty, virtue and humility which priests and religious provided was maintained in the home through a growing devotion to Our Lady. Our Lady was popular in Ireland before the nineteenth century, but it was then, as part of the devotional revolution, that the rosary, novena, May and October devotions, as well as shrines, processions and pilgrimages made in her honour, became common practices.[39] These practices reached their peak in 1879 in Knock, County Mayo, when she appeared to fifteen people. Our Lady occupies a unique position in the history of the Catholic Church because of her dominance in an otherwise patriarchal institution. Taylor argues that devotion to her was introduced as a deliberate strategy by the Church to counteract heretical movements, mainly towards orgiastic, sex-imbued pagan practices.[40] She was a mother figure who was at the same time completely desexualised. In other words, it was crucial that the pagan practices which were rampant in pre-Famine Ireland be replaced by an ideal-type figure that was fecund and female, and yet remained virgin and pure. The chaste, modest and humble virtues of Irish women and mothers grew apace with their penitential devotion to Our Lady. The rosary – those penitential beads which rarely left her hand or pocket – became the means by which the mother maintained her own soul, and those of her family. It was a penitential practice that bound the family together. Griffith painted the following picture of holy Catholic Ireland. 'Come with me some evening to, it may be a humble, but always a hospitable home in holy Ireland. The mother is there, surrounded by her family, generally a large one. She has (to use Our Lord's beautiful comparison) gathered them together around her as the hen doth gather her chickens under her wings (*Matt.* 23:37). Each kneels with beads in hand.'[41] The rosary was a time when the mother exercised her moral power and called her husband and children to the attention of God and Our Lady. It strengthened her position as the sacred heart of the home. It bound the family together in ritual practice. Such ritual practices were essential to the maintenance of pious devotion to the mother and family and the suppression of individual interests. It is slightly romantic, but quite reasonable, for Lockington to describe the rosary, and the devotion to Our Lady, as the girdle that lifted Ireland out of the blackness of pestilence and famine.[42] It was through such devotional practices as the rosary that the mother retained her power in the home. It was through a devotion to Our Lady that she fostered a devotion to herself and motherhood in general. But most important of all, she developed a notion of the chaste mother. It was through a devotion of Our Lady that women gave control of their bodies to the Holy Spirit. Sex itself became a penitential practice. Just how successfully these practices and beliefs were inculcated over the years can be judged from one of Humphreys's respondents:

I think there is something wrong with sex and nothing will ever change me. . . . And I think that is the general attitude. One woman friend of mine who is married told me that she felt that after she was married that the loss of her virginity was the greatest loss of her life. And I felt the same way about it. . . . There is something repulsive about it and nothing will get that out of my system. And the women will tell you that it is the men who enjoy it, not the women – they get no enjoyment out of marriage that way.[43]

Throughout the late nineteenth and twentieth centuries, the Church, faced with the threat of an economic individualism associated with urban industrialisation, came to depend more on maintaining control of the family. This it did by developing its alliance with the mother and keeping her within the home. As part of this strategy, the Church perpetuated a notion that women had a natural vocation as housewives and mothers, and should not indulge in matters of the mind and reason, even if they were capable of such things. As a priest at the turn of the century put it: 'Let it first be supposed that girls are capable of such higher studies as Greek, mathematics, philosophy, etc., and are a success in them; is it too much to surmise that this success would be gained at the cost of other studies which are better calculated to make them good heads of houses?'[44] The Church's message was consistent: if a mother went out to work, family life would be destroyed. Worse still, as Pope Pius XII claimed, it would give bad example to the daughter and her preparation for real life, for she would not feel the slightest inclination for austere housekeeping jobs and, consequently, could not be expected to appreciate their nobility and beauty and to wish one day to give herself to them as a wife and mother.[45] But Pope Pius XII was writing about the dangers of an urban industrial society which was to remain foreign to Ireland until the 1960s. If he had read Griffith's description of the Irish mother, he would have realised that, as regards Ireland, there was at that time little to worry about.

You may enter, almost at random, any of the thousands of Catholic homes in the land, and there you will meet the ideal mother, modest, hospitable, religious, absorbed in her children and motherly duties. The outside world, the masculine woman and her antics, have little attraction for her. She feels herself placed in a position by God, her life and actions their model. She is the class of woman who makes her home a home in the truest sense, a house in which her children are happy, and to which they ever look back with love when they have left it for a home of their own.[46]

Irish Mothering Practices

From the above description we can gain some insight into how the power alliance between the Catholic Church and the Irish mother was created and maintained, and how the mother instilled in her children a pious devotion to the Church and Our Lady which were central to maintaining the chastity and modesty necessary for postponed marriage and permanent celibacy. But this still does not give an adequate account of how these practices were successfully maintained over the years. To gain some understanding of how this was achieved it is necessary to focus on some of the more specific child-rearing practices of Irish mothers.

In traditional Irish families, mothers were not only responsible for child-rearing and moral instruction, but also for the more general task of emotional management. In their study of the extent to which traditional family roles had changed in Ireland from the 1930s, Hannan and Katsiaouni found that in a quarter of all families the father played almost no part at all in such 'emotional management' tasks and in over half the cases played a minimal role.[47] This is supported by McNabb who noted that there was some evidence that fathers believed that the expression of too much interest in children was a sign of immaturity.[48] Scheper-Hughes suggested that it was through the control of the moral emotional sphere that the mother not merely instilled the prerequisites for postponed marriage and permanent celibacy, but through the various psychological strategies that she employed she tended to identify those sons who would do well by becoming priests, teachers, civil servants, etc.; those who would emigrate; and the one who would stay on and look after her and the farm. Her daughters were reared to the tasks of mothering, but they were also taught a sense of independence which would allow them to emigrate. Scheper-

Hughes argued that it was no longer the case that a number of sons waited around in competition to see who would get the land, but rather that the one who failed to escape got stuck by default with the land and saddled with a life of almost certain celibacy and self-negating service to the old people. This led to a change in psychological strategies. 'An Irish mother has always had special endearments for her favourite child and it appears from the life histories of older villagers that, in former generations, the family pet was often the first-born son, traditionally named after his paternal grandfather and reared in order to fill his projected role of farm heir.'[49]

Scheper-Hughes argued that by the 1970s the first-born were reared for export – for the occupations of schoolteacher, civil servant, successful emigrant, possibly the priesthood. She detailed the justifications and rationalisations which were used to give preferential treatment to the mother's pet, and how often the last-born son, often jokingly referred to as the 'runt', the 'scraping of the pot', the 'bottom of the barrel', was encouraged to end his education in primary school.[50] Connell has described this practice in detail:

> Many a mother too, though happy enough to see her daughters settle down – even the sons who had left home – resisted the marriage of their heir. Perhaps with justification, she pictured herself the object of his affection over 40 years and dreaded her relegation; she dreaded, too, the daughter-in-law, scheming not only for her son, but for the kitchen and yard she had ruled so long. By rousing a sense of sin, by ridicule, even by words unspoken, she kept her boy from girl-friends, leaving him awkward with women, perhaps incapable of courtship – a bridegroom, if at all, in a match made for him when her day was done.[51]

These strategies of keeping a son on the farm were extended to the wider community. Males used 'slagging' and 'taking the mickey' as a means of cutting each other down to size, and to censure those young men who tried to shake off village apathy by making an effort to get ahead or to demonstrate feelings for others. But, as Scheper-Hughes indicated, these strategies of creating inhibition through ridicule were first learnt in the family, where the mother, often purely for reasons of economic survival, brought up one of her sons with a sense of dependency on her and an inability to survive in the wider world without her.[52] Hutchinson argued that not only was the Irish mother a stifling influence on individual initiative and innovation, but that in this respect she is an exception in Western society:

> Restrictions imposed upon the son by a father jealous of his status were not counterbalanced (as they have been in other western societies) by contrary influences emanating from the mother. If the Irish mother's influence upon her son was a powerful one, it operated, nevertheless, in a direction opposed to economic development based upon individual initiative and innovation. Her influence set limits to her son's freedom which, while different from those imposed by his father, were equally difficult to circumvent.[53]

Daughters, on the other hand, were reared to be responsible, competent and independent, which gave them a greater sense of autonomy, prepared them for early emigration from the village, and allowed them to feel less guilty about severing ties with old people. More important, Scheper-Hughes's research gives us an understanding of how the emotional distance and sexual 'flatness' of the Irish were maintained. She argued that both sons and daughters were reared in a harsh, unphysical, comfortless manner by the mother. Loneliness, lack of tenderness, and consequent feelings of psychological abandonment and loss had, she argued, become basic components of the Irish personality structure, and were learned at an early age through the experience of a less than satisfactory relationship to the first love object – the mother. The basic line of Scheper-Hughes's argument is as follows: The reason why the Irish were so often schizophrenic, shy, withdrawn and uneasy in the company of others, especially members of the opposite sex, was that their mothers, as part of a traditional, cultural practice, denied physical gratification and stimulation to their children whom they left for an inordinate amount of time by themselves, not rocked, held, and reassured. Besides being excessively preoccupied with controlling their children's sexuality – which she linked to the ascetic Jansenist tradition of Irish Catholicism – Irish mothers tended to be schizophrenogenic because, while they were too protective and extremely possessive of their children, they were at the same time unconscious of – and ignored – their expressed needs and demands.[54]

Stivers also picked up on this ambivalence: 'A puritanical sexual code is upheld by the mother in the Irish family: in fact, sin in general comes close to being equated with sexual sin in particular. The Irish mother often functions as an autocrat in the home, although she is often gentle and overprotective toward her children.'[55] The reason for this ambivalence was that from the time they got married, mothers came under a traditional, cultural pressure from their own mothers, other women, and the Church, to have children, even though they often expressed resentment at having had more children than they wanted or needed. This was the double bind that Irish women experience in their struggle for power.[56] It was this double bind which was transmitted in terms of overprotection but emotional coldness. The lack of fondling, cuddling, and emotional intimacy which Scheper-Hughes documented as still being practised by Irish mothers in the 1970s had its roots in the transformations that took place in Irish society in the nineteenth century. The domination and control of women by the Church, and the necessity for women to ally themselves with that dominating power if they themselves were to have any power, led to their high level of marital fertility which, in turn, created the need for postponed marriage, permanent celibacy and emigration among their children. These practices were encouraged by the mother in the home through a devotion to the Church, a rigorous sexual morality, and a physical and emotional distance from her children. It is this scenario, re-enacted over generations, that is the essence of the dialectical relationship of power between the Church and family in modern Ireland.

Conclusion

When we come to explain why it was that from the beginning of the nineteenth century successive generations of Irish Catholics began to adhere strongly to the rules and regulations of the Church, it is necessary to go beyond the extension of the modern European civilising process into Ireland and the interest in consolidating farm holdings and improving the standard of living. It is also necessary to go beyond the changes that took place within churches and schools, and examine what was happening to individuals within families. It is the family which has been the continuing link between the Church and individual Catholics. More specifically, it has been Irish mothers who have produced each new generation of devoted Catholics. When, as has been happening since the 1960s, Irish women are no longer dependent on the Church for power (having gained access to political and economic power), and, consequently, the Church loses its ability to control them and their sex, then one of the pillars, if not the foundation, of what has held the Church above modern Irish society begins to crumble and decay.

Irish motherhood as primarily involving the sentimental and moral education and care of children within the home, did not exist among the majority of the population at the beginning of the last century. It was constituted, like the power of the Church itself, through the conjuncture of a number of processes and events. The first of these was the termination of the economic power which women had held through various jobs, mainly involving spinning and weaving. The second was the gradual shift from tillage to pasture farming. This was part of a third process which involved the consolidation of a new class of substantial tenant farmers who refused to subdivide their farms and insisted that their offspring either postpone marriage, not marry at all, or emigrate. These practices depended upon numerous other processes, one of the most important of which was the separation of the religious from the social sphere and, in particular, a separation of Church and home. The priest became a formal, austere figure; a man of Roman precept, civility and morality who helped develop, especially among those large tenant farmers from among whom he came and with whom he socially interacted, a rigorous discipline over the body and its passions which was the key to the Irish stem-family. It was he and the

Church who helped transform rough, uncouth girls into fragile, delicate colleens who had to be protected from the sexual evils that lurked deep within them, and who made good Irish mothers chaste and fertile in the image of Our Lady.

A new regulation and supervision of the body and its passions also began to be exercised by teachers in schools. It was here that girls, who until the advent of the National School system were mostly illiterate and less educated than boys, began to learn not just to read and write but the specific tasks and duties of mothers. Increasingly confined to the house, increasingly losing any specific economic role, and increasingly being supervised by priests, nuns and teachers, Irish women began to take on motherhood and helped transform Irish houses from a mass of mud cabins into substantial farmhouses in which, as in the school, time and space were regulated and in which there was a proper time and place for everything, and everything was in its proper time and place. It was within the home that a new power alliance between priest and mother began to emerge; an alliance that was founded on her dependence on the Church for moral power. The result of that alliance was an embodiment of the rules and regulations of the Church among successive generations of Catholics. The price of that alliance was a chaste motherhood with unregulated fertility. Most of the children were reared for export; some as examples of local pride and joy; and some as good-for-nothings who would always be dependent on their mother, as she herself was on the priest and the Church.

PART THREE
Decline in the Power of the Catholic Church in Ireland

9

The Decline in the Catholic Church's Monopoly over Irish Morality 1986–1997

[handwritten in margin: New Catholic]

There are two opposing views when it comes to deciding the current condition of the Catholic Church in Ireland. There are those who look at the indicators and declare that the Catholic bottle is still quite full and there are those who argue that it is almost half empty. In his analysis of the Catholic faith in 1983, Ryan concluded that a new Catholic was emerging in Ireland. He concluded that there was an increasing number of people in Ireland 'who see themselves as having the Christian faith, who wish to remain within the Church, who are weekly church-goers, but who question the Church's authority over their private lives.'[1] This view was reiterated by Hornsby-Smith and Whelan in 1994. Their analysis of the evidence from the European Values Study in 1990 indicated to them that there was indeed a new type of Catholic in Ireland who had the following characteristics:

1. An informed appreciation of the value of the supernatural and sacramental life of the church, including an increasing tendency to think in terms of a spirit or life force rather than a personal God.
2. An outlook that questions the church's right to speak with absolute authority on matters of personal morality or to speak out on Government policy while at the same time considering it appropriate that the Church should be outspoken on social issues.
3. A liberal attitude on sexual matters, which can be coupled with an adamant rejection of abortion except in circumstances where the mother's health is at risk.
4. An optimistic interpretation of religion, one's standing before God and the world; Hell, the Devil, sin and doom-and-gloom fears of damnation have all taken a bad beating.[2]

Greeley has also questioned whether a decline in institutional adherence, or a secularisation process, is taking place. He points to the fact that there was no change between 1981 and 1990 in: the level of prayer; belief in life after death; belief in God; belief in the human soul; belief in hell, heaven, and sin; or the importance of God to human life. He goes on to point out that the proportion (85 per cent) of Irish Catholics who went to Mass every week in 1990 was still the highest in the world.[3] In a separate and more detailed analysis, Hornsby-Smith argues that historically there has always been an acceptance of a wide variety of ways of being a Catholic in Ireland. Nor has there ever been a simple top-down imposition of orthodoxy. Catholics, he argues, have disregarded Church teaching on some issues in the past, for example boycotting, as much as they do today in relation in contraception. He claims that 'there is growing evidence of a more participative and socially aware laity seeking ways of realising a Christian dimension in their everyday lives. Finally, he argues that the institutional church has also changed. 'In the maintenance of its "moral monopoly", the church has shifted its strategy from one of coercion to one of being the "conscience of the nation".'[4]

Greeley is adamant that, given the rich tapestry of religious images which persist among Irish Catholics in the stories they tell, to talk of their undergoing a secularisation process is erroneous. He maintains that despite the authoritarian and insensitive promulgations by priests, despite the Vatican's obsession with sex and birth control, and despite its discrimination against women and homosexuals, Catholics stay in the Church because of Catholic metaphors, stories and imagery. He believes that the imagery is positive and powerful; that it creates a gracious image of God which is so strong that it overcomes the formal, negative, diatribes the institutional church has about the human condition. Of the four religions of Judaism, Catholicism, Protestantism and Islam, Greeley argues that 'Catholicism has the most richly developed popular tradition because it is least afraid of the imaginative dimension of religion.' He emphasises, in particular, the importance of the concept of Our Lady in Catholicism – that is, of God having a mother.[5] So strong is the imagery that despite institutional attempts to repress it, Irish-American Catholics are more adventurous and playful when it comes to sex; engage in it more frequently and enjoy it more than people from other ethnic-religious backgrounds.[6]

In this chapter I will argue that these interpretations of the condition of the Church are not only optimistic, but are a limited if not erroneous reading of the evidence. The power of the Catholic Church has been eroded significantly over the past ten years. This continues a process which began thirty years ago. It is part of the reformation of the Catholic Church, or the Protestantisation of Catholic belief and practice. It is also part of wider process – the secularisation of Irish social life. The reality is that despite claims of rich tapestry of religious imagery, the sacred supernatural canopy which hung over Irish social has been gradually lifting. Religious language, symbols and rituals no longer frame Irish social life as they did in the past.

The lives of Irish Catholics are no longer lived within the rigour of religious seasons and holy days. There is not the same invocation and recourse to saints. People are less concerned about blasphemy. Irish Catholics live in a rational, predictable world, which they believe can be mastered and controlled. This is not to deny that they have spiritual feelings and supernatural experiences, but it is to assert that, in comparison with the past, they are occasional rather than regular.[7] I will argue that the influence of the Church in the religious field has declined significantly and that this has been linked with a decline in its influence in other social fields.

As discussed in chapter 1, Irish society is best analysed in terms of different, overlapping social fields. Each field has a specific type of discourse with its own experts and professionals as well ordinary practitioners. In the religious field, the discourse is about the existence and nature of the supernatural, the meaning of life and how to lead a good life in this world in order to gain entry to the next. Different languages are used within the overall discourse. So, for example, the language of Hinduism is quite different from Catholicism, even though they are both within the field of religion and religious discourse. There is, then, a huge diversity within religious discourse; and even within the language of Catholicism there are different voices, sometimes conflicting, sometimes consensual. My argument is that while Catholicism still dominates the religious field in Ireland, in that the religious experts are still considered to be bishops, priests, nuns and brothers, they no longer exercise the same power over the minds and hearts of Irish Catholics and the way they think, understand, read and relate to the world in which they live. Moreover, if we follow Weber and think of the world's main religions as being ethical salvationary – that is, they are based on prescribing how to live a good life in this world in order to gain entry to the next – then we can say that the institutional Church is losing its ability to determine the way Irish Catholics are religious.[8] As Bourdieu would suggest, while the acquisition of religious capital in the religious field is still based on being people being spiritual and ethical, Irish Catholics are increasingly devising their own paths to spirituality and morality.[9]

But Irish Catholics are not only becoming more Protestant – that is, devising their own spiritual and moral path to salvation – they are also becoming more secular. The decline of the influence of the institutional Church in the religious field has been matched by a decline in its influence in other social fields, particularly in politics, education, health, social welfare and the media. In terms of individual behaviour, being religious or acquiring religious capital is no longer necessary to the acquisition of other forms of capital. Irish Catholics can attain status, honour and respect, and they can attain political, economic and social power, without having

to have Catholic religious capital or to have their forms of capital symbolically legitimated by the Church.

As we saw in previous chapters, the religious field in Ireland has been
characterised by ongoing struggles by various religious denominations,
sects and cults to disseminate their beliefs and values; to have them recognised as legitimate; and to get people to change or maintain their allegiance.
There is a continual struggle to be recognised as exceptional, to have rites
and beliefs accepted and churches and schools built. Many religious
groupings have reached the first stage and have been symbolically accepted
as legitimate. Some cults and sects have not. Most religious groupings
in Ireland have failed to achieve widespread adoption of their beliefs,
practices and morals. The result is that the Catholic Church has dominated
the religious field in Ireland for the past one hundred and fifty years. The
Church of Ireland's attempts in the eighteenth and nineteenth centuries,
aided by the British state, failed miserably to persuade the Irish to change
their religious allegiance. The opposite happened. The Church of Ireland
and other Protestant denominations declined dramatically after the formation of the new Irish State in 1922. There was, of course, some ongoing
opposition, and some new sects and cults emerged, but by the middle of
the twentieth century the vast majority of people in the Republic aligned
themselves with the Roman Catholic Church.

It is also important to remember, as has been emphasised in this book,
that the attempt by the Roman Catholic Church to dominate and control
the religious field in Ireland involved the systematic elimination or assimilation of religious languages, beliefs, practices and morals which were
opposed to its position. The struggle of the Church in the nineteenth century was to establish Roman orthodoxy. This involved in some cases trying
to eradicate pagan beliefs and practices and, in other cases, incorporating
them within the institution.[10] However, any detailed ethnography of
religious life in Ireland, particularly in rural areas, would find evidence of
pagan practices and beliefs, particularly among the elderly. These beliefs
and practices have been central to Irish religious consciousness for hundreds of years. It is embodied in the landscape, the home, the language and
the habitus of the Irish religious field. It is a cultural residue which does
not go away either in the society or the individual and which can be re-
enacted at any time in any place. Religion may constantly take on new
forms, but as Taylor points out, 'each time a new religious form takes shape
it does so with pre-existing materials – language, objects, places, notions.'[11]
Despite its best efforts the Church has never developed a 'monopoly either
of the interpretation of the supernatural world or the manipulation of
forces it contained.'[12] In this respect the Church can be seen as an institutional force which adapts to the changing conditions of Irish people's

beliefs and values. For the past one hundred and fifty years it has had a determining influence on the way Irish people read the world in which they lived. Now these beliefs and values are changing rapidly and in a different direction from what Rome teaches. But it is argued, particularly by the Church's optimists, that the Church is an adaptive organism. As much as it moulded Irish beliefs and values in the past, it has always adapted its message to suit the needs and interests of the people. The Church is now seen by the optimists as going through a period of rapid change. As an institution it is learning to mould itself to the beliefs and values of Irish Catholics. The problem for the Church is how the institution can be maintained, especially as the one, true, universal institution, when its members are becoming increasingly Protestant and secular? While the increasing number of people who reject the Roman Church as the one true path to salvation may not be a sign of secularisation, it is a sign of Protestantisation and a decline in the institutional Catholic Church and its monopoly over morality. On the other hand, if when making a moral decision, Irish Catholics do not refer to God, sin, or a life after death, then that is indeed a sign of secularisation.

This is linked into a problem for sociological analysis: whether to develop and adhere to substantive definitions, for example that religion pertains to something supernatural, or whether to adopt a more hermeneutic approach which follows people's own definition of religion and what it is to behave religiously. In a substantive approach, we cannot regard people as religious if they are not oriented towards the supernatural. On the other hand, in a hermeneutic approach what matters is whether Irish people define and classify themselves as Catholic and see themselves as religious. In other words, if Irish people define themselves as Catholic and religious then *their* definition has real consequences and is the one which really counts. The task of good sociology is to marry an objective analysis of the structure of Irish Catholic belief and practice with the logic of that belief and practice as it operates in Catholic people's minds and hearts, and to show how it is worked out between them in everyday life.[13] It is necessary to go beyond the logic of people's beliefs and practices and link it into an explanation of the broader, macro-structures from which it emerges and in which it operates.

It would be wrong, then, to reduce an understanding of the reformation of the Irish Catholic Church or the secularisation of Irish society simply to changes in people's beliefs and practices. Secularisation also takes place at the level of the institution, particularly in terms of the decline in numbers of vocations and religious personnel and in the decline of the influence Church and religion in other social fields.[14] Again, following a substantive realist approach, we can say that insofar as there is no supernatural reference in people's behaviour in these fields, particularly in deciding what is right and wrong, this reflects not just a decline in the influence of the Catholic Church, but a process of secularisation. In effect, the main change in Irish society is the decline in the symbolic domination of the Catholic Church and the rise in the symbolic domination of the media. But before analysing these changes, it is necessary to review and reinterpret some of the data concerning the belief, practice and morals of Irish Catholics.

Decline in Catholic Belief

Those who argue that little secularisation is taking place in Ireland point to the continued high levels of belief in God (96%), Life after death (78%), a soul (85%), Heaven (85%), Hell (50%), the Devil (53%), and Sin (84%). They emphasise that there has been little change in these figures in recent decades, and they remain significantly higher than the European average.[15] But there are some changes in the nature of Irish Catholic belief. For example, the proportion who believed in a personal God decreased from 77 per cent to 66 per cent in the nine years between 1981 and 1990.[16]

Although Hornsby-Smith and Whelan note that Irish Catholics are exceptional in their attachment to traditional orthodox beliefs, they do not comment on whether or not they are beginning to resemble their European counterparts who appear to be becoming more Protestant if not secular and only Catholic in name. Are Irish Catholics becoming more like French Catholics, among whom, for example, only 48 per cent believe in life after death and only 43 per cent believe in heaven? What is the nature of this ethical, salvationary type of Catholic religion? If, following Durkheim, we define religion as a unified system of beliefs and practices relating to sacred things which unite into a Church all those who adhere to them, then what type of Church is it in France, when less than half of the Catholics believe in fundamental beliefs such as life after death and less than half go to Mass once a week?[17] It would appear that being a member of the Catholic Church in France, like being French itself, has more to do with being a member of an imagined community rather than of a real community centred on shared beliefs and practices.[18]

But whatever may be true about the decline in traditional Christian beliefs, particularly concerning the nature of God and salvation, the greatest decline would appear to be in institutional beliefs about the Church. In 1974, 83 per cent of Catholics fully accepted that the Church was the one true Church and 69 per cent fully accepted papal infallibility. By 1984, these percentages had dropped to 73 per cent and 61 per cent respectively.[19]

Decline in Catholic Practice

Writing in 1994, Greeley noted that the weekly Mass attendance by Irish Catholics – which in 1990 was shown to be 85 per cent – was the highest in the world.[20] This also meant that the decline in twenty years – 6 per cent since 1974 – was only marginal. But recent opinion poll results would indicate that the decline since 1990 has been quite dramatic. A poll conducted in 1995 showed that weekly mass attendance had fallen to 64 per cent.[21] A different poll a year later showed weekly mass attendance to be 66 per cent. This poll also found that 69 per cent of those surveyed believed that in 20 years time 'Ireland will be Catholic in name, but only a minority will be practising their Catholicism.'[22]

The most rapid decline in religious practice has been in attendance at Confession. The level of attendance at monthly Confession decreased from 47 per cent in 1974 to 14 per cent in 1995. This decline in the institutional forgiveness of sins may be more an indication of Protestantisation than of secularisation – that is, of people deciding more for themselves what is right and wrong and how to live a good life that is pleasing to God. It also verifies a decline in the doom-and-gloom, fearful, fire-and-brimstone type of beliefs associated with the devil and hell; and the rise of a feel-good ethos within the Church. This is reflected in the rise in the participation in Holy Communion at Mass, which rose from 28 per cent in 1974 to 43 per cent in 1989, although it has decreased since then to 39 per cent in 1995.[23] The level of daily prayer has remained high. It rose from 80 per cent in 1974 to 84 per cent in 1984, but declined to 71 per cent in 1989.[24] What is not known, however, is if there has been a change in the nature of people's prayers. To whom do Irish Catholics now pray? Is it to God, Jesus, Mary or some of the other hundreds of saints in the Church? When, where and how do they pray? For what do they pray? Has family prayer declined? Do families say grace before meals? Do they still say the rosary together? Have traditional aspects of Catholic devotional life such as wearing medals and scapulars, using holy water, putting up religious pictures and statues, gone into decline? The evidence is conflicting. There is evidence which suggests that pilgrimages whether to Knock, Lough Derg or Croagh Patrick are still popular. There is also evidence that the traditional nine-day solemn novena to Our Lady of Perpetual Help is growing in popularity. It may well be that there is a core group of traditional, committed Catholics who are becoming more assertive and public in their faith. But there are also *à la carte* Catholics who are choosing what they like best from within the traditions of the Church, without accepting other crucial doctrines and practices.

Almost all surveys show that religious practice in Ireland is declining among: men; the young; the better educated (those under forty); those living in urban areas (especially the unemployed); those who have emigrated at some time; and those with a higher level of consumption of foreign media. If present trends continue, this would allow us to predict that religious practice among Irish Catholics will continue to decline in the following circumstances: the more women attain power; when the present generation of young people grow older (even allowing for the fact that people become more religious as they get older); as people become better educated; the more people live in towns and cities; the higher their social class; and the greater the exposure to different ideas, interests and lifestyles through the media and travel.[25]

Decline in Moral Authority

Given that morals and rules about how to live the good life are central to an ethical salvationary religion like Catholicism, and since most Irish Catholics have been traditionally 'conventional, rigid and legalistic', it might be expected that they would be guided by the Church when deciding what is good and bad, and right and wrong behaviour. Certainly this seemed to be the case in 1974 when 86 per cent said that being a Catholic was very important to living a happy family life, and 70 per cent that it was very important to them being honest and sincere with others. Similarly, 73 per cent said that their religious principles always guided their behaviour in family life, while two-thirds said their religious principles guided their behaviour in their spare-time activities and in their occupational life.[26] These findings were a clear indication of a strong religious foundation to Irish society. Religion was integrated into everyday social life; it was not compartmentalised into specific occasions, times and places. The findings suggested, perhaps even more than the fact that 90 per cent of Catholics went to Mass on Sundays, that the Church's moral monopoly was still intact. They indicated that Irish Catholics listened to what the Church taught about the good life and endeavoured to embody these principles in the way they lived their lives.

An examination of recent survey data shows a major decline in the influence of the Church on the lives of Catholics and in its monopoly over Irish morality. Less than half (42 per cent) felt that the Church gave adequate answers to moral problems and the needs of the individual. Slightly more (49 per cent) felt that the Church gave adequate answers to social problems, while just over half (54 per cent) felt that it helped answer problems of family life (54 per cent).[27]

While it is recognised that the questions asked in these two surveys were not the same, the figures do suggest that when it comes to providing guidelines as to how to live a good life, the Catholic Church is increasingly seen as irrelevant, by Catholics themselves. This trend was verified by an opinion poll in 1996 which found that when it came to serious moral problems, 78 per cent of Catholics followed their own conscience rather than the teaching of the Church.[28]

To understand the reversal in the moral power of the Catholic Church in twenty years, it is necessary to realise that it was part of a wider process of rationalisation and differentiation. At one time, being a good person was easily equated with being a good Catholic. Over the next twenty years, particularly owing to the increasing influence of the media, rising educational standards, travel and becoming part of Europe, these quickly became separated. It was no longer necessary to have the symbolic blessing of the Church in order to be accepted as a good moral person. The moral field gradually became distinct from the religious field. In this process, being a good Catholic remained a significant, but no longer a necessary, way of attaining honour and respect. In other words, although the Catholic Church no longer has a monopoly in the field of morality, it is still a major player. Whereas the links between institutional Church teaching and the moral habitus used to be obvious and direct it has now become indirect. For example, within the new moral habitus, people may continue to practice humility and self-deprecation. They may continue to humour, please and put others first as a means of being considered a good person and attaining honour and respect. These strategies, although in many instances derived from Church teaching, have become increasingly separated from it at least at a conscious level.

Decline in the Institution

In the heyday of the Catholic Church in Ireland there were a priest, nun and brother in every corner of society. They presided over schools, hospitals and a wide variety of social welfare institutions from orphanages, homes and hostels to hospices and reform schools. Most important of all, they presided over Irish family homes. Like all good authority figures, their supervision and control persisted even in their absence. In the most subtle and yet penetrative form of power, the supervisory eye of the Church was internalised in the minds and hearts of Irish Catholics.[29] The authoritarian, superego figure of the father became replaced, with the aid of the mother, by the figure of the priest.[30] When it came to moral matters, what really counted was not so much 'what will father say?' as 'what would the priest think?'. But the maintenance of this moral control is dependent on having a reliable number of active, well-trained, vigilant religious personnel. Consequently, the decline in Catholic faith, practice and morals can be linked to the decline in the numbers of priests, nuns and brothers. The decline which began in the 1970s has become more dramatic in recent years.

Table 10.   Changes in Human Resources of the Catholic Church in Ireland,
1970–1995

	1970	1981	1995	Decrease 1970–1995	Percentage decrease 1970–1995
Diocesan Clergy	3,944	3,762	3,659	285	7.2%
Clerical Religious Orders	7,946	6,711	4,564	3,382	42.6%
Sisters	18,662	14,878	12,104	6,558	35.1%
Brothers	2,540	1,719	1,061	1,479	58.2%
Total	33,092	27,070	21,388	11,704	35.3%

Sources: Research and Development Commission, *Irish Priests and Religious 1970-1975*; Research and Development Commission, *Vocations Returns 1996*.

Between 1970 and 1995, the number of priests, nuns and brothers in Ireland decreased by over one-third (35 per cent). What is remarkable in this general decline is the difference between the fate of nuns and brothers compared with priests, particularly diocesan priests. While the number of nuns decreased by over one-third (35 per cent) and the number of brothers by over a half (58 per cent), the number of diocesan priests declined by only 7 per cent. If the present rate of decline continues, in twenty-five years time there will be fewer than fourteen thousand priests, nuns and brothers in Ireland. In fifty years, the number of religious will have declined by over 50 per cent.[31]

The decline in numbers is reflected in the decline in vocations. In the thirty years between 1966 and 1996, the number of vocations dropped from 1,409 to 111, a decrease of 92 per cent.

Table 11.   Changes in Numbers of Vocations to Religious Life, 1966,
1985 & 1996

	1966	1985	1996	Decrease 1966—1996	Percentage decrease 1966–1996
Diocesan Clergy	254	169	52	202	79.5%
Clerical Religious Orders	390	151	39	351	90.0%
Sisters	592	123	19	573	96.8%
Brothers	173	28	1	172	99.4%
Total	1,409	471	111	1,298	92.1%

Sources: Research and Development Commission, *Irish Priests and Religious 1970–1975*; Research and Development Commission, *Vocations Returns 1996*.

Again the decrease is most dramatic among nuns and brothers. There was only one vocation to the various orders of religious brothers in Ireland in 1996. This is remarkable given the long tradition of orders such as the Christian Brothers in Irish society. The drop in the number of female vocations is equally dramatic. Whereas there were nearly six hundred vocations to orders of religious sisters in 1966, thirty years later there were only nineteen. If the present trend continues, a year will soon come in which there are no new entrants to orders of nuns and brothers.

Another problem is that despite a rigorous selection procedure – only 40 per cent of applicants were taken in 1996 – there is still a high level of departures before ordination or final profession. More students are leaving than are beginning training. In 1995, 134 students for the religious life left before completing their training. This was twenty more than the number which entered that year. If we add in the 95 priests, nuns and brothers who left religious life when they were fully ordained or professed, then the number of departures is more than twice the number of entrants. Even more problematic is the high number of deaths. In 1995, there were 606 deaths. There is, then, a net annual loss of over 700 personnel through deaths and departures.[32]

The rapid decrease in numbers has had other implications. It has brought new interpretations of what it means to have a vocation and live a religious life. Convents and religious houses are regularly up for sale. The religious are being forced to abandon the large houses which set them apart, and to move into ordinary houses within the community. The aura of sacred difference, which came from being in but different from the community and which was at the heart of their symbolic power, is being eroded. In losing control of health, education and social welfare services, the Church is losing its source of cultural and political capital. It is also losing the symbolic capital which legitimated its moral monopoly. There is a danger that in years to come, instead of religious and clerical difference being seen as sacred, they will be seen as odd. The reality behind the image of religious life is that priests, nuns and brothers are becoming old and grey. The institutional Church is literally dying off.

But to understand the decline in the institution, it is necessary to go beyond the fall in numbers and understand the impact which an increasing age profile is having on the image and morale of the Church. It is not only that the gap between the average age of priests and members of the laity is growing, but there is a generation gap in the beliefs and attitudes of young and old priests. The majority of the religious personnel who occupy powerful positions were brought up and trained within a pre-Vatican II Church in which there was a legalistic adherence and deference to power. Debate and discussion about key issues such as the nature of the Church, faith, self and sexuality were quelled. Although Vatican II was about the Church in the modern world, it came too early to deal adequately with the growth of individualism and, later, postmodernism. The issue of individual conscience has been greater for members of the religious life than it has for members of the laity. Following one's own conscience was outside the language and practice of the authoritarian, legalistic religious houses and seminaries which were dominant up until the 1970s. Flannery argues that life in the institutional church was based on the systematic elimination of individuality and initiative. The most minute details of life were monitored and controlled. There was a strict timetable, and any deviation required the consent of the superior. He argues that these strictures had their roots in a particular language of theology and spirituality. The concept of God was one of a 'severe distant being, pure and undefiled, and not easy to approach.' At the same time, the spirituality of the Church was founded on establishing a conflict between the world and the spirit, between body and soul. The world was evil; humans were all sinners and this life was not important in itself, merely a preparation for eternity.[33] Such was the Church's monopoly over the meaning and interpretation of life, that there was, as Flannery argues, no significant difference between the mindset or *habitus* of those living in religious houses and those living in wider society.

One of the strengths of the form of religious life that was lived at that time was its harmony with the society around it. It too was very authoritarian, and it strongly promoted the value of self-denial, or self-abnegation as the spiritual books called it. This approach to life has, of course, strong roots in Christian teaching and tradition. Christ 'humbled himself and became obedient unto death'. 'Not my will, but yours be done,' were some of his final words.[34]

But while the denial of self was central to maintaining a one, true, universal and apostolic Church, it began to run into increasing contradictions with the culture of narcissism and the modern era of the ego.[35] The traditional Church soon became a fish out of water in a society saturated with media messages of self-development. The contradiction within the Church between an institution based on silenced, repressed egos and one based on self-revelation, debate and discussion began to emerge in the 1970s. It is manifested in the debate about individual conscience. The problem described by Flannery has not gone away. 'We were told that yes, a person's conscience is the ultimate arbiter. But that conscience needs to be informed. And one must inform it by finding out and obeying the teaching of the Church.'[36]

The contradiction between dogma and individual conscience is reflected in the conflict surrounding debate and discussion as a means of reaching consensus within a divinely inspired hierarchical institution. We live in an age when people are encouraged to leave entrenched positions and to come to the negotiating table to discuss differences and, hopefully, to reach a compromise, if not consensus. As Habermas points out, the notion of proceduralised popular sovereignty goes hand-in-hand with the notion of a decentred society.[37] The reality of the hierarchical institution of the Catholic Church is that it is highly centralised, is not based on popular sovereignty and, consequently, has had no need for establishing procedures for deliberation. What is the purpose of discussion within the Church when the Pope pronounces that, for example, women cannot become priests, priests cannot marry, and that contraception is intrinsically evil? The maintenance of dogmatic truth is central to the Church. A paedophile priest who commits the most horrific crimes against children can maintain his holy orders and even be forgiven, but a priest or theologian who challenges central tenets of Church doctrine will be excommunicated. The issue of what can be debated, when, where and by whom, was central to the conflict which emerged between Bishop Comiskey and Cardinal Daly on the issue of priestly celibacy. Bishop Comiskey's remarks that the Church, in light of the huge drop in priestly vocations, might have to consider a change in the celibacy rule, led to a public controversy with Cardinal Daly and a summons to Rome to explain himself.[38]

The low status of debate and discussion in the Church makes its teachings and pronouncements appear more fundamentalist. In the same way that the denial of self is in contradiction with the present era of the ego and the culture of narcissism, so fundamentalist pronouncements are in contradiction with a postmodern culture in which truth is seen not only as relative, but arbitrary. Truth is elusive, polymorphous, inward and subjective. Salvation in the post-modern world involves continually questioning accepted truths. If truth exists, it is a revolving process of deconstructing statements of truth. The task, so to speak, is not to keep the faith.[39]

The decline in the numbers of priests, nuns and brothers is linked to the Church being caught in a series of double-binds relating to individual conscience and fundamentalism. It tells individuals to follow their own conscience, but at the same time insists that it is the final arbiter of what is right and wrong. It encourages and listens to different points, but at the same time claims to provide the only true interpretation of the Natural Law. But perhaps the main contradiction on which the Catholic Church in Ireland has floundered, as it has elsewhere, is that some bishops, priests and brothers have not only failed to practice what they preach, but blatantly contravened it. It was these contraventions, founded on inherent contradictions concerning sexuality, which have had an enormous effect on the position of the Church in Irish society.

A comparison of newspaper headlines in 1996 with those of 1987 show clearly that while the number of stories about the Catholic Church did not change significantly, the number of stories about controversies and scandals in the Church increased dramatically (see Appendix). In 1987, there were no scandals concerning the personal sexual behaviour of priests and religious. In effect, there were only two stories during the year about the personal behaviour of priests. One had to do with a curate in Wexford not paying his taxes and the other concerned the appointment by a bishop of a parish priest against the wishes of the parishioners. There was little controversy and certainly no scandal within the Church. The ongoing dispute about the decision to build a new church in Rush in North Dublin against the wishes of some of the parishioners received widespread coverage. But it is an indication of the institutional strength of the Church that this was the only controversy which could be said to exist. Despite the attempts by the Church to see itself as the caring conscience of Irish society, there were more stories about the Church's statements on sexual moral issues than on issues to do with poverty, disadvantage and inequality. For example, during the year there was considerable coverage given to Church statements about AIDS, test tube babies, the Virgin Mary, and homosexuality. But there were only a handful of stories about the Church calling for a better deal for the poor. The largest amount of coverage concerned events within the Church. There were, for example, 33 stories about the death, retirement and appointment of bishops. The longest running story during the year concerned the appointment of a new Archbishop to Dublin after the death of Dr McNamara in April.

The type of stories being told about the Church in 1996 was quite different. What would have been considered unbelievable stories in 1987, had by then become commonplace. There were stories about: (*a*) a Donegal priest charged with child sex abuse; (*b*) victims complaining of a sexually abusive priest in Co. Wexford; (*c*) the jailing of a paedophile priest in Kilkenny; (*d*) the resignation of Bishop Wright in Scotland; (*e*) a file on sex abuse by Dublin priests being sent to the Director of Public Prosecutions; (*f*) a Brother walking free after child sex abuse charges were dropped; (*g*) two cases of Wexford priests charged with sexually assaulting young males and (*h*) a Dublin man telling of his abuse as a child by a priest. In contrast to 1987, when there were only two stories concerning celibacy or homosexuality, there were 34 different stories – one in six of the total – concerning the sexuality, celibacy and misconduct of clergy and religious. This does not include the eight stories which appeared in February around the time that the controversial Bishop Brendan Comiskey who, among other things, was accused of protecting a paedophile priest, returned to his diocese.

In making these comparisons it should be remembered that *The Irish Times* is a daily newspaper with a Protestant, Anglo-Irish tradition which is read mainly by urban middle-class, well-educated liberals. But nevertheless, in 1987, there was an institutional deference to the Church. Most of the stories covered appear to derive from Church sources. There were few investigative reports or feature articles criticising or commentating on the position of the Catholic Church in Ireland. The language and content changed dramatically over the next nine years. Not only is there in 1996 a series of controversial, negative stories being told about the Church, there is an ongoing debate about the position and role of the Church in Irish society and of the way it handles its own affairs. Suddenly, the Church has lost its sacredness and has become another interest group in civil society which is open to the same inspection as any other. But the reason why it has attracted so much attention is because for so long it spoke longest and loudest about the sacredness of marriage, the innocence of children and the need for strict sexual morality. This is not to deny, however, that the media have been pushing a secular, liberal agenda over the last thirty years.[40]

Although the number of sex scandals which have emerged in the last decade may not have been so large in absolute terms, they were a radical rupture in what for two hundred years had appeared to have been a seamless, uniform and total commitment by the clergy to the teachings of the Church. It was not so much that the members of the clergy were shown to be guilty of the sins of promiscuity, adultery, fornication, paedophilia, rape and buggery, but that for centuries they had been castigating these contraventions of the Natural Law not just as intrinsically evil, but as the greatest of sins. A Church which emphasises the necessity to confess sins had enormous difficulty in confessing its own sins. This inability, as Fahey pointed out, stood in contrast to the state. 'The Catholic Church teaches that penitential renewal involves confession, contrition, penance and a firm purpose of amendment. In responding to the Smyth affair, the state has provided all those things, including penance, in full television colour. . . . The church, by comparison, has dithered in half-measures.'[41] There is still a reluctance to see the sins which were committed as institutional. Instead there has been willingness to blame the individuals concerned. There was equally a delay and a reluctance in seeking forgiveness and making atonement to the victims. This relates to perhaps the biggest contradiction: between the Church representing itself as the people of Christ and at the same time operating as bureaucratic, legal and financial institution determined to maintain its power. The divine, authoritarian institution has had difficulty in returning to its frail, humble, human roots.

The foundation of the moral monopoly of the Roman Catholic Church in Ireland over the last two hundred years was discipline. Bishops, priests, nuns and brothers were predictable. There might have been character differences and perhaps weaknesses, but there was a uniformity to what they did, what they said, where they went, the way they dressed and, in general, the way they represented the Church. What happened in the case of Bishop Eamon Casey was that, for the first time in a long time, this uniformity was shattered. It was not that he drank, drove fast cars or fancied women. The Church was big and strong enough to deal with such failures and there was a moral tradition within the media of not touching these stories. But when it emerged that he had had an affair with a young American divorcee, that she had given birth to a boy, and that he had had a son for sixteen years, the media broke the silence. It was no coincidence that the way the Church dealt with Bishop Casey was to silence him and banish him from the country. This was the same strategy which had been used to deal with sex. Whether in the seminary, the classroom, or the home, sex could not be talked about. Now, in the era of the ego, in the new age of information and communication, and at a time when there is an expectation and a demand to talk, the Church could not allow a priest, let alone a bishop, to be heard to talk about sex, desire, passion, contraception, pro-creation, becoming a father and acting as a father. The Church which for so long had insisted on confession and had extracted the most exact details concerning the nature of sexual sin, was not itself able to confess. Instead of the Church being able to talk openly and honestly about the problems with celibacy and engaging in critical self-reflection about the way in which it has talked and taught about sex, there was a denial of what had happened, especially its significance, and an attempt to discredit the individuals involved. The fact that Bishop Casey was not allowed to confess stood in stark contrast, for example, with the way a government minister Emmet Stagg and a businessman Ben Dunne confessed quickly and openly to the media about their sins. It is important to recognise in this process that it is the media which now extracts public confessions, since it is they who now dominate the field of morality.

The inability of the Church to develop a new and appropriate language to talk about what had happened and what was continuing to happen about sex, is linked to its having talked in a unified, Roman way for over a hundred and fifty years. Much was said informally but whatever was said publicly had to fit in with the one true universal statements from Rome. It was not possible for the Church to develop a new alternative language; to talk differently about itself, about celibacy and about sexuality.

The difficulty in talking about and dealing with sex in the Church as opposed to in society reached a peak with the Fr Brendan Smyth affair.[42] At one level this was a betrayal of trust and the exploitation and rape of innocent children. But it was also an indication of how the Church's monopoly on sexual morality gave rise to a situation in which children were ushered into rooms by nuns to be abused by a priest, and who then had no competence, means or resources to be able to announce to themselves or others what had happened. The Church itself had no language to talk about let alone critically reflect about the unmentionable and the unthinkable. The Church is caught in a contradiction between ethics and politics. The interest in maintaining its position as the final arbiter of the Natural Law means that children have to be taught what is sexually right and wrong. The emphasis is on teaching them what *should* happen rather than enabling them to debate and discuss what *is* happening.

Not only was the sacred image of the Church as the protector of innocence shattered, but the Church was unable to engage in critical self-reflection in the public sphere about homosexuality within the Church, about the repression of desire, or about the strategic silencing of sexuality. It is no coincidence that when such a debate did take place it quickly ran into the contradiction that debate and discussion as a basis for creating changes is hindered by the Church being a divine rather than a democratic institution.

While there were many other scandals which have emerged about the Church in the last ten years, the Bishop Casey and the Fr Smyth affairs did the most damage.[43] An opinion poll in 1995 showed that 65 per cent felt that Bishop Casey affair and 59 per cent that the Smyth affair 'undermines the position of parents in giving advice to their children on moral and social attitudes.' The poll also found that 42 per cent of Catholics had lost some respect for the Church because of the revelations, while 45 per cent of priests thought that teaching on moral issues had been undermined.[44] But the decline in the institutional church is indicated not only by the fall in numbers and the decreases in levels of belief and practice, but also in the language with which the Church now speaks of itself and its role in Irish society. In a speech given at the 1997 Merriman Summer School, Bishop Willie Walsh of Killaloe said that the scandals involving priests and religious had been devastating for the Church. He linked these to the significant decrease in religious practice and to the fact that many Catholics were ignoring the Church's teaching on sexual morality. He believed that the Catholic Church was, as a result, weaker as an institution, but a more humble and honest church which recognises its own sinfulness. He said that 'a weaker church is a less oppressive church and the "strong" church of 1920s to the 1960s was at times quite oppressive.'[45] This is a very different speech for a bishop and a very different language to describe the Catholic Church. Traditionally not only has the Church been blameless, but it has blamed everyone else for the ills of society. For example, in an interview in June 1994, the Bishop of Meath blamed the Labour Party for trying to take the church out of Irish education; a Dublin 4 mentality for promoting a liberal agenda on socio-sexual issues; the US and Europe for a new form of cultural imperialism; and the media for looking for scandal involving the church.[46]

The Decline in the Political Field

One of the key arguments in this book is that moral monopoly of the Catholic Church in Ireland was founded not just on its monopoly of the religious field, but also on its being a major player in many other social fields. Primary among these was the political field. The Church's ability to preside within the political field was crucial to its monopoly on morality. In other words, not only did the Catholic Church develop a monopoly on the way Irish people were spiritual and moral, it also had considerable influence on the state, political parties, politicians and the electorate. This enabled the Church to have considerable influence in the formation and acceptance of the Irish Constitution, the type of referenda which have been proposed and voted on, and the type of social and cultural legislation which the Dáil has passed.

As Keogh has argued, the basis of Church-state relations in Ireland after 1922 was an informal consensus among bishops, priests and politicians about the nature of Irish society and what Irish people needed. Within the Catholic nationalist mindset, there was a similar vision of Irish society.[47] This informal consensus began to break down in the 1970s and is now fast disappearing. In the 1980s it could be said that in the struggle to know, understand and represent the minds and hearts of the Irish people, the Church won out over the state and the main political parties. Given the success of the referenda on abortion (1983) and divorce (1986), the Church could have rightly claimed that it still represented the moral conscience of Irish society. Indeed in the newly emerging pluralist society of Ireland in Europe, this was the role the Hierarchy had identified for itself.[48] However, in the last ten years there is evidence that the Church is no longer fulfilling this function, even though it is still operating within an almost homogeneous Catholic society. The two main issues on which Irish voters clearly went against the teachings of the Church were, again, abortion and divorce. Following the famous 'X' case in 1992 when a fourteen year old girl who had become pregnant through sexual molestation was prevented travelling to Britain for an abortion, the Supreme Court ruled that abortion was lawful in certain circumstances. In a subsequent referendum in November, the electorate rejected the substantive clause which would have permitted abortion when there was an illness or disorder of the mother which gave rise to a real and substantial risk to her health. However, the electorate voted in favour of the right to travel to another country to have an abortion and to the right to information about abortion services outside Ireland.[49]

The other major issue on which Irish Catholics did not follow the teaching of the Church was in the second referendum on divorce in 1995. As in previous referenda, much of the argument made in the media against divorce was produced by members of the Catholic laity who belonged to the different anti-divorce groups. As had happened in previous referenda, the Irish Conference of Bishops issued a statement.[50] But, as also happened in previous referenda, individual bishops spoke differently. Archbishop Connell emphasised that the Catholic principle of the sacredness of marriage could not be forsaken for pragmatic ends. He stated that a Catholic must inform his or her conscience according to the teaching of the Church as put forward by the Bishops. Towards the end of the campaign Bishop Flynn, the Hierarchy's spokesman, declared that the Church would refuse all the sacraments, including the last rites, to people who had divorced and remarried. It was later revealed that this declaration followed on from a letter issued by the Vatican's Congregation for the Doctrine of the Faith which had stated categorically that divorced and remarried people whose first marriages had not been annulled by the Church could not receive Holy Communion. But these pronouncements stood in contrast to Bishop Walsh's statement that he might repeat the pro-divorce vote he made in the previous referendum. The result of the referendum was extremely close; 50.3 per cent voting in favour with 49.7 per cent voting against. A survey carried out on the day of the referendum showed that support for divorce was strongest among Dubliners (64 per cent) and 18–34 year olds (66 per cent).[51]

But it has not only been in constitutional referenda that Catholic Church teaching has been ignored. Successive governments have brought in legislation which does not correspond to the concept of good Catholic law for good Catholic people. In 1993, legislation was passed legalising homosexuality. The necessity for such legislation had arisen from a ruling from a judgement from the European Court of Human Rights, which had insisted on the decriminalisation of homosexual acts between consenting adults. The final bill passed defined adults in this instance to be 17 years old, which made the piece of legislation one of the more liberal in Europe. A statement issued by the Irish Conference of Bishops noted:

This teaching of the Church is independent of State law. No change in State law can change the moral law. New civil laws cannot make what is wrong right. Laws relating to homosexuality, like other laws which bear on moral issues, should not be seen in terms of the State's upholding or not upholding Church teaching.

The Church does not expect that acts which are sinful should, by that very fact, be made criminal offences. All such laws bearing on moral issues must be assessed in the light of the way in which they contribute or fail to contribute to the common good of society.[52]

The reasons for the decline in influence of the Catholic Church in the political field centre on four main processes. The first is the ongoing separation and differentiation of the religious from the political field, and follows the general trend in Western European society. Whereas religion, morality and law used to be closely intertwined, they have gradually separated into distinct social fields. The second process involves the Church not having a clear, unified vision of the future of Irish society. The Church is obviously against the 'permissive' society. It is for the common good and against a liberal, pluralist society in which the rights and interests of minorities threaten the common good. But whereas it is definite about the common good in relation to sexual morality, it is vague about political common good. As Peillon has pointed out, the Church speaks in many different languages on social issues and is ambivalent about capitalism, the state and urban society.[53] Other items which might be added to this list are Europe and environmental issues.[54] In recent years, the work of agencies such as the Conference of Religious in Ireland in promoting social equality, the Commission for Justice and Peace in promoting social justice, and *Trocaire* in promoting Third World development, have indicated to some commentators that the Church has become a 'left-of-centre' social critic on behalf of the poor, deprived and those oppressed and vulnerable as a result of social and economic change.'[55] However, as Nic Ghiolla Phádraig points out, one of the problems the Church has in dealing with social inequality is that it is itself an elitist, hierarchical institution. She argues that it has tended in the past to legitimate, if not directly reproduce, inequality and that its main goal has been maintaining social stability through a legitimisation of the state.[56] Eipper goes further and argues that while the Church has seen itself as the guardian of the common interests and values of both rulers and ruled, it has functioned to reproduce the interests of a dominant bourgeois class.[57]

The decline of the Church's influence in the political field is related to two other processes. The first is the absence of representatives of religious life in debate and discussion in the public sphere, specifically within the media. While lay groups have produced some outstanding speakers, such as William Binchy who has led the pro-Catholic position in the abortion and divorce referendums, the contribution of priests and religious to debate and discussion on social and political issues has been insignificant. The Church still speaks and teaches from a distance. The second process is that is no longer necessary for many politicians to be seen to be involved with members of the clergy and to have them symbolically legitimate their political position. In comparison with thirty years ago, politicians and clergy no longer mix in the same social circles. The diminishing presence of priests and bishops in the elite, inner circles of Irish society has also contributed to the decline of the Church's influence in the political field. De Valera may, as Keogh argues, been an *à la carte* Catholic, but he mixed regularly in clerical company. Moreover, he sought the symbolic legitimation of the Church for himself, his party and his government. Irish politicians no longer seek this symbolic legitimisation, or at least not to the same extent. De Valera was quite willing to bend down and kiss a bishop's ring and to be photographed doing so. This is not the case today among most Irish politicians. The kissing of bishop's rings by Catholic politicians has ceased to be politically correct. Catholic politicians used not to say publicly things which were contrary or offensive to the Church. But now it is a regular occurrence. For example, the bill for homosexuality included a provision to decrease the penalties for prostitution. During the debate Austin Deasy, a rural Fine Gael deputy, made the following argument for the legalisation of prostitution:

It is, after all, the oldest profession in the world, older than politics. We don't want members of the Oireachtas emerging from such premises if they are illegal. We would like to see members of the Oireachtas doing things within the law.[58]

Another indication of the decline in the Church's influence in the political field was the announcement in 1996 by the Minister for Finance Ruairí Quinn, that Ireland was a 'post-Catholic, pluralist republic'. The implication that the Church had little influence in the social field, let alone the political field, was attacked by Archbishop Connell.[59] But what was remarkable was the Minister's ability and willingness to make the statement. It could be argued that in a rapidly changing political field, attacking rather than ignoring or defending the Church has become a new strategy by politicians to attain political capital. Finally, during the Divorce Referendum, Proinsias De Rossa, the Minister for Social Welfare, became embroiled in a clash with the Archbishop of Cashel, Dr Clifford about the statistics for marriage breakdown north and south of the border. As one commentator put it:

It would have been unthinkable even ten years ago for a left-wing minister in a Fine Gael-led coalition to call a Catholic Archbishop a liar, and get away with it – without either any Fine Gaeler repudiating his remark or the other bishops rallying in outrage in their colleague's defence.[60]

Decline in the Educational Field

The dominance of the Catholic Church in the educational field has been central to preventing a more rapid decline in its position in Irish society. Having direct access to successive generations of young people and to the formation of their religious and social personalities has helped maintain its dominance in the religious field and stem the flow of secularisation. The Church's dominance in education has been sustained by the reluctance of the state to change the existing system, particularly in relation to the way schools are funded and managed. The 1995 White Paper on Education proposed some minor changes in relation to the management structure of primary schools, but none in relation to secondary schools.[61] The White Paper concluded that the scope for the state introducing new legislation is restricted, given that the Constitution recognises the rights and duties of parents as the primary and natural educators. The Constitution also recognises property rights (the vast majority of schools are owned by the Catholic Church), and the rights of religious denominations to manage their own affairs.[62] The White Paper recognised that there may be a conflict between the articles of the Constitution in that, on the one hand, the Constitution prohibits discrimination on the grounds of religion and, on the other, recognises the rights of denominational schools to preserve their particular ethos. In effect, this last issue was resolved when the Supreme Court found that a proposed Government Bill prohibiting denominational schools from discriminating against teachers on the grounds of their religious beliefs and values was not constitutional.[63] The special position of the Catholic Church in Irish education is then enshrined in various articles of the Constitution, so unless there is a new Constitution, it is unlikely that the special position of the Catholic Church and other religious denominations in the educational field will be eroded in the near future.

In a social field such as education, struggles are continually taking place between the different players or organisations as they attempt to maintain or improve their position. The Church has been involved in a number of struggles, particularly with the state, over the past decade. These have included, for example, the establishment of multidenominational National Schools and the appointment of chaplains to non-denominational secondary schools. The longest running struggle concerned the attempt by the state to build a Community College (over which the Church would have less influence) instead of a Community School on a site which the Church owned.[64] It is an indication of the Church's strong position in the field that most of the struggles have been minor.

Although the Church has lost little ground in the funding and the control of schools, it has lost some ground in its control over the curriculum. The Church may have been able to maintain the religious ethos of its schools, but it has not been able to prevent an erosion of the religious atmosphere. Religious studies has become a recognised subject for the Leaving Certificate, but this reflects the decline of teaching religion as non-examination subject. The competitive ethos of the Leaving Certificate and the points system for entry to third level education dominate the atmosphere of all secondary schools.[65] Another issue on which the Church has ceded territory is in relation to teaching children about sex. The *Stay Safe Programme* which was set up in 1989 to help prevent child abuse, particularly sex abuse, is now operating in the majority of primary schools.

Although the Programme has been generally supported by the Church, it is a direct challenge to its moral teaching, in that the programme tends to invest the decision as to what is right and wrong, what are good or bad feelings, with the child rather than with parents, priests or teachers. This overrides the position of the Church as the final arbiter of what is right and wrong in sexual morality. Similarly, the Church has given support to the *Relationships and Sexuality Education* Programme which commenced in 1997. The attempt by the Church to have the programme taught within existing religion classes failed. Instead it was agreed by the state that there would be no specific curriculum, but rather a set of guidelines and resource materials. The content of the programme was to be worked out by the parents, the teachers and the school management in accordance with the ethos of each particular school. But in the guidelines for the programme issues, areas of sexuality are covered which Church teaching designates not just as morally wrong but as intrinsically evil. The difficulty for the Church is that it may have to stand by while discussion takes place and advice and information are given on such issues as pre-marital sex, contraception and homosexuality.

The main problem facing the Church in its struggle to maintain its influence in the educational field is the decline in the numbers of priests and religious. As discussed earlier, the decline in numbers has been largest among orders of religious sisters and brothers. Over the past 150 years they have been the linchpin of Catholic education. The proportion of religious as full-time teachers in secondary schools fell from 48 per cent in 1965 to 9 per cent in 1991.[66] As Nic Ghiolla Phádraig points out, the decline has occurred at a time when there has been a dramatic increase in numbers in the school system because of an increase in the birth-rate and free second level education.[67] Although Catholic schools may still be able to insist that teachers practise their religion and adhere to the moral code of the Church, the day-to-day religious ethos of the school is being left to lay teachers and the one or two nuns, brothers or priests who manage the school. The absence of religious teachers undermines the religious habitus in the schools. Nuns and brothers are no longer there as authority figures and as symbols of the Catholic Church. Consequently, it is no longer necessary for lay teachers to embody the language and practice of the Church as a means of gaining the honour and respect of others and of gaining recognition and promotion. Being religious has become less significant and necessary as a strategy employed by teachers to gain the cultural and symbolic capital needed to attain and maintain their social position.

Decline in the Health Field

The Catholic Church has had enormous influence in the health field in modern Ireland. Orders of religious sisters were responsible for establishing and running a Catholic health care service over the last two hundred years. Many of Ireland's hospitals, nursing homes, homes for the disabled and hospices are still owned and run by nuns and brothers. Twenty-six of the 63 hospitals in the Republic are Catholic voluntary hospitals. The ownership and control of hospitals and the representation of Catholic religious on the boards of public hospitals has meant that the Church has been able to exert considerable influence on the way medicine is practised, written and talked about; on the teaching, training and appointment of doctors and nurses; and over hospital ethics and the type of medical procedures available to patients.

Many struggles over the past ten years have demonstrated the ongoing conflicts and struggles between the Church and other organisations or players in the health field. With some exceptions, the Church has been successful in delaying or preventing procedures such as sterilisation, artificial fertilisation and amniocentesis from being introduced not only in Catholic voluntary hospitals, but in public hospitals run by the Regional Health Boards. But the tide is turning and there is increasing evidence of politicians, doctors and the state taking a stance against the Church. An example of the changed climate in the field of health was the controversy regarding the provision of a vasectomy clinic in Letterkenny General Hospital. The clinic opened on 14 March 1997, but was picketed by members of the Pro-Life Campaign and Family Solidarity, and by two consultant doctors who worked at the hospital. The service was suspended by the Health Board on 20 March. In a homily on Easter Saturday, 29 March, Bishop Boyce of Raphoe said that 'nobody has the right to harm, to prevent or destroy the life or the ability of producing life with which we are endowed'. He continued by saying that 'directly intended mutilation of our bodies such as amputation or sterilisation is against the moral law and is a rejection of God's gift of life.'[68] The Taoiseach, John Bruton regretted the suspension of the vasectomy services and said such a clinic would be provided in the area, if not in Letterkenny then somewhere else.[69] Ten days later the Health Board voted to reopen the clinic.

However, the main area in which the Church lost control was in the area of the promotion of artificial contraception. The fear of an AIDS epidemic led the Health Promotion Unit in the Department of Health to broadcast a series of advertisements on radio and television which promoted safe sex through the use of condoms. The orientation of the advertisements was towards people engaging in sexual intercourse outside of marriage.

Seven different advertisements were produced, each of them based on a presenter giving a blatant message straight to camera about the need to wear condoms. There was never any mention of alternative forms of protection, such as abstaining from sex outside marriage. For example, a mother of a person with AIDS says 'I urge all mothers to talk to their children about safer sex and I ask them to please, please tell your children to use a condom if they are having sex.'[70]

Tied in with this loss of symbolic power and the ability to limit and control what is said within the field of health, is the decline in vocations and the ability to put nuns and brothers in important positions within the various health organisations run by the Church. Again, as in the educational field, there are fewer doctors and nurses thinking and acting automatically within a Catholic moral framework when it comes to medical decisions. The coded remarks and reminders, together with the supervisory eye of priests, nuns and brothers, have been removed. It may well be that some lay doctors and nurses will turn out to be 'more Catholic than the priests, nuns or brothers'. On the other hand, it may turn out that the changing structure of Catholic-run religious organisations is such that once the fear of not complying with or deferring to Catholic authority is removed, these hospitals and homes will become Catholic only in name.

Decline in Social Welfare

On her last day as President of Ireland, Mary Robinson opened a social housing project which had been developed by the Presentation Sisters.[71] Sr Stanislaus Kennedy, Director of Focus Ireland and a well-known activist and spokeswoman on poverty and homelessness, emphasised the contribution of the nuns to Irish society. The last function of Mary Robinson as President was to legitimate symbolically, as she had done for thousands of other projects, the work being done by nuns and the Church. Some years earlier, this would have been just another good story told about the work of the nuns in looking after the vulnerable and disadvantaged. But times have changed in Ireland, and the story was now being told in the context of a series of negative stories which had emerged in the previous five years. Most of these centred on the abuse of children, usually from deprived backgrounds, who ended up in the care of religious. These stories have done most to erode the symbolic power of the Church in the last decade. The series of scandals, pursued and developed by the media, has tainted the role as the Church as carer, and portrayed it instead as an abuser. The scandals had key common ingredients. They involved religious orders; they centred on sexuality and moral failure; and they pertained to maintaining the traditional nuclear family as the basis of Irish society.

In 1993 a major debate took place in the media and the public sphere about women, the Catholic Church, nuns and immorality. The debate was sparked by the decision of Sisters of Our Lady of Charity in Drumcondra in Dublin to sell off a graveyard to pay their debts. The graveyard contained the bodies of 133 abandoned women who had worked in the convent laundry. Some were unmarried mothers rejected by the family and community in which they lived. Some were women who had become destitute through mental illness or alcoholism. Others were girls who were considered to be wild.[72] The debate and the media coverage enabled the story of these 'fallen' women, some of whom lived to tell the tale, to be told differently. It led to critical debate and self-reflection inside and outside of the Church about the position of the Catholic Church in Irish society, the position of women, and the nature and function of religious sisters. Bringing to the surface the bodies of the dead women had the unintended consequence of bringing to the surface a whole series of stories about the experiences of people who had lived their lives in institutions run by the Church. The Church became exposed in a different light. As the following stories show, however, the Church did not willingly engage in a critical reflection about its power; rather it was forced to do this by some other power, in this case the media.

Madonna House was a residential home for disadvantaged children operated by the Sisters of Charity. Fifteen former residents made specific allegations of assault to the police and the Eastern Health Board against a maintenance man who worked at the home. An inquiry was set up by the Sisters of Charity. The case received widespread publicity and was subject of numerous stories in the media. When the report was finally released – but not published in full – some of the comments on the work of the Sisters of Charity and the way they managed Madonna House were very negative. The social affairs correspondent of the *The Irish Times* asked: 'And what of the Sisters of Charity? Did they know that children were physically assaulted, deprived of food and made to wear pyjamas during the day.' The editorial the same day criticised the report 'for what it does not say about the sexual abuse of the children' in the House, and the 'omission of any detailed analysis of the stewardship of the Sisters of Charity.'[73]

The Goldenbridge controversy centred on a television documentary 'Dear Daughter' which was shown in February, 1996. It portrayed life in a Dublin orphanage run by the Sisters of Mercy (the largest order in Ireland) in the 1950s and 1960s as brutal and uncaring. It was argued that the authoritarian regime of discipline and punishment in orphanages was institutionalised in the Mercy Order.[74] The power of the media to influence the perception and understanding of nuns and the Catholic Church in the field of Irish welfare was evident. The documentary also indicated how the perception and understanding of nuns and the Church had changed in RTÉ. It is unlikely that such a programme would have been broadcast ten years previously, particularly since it took such a negative, one-sided view. It indicated that there was a change within RTÉ regarding stories about the Church. In the changed climate of opinion, it was not only permissible to produce programmes critical of the Church, it became a mechanism of increasing one's symbolic capital. It was as if it was open-season on the nuns and the Church.

The response of the Mercy nuns was as dramatic as the documentary. The Provincial of the Congregation appeared on the Kenny Live Show (a Saturday night television chat show), to explain the background to the orphanage and to apologise to those who at any time or place in the care of Sisters of Mercy, had been hurt or harshly treated. The Order placed advertisements repeating this message in the Sunday newspapers. It established a confidential telephone hotline to respond to victims.

Two weeks after the documentary the nuns released, through a media consultant, a list of names of former pupils willing to tell positive stories about their childhood in Mercy orphanages.[75] This led to some criticism of the way the documentary had been built up by the media in the week prior to being broadcast to increase both the number of viewers and secondary coverage in the print media. There was also criticism of how the narrative structure of the documentary was based on a simplistic 'goodies and baddies' format.[76] But at this stage not only had the story been told, but the reputation of the Mercy nuns as the unsung, caring heroes of Irish society had been badly damaged.

The story of Goldenbridge is really a story of the power of the media in Irish society and how it has become a dominant player in every social field. It demonstrates the ability of the media, particularly television, to change the language and the stories about nuns and the Church and thereby to shatter the myth which had been established. The ongoing, unquestioned, predisposition through which nuns were perceived, known and understood was broken. The documentary reflected the demise of the Church's ability to have only good stories told about itself. The process of criticism within the media was a sign of entering a new era when previously untold stories could begin to be told. The telling of the Goldenbridge story was part of a process of revealing that which was once hidden and silent. The documentary was part of process through which the myth was broken that the family is a sacred haven and the orphanage is a safe refuge for innocent deprived children of sacred havens. But although the state was directly involved in all of these stories – in that it was state agencies which referred cases to the institutions involved – the stories were told not against the state, but the Church. It would appear that the backlog of stories had built up so much that once the climate changed, the lid was suddenly lifted, and what had remained private and individual quickly became public.

A final story which damaged the symbolic power of the Church concerned the export of babies for adoption, primarily in the United States.[77] These babies were mainly born to unmarried mothers. The export process was operated by nuns. It was sanctioned by the Archbishop of Dublin and administered by the Department of External Affairs. The export of babies for adoption arose because the idea of an unmarried mother looking after her child was outside the realms of morality as set down by the Church and embodied by the laity. The head of the Catholic Social Welfare Bureau described single mothers as 'fallen women' and 'grave sinners' whose children were the victims of 'wickedness'.[78] The story reveals the collusion between the state and the Church and the determination of both institutions to create a secret Irish solution to breakdowns in Catholic morality. Instead of women being exported for abortion – the present solution – their babies were exported for adoption. Such was the Church's moral monopoly in the 1950s and such was the state's willingness to acquiesce in this, that the Archbishop of Dublin was able to lay down strict guidelines which demanded that the adopting parents not only be Catholic, but well-off and be willing to guarantee that the baby be brought up as a Catholic, be sent to a Catholic school and, if it arose, to a Catholic university.[79]

But the story was told only as part of a process of critical reflection about the Catholic Church's monopoly on morality and its control over women and their social welfare. Its emergence into the public sphere in 1996 led to further debate about the Church, the state and patriarchal society limiting and controlling women's sexuality and fertility. It raised further questions about the position of women in Irish society, the nature of the Irish family, and the right of access to contraception and abortion. In much of this debate, the Church was under direct or indirect attack.

The extent to which the Church is still a major player in the field of social welfare is in doubt. Peillon maintains that the Church still has control over a range of social services in which it has historically played a central part.[80] Provision of these services, he argues, enables to the Church to penetrate not just into the private sphere of families, but creates a position for it in civil society outside of the religious field. However, the Kilkenny Incest Inquiry gave a good insight into the structure of the field of social work and the habitus of the people involved. The report makes no mention of Church or religious personnel being directly involved in the case.[81] The social worker has taken over much of the power previously held by the priest. The power the priest once had to knock unannounced and gain entry to private homes and then to ask mothers and fathers personal questions about the way they were rearing their children, has now transferred to the social workers. The supervision and control of what is permissible for parents to say and do with their children, particularly in relation to what fathers can and cannot do with their daughters, has moved from the Church to the state.

Decline in the Media

Until 1960s, there was a homology between the way bishops and priests viewed and understood the world and the way the world was portrayed in the media. Indeed, such was the level of symbolic domination that when a commission was established in the 1958 to look into the development of a national television station in Ireland, not only the Vatican but the Pope himself welcomed and took a personal interest in the project. Pope Pius XII believed that 'practically all broadcasting and television systems everywhere were under the control of groups who, at best, were not greatly concerned about moral issues.'[82] He felt that the influence of radio and television had been particularly bad in traditionally Catholic countries. However, the Pope felt that because of its geographical position, Irish television would have the potential to broadcast the Christian message to both sides of the Atlantic. De Valera who was Taoiseach when Irish television began broadcasting in 1961 and who had a very Catholic view of the world, was not as optimistic as the Pope. He likened television and radio to atomic energy – they could be used for incalculable good but could also do irreparable harm. He felt that television 'can lead through demoralisation to decadence and disillusion.' He went on to argue that competition to give the people what they want often led to bad taste and lower standards.[83] In retrospect, de Valera probably had less hope but a better vision of the future than did Pope Pius XII. Four years after the television station opened, an incident occurred which became legendary in the history of Irish broadcasting and which indicated how the language of television with its emphasis on being sexy, exciting and entertaining was fundamentally at odds with that of the Church.

The incident took place on the *Late, Late Show* which was hosted by Gay Byrne, and became known as the episode of 'The Bishop and the Nightie'. As part of the programme, husbands and wives were asked what they knew about each other. One woman was asked what colour nightie she had worn on her wedding night and when she said she could not recall and that perhaps she had not worn any, there was laughter and a round of applause. Bishop Tom Ryan had been watching the programme and was infuriated by this. He sent a telegram to RTÉ saying he was disgusted, and the following day gave a sermon on the episode and the show. The Sunday newspapers covered the incident in full, and it became a major issue of debate in the public sphere. The incident attained mythical status for many reasons. It was, as Kenny argues, an announcement that honeymoon nights were not just about bridal bouquets and perfumed lingeries, but fundamentally about something more primitive, sex. What could not be countenanced in thought, word or deed had been announced. The bishop in his protest could not even announce it and said 'Everybody will know what I am referring to'. As much as the woman's revelation was a spontaneous public expression of self and pleasure which matched a new era in Irish social life, so too did the spontaneous disgust of the bishop at the reference to sex match the old era. A woman had confessed her sexual secrets to a man, but Gay Byrne was no priest and the television was no dark confessional.[84]

The 'bishop and the nightie' episode was an indication of how the Church's interpretation and control of the Irish social life was being undermined by the media. The state had led the way in the late 1950s not only by developing television, but developing an economic policy based on economic growth and a consumer society. Moreover, the development of a consumer society was intrinsically linked to the penetration of the family by television and the creation of demand through advertising. The arrival of television brought a new symbolic structure, habitus and practice to Irish homes. The alternative conceptions of self to which filmgoers had been exposed on an occasional basis, now began to broadcast nightly directly into people's homes. The language, symbols and lifestyles portrayed in programmes imported from the United States and Britain were incompatible with the way the Catholic Church represented the world. Television, radio and the media in general encouraged self-realisation and self-expression while the message of the Church was essentially of self-abnegation or denial.[85] It was not just radio and television. For over one hundred years, religious magazines such as *The Irish Messenger of the Sacred Heart* had been received into Irish homes. From the 1960s these began at first to co-exist with, but gradually to be replaced by women's and teenagers' magazines.[86] Magazines providing knowledge and information about the Catholic Church began to replaced by glossy magazines promoting consumerism, pleasure, sex and self-expression.

Within the public sphere, the media gave publicity to intellectuals who were developing a new language, alternative to that of the Church, which people appropriated to read and interpret their lives. The language of these writers, doctors, psychologists, educationalists and programme makers was often at variance with the Church's language. In other words, the very language through which issues were discussed in the public sphere began to change through the media. Moreover, the nature of the discourse within the media changed from the imparting of knowledge and information to a greater emphasis on dialogue, debate and discussion. What was emphasised in this approach was that nobody had a monopoly on knowledge or truth and that there were different arguments and positions which had to be recognised and heard. But it is important to recognise that this was not the end of symbolic domination. What was happening was that the symbolic domination of the Church in the public sphere was being replaced by the symbolic domination of the media. The knowledge produced about social life and the way of reading and interpreting it and debating it in the public sphere shifted from bishops, priests and theologians to journalists, commentators, producers and spin-doctors.

The third factor was that the type of person who sought and gained access to the media, received publicity and contributed to debate in the public sphere tended to be more self-confident and extravert and skilled in speaking in the media's preferred format – keeping their sound-bites simple, short and sexy. Furthermore, a shift took place in the nature of symbolic power. It used to be that people who were close to the centre of religious power, who led spiritual and ethical lives, were those who not only had the most prestige, but were given the widest audience. As the media grew, there was a shift in the nature of social prestige. Increasingly, it was those who appeared in the media who attained prestige.

The final factor in the decline of the Catholic Church in the public sphere was the direct challenge by the media to the authority of the Church. With the growth of the media in the 1960s and 1970s there was still a respect for the sacred authority of the Church. Slowly with the development of the media's own language and form of discourse, there was a direct questioning of the Church's stance on social and moral issues. The debates on contraception, abortion and divorce gave voice to a developing social movement which publicly challenged the Church in newspapers and on radio and television. The questioning and challenging of the Church's authority reached a peak when the media revealed the scandals of religious life which in form and content were a direct challenge to the Church.

The central interest in the public sphere is the dissemination of knowledge and information across rather than within, particular social fields. Groups and individuals compete to have their ideas and interests recognised and accepted as public knowledge. According to the theory of civil society, the public sphere is founded on a competitive symbolic struggle in which debate and discussion is based on the strength of the reasoned arguments of private individuals. If individuals come to debate and discussion in the public sphere not so much as private individuals but as representatives of groups pursuing specific interests, rather than engaging in reasoned debate with the intention of reaching a consensus, then the public sphere and civil society are undermined. Looking at public debate and discussion in terms of a sphere, it is realised that it is always groups and individuals with already accumulated capital who dominate the language and the content of the debate. What has characterised the Irish public sphere in the last thirty years is the decline of the dominance of the Catholic Church and the rise of the media. One of the reasons for the decline in the Church's influence in the public sphere is its inability to produce clerical and lay intellectuals who are able to speak within the language of the media.

The problem which the Catholic Church faces in contributing to debate in the public sphere is that it is a hierarchical institution which claims to be divinely ordained. Priests and members of the laity can contribute to debate and discussion as long as they do not claim to speak on behalf of the Church. The authority of the Catholic Church necessitates that only those with designated authority speak on its behalf. This emphasis on hierarchical authority and the inability to use the language of the media has weakened the Church's position in the public sphere. The hierarchical structure of the Church, as an institution which structures discourse in the religious and public spheres, creates a contradiction between the necessities of preserving divine authority and developing free, open debate and discussion.

A good example of the way the Church seeks to control debate and discussion internally was the Hegarty affair. In January 1995 an internal row within the Church spilled into the media, particularly the letters column in the *The Irish Times*. In 1991, Fr Kevin Hegarty was appointed editor of *Intercom,* a pastoral and liturgical journal published by a Commission of the Irish bishops. He began to publish a series of articles which critically reflected on the nature of the Catholic Church in Ireland. In 1993, one of these articles challenged the Church to deal with clerical sexual abuse. Shortly afterwards, he was told by a bishop to make sure that such an article did not appear again. Around the same time, an unsolicited homily from another bishop was sent to him for publication. Fr Hegarty decided that it did not warrant publication, but published an edited version of it. An internal report was produced which concluded that Fr Hegarty was damaging the morale of his fellow priests and religious. The Conference of Irish Bishops discussed the matter and in 1994 Fr Hegarty was transferred from Dublin to a remote parish in the west of Ireland. Fr Hegarty felt that this sudden and unusual transfer made it impossible for him to fulfil two jobs at the same time and, and reading it as a lack of confidence in him, resigned as editor.

What was effectively a private internal affair moved into the public sphere when the Catholic Press and Information Office wrote a letter to *The Irish Times* giving the official Church version of what had happened. Three days later a very contradictory version was given in a letter from Fr

Hegarty.[87] Over the next month, there was a series of letters from priests, bishops, nuns and other citizens about the issue, as well as feature articles and, finally, *The Irish Times* published an editorial. The editorial noted that Fr Hegarty believed that a religious magazine 'should be a place where different views are aired, where positions are argued forcefully but courteously, where those alienated from church structures are given a voice, where there is a respect for dissent and nobody is excluded because of perceived unorthodoxy.' However, the editorial concluded: 'It appears that such praiseworthy sentiments are seen as dangerously subversive in some leading church circles.'[88] The editorial went on to note:

The Catholic Church makes a virtue out of being a hierarchical organisation, accountable only to God and to His Servant on earth, the Pope. When it moves its priests around – justly or unjustly – it is not answerable to the secular, democratic society in which it operates. This may be so, but perhaps it could learn something from the better practices of that society, such as the value placed on freedom of speech and expression, or the value of open, honest debate.

The affair came to a close when the Bishop of Fr Hegarty's diocese issued a statement saying that he regretted not offering him a less demand-ing curacy which he could have combined with editing the magazine and that when the existing editor's contract was finished, he would propose Fr Hegarty for a second term.

The Hegarty affair indicates the fundamental contradiction which lies at the heart of debate and discussion within a centralised, hierarchical organi-sation such as the Catholic Church. While the Pope and bishops may engage in debate and may listen attentively to what is being said by priests, theologians and the laity, this cannot interfere with the Pope's divinely inspired interpretation of the truth. Consequently, when Ryan argues that the Catholic Church acts as the conscience of Irish society, it is not a collec-tive conscience formed through debate and discussion. Nor is it formed through the unforced force of reason, but rather through symbolic domina-tion. Debate and discussion are acceptable within the Church as long as they do not challenge the process by which Church truth is revealed.

In the past, the certainty of the truth propagated by the Church has not necessitated debate and discussion. Debate and discussion must be orientated towards preserving rather than undermining the faith. This protective attitude to the faith helps explain why religion or religious studies has only recently been accepted as an official subject in Irish second-level education. The promulgation of truth, rather than debate and discussion is also reflected in the way the Irish bishops communicate with the laity through issuing pastoral letters.[89] These often become the basis of Sunday sermons, but in effect they are letters to which no response is expected – a normal association within civil society. If the Church were a civil society there would at least be an expectation, if not positive encouragement, to have a discussion which could provide grass-roots reaction and lead to changes in policy.

The way the Church communicates internally and with its laity is reflected in the way it communicates with the wider public through the media. Recognising the growing importance of the media, the Irish bishops established the Catholic Communications Institute of Ireland in 1969. As part of the Institute, a Press and Information Office was opened in 1973. But as O'Toole notes, Church leaders tend to look on the media simply as a conduit through which their ideas and instructions can be fed to the masses.[90]

Not only has the Church been unable to operate with the language and structures of the news media, but in recent years instead of the Church being the moral guardian of the media and Irish society, it is the media which have become the moral investigators of the Church and the defenders of the common good against the Church. Over the last thirty years in Ireland, but particularly in the last ten years, the news media have been telling stories which are against the interests of the Church. When these stories break, the Church has tended to be slow and cautious in its reactions. Unlike politicians, bishops are not used to preparing immediate responses to developing stories and making themselves available to reporters. Even if they did, they have difficulty in fitting in with the language and format of news construction, particularly in radio and television. There are numerous priests who have a high profile in the media and would be able to meet the demands of modern news reporting – but the problem for the Church is allowing those without authority to speak with authority.[91]

These conflicts which revolve around issues of hierarchy, authority, media priests, and civil society were revealed during a programme on Irish television (4 November 1995). The programme brought together a wide variety of Catholics, including bishops, priests, nuns, brothers and members of the laity to discuss the state of the Catholic Church in Ireland. The discussion took place on the *Late, Late Show,* which is the longest running and most famous programme in Ireland's television history. Many issues were raised during the discussion, particularly the scandals of paedophile priests, priests having sexual relationships and children, celibacy, and women priests. What was unusual about this show was that, in effect, the Church not only came into the media to openly confess its problems, but that the bishops allowed themselves to be challenged and questioned by priests and members of the laity. A central problem for the lay members of the audience was that while the laity was constantly told that the people were the Church, the people had no voice. This was linked to a general absence of debate within the Church and a fear, particularly on the part of priests, of speaking out and expressing their opinions. The laity felt that they had been dominated by the institutional, clerical Church and that they had no power to instigate change.

Cardinal Daly came onto the programme for the final part of the show. He played down the claim that there was a crisis in the Church and pointed to the healthy collaboration between laity and priests taking place throughout the country. However, when asked, he said he could never foresee an end to priestly celibacy or women being allowed to become priests. He was challenged to reconcile the claim that the people are the Church with his announcement that the Church could not allow women to become priests. A national opinion poll had shown that half of the respondents would welcome women as priests. This revealed the inherent weakness of dialogue and debate in the Church orientated toward reaching a normative consensus. When asked why there could not be women priests when the people who were the Church wanted them, he replied:

The Pope after reflection and out of his full responsibility as the one who was appointed by the Holy Spirit to confirm his brethren and sisters in the faith says that the Church does not feel authorised by Our Lord to ordain women to the priesthood and that there are valid reasons for this decision; the Church has to listen but it first has to listen to what the Spirit says.

There is, then, a fundamental contradiction between the constitution of the Catholic Church and debate and discussion as the basis of communicative action orientated towards reaching understanding and a normative consensus. The Church's contributions to debate, both within its own structures and in the wider civil society, have to be seen as limited by its claims to divine truth. This claim to divine truth creates a fear of liberal individualism and self-expression – a fear which because of its theological base, is not so evident within Protestantism. This fear of self-expression, so anathema to operating within the public sphere, contributes further to the incompatibility between the Church and the media. On the other hand, although it is fragmented into different churches and sects, what links the diversified world of Protestantism is that ultimate authority in temporal and spiritual matters is seen to rest with the individual. Indeed, the individual quest for truth, salvation and the common good may make Protestants more receptive to the marketplace of ideas produced within the media. It may even be that at a structural level there is an elective affinity between Protestantism and the media which does not exist within the Catholic Church. And it may well be that this links into a greater contradiction not just with the media but with democratic participation, pluralism and ethical relativism which are essential ingredients of civil society.

Yet while the inability of the Church to adapt to and perform well in the media has contributed to its decline, it is the dominance of the media within the family which has contributed most to the erosion of its moral monopoly. The Church has been fighting a losing battle in trying to protect the family from the inroads of the state. But there was never really a battle with the media. Within thirty years of its arrival, the mass media, in particular television, had wrested control of the family from the Church. Catholic thought, images and practices used to dominate schools, hospitals and other institutions, as well as public life at large. But most of all the Church dominated imagery, thought and practice within Irish homes. All of this changed with the arrival of newspapers, magazines, radio, cinema, television, video, and more recently computers. For a long time there was – and still in many places is – an accommodation between the two. However, the mass media are tied into a view of the self and social life radically different from that of the Catholic Church. Radio, television, newspapers and magazines are constantly broadcasting messages into the heart of Irish homes which are based on self-expression, pleasure, entertainment, consumption, debate, discussion and controversy. It is no longer a question of which is more symbolically dominant in Irish homes. It is a question of how the Church can produce messages so that it continues to be heard and listened to. It is being forced into producing its own media gurus, its own advertisements selling its products. Images of pop, film and sports stars have replaced the images of Our Lady, Christ and the saints. The thought for the day, broadcast at least four times each hour, is the need to consume, to express, entertain and satisfy yourself. The focus is on active involvement in the here and now. It is not about an orientation towards or escape into another supernatural world. There are constant messages about how to live the good life; to be a good person and citizen. But it is not priests and religious who are giving out these messages; it is not priests who are listening to the confessions of Irish Catholics. It is a plethora of media gurus.

Decline in the Family

In his analysis of why Ireland became and remained so Catholic, Fahey pointed to the importance of religion becoming 'a women's business, particularly within the confines of the home and in connection with the socialisation of children.'[92] I have argued that the mother was the linchpin in the creation, development and maintenance of the Catholic Church's moral monopoly. She was the crucial link between the institutional structure and the religious devotion of each new generation of Irish Catholics. The decline of the traditional Irish mother, selflessly devoted to her family and the Church, has been directly instrumental in the decline of the Church's moral monopoly. The decline in religious belief and practice, in the commitment to the Church's moral teaching, and in the number of vocations can be directly linked to Irish women abandoning the traditional role of mother as constructed by the Church. Irish women are abandoning the notion that their lot in life is to get married, to get pregnant and to beget a large family. Increasing numbers of Irish women are going on to third-level education; breaking free from traditional female employment; having sex before marriage; using contraceptives; having children outside of marriage; staying on at work after marriage; having smaller families and returning to work when the children are reared. It would also seem that many Irish mothers have encouraged their daughters in this direction. What is certain is that mothers are no longer fostering the number of vocations which were central to maintaining the institutional strength of the Church. The Church's decline in the fields of politics, education, health, social welfare and the media can be directly linked to Irish women abandoning the traditional image of virgin and mother which the Church created and maintained over the last two hundred years. Women have increasingly found their voice, themselves and their needs, interests and pleasures. Women have fought for and gained increased participation in the labour market before and after marriage, and the differential between men's and women's pay is steadily decreasing. Between 1971 and 1996 the number of women at work rose from 212,000 to 488,000, an increase of 130 per cent. In the same twenty-five year period, the proportion of men at work increased by only 3 per cent. More important, the proportion of married women in the total female labour force has risen from 14 per cent in 1971 to 50 per cent in 1996. There has also been a steady increase in the number of mothers at work. In 1991, a quarter of all mothers were in the labour force. By 1996, this had risen to 37 per cent.[93] Women have also gained key political rights and increased political participation, most of these due to struggles waged in civil society by various strands of the women's liberation movement. Among these were the lifting of the ban on the employment of married women in the Civil Service in 1973, the right to equal pay in 1976, and the Employment Equality Act which prohibited discrimination in employment on the grounds of sex or marital status. There was also an increase in the number of women's organisations, increased participation in party politics, and representation on boards of management. Most important of all, in terms of symbolic power, voters elected Mary Robinson the first woman President of Ireland.[94] In the field of education, girls have always participated more and succeeded better in second-level education and increased numbers of them are going on to third level. But also significant, in terms of young mothers leaving the home, is the increase in the number of women participating in and changing the structure of adult education.[95] In the field of health, women have gained access to contraception and the right to receive information about, and travel abroad for, an abortion. In social welfare, women gained the right to divorce and remarry.

All of these changes have arisen from the agency of Irish women, often working from within their own homes, and have then been filtered back down to homes. The image of the traditional Irish mother being at home with four, five or more children, devoting herself to them and her husband's needs, is becoming less a reality. The number of children born to married women has declined significantly, from 207 per 1,000 in 1961 to 112 in 1991, a drop of 46 per cent. There is definite evidence of a decline in fertility among older women, and there is also evidence which suggests that women are not having children immediately after marriage.[96] But at the same time that the fertility of married women has been declining, the fertility of unmarried women has been rising. In 1961, 2 per cent of births occurred outside of marriage. This has now risen to 20 per cent. Furthermore, one in three of first births are to unmarried mothers.[97] However, not only have there been these changes in the position and role of Irish women and mothers, but the basic concept of the family has, as Ryan argues, 'broadened to include unions based on cohabitation, one-parent families, homosexual and lesbian unions.'[98]

There has, then, been a fundamental change in the attitude to women, mothers and the family in Irish society. The European Values Survey in 1990 showed that Irish people are no more likely than other Europeans to see women in traditional sex roles. The majority of Irish respondents were positive that having a job is the best way for a woman to be an independent person and that a working mother can establish a warm and secure relationship with her children. On the other hand a majority also agreed that a pre-school child is likely to suffer if his mother works and that being a housewife is just as fulfilling as working for pay. But it is important to note that women, especially those in employment, were less likely to have a traditional view of themselves. Similarly, young people and those with a higher level of education were also less likely to have a traditional image of women.[99] The mainstay of the Catholic Church, which the Church strove for so long to support and protect, was the traditional family based either on household economy of a farm or small business or with the husband going off to work while his wife stayed at home to do the housework and mind the children. Increasingly, Ireland is moving to another level of family life in which a large proportion of married women work outside the home. At the same time, many men and women still want to have a large family (four children) and seem to hanker after and romanticise about a traditional nuclear family lifestyle.[100]

Conclusion

The Catholic Church's monopoly on Irish morality has been broken. It no longer commands the same awe and respect as it did thirty years ago. In civil society it has moved from having a close relationship with the state, especially in relation to social and moral issues, to being one interest group among many others. It is no longer the conscience of the Irish people. The Church may hold that it is the duty of Catholics to be informed about Church teaching when making moral decisions, yet most Irish Catholics consider the Church's moral teaching to have little relevance in their everyday lives. Catholics appear as likely to be more informed and guided in what is right and wrong by what they hear discussed in the media, as by what they are told by priests and bishops. Most Catholics no longer see it as necessary to confess their sins to a priest, at least not on a regular basis. There has been a sharp decline in attendance at Mass. The level of baptisms, marriages and funerals within the Church may not have diminished, but this could be a ritualistic shell which has lost the core loyalty and commitment to the Church which used to sustain it. Perhaps the most dramatic change in the last ten years, particularly in relation to the future of the Church, is the drop in vocations. Not only have numbers of priests, nuns and brothers decreased by one-fifth in fifteen years, the age profile of religious personnel is growing much older. These changes have all had a major impact on the power of the Church to direct the moral attitudes and practices of Irish Catholics. And yet, perhaps, they are only the tip of an iceberg, for what has rocked the foundation of the institutional Church more than anything else in the past decade has been the scandals of adulterous priests and bishops, homosexual priests and, most of all, priests who have sexually abused young children. It may have been that the way the institutional church responded to these events, particularly its slowness to apologise and admit certain culpability, which has been most damaging. It was as if it was caught between being a legal and financial institution and, at the same time, a voice of the people, particularly of the marginalised and oppressed. And, finally, there seems to be a lasting overall image of fragmentation. Whereas thirty or forty years ago the Church and all its priests, nuns, brothers and laity tended to speak with one voice, over the last ten years a dozen different voices seem to speak on behalf of the Church, some liberal, some conservative, but increasingly at odds with one another.[101] Increasingly, when some priests and religious, including bishops, speak in the public sphere, it is not only in a self-reflective way about the Church, but in an conciliatory if not apologetic voice.

There is, then, definite evidence that the moral power of the Catholic Church has declined significantly in the last decade. But this must be put into perspective. The Church may no longer have a monopoly over what Irish Catholics consider to be right or wrong, good or bad behaviour, particularly in the area of personal and sexual morality. But the decline in the influence of the Church in the moral field is not matched by a similar decline in the religious field as a whole. If we consider that being religious is made up of two main dimensions – being moral and being spiritual – then there is less evidence of the Church's decline in the spiritual field. There may be fewer people going to Mass and Confession, but the numbers going to Holy Communion and praying have not decreased as significantly. Moreover, the level of belief in God, Christ and Our Lady has remained very high. What seems to be occurring is that whereas back in the 1970s there was a little difference between the level of belief and the level of practice, a considerable gap has begun to appear. In this respect, Ireland is becoming more like other European countries which are predominantly Catholic. This gap between belief and practice may be seen as part of a growing secularisation. Less and less of what the Catholic Church says about spiritual, as well as moral, matters has relevance to the everyday life of Irish Catholics. They live in a secularised, commercial world which is dominated by reason and rationality and in which a transcendental or supernatural orientation is compartmentalised into specific times and places. Catholic icons and rituals no longer dominate public life; priests and bishops no longer dominate debate and discussion in the public sphere.

There are, however, important caveats to the above argument. The first is that the Catholic Church has been operating in Ireland for over fifteen hundred years and while the present downturn in its fortunes may mirror what has happened in other European countries, it would be wrong to consider ongoing secularisation as inevitable. Secondly, despite the scandals and the decline in the Church's moral monopoly, most Irish Catholics still go to Mass on Sundays, have their children baptised, make a fuss of the first holy communions and confirmations, are married in church and buried by the Church. In other words, within the religious field in Ireland, the Catholic Church is still without any significant competitors. Thirdly, while the Church may have become an interest group like any other in civil society, it still has a dominant influence in the fields of education, health and social welfare. Moreover, although it has received a certain amount of negative publicity in the last ten years, it still receives a considerable amount of neutral and even favourable coverage in the media for its messages and activities.

10
The Influence of the Catholic
Church on Modern Irish Society

I rish people behave in much the same way as people from other Western societies. They work at the same kind of jobs. They are taught the same things at school. They live in similar kinds of houses. They have similar manners and habits. They eat the same foods. They drink the same beer. They watch the same television programmes. They follow the same football matches. They read the same articles and stories in newspapers, magazines and books. They speak the Queen's English. Ireland has moved from the periphery to the centre of Western culture.

But in this vast ocean of similarity the Irish are also different. The traditional image of the Irish, which is sometimes denigrated but which many Irish like to live up to, is of an easy going, happy people who are outgoing and caring; who have a deep devotion to their family, community and Church; and who, compared with other Westerners, have a greater interest in the spirit of things – that is, in being social, cultural and artistic, rather than having a selfish concern for material success. This image is grounded in habitus, in an orientation to life and to people, which, sometimes unintentionally, was fostered and developed by the Catholic Church and was, in part, a result of its symbolic domination of Irish life. The traditional image, like the Catholic Church, is in a period of rapid transition and is blending with a new image. The new image of Ireland is of a Celtic tiger which has the fastest growing economy in Europe. If we are as others see us, then we are no longer, as the English cartoonists used to depict us, the untamed savages of the West. We have become what we always were, a spiritually sophisticated Celtic people who are educated, cultured, disciplined and innovative. In some respects, then, Catholic Ireland is going through a process of assimilation in which the best of the old is being married with the best of the new. There is new self-confidence. There is no longer the same fear. There is a willingness to open and look behind doors which were previously shut tight. The silence that reigned over sex, pleasure and the expression of oneself has been broken. There may well be a new Irish Catholic emerging from the orthodox cocoon of rules and regulations in which they were enmeshed. But what is the position of the institutional Church? Are the two images of Ireland, which I have represented, two realities passing each other by like ships in the night? Do they correspond to Flannery's description of two generations of Irish priests passing each other on the stairs of their religious house early in the morning, one generation descending to say early morning Mass, the other going up to bed after a hard night on the town?[1]

While there is definite evidence of the decline of the influence of the institutional Church in many fields of Irish social life, it would be wrong to think that Irish Catholicism is dying, especially when the Church still has such control in education. There is no doubt that the institutional religious life of priests, nuns and brothers, as it was thirty years ago, is rapidly fading away. There is no doubt that the absolute religious power of the Catholic Church in Ireland is dying, if not already dead. But we live in a rapidly changing culture in which, increasingly, fundamentalism is being pitted against postmodernism – the absolute against relative truth. It would be a foolish Christian who did not believe in the power of the institutional Catholic Church to resurrect itself.

So what can be said of the religion of the people? In the same way that there was a general movement away from magical-devotional religion in the last century to a more legalist-orthodox way of being religious, so towards the end of this century there has been an ongoing, gradual move away from both of these towards individually principled ethics. Irish Catholics are becoming more Protestant and probably more secular. But it would also be wrong to think that this is some kind of definite, irreversible trend. We live in a disenchanted world, but it could easily be re-enchanted. The different ways of being religious which I have described can be seen as points on a path towards rational, secular society. They can be also be seen as universal elements of being religious which become embodied in specific rites and rituals which are re-enacted and given emphasis at different times. They are points around a circle rather than in a straight line. Irish Catholics are, in Weber's terms, moving more towards an inner-worldly, ascetic type of religion in which people work hard and focus on what is happening in this world. But the residues of orthodoxy and devotionalism remain deep with the system. They have been embodied from a young age. They linger in the individual personality as well as the social system and can be reactivated at short notice.

Most Irish Catholics still adhere strongly to the teachings and practices of the Church, and for many their religious life is enlivened with holy water, statues, shrines and pilgrimages. The priest is still treated with respect, but maybe not with the same awe and reverence as a holy man from a peasant society. His word is one among many. It may be the word of God, but it now has to compete with the word of the media whose messages may not be completely secular, but certainly correspond less and less to the teaching of the Church. It was the dominance of the Catholic Church in everyday social life, but particularly within the family, which was associated with the pious humility of the Irish, their practice of self-denial and the surrender of individual interests to those of family and community. Irish mothers were seen as paragons of Christian virtue who were happy to stay at home rearing their children in the love and sight of God, and who fussed and worried about their husbands spending too much time in the pub. The surrender of self in religious and family life was mirrored in the pub. What made male community life in Ireland different was not so much that they drank more, but the way they drank. Hard drinking is about the elimination of the self. This was done in an atmosphere in which nobody was powerful enough to avoid having their leg pulled. Like the pub, and teasing, many of the practices which make the Irish different, and yet as civil and as moral as other Western people, may be linked to the cultural traits inherited and adapted from Catholic Church teaching. Indeed it is because the Irish became the same as other Westerners in and through the Catholic Church that they have remained different.

In order to explain the position of the Catholic Church in modern Irish society, this study has posed and sought to answer four main questions. What was the nature of the Church's power in Irish society? How has this power been maintained? When and how did its power become established? How has its power diminished? In attempting to answer these questions, I have developed a particular theoretical perspective on the Church and social life in general. I have avoided looking at the power of the Catholic Church in Ireland as being founded simply on people's commitment to a supernatural faith in God and Christ. Instead, I have developed a more sociological perspective which, following the work of Weber and Bourdieu, has examined the field of Irish religion and how it relates to other social fields. The dominance of Catholicism was linked to the institutional struc- ture of the Catholic Church and the strength of its human and physical resources. An understanding of the institutional structure of the Church enables us to understand how it was able to dominate the religious field in Ireland and have such an influence on the way Irish Catholics were religious. But in the heyday of the Catholic Church's power, particularly during the fifty years after the foundation of the state, its influence expanded beyond the religious field into the field of politics, economics, education, health, social welfare, the media and many other fields. The power of the Church meant that it structured not just the religious life of the Irish people, but their social, political and economic life as well. Consequently, the strategies through which Irish Catholics struggled to gain cultural, social, political, economic and cultural capital were linked in with living a good Catholic life.

However, this moral power has been declining since the 1960s. Irish Catholics are becoming less influenced by the Church in their struggle to attain power. It is no longer as necessary as it was in the past to adhere to Catholic rituals in order to seem the same and to be treated with respect. This decline in the Church's moral power cannot be separated from the growth in the power of the state and the media. The state abandoned the Church's ideal of a self-sufficient, rural society based on small-scale production in which family, community and religious life took as much precedence as the acquisition of material possessions. From the end of the 1950s the state began to pursue economic growth through increased industrialisation, urbanisation, international trade, science and technology. The growth of the media brought enormous changes to family and community life. It is the media which symbolically dominate the lives of Irish people. The media and the Catholic Church have changed positions. People used to make a trip to read a newspaper, listen to the radio or, more recently, watch television. God, Christ, Our Lady, the saints, as well as their priestly representatives on earth, were more on their minds, in their hearts and on their lips than what was said by Gay Byrne, Gerry Ryan or other media gurus. Instead of going out to the church or kneeling down to say the rosary, Irish families now sit down and watch television. Many of the programmes portray rich, glossy American and British lifestyles in which priests and religion have little or no representation or influence. Television changed the nature of social discourse and practice in Ireland, because watching television in the privacy of one's home became the main family ritual. Television programmes rather than Church rituals became the basis of shared experiences about which people communicated and related to each other. It is now the media more than the Church that form and inform consciences and expand or limit how people perceive the world. It was the development of television, film and magazines which were mainly responsible for loosening the censorship on sex. It was the growth of the media which forced the Church into confessing its sins in public.

The other question which this study has sought to answer is when and how did the Church manage to attain such a powerful position in Irish society, and how this power was developed over successive generations? The growth of the power of the Catholic Church in Ireland cannot be attributed to one or two factors. Rather has it been the result of numerous events and processes coming together over a period of time. One of these was a transformation in the way in which the British state sought to control the Irish population. There was a shift away from repressive Penal Laws and the systematic attempt to subjugate Irish Catholics, to softer, more indirect forms of control centred on policing, emigration and education. Once it was realised that the attempt at Protestant evangelism was doomed to failure, and once the reports from various investigative commissions began to be submitted, the state started to hand the task of educating and civilising Irish Catholics over to the Catholic Church. One of the reasons which precipitated this capitulation was that the Irish Church, in and through Rome, was already emerging as a cohesive, bureaucratically organised power bloc, able to challenge and harangue the state.

But again it would be too easy to explain the growth in Church power simply as something which was imposed on an unwilling people by power blocs, in this case the Roman Catholic Church and the British state. Hierocratic power, or the power of priestly religion, cannot be considered coercive in the same way as the power of the state, even though the threatened denial of salvation is often as effective as the threat of death itself in attaining compliance to commands. One of the reasons why the Church was able to attain compliance with its teachings and practices was because it afforded the ability, denied during the Penal Laws, for Irish Catholics to become the moral equals, if not the superiors, of the Protestants who had dominated them for so long. Indeed Irish Catholics are a good example of a traditional people who, in the transition to modernity, place primary importance on becoming the same, as civil and refined as those who have dominated them, but who use a different means – in this case the Catholic Church – to attain that end. In some respects the Penal Laws were a failure in that they made Irish Catholics more Roman and attached to the Church than they might ever have been. On the other hand, they were a success in that once they were abolished there was such an intense interest in becoming as civil and moral as modern Europeans and in creating a Catholic nation-state, that with the exception of the struggle to attain ownership of the land, economic development was of secondary importance. In other words, the abolition of the Penal Laws may have had the unintended consequence of fostering the very economic backwardness which they had been intended to establish among Irish Catholics.

The interest in becoming as moral and civil as Protestants, and in worshipping in large, ornately furnished churches rather than in secluded back-streets (or worse still in the open air) was a major factor in the physical growth of the Church in the first half of the nineteenth century. But the interest in being civilised had much deeper roots. The modern civilising process had been spreading throughout Europe since the sixteenth century. In its early stages, it essentially involved the imitation of the manners and customs that characterised the court behaviour of aristocrats, by the bourgeoisie and later by other classes. What is coincidental is that the development of this civility involved a moral discipline over passions and instincts which was best achieved through an internalisation of shame and guilt about the body – a process which, in part, had been developed and exported to the Continent by Irish monks back in the sixth and seventh centuries. The most rationally developed forms of this morality were Puritanism and Jansenism. Now while there is no evidence that Jansenist doctrines were ever preached or adhered to in Ireland, there is little doubt that a Catholic brand of Jansenist practices was imported under the umbrella of rigorism. It is a matter of debate whether this rigorism was Roman or French in origin or whether it was a development within the Irish Church itself. Whatever its exact origins – and again it was probably a combination of all three – this new morality began to develop from the middle of the last century, first in churches and later in schools and homes.

The strict adherence to the rules and regulations of the Church became the means of halting the impoverishment which had been caused by the subdivision of farms. There was little differentiation of time and space in the mud cabins which dominated Irish housing until the Famine. There was a differentiation between animals and humans, but the pig was often given the right to his space since he at least helped pay the rent. It was in and through the church and the school that the child began to take precedence in Irish homes, and the pig was removed to the out-house. The new moral discipline aided the adoption of postponed marriage, permanent celibacy and emigration. These practices became the principal means of consolidating farm sizes and raising the standard of living. Homes, like churches and schools, became well-ordered, supervised spaces in which there was a time and place for everything, and everything was in its proper time and proper place. The transformation in the size, quality and durability of Irish houses during the second half of the nineteenth century involved an internal revolution of time and space centred on body discipline. It was paralleled by an initial differentiation of spaces; of churches from schools; of churches from homes; and, within homes, of kitchens, bedrooms and living-rooms. It was because this initial differentiation of space took place in and through the supervision of the Church, and because the Church continued to be able to determine what went on in schools and homes, that the rational differentiation of social fields in Irish society was delayed and, consequently, the full modernisation of Irish society did not commence until the latter half of this century.

But for all the priests and teachers, the development of the Church and a rigorous moral discipline could not have been attained without the Irish mother. She became the sacred heart of the Irish home. It was she who inculcated a ritualistic and legalistic adherence to the rules and regulations of the Church. She brought the family to prayer and enforced the Church's code of morality. She was the Church's representative in the home who supervised the moral conduct of her husband and children. She became the living embodiment of Our Lady – humble, pious, celibate and yet fecund. She gave herself to the Church, and in each succeeding generation produced the religious vocations that sustained the Church. Her moral power in the home was sanctioned by the priests, nuns and brothers that she bore.

The mother maintained her power within the home in the same way as the Church did in wider society. She did the dirty, menial tasks involved in the care of members of the household. She looked after the young, the sick, the elderly, the weak and the distraught. In Humphreys's terms, she 'dominated by affection'.[2] She slaved, especially for her husbands and sons. She encouraged her daughters, as part of their training, to be good mothers, to do likewise. By doing everything for her sons, the mother made them dependent on her. But by limiting and controlling the physical expression of her affection, she inculcated an emotional awkwardness in her children. This denial of the physical expression of affection was a major child-rearing practice in the preparation for emigration, postponed marriage and permanent celibacy. The segregation of the sexes, the lack of physical contact between bodies, the denial of emotional expression, the ridicule and teasing about affection, especially in the male bachelor drinking group, partly accounts for the awkward distance between the sexes in Ireland. This also explains the cold and often formal relationship that has existed between husband and wife in Ireland. Whatever possibility there was of a warm, physical relationship, there was little or no possibility of any open, honest communication about sex. This helped perpetuate the high level of fertility which has continued to be a major characteristic of Irish marriages. Only since the 1960s has the reproductive cycle of high marital fertility, maintaining the need for postponed marriage, permanent celibacy and emigration, begun to be broken. It has been broken because women have begun to acquire a knowledge of sex and a control over their bodies which has been instrumental in attaining economic and political power, thereby shattering the bonds that made them dependent on the moral power of the Church.

The Modernisation of Irish Society

Two questions which arise from this study are how did the modernisation Irish society take place, and what role did the Church play in the process? The answers to both of these questions are interrelated but depend on what one means by modernisation. If one means the end of magic as a dominant form of ethical behaviour; the end of people living with and like animals in mud cabins; the beginning of a new control over life and death; the adoption of many of the manners and practices of modern Europeans; and the adoption of a new discipline over the body – then Ireland can be said to have modernised during the nineteenth century and the Catholic Church to have played a major role in the process. If, on the other hand, one means by modernisation the advent of an industrial type of society in which religion becomes rationally differentiated from the rest of social life, the state becomes separated from the Church, religious belief and practice become a private rather than public affair, the rational choice of individuals in the market place takes over from the pressures of tradition and community to conform; and production and consumption take primary importance over being spiritual – then it might be said that Ireland did not begin to modernise until the 1960s. It might also be argued that the Catholic Church, because of the nature of its teachings and practices, in particular its opposition to materialism, consumerism and individualism, was an inhibiting factor in modernisation and industrialisation of Irish society. In other words, Ireland went through two stages of modernisation. The first stage was the creation of a new class of civilised, educated and disciplined tenant farmers, a latent bourgeoisie. But because this initial stage of modernisation took place in and through a form of external constraint towards self-constraint, operating through a rigorous morality which centred on self-denial, this bourgeois class did not fully realise itself and, consequently, the state remained Catholic rather than becoming capitalist, and agricultural production remained within a peasant subsistence rather than modern entrepreneurial type model.[3] In other words, I am arguing that the socio-religious context in Ireland, particularly the dominance of the Catholic Church's vision of self and society, did influence the world of work and politics (particularly the vision of the state) as well as family and community. However, it should be pointed out that most commentators argue by default (since they rarely give it any space) that socio-religious culture did not have much to do with Ireland's late development as an industrial society.[4]

If it is accepted that modern industrialisation is to a certain extent dependent on the prior and full development of agriculture along the lines of small-scale petty commodity production, then we might ask what were the social and cultural practices that existed in Ireland which inhibited the development of this form of production, and what role did the Catholic Church play in maintaining this inhibition? In other words, accepting the dominance of external and internal economic and political factors, what were the internal socio-cultural factors that may have inhibited Irish farmers from modernising their holdings, capitalists from being more expansionary, intellectuals from being more critical and visionary and the state from being more supportive of capitalist economic growth?

Some analysts have emphasised the impact that of socio-cultural factors in Irish underdevelopment. In attempting to explain why more mature capitalist agricultural production developed in Northern Ireland and how, by the end of the nineteenth century, that region became one of the core industrial areas of these islands, some commentators have argued that people in the south were generally more interested in leisure than work. Black, for example, claims that 'the people of the north did devote more time and energy to their work and less to fairs and race-meetings, patterns and wakes than did the people in the south.'[5] The implication is that, in the south, being sociable, engaging in collective rituals and surrendering the self to community and tradition had an equal, if not higher, priority to being productive.

Lee points out that there was no shortage of capital in nineteenth-century Ireland but that farmers were inclined to keep it for dowries, to give it to their children for a professional education, or simply to put it in the bank, rather than invest it in their farms. He associates this with Irish Catholics always trying to emulate their social betters, the Protestant upper classes, and says that they were more interested in the veneer of respectability than in developing trade.[6] The traditional lack of respect and support for working class trades may be linked to an obsession which successful farming families had for getting their children into professional employment – or at least non-manual work – and the extent to which this was reinforced through the classical education given in the schools run by priests, nuns and brothers. Larkin attempted to draw a more direct link between the interest in social and moral respectability and economic underdevelopment. His argument was that capital which could have been invested in enterprises was directed towards the Church. He claimed that in the second half of the nineteenth century the Catholic Church absorbed almost 15 per cent of the surplus available over subsistence for the Catholic population.[7] However Kennedy has argued that, far from inhibiting economic growth, the Catholic Church made a positive contribution:

The Catholic Church was itself a major consumer of goods and services. It had strong linkages to enterprises in the local economic context. By raising the level of economic demand for such services as building and maintenance services, as well as requiring steady supplies of food and food products – outputs which, on the whole, could only be provided by native industry – it is quite probable that the Church contributed to economic growth rather than the reverse.[8]

Whatever the merits of this Keynesian economic argument, more important from the perspective of the present study is that Kennedy goes on to claim that the intensive and systematic propagation of Catholic

Church teachings did not have any major effect on the modernisation of Irish agriculture. He argues that although high marital fertility 'might be seen as increasing the economically dependent proportion of the population and as straining the productive resources of the country', this cannot be linked to the Church's prohibition on forms of birth control since 'the people of nineteenth century Ireland possessed neither the desire nor the techniques to practise family limitation.' He also claims that there was a 'relative autonomy of the religious and economic spheres' which is evidenced by the fact that 'the growth of piety was paralleled by a growing consumer consciousness, rising material expectations, and a ruthless commitment to land possession, almost irrespective of the human costs involved.'[9]

My argument is very different. I maintain that the ethos and teaching of the Catholic Church were the reason why contraceptives were not legally available until 1979 and that the desire to have large families was exactly because married people, but particularly mothers, operated within a Catholic habitus in which there was an inherited predisposition reinforced by other women towards having children. It is not enough to say that Irish fertility was so high simply because Irish people wanted to have children. The question is where this desire came from and how it was maintained over generations. I have argued that the image women had of themselves, and the way they lived their lives, cannot be separated from the Catholic Church's image of women. But, more importantly, I argue that the type of personality – the understanding that people had of themselves, their hopes, their felt needs and desires, their interpretation of what it was to be good person was constructed within a Catholic habitus.

In his analysis of twentieth-century Ireland, Lee dismisses the idea that the Catholic Church or Irish religiosity had anything to do with Ireland having the least impressive economic performance in Western Europe. He argues that the 'image of Ireland as an island sublimely submerged in a sea of spirituality carries little conviction' and that the real cultural explanation for lack of economic growth was not that we were not opportunistic materialists, but that we were lazy and inefficient.[10] Lee goes on to blame what he refers to as a possession mentality (holding onto land, possessions and jobs) rather than a performance mentality (making enterprising use of resources) among the Irish. He links the persistence of this habitus not to the Catholic Church but to the failure of Irish intellectuals, particularly those working in the social sciences, to provide the necessary critical reflection which would have formed the basis for a vibrant civil society.[11] But again, we have to ask what socio-cultural forces created and maintained a possession mentality among the Irish, and why it was that social critique remained underdeveloped for so long.

Fahey follows a somewhat different line. He argues cogently, using America as a primary example, that there is no necessary opposition between a society being religious and being modern and industrial. However, he accepts that the Irish Church 'was committed ideologically to a rural fundamentalism which was suspicious and fearful of the industrial city and it glorified the family farm and the little village as the pillars of social and economic life.'[12] But he does not say if this fundamentalism had an impact on Irish modernisation. Other analysts have pointed out that the distinctive combination of religious orthodoxy, family based production, and the Church's unrivalled prestige and legitimacy, resulted in the goals of state policy being by and large those of the Church. A consequence of this was that the Catholic education system remained unsuited to the needs of a modern, industrial economy.[13] Daly has shown that the Catholic vision of Irish society being founded on spiritual ideals of frugal comfort lived out in the fellowship of family, friends and neighbours was a central feature of Irish political philosophy up until the 1960s. She insists that 'while cultural attitudes may not provide the major explanation for Ireland's poor economic performance, ideals did influence policies and, indirectly, performance.'[14]

The argument here is that up to the 1960s and in many cases after then, religious belief and practice were often not rationally differentiated from economic and political activity. If it was differentiated it was quietly at the level of practice, but what was done economically and politically was within the ethos and rhetoric of the good Catholic life. There was a sacred Catholic canopy which hung over most aspects of Irish life. It could be bypassed in what was done, but not in terms of what was said. But the impact of Catholic values and practices was primarily through social and political activity. The constant invocation and support for surrender to God and the Church, for the surrender of the self to family and community, and for the good life being one of humility and self-denial became ingrained in the hearts and minds of Irish Catholics. It became their second nature to put themselves down. This had a direct impact on people not seeking success and considering their success to be undesirable and unjustified. Even if people were ambitious and successful, they had to deny continually that they had done so deliberately. The state may have decided in its economic policies to pursue unashamedly economic growth and success. But the residues of Catholic culture lingered for longer in the Irish collective consciousness, in their view and understanding of the world and of what constituted the good life and a good person.

Surrender to Church, family, community and nation – the daily life of Irish martyrdom – created a disposition in which people were not encouraged to think for themselves. In the same way that in religious life salvation was not in one's own hands, but was attained through adherence to the

Church, so too in political life people were dependent on persuading local and national politicians to get things done for them. In the same way that the priest was seen as the mediator with God, the politician became the mediator with the state. In the same way that if people put faith in the priest it was believed he would lead them into heaven, so if people put faith in the politician, it was believed he would get them all kinds of pardons, permissions and pensions. Flannery describes the link between God and state, priest and politician as follows:

The notion of God at that time was one of a severe distant being, pure and unde-filed, and not easy to approach. The average Catholic regarded themselves as unworthy to approach and be heard by this God. They needed somebody 'holier' than themselves to speak on their behalf. In an uneducated society this notion of having someone to intervene for you with the people in power was common. Politicians, with their clinics, played the part in secular life. Religious and priests filled that need with God. People came to them with their worries, problems and sins, and asked for their prayers. Because religious were believed to live a partic-ularly pure and good life, God would listen to them.[15]

There is, then, a link between the decline in the image of and trust in the priest being holier than thou and the decline in the image of and trust in the Irish politician being honest and incorruptible. In moving away from the Catholic Church and thinking morally for themselves, Irish people are no longer as much dependent on priests and politicians and no longer see them as the great heroes in and saviours of their lives.

But it is argued that the impact of the Catholic habitus has lingered longest and still has most impact on the way Irish people view and under-stand themselves and socially interact with each other. The residues of Catholic belief, thought and practice are still to be found in Irish people's immediate orientation to denying, surrendering and putting themselves down. This is reflected in the humour, banter and repartee of Irish social life. It revolves around strategies which reinforce the belief that nobody is bigger than the social group, family or community to which they belong. Those who 'get beyond themselves' are saved through a generally gentle but sometimes harsh strategy of teasing and ridicule. It is, of course, the ability of the Irish to surrender themselves to the collective conscience and consciousness of the group which brings a unified way of seeing and inter-preting the world; and which gives them such a strong sense of purpose, meaning and identity and enables them to let go and enjoy themselves. But, I argue, the origins of this social self lie back in a series of institutional changes and social processes and strategies which have their origin in the nineteenth century.

In this book I have argued that the teachings and practices of the Catholic Church did have a significant influence on the economic outlook and performance of Irish people, but that this influence was rooted not just in ideals but in the Irish habitus and the practices of family and community life. It was through a rigid disciplining of the body, which was propagated in and through the Church, that Irish farmers embodied the discipline that was central to increased production. It was through a rigid adherence to Church teaching on sexual morality that Irish mothers were able to inculcate in their children the type of stem-family practices which were essential to the consolidation of farm sizes and an improvement in the standard of living. These practices centred on the inculcation of piety and humility and the systematic surrendering and denial of self. This strategy would have worked except that each successive generation of couples who did marry continued to have very high levels of fertility. This necessitated ongoing strategies such as postponed marriage, permanent celibacy and emigration. Lee is partly correct when he argues that the Irish were as materialist and economically strategic and calculating as any other European. But he fails to recognise that they were materialist and calculating in ways which the peculiar socio-economic environments necessitated. When he states that 'few peoples anywhere have been so prepared to scatter their children around the world in order to preserve their own living standards', he reveals something crucial about the nature of Irish society and the calculating materialist strategies which people adopted to create a decent standard of living.[16] How was it that successive generations of Irish farm families ended up encouraging, if not enforcing, emigration as a strategic means of maintaining a decent standard of living? Emigration was a strategic solution to what had become a peculiarly Irish problem of persistent high levels of marital fertility.

I argue that the Catholic Church had an important influence on Irish modernisation and, consequently, on developing the type of social relations associated with mature capitalist societies. Because the Church played a crucial role in the initial phase of modernisation, it came to have a dominant influence in the sphere of family life, particularly in relation to mothers and, simultaneously, in the relations between husbands and wives, the level of fertility, the circumstances and manner in which children were reared and the resulting type of personalities which emerged. The role the Church played in this first period of modernisation meant that its influence in social, political and economic life continued to grow and develop late into the twentieth century at a time when in more mature capitalist economies, the role of religion and churches in social life was being systematically reduced. This dominance manifested itself in two ways. At a structural level it meant that the Church maintained control of important fields such as education, health and social welfare. This meant that the Church had a crucial influence on certain aspects of state policy. It meant, for example, that up until the 1970s middle-class schoolchildren received a classical rather than a scientific education and that contraception did not become widely available until the 1980s. It was this Catholic version of what was the good life which had a significant impact on political and economic life. The absence of mechanisms of fertility control, combined with a lack of knowledge or communicative competence about sex, maintained a high level of marital fertility among Irish women until the 1960s. The high level of marital fertility not only increased the economically dependent proportion of the population, but led to the persistence of a labour intensive form of agricultural production. The persistence of large families was also characterised by a need for a set of child-rearing practices which inhibited self-confidence, ambition and achievement. These became extended into practices such as teasing and ridicule which became established within the wider community. These practices prevented the development of an economic individualism that is the prerequisite for modern Western risk-capital production. The curtailment of individuality, combined with an unquestioning obedience to the Church, led to what Hutchinson has called 'a dominance of familial and social conformity'.[17] It was a rigid conformity that led to, and maintained, an interest in social prestige that was equal to, and sometimes greater than, economic and political interests. In other words, as well as having an influence in the social structure of Irish society, the Church had considerable influence on the Irish habitus, that is the way Irish people saw and understood themselves and the family, community and society in which they lived. The Church was instrumental in creating and maintaining the understanding of what was a good man and woman and what was acceptable and unacceptable behaviour. In many ways, it was because the Catholic Church was responsible for the initial modernisation of Irish society that Irish Catholics became legalistically moral rather than secularly civilised. It was not until a new urban bourgeoisie achieved dominance, and through the state broke free from the shackles of rigid moralisation, that men and, in particular, women broke free of the Church's image and understanding of themselves, that Catholics unashamedly began to express themselves in languages and practices which did not conform with Church teaching and, to openly seek and recommend sensual pleasures and material comfort.

The long nineteenth century of Irish Catholicism is, then, drawing to a close at the end of the twentieth century. A transformation is occurring in present-day Irish society as dramatic as that which occurred during the middle of the last century. The monolithic Church which brought a holistic view to Irish social, economic and political life is beginning to fragment. The days of the unquestioned moral power of the priest are over. The awe, reverence and obedience which the priest enjoyed during the heyday of holy Catholic Ireland have begun to dissipate, sometimes into open disre-gard, sometimes in open hostility. At the end of the first edition, I went on to say that 'Irish Catholics are still a long way from publicly criticising and challenging priests and bishops'. The events of the last ten years are testimony that this is no longer the case. The media have driven a stake into the heart of the institutional Church from which it will recover, but never fully. It is unlikely that we will ever see the likes of the Catholic Church's moral monopoly again. Not only do the media symbolically dominate public and private life in a way that is far more pervasive and effective than the Church ever achieved, but it is the media which calls the Church to come to it to give an account of itself. One of the main prob-lems facing the Church, as Peillon pointed out fifteen years ago, is that it no longer has a vision of the future of Irish society. It has never managed to adapt its social philosophy to the needs and interests of contemporary Irish society. It can hold firm to its traditional conservative teaching based on the Natural Law, or it can try and adapt its message to suit the needs of a more Protestant, secular, liberal, pluralist society. The Church in general is facing a dilemma which has been growing rapidly in recent years; how to contain all the different, divergent trends which have appeared within it and yet maintain itself as a monolithic, multinational organisation? In Ireland, the future power of the Catholic Church will depend on its ability to reconcile the demand for an adherence to its rules and regulations as the criterion of Church membership with the more Protestant do-it-yourself type of ethic which is becoming dominant among the younger generation.

A related problem for the power of the Catholic Church in Ireland is the increasing demand for status by the laity. The shift from a legalist to an individually principled ethic has led at some levels to disaffiliation from the Church; at other levels it has led to a demand for more power by the laity. The days of a rigid, hierarchical division between the permanent, celibate members of the Church and the laity to whom they ministered, are coming to an end. The recent decline in vocations and, consequently, in the num-ber of religious personnel, has necessitated the incorporation of some members of the laity into the inner core of power. But an increasing role for the laity threatens the organisational cohesiveness of the Church as a power bloc, especially at a multinational level. It could threaten not just an acceptance of papal infallibility, but of the rules and regulations by which the universal power of the Church has been maintained. It could lead to a Protestant-style situation of sects and churches doing and saying their own thing. It is this threat which has led to the recent Ultramontane campaign of Dr Connell which in many ways is similar to that waged by Cardinal Cullen in the last century. Yet the reality is that this campaign will alienate 'lapsed' Catholics even further.

The Catholic Church in Ireland is also threatened by the encroachment of the state into areas in which it previously held a monopoly, especially the provision of education, health and social welfare services. This is not to suggest that the vast organisational network of schools, hospitals and other institutional buildings will not continue to be a major aspect of the Church's power, but it is to suggest that the more there is a revolt by 'lapsed' Catholics against the power of the Church, and that the less dependent the state becomes on the Church for legitimating and maintaining its power, then the more likely it is that state financial support for these institutions will dwindle. The state will continue, as it has been doing, to set up its own schools hospitals and welfare systems. Catholic institutions will be forced increasingly to rely on private, necessarily middle-class, support. Until now the Catholic Church in modern Ireland has received support from every economic class. The Church was able to educate and legitimate the position and possessions of the rich, and discipline and compensate the poor for their lack of possessions. In the days when the Church dominated education, when the media were there to support and not to challenge the Church, and a rigid adherence to the rules and regulations of the Church was the dominant ethic, these inequalities in wealth and power were easily explained and justified. However, the more withdrawal of state funds forces the Church to depend on private support, and the more the supporters of liberation theology side with the poor and oppressed (whose poverty and oppression is often caused in part by an exploitative bourgeoisie within their own Church), the more the cohesion and unity of the Catholic Church in Ireland will continue to fragment.

There was a time, until quite recently, when there was a unified, holistic view of life in holy Catholic Ireland, in which the Church put forward a vision of an ideal society of saints and scholars. It was a vision of a democratic, decentralised society in harmony with nature in which the interest in materialism and economic growth was limited by a sense of spiritual well-being centred on Church and family. The non-rational acceptance of the values on which this vision was based depended on people being content with the possessions and positions they held. It has been the state, and the science and technology by which the state has sustained economic growth, that have done more than anything else to destroy this vision. In accepting the rational differentiation between religion and politics, between what the Church does and what the state does, the Church has lost the possibility of maintaining a unified, holistic vision of Irish society. A holistic view of life may be necessary for the salvation not just of Irish society but of all human societies and living species. But for such holism to become a reality the Church needs to challenge the power of the state directly. It also needs to challenge the media which, like the Church itself formerly, are increasingly attaining the position of being accountable to none other than themselves. More importantly, the Irish Church will have to transcend its interest in an unquestioning, legalistic adherence to its rules and regulations. It must adopt an ethic of individual responsibility, leaving behind its obsession with sexual morality and individual salvation to embrace an ecological ethic of global responsibility and, perhaps, the salvation of the earth.

Notes

Full references are given at the beginning of each chapter (including those cited in previous chapters). Second citations within chapters are given in abbreviated form.

Chapter 1. Introduction,

1. Bishop Jeremiah Newman, quoted in the *The Irish Times*, 29 September 1984.
2. See, for example, Paul Blanshard, *The Irish and Catholic Power*, Boston: Beacon Press 1953; John Messenger, *Inis Beag*, New York: Holt, Reinhart & Winston 1969.
3. See, for example, Eoin Cassidy, ed., *Faith and Culture in the Irish Context*, Dublin: Veritas 1996; Séan MacRéamonn, *Pobal: The Laity in Ireland*, Navan: Columba Press 1986; Séan MacRéamonn, ed., *The Church in a New Ireland*, Navan: Columba Press 1996.
4. Joseph Dunn, *No Lions in the Hierarchy*, Dublin: Columba Press 1994, 20–2. He subsequently wrote a second volume of stories, *No Vipers in the Vatican*, Dublin: Columba Press 1995.
5. Tony Flannery, *The Death of Religious Life?*, Dublin: Columba Press 1997, 76–80.
6. Pat Buckley, *A Thorn in the Side*, Dublin: O'Brien Press 1994. Fr Buckley received considerable media attention again in September, 1997 when the Archbishop of Dublin refused to allow him officiate at his cousin's funeral and then would not give assurance that he would be allowed officiate at his mother's funeral. This story has to be read in the context surrounding the life and death of the paedophile priest, Fr Brendan Smyth whose right to administer the sacraments was never taken away.
7. As Dunn notes, one of the main failings of the institutional Church, especially the Curia, is to deal with loyal opposition. Dunn, *No Lions in the Hierarchy*, 322.
8. Mary Condren, *The Serpent and the Goddess*, New York: Harper & Row 1989, 204.
9. Condren notes that nothing changed with Vatican II and comments ironically that while women had hardly been allowed to speak at this event, the closing message of the Council was 'Women of the entire universe, you to whom life is entrusted, it is for you to save the peace of the world.' Condren, *The Serpent and the Goddess*, 207.
10. Mary Kenny, *Goodbye to Catholic Ireland*, London: Sinclair-Stevenson 1996, 387.
11. C. Whelan and T. Fahey, 'Religious Change in Ireland 1981–1990', in *Faith and Culture in the Irish Context*, ed. Eoin Cassidy, Dublin: Veritas 1996, 115.
12. See T. Fahey, 'Catholicism and Industrial Society in Ireland', in *The Development of Industrial Society in Ireland*, ed. John Goldthorpe and Chris Whelan, Oxford: Oxford University Press 1992, 241–63; C. Whelan and T. Fahey, 'Marriage and the Family', in *Values and Social Change in Ireland*, ed. Chris Whelan, Dublin: Gill & Macmillan 1994, 45–81.
13. The use of the term 'field' here follows Bourdieu. See Pierre Bourdieu, 'Some Properties of Fields', in *Sociology in Question*, London: Sage 1993, 72–7; Pierre

Bourdieu, 'The Intellectual Field: a world apart', in *In Other Words*, Cambridge: Polity Press 1990, 140–9; Pierre Bourdieu, *The Logic of Practice*, Cambridge: Polity Press 1990, 66–8. A social field such as the religious field, consists of a set of objective, historical relations between individuals, organisations and institutions which are based on certain forms of power, or capital. Bourdieu often uses the analogy of a game to describe a social field. Consequently, the religious field centres around people playing or struggling to be spiritual and moral. There is a certain logic to the religious field. It has its definite patterns and regularities which mark it out as different from other social fields. Even though beliefs and practices change within different churches, denominations and sects, it is almost universally recognised that being religious means being spiritual and moral. This is not deny that playing at or struggling to be a Catholic in Ireland requires a knowledge of local logics and regularities. Success in the religious field, that is being able to control if not dominate the game, depends on the accumulated capital which players bring. Obviously the Catholic Church as an institution has dominated the religious field in Ireland, as has its bishops, priests, nuns and brothers. Not only are they accepted as being spiritual and moral, their control is such that they have been able to set the beliefs and practices necessary for others to acquire religious capital and be seen as spiritual and moral people. For a more detailed discussion of a 'game' being an analogy for what takes place in a social field, see Pierre Bourdieu and Loïc Wacquant, *An Invitation to Reflexive Sociology*, Cambridge: Polity Press 1992, 94–115.

14. Max Weber and Émile Durkheim, two of the greatest sociologists, both studied religion in depth and both came to different conclusions about the need for a definition. Weber declined to give a definition of religion arguing that it was not possible at the start of his research to say what something was, and anyway it was the conditions and effects of religion which were important rather than its essence. Max Weber, *Economy and Society*, Vol.1, Berkeley: University of California Press 1978, 399. Durkheim, on the other hand, gave a precise, detailed definition of religion saying that it is 'a unified system of beliefs and practices relative to sacred things, that is to say, things set apart and forbidden – beliefs and practices which unite into one single moral community called a Church, all those who adhere to them.' Émile Durkheim, *The Elementary Forms of the Religious Life*, London: George Allen & Unwin 1976, 47. For a detailed discussion about the need for and type of sociological definitions of religion, see Roland Robertson, *The Sociological Interpretation of Religion*, Oxford: Basil Blackwell 1970, 34–51.

15. Max Weber, 'Religious Rejections of the World and Their Directions', in *From Max Weber*, ed. Hans Gerth and C. Wright Mills, Oxford: Oxford University Press 1946, 323–59.

16. A. Greeley,'The Persistence of Religion', *Cross Currents*, Spring (1995), 39, 27.

17. For an analysis of the rise of power of priests, see J Goudsblom, 'Ecological Regimes and the Rise of Organised Religion', in *Human History and Social Process: Economic Growth, Social Process and Civilization*, ed. Johan Goudsblom, E.L. Jones and Stephen Mennell, London: M.E. Sharpe 1996, 31–47; Ernest Gellner, *Plough, Sword and Book: The Structure of Human History*, London: Collins Harvill 1988.

18. This was the approach Weber followed in his empirical studies of religion in China, India, Ancient Judea and Modern Europe. See Max Weber, *The Religion of China*, New York: Free Press 1951; Max Weber, *The Religion of India*, New York: Free Press 1958; Max Weber, *Ancient Judaism*, Glencoe: Free Press 1952; Max Weber, *The Protestant Ethic and the Spirit of Capitalism*, New York: Scribner 1958.

19. This mirrors Weber's main question in relation to Western civilisation, and explains his study of world religions. When, where, how and why did cultural phenomena, particularly the Protestant ethic, emerge in Western civilisation which were to have

universal significance, playing a part in the rise of world capitalism? In the present study the question is how, when, where and why did the Catholic Church and Catholicism emerge in Irish society, and come to have such national significance to the end of the twentieth century? See, Max Weber, 'Author's Introduction', in *The Protestant Ethic*, 13. Answering these questions helps fulfil what Mills saw as the promise of sociology, to enable ordinary people see the connection between the patterns of their own lives and the course of world history. C. Wright Mills, *The Sociological Imagination*, London: Oxford University Press 1959, 4.

20. E. Larkin, 'The Devotional Revolution in Ireland 1850–1875', *American Historical Review* LXXVII (1972), 649. Cullen has argued similarly that the concept of Ireland being an island of saints and scholars was a romantic construct developed to deal with rapid social change. L.M. Cullen, *The Emergence of Modern Ireland 1600–1900*, Dublin: Gill & Macmillan 1983, 255.

21. D. Miller, 'Irish Catholicism and the Great Famine', *Journal of Social History*, IX (1975), 81–98.

22. S. J. Connolly, *Priests and People in Pre-Famine Ireland 1780–1845*, Dublin: Gill & Macmillan 1982, 278.

23. E. Hynes, 'The Great Hunger and Irish Catholicism', *Societas*, VIII (1978), 81–98.

24. I am grateful to DBK for his help in formulating this Marxist interpretation.

25. The primacy of religious symbols and language in terms of classifying, reading and operating in the social world has been long recognised by sociologists, particularly those in the French structuralist tradition, and especially Durkheim and Lévi-Strauss. Religion is the primordial force through which consensus is generated about the way the world is classified and objectively understood and, at the same time, becomes the symbolic medium through which this knowledge is communicated. Bourdieu, although always trying to overcome what he sees as the false dichotomy between structuralist and hermeneutic or symbolic interactionist theories, is nevertheless rooted in the French tradition. The task for contemporary sociological analysis of religion, according to Bourdieu, is to link religion in with the overall process of symbolic production in highly differentiated, class divided, societies. See P. Bourdieu, 'Genesis and Structure of the Religious Field', *Comparative Social Research*, 13 (1991), 3.

26. Bourdieu, 'Genesis and Structure of the Religious Field', 13, 2. For an overview of Bourdieu's analysis of the relation between structure and agency, see P. Bourdieu, 'Men and Machines', in *Advances in Social Theory and Methodology*, ed. K. Knorr-Cetina and A.V. Cicourel, London: Routledge & Kegan Paul 1981, 304–17.

27. Bourdieu, 'Men and Machines', 309–12.

28. Weber, *Economy and Society*, 1, 439–67.

29. Weber, *Economy and Society*, 1, 419; Max Weber, *Economy and Society*, Vol.2, Berkeley: University of California Press 1978, 1178–9.

30. P. Bourdieu, 'Legitimation and Structured Interests in Weber's Sociology of Religion', in *Max Weber, Rationality and Modernity*, ed. Sam Whimster and Scott Lash, London: Allen & Unwin 1987, 126 (emphasis in original).

31. For an overview of Bourdieu's concept of habitus, see Bourdieu, *Logic of Practice*, 54–65.

32. For an overview of Bourdieu's concept of capital, see P. Bourdieu, 'Forms of Capital', in *Handbook of Theory and Research for the Sociology of Education*, ed. J. Richardson, Westport [Conn.]: Greenwood Press 1986, 241–58.

Chapter 2. The Religious Habitus of Irish Catholics.

1. Robert Kennedy, *The Irish*, Berkeley: University of California Press 1973, 110.

2. Máire Nic Ghiolla Phádraig, personal communication of unpublished findings from 1973–74 national survey. For details of the sample see M. Nic Ghiolla Phádraig, 'Religion in Ireland: Preliminary Analysis', *Social Studies*, V (1976), 116–19.

3. B. Walsh, 'Religion and Demographic Behaviour in Ireland', (Paper 55), Dublin: Economic and Social Research Institute 1970, 33.
4. Jack White, *Minority Report*, Dublin: Gill & Macmillan 1975, 130.
5. Walsh, 'Religion and Demographic Behaviour', 32.
6. See Kennedy, *The Irish*, 187–8; Damian Hannan, 'Displacement and Development: Class, Kinship and Social Change in Irish Rural Communities', (Paper 96), Dublin: Economic and Social Research Institute 1979.
7. Research and Development Commission, 'Students and Religion 1976', Dublin 1978, 22–5.
8. There has been considerable debate in the sociology of religion concerning the different dimensions of religiosity, or ways in which people can be religious. For a discussion of these in relation to Irish Catholicism see, T. Inglis, 'Dimensions of Irish Students' Religiosity', *Economic and Social Review*, XI (1980), 237–56.
9. L. Ryan, 'Faith Under Survey', *The Furrow*, January 1983, 10.
10. Ryan, 'Faith Under Survey', 9.
11. See Séan Connolly, *Religion and Society in Nineteenth Century Ireland*, Dundalk: Dundalgan Press 1985, 49–50.
12. This typology is adapted from Max Weber, *Economy and Society* Vol. 1, ed. Guenther Roth and Claus Wittich, Berkeley: University of California Press 1968, 422–39. See also Wolfgang Schluchter, *The Rise of Western Rationalism*, Berkeley: University of California Press 1981, 43–48.
13. Weber, *Economy and Society* 1, 422.
14. Weber, *Economy and Society* 1, 426, 432, 438; Schluchter, *Western Rationalism*, 44, 168.
15. Max Weber, *The Protestant Ethic and the Spirit of Capitalism*, New York: Scribner 1958, 117.
16. Max Weber, *Economy and Society* Vol. 2, ed. Guenther Roth and Claus Wittich, Berkeley: University of California Press 1968, 1165.
17. *A Catechism of Catholic Doctrine*, Dublin: Gill 1951, 101.
18. N. Abercrombie *et al.*, 'Superstition and Religion: God and the Gaps', in *A Sociological Yearbook of Religion in Britain* Vol.3, London: SCM Press 1970, 98.
19. David Martin, *The Religious and Secular*, London: Routledge & Kegan Paul 1969, 107.
20. S. J. Connolly, *Priests and People in Pre-Famine Ireland 1780–1845*, Dublin: Gill & Macmillan 1982, 148.
21. Patrick Logan, *Making the Cure*, Dublin: Villa Books 1972, 1.
22. Patrick Logan, *The Holy Wells of Ireland*, Gerrards Cross: Colin Smythe 1980, 14.
23. See Weber, *Economy and Society* 1, 422.
24. Nic Ghiolla Phádraig, personal communication of unpublished findings from 1973–74 national survey. See note 2 above.
25. See Colm Tobín, ed., *Seeing is Believing: Moving Statues in Ireland*, Mountrath: Pilgrim Press 1985.
26. Lawrence Taylor, *Occasions of Faith*, Dublin: Lilliput 1996, 35–6; 162; 218; 226.
27. Research and Development Commission, 'Solemn Novena to Our Lady of Perpetual Succour', Dublin 1980.
28. Hugh Kelly, *A History of the Novena of Grace*, Dublin: Irish Messenger 1965, 15.
29. Research and Development Commission, 'Report No. 1: Religious Practice', Dublin 1975, 63.
30. *Catechism of Catholic Doctrine*, 67.
31. Tony Flannery, *The Death of Religious Life?*, Dublin: Columba Press 1997, 10–11, 15.
32. Mary Kenny, *Goodbye to Catholic Ireland*, London: Sinclair-Stevenson 1997, 229.
33. Research and Development Commission, 'A Survey of Religious Practice, Attitudes and Beliefs: Report No. 3, Moral Values', Unpublished report. Dublin 1976, 79.

34. M. Hornsby-Smith and C. Whelan, 'Religious and Moral Values', in *Values and Social Change in Ireland*, ed. Christopher Whelan, Dublin: Gill and Macmillan 1994, 21.
35. T. Inglis, 'Dimensions of Irish Students' Religiosity', *Economic and Social Review*, XI (1980), 244, 247.
36. Research and Development Commission, 'Report No.21, Religious Beliefs, Practice and Moral Attitudes: A Comparison of Two Irish Surveys 1974–1984' Maynooth: 1985, 35, 61.
37. M. Nic Ghiolla Phádraig, 'Alternative Models to Secularisation in Relation to Moral Reasoning', *CISR Religion, Values and Daily Life*, Lausanne: Acts of the International Conference on the Sociology of Religion, 1981, 367–8.
38. Inglis, 'Dimensions of Irish Students' Religiosity'.
39. Irish Episcopal Conference, *Conscience and Morality*, Dublin: Irish Messenger 1980, 22, 16.
40. Bishop Jeremiah Newman, quoted in the *The Irish Times*, 30 September 1981.
41. Irish Episcopal Conference, 'Conscience and Morality', 16.
42. K. O'Doherty, 'Where Have all the Faithful Gone?', *The Furrow*, XX (1969), 588.
43. Nic Ghiolla Phádraig, 'Religion in Ireland', 121.
44. Nic Ghiolla Phádraig, personal communication.
45. Nic Ghiolla Phádraig, 'Religion in Ireland', 144.
46. M. MacGréil, 'Church Attendance and Religious Practice of Dublin Adults', *Social Studies* III (1974), 181.
47. Inglis, 'Dimensions of Irish Students' Religiosity', 247.
48. See Michael Fogerty, Liam Ryan and Joseph Lee, *Irish Values and Attitudes*, Dublin: Dominican Publications 1984, esp. 125–6.

Chapter 3. Church Organisation and Control.
1. Max Weber, *Economy and Society* Vol. 1, ed. Guenther Roth and Claus Wittich, Berkeley: University of California Press 1968, 603.
2. Max Weber, *Economy and Society* Vol. 2, ed. Guenther Roth and Claus Wittich, Berkeley: University of California Press 1968, 1393.
3. For a detailed description of the Irish Hierarchy's decision-making process, see D. Keogh, 'Episcopal Decision-Making in Ireland', in *Education, Church and State*, ed. M. O'Connell, Dublin: Institute of Public Administration 1992, 1–18.
4. *The Irish Times*, 18 August 1983.
5. Quoted in L. Ryan, 'Church and Politics: The Last Twenty-Five Years', *The Furrow*, XXX (1979), 12.
6. Jean Blanchard, *The Church in Contemporary Ireland*, Dublin: Clonmore and Reynolds 1963, 17, 19.
7. Research and Development Commission, 'Report No.4: Attitudes to the Institutional Church', Dublin 1976, 67.
8. Blanchard, *The Church in Contemporary Ireland*, 20.
9. For a discussion of the gap between the Internal Forum and External Forum in relation to sex, see Kate Saunders and Peter Stanford, *Catholics and Sex*, London: Mandarin 1992, 155–60.
10. T. Inglis, 'Decline in Numbers of Priests and Religious in Ireland', *Doctrine and Life*, XXX (1979), 87.
11. Research and Development Commission, 'Irish Catholic Clergy and Religious, 1970–1981', Maynooth 1983, 4.
12. For an overview of the structure and patterns of symbolic power, see Pierre Bourdieu, *Language and Symbolic Power*, Cambridge: Polity 1991, esp. 163–70.
13. For a description of how priests operated at parish level in civil, political and economic matters see, Chris Eipper, *The Ruling Trinity: A Community Study of Church, State and Business in Ireland*, Aldershot: Gower 1986, 98–108.

14. J. Abbot, 'Visitations by Priests in Irish Rural Parishes', *Irish Ecclesiastical Record*, XCVI (1961), 10.
15. Research and Development Commission, Report No. 4, 25.
16. Abbot, 'Visitations by Priests', 3.
17. For a discussion of the structural homology between social life inside and outside the home, see Pierre Bourdieu, 'The Kabyle House or the World Reversed', in *The Logic of Practice*, 271–83.
18. Abbot, 'Visitations by Priests', 9.
19. Ryan, 'Church and Politics', 5.
20. T. Inglis, 'Dimensions of Irish Students' Religiosity', *Economic and Social Review*, XI (1980), 244, 247. Research and Development Commission, 'Students and Religion 1976', Dublin 1978, 24.
21. This fault is beginning to be rectified. See, for example, Catriona Clear, *Nuns in Nineteenth Century Ireland*, Dublin: Gill & Macmillan 1987; T. Fahey, 'Nuns in the Catholic Church in Ireland in the Nineteenth Century', in *Girls Don't Do Honours*, ed. Mary Cullen, Dublin: Women's Education Bureau 1987, 7–30; M. MacCurtain, 'Late in the Field: Catholic Sisters in Twentieth Century Ireland and the New Religious History', *Journal of Women's History*, 6.4 (1995), 49–63.
22. Again this fault is beginning to be rectified, see Barry Coldrey, *Faith and Fatherland: The Christian Brothers and the Development of Irish Nationalism 1838–1923*, Dublin: Gill & Macmillan 1988.
23. Inglis, 'Decline in Numbers', 87.
24. Research and Development, 'Irish Catholic Clergy', 83.
25. Inglis, 'Decline in Numbers', 98.
26. Research and Development Commission, Report No. 4, 30.
27. Evelyn Bolster, *The Knights of St Columbanus*, Dublin: Gill & Macmillan 1979, 32. See also, Emily O'Reilly, *Masterminds of the Right*, Dublin: Attic Press 1992, esp. 23–9.
28. Desmond Clarke, *Church and State*, Cork: Cork University Press 1984, 202.
29. Quoted in Christina Murphy, *School Report*, Dublin: Ward River Press 1980, 155.
30. Quoted in John Whyte, *Church and State in Modern Ireland*, 1923–1970, 1st edn., Dublin: Gill & Macmillan 1971, 306.
31. See Sheelagh Drudy and Kathleen Lynch, *Schools and Society in Ireland*, Dublin: Gill & Macmillan 1993, 76–8.
32. The White Paper on Education proposed to change this structure to a core board of two nominees of the patron, two parents, one staff member and the principal who would be *ex officio*. The core board would then nominate two members of the wider community to join it. See *Charting Our Education Future*, Dublin: Government Publications 1995, 148.
33. *Solas* No. 6 (Easter, 1985), 4.
34. *The Irish Times*, 20 November 1985.
35. Charles McCarthy, *The Distasteful Challenge*, Dublin: Institute of Public Administration 1968, 109.
36. *List of Post-Primary Schools 1982–1983*, Dublin: Government Publications 1983, 1–11. This does not include schools under the Vocational Education Committee system. There has also been a decline in recent years in number of Catholic schools. See Drudy and Lynch, *Schools and Society*, 6–16.
37. Nic Ghiolla Phádraig, 'Religion in Ireland', 144.
38. Whyte, *Church and State*, 18.
39. *The Irish Times*, 9 March 1985.
40. E. Brian Titley, *Church, State and the Controlling of Schooling in Ireland 1900–1944*, Dublin: Gill & Macmillan 1983, 153.
41. Clarke, *Church and State*, 215.

42. Ryan, 'Church and Politics', 15.
43. For an example of the extent of this control, see O'Reilly, *Masterminds of the Right*, 7–9.
44. See Whyte, *Church and State*, 281.
45. Letter from the Irish Hierarchy to the Taoiseach, 5 April 1951, quoted in Whyte, *Church and State*, 426.

Chapter 4. Power and the Catholic Church in Irish Social, Political and Economic Life.

1. Bourdieu sees the struggle to attain economic capital as primary, but sees the struggle to attain other forms of capital as independent and not reducible to the attempt to gain economic capital. On the other hand, he refuses to see, for example, the struggle to attain religious capital as having nothing to do with trying to attain economic capital. See P. Bourdieu, 'Forms of Capital', in *Handbook of Theory and Research for the Sociology of Education*, ed. J. Richardson, Westport CT.: Greenwood Press 1986, 252–3.
2. For a detailed discussion on the volume and structure of an individual's accumulated capital and how this defines his or her position in society, see Pierre Bourdieu, *Distinction*, London: Routledge & Kegan Paul 1986, esp. 99–168. Although Bourdieu recognised religious capital as central to cultural and symbolic capital, he rarely refers to it in contemporary analyses. This may simply be that it is no longer an important component in defining a person's social position in French society. See P. Bourdieu, 'Genesis and Structure of the Religious Field', *Comparative Social Research*, 13 (1991), 22–3.
3. Bourdieu, 'Forms of Capital', 243–8.
4. Bourdieu, 'Forms of Capital', 248–52.
5. Bourdieu refers to political capital simply in terms of having 'political clout', but this derives from being able to mobilise people which, following Weber, derives from the functional necessity or professional capacity of the position on the one hand, and personal charm or charisma on the other. See Pierre Bourdieu, *Language and Symbolic Power*, Cambridge: Polity 1991, 194–7. Peillon has developed the concept of political capital to include the ability to control what is done, to mobilise followers, and to mould their behaviour. See M. Peillon, 'Constructing Irish Welfare as an Object of Sociological Investigation', Paper presented at Sociological Association of Ireland Annual Conference, Dundalk, May, 1996.
6. See P. Bourdieu, 'Social Space and the "Genesis of Classes"', in *Language and Symbolic Power*, Cambridge: Polity 1991, 239–43; P. Bourdieu, 'On Symbolic Power', in *Language and Symbolic Power*, 164–70; P. Bourdieu, 'Social space and symbolic power', in *Sociology in Question*, London: Sage 1993, 122–39.
7. M. Nic Ghiolla Phádraig, 'Religion in Ireland: Preliminary Analysis', *Social Studies*, V (1976), 120.
8. Research and Development Commission, 'Students and Religion 1976', Dublin 1978, 39.
9. This, of course, is a central thesis of Elias. See N. Elias, *State Formation and Civilization*: Vol. 2. *The Civilizing Process*, Oxford: Basil Blackwell 1982, 247–58.
10. Nic Ghiolla Phádraig 'Religion in Ireland', 148–9. MacGréil found that in the case of monthly Holy Communion, 'manual workers are almost 20% less frequent participants than the higher status occupations'. M. MacGréil, 'Church Attendance and Religious Practice of Dublin Adults', *Social Studies* III (1974), 185, 181.
11. Pierre Bourdieu, *Reproduction In Education, Society and Culture*, London: Sage 1977. P. Bourdieu, 'Cultural Reproduction and Social Reproduction', in *Knowledge, Education and Cultural Change*, London: Tavistock 1973.
12. Research and Development Commission, 'Report No.4: Attitudes to the Institutional Church', Dublin 1976, 4.

13. P. Ó Healaí, 'Moral Values in Irish Religious Tales', *Bealoideas*, XLII–XLIV (1974), 212.
14. E. Leyton, 'Conscious Models and Dispute Regulations in an Ulster Village', *Man*, I (1966) 535–6.
15. P. McNabb 'Social Structure', in *Limerick Rural Survey*, ed. Jeremiah Newman, Tipperary: Muintir na Tíre 1964, 198.
16. Damian Hannan and Louise Katsiaouni, *Traditional Families?* Dublin: Economic and Social Research Institute 1977, 84. Hutchinson cites examples from USA, Portugal, Brazil and Mexico. He argues that the chief function of mutual aid in Ireland, as in other similar societies, 'was not that of easing a man's personal burden of labour; it was that of providing a degree of security to the people. . . .' B. Hutchinson, 'On the Study of Non-Economic Factors in Irish Economic Development', *Economic and Social Review*, I (1970), 522. Gibbon, however, rejects the notion that the mutual aid system has the function of providing security, or that it is part of the struggle to attain social prestige, and claims that it was part of the exploitation of small farmers by large farmers. P. Gibbon, 'Arensberg and Kimball Revisited', *Economy and Society*, II (1973) 487.
17. Nic Ghiolla Phádraig, 'Religion in Ireland', 135. Heeran found that 58 per cent of her school-leaver respondents perceived their mother as extremely or very religious, compared with 34 per cent who so described their fathers, see Rita Heeran, 'Attitudes of School Leavers to Missionary Religious Vocation', Dublin: Irish Missionary Union 1976, 34A.
18. E. Viney, 'Women in Rural Ireland', *Christus Rex*, XXII (1966), 334.
19. P. McNabb in *Limerick Rural Survey*, 199.
20. These issues are dealt with in more detail in chapter nine.
21. Paul Blanshard, *The Irish and Catholic Power*, Boston: Beacon Press 1953, 186.
22. See John Whyte, *Church and State in Modern Ireland*, 1923–1970, 1st edn., Dublin: Gill & Macmillan 1971, 44–7.
23. *The Irish Rosary* (March 1951), 70. Carty notes that the writer John McGahern was told that the reason he was dismissed from being a national school teacher was not so much for having written his book *The Dark*, but for having married a foreign women in a registry office. Ciarán Carty, *Confessions of a Sewer Rat*, Dublin: New Island Books 1995, 19.
24. Brian Inglis, *West Briton*, London: Faber & Faber 1969, 107.
25. Whyte, *Church and State*, 368n, 313.
26. *The Irish Times*, 22 August 1983.
27. M. Daly, 'The Economic Ideals of Irish Nationalism: Frugal Comfort or Lavish Austerity?', *Éire/Ireland*, XXIX.4 (1994), 77–100. Lee, on the other hand, has argued that the Irish person was as rationally calculating and strategically economic as any other European. Joseph Lee, *Ireland 1912–1985*, Cambridge: Cambridge University Press 1989, 517. But it is important to realise that Irish people were strategically calculating in a way and in circumstances beyond their own choosing. It was for this reason that, as Lee himself points out, they were 'prepared to scatter their children around the world in order to preserve their own living standards.' Lee, *Ireland 1912–1985*, 522. It was because they were symbolically as well as politically dominated by the Catholic Church that they ended up having to strategically export their children.
28. Whyte took only 'those measures in regard to which I have evidence that, at any stage, one or more bishops were consulted or made representations.' He was thus able to conclude that the influence of the Catholic hierarchy on state policy 'has been fairly rarely exercised'. Whyte, *Church and State*, 363, 362.
29. Keogh refers to this symbiotic relationship as an 'informal consensus'. As an example of this relationship, Keogh quotes from *Preface to Statecraft* by Desmond

FitzGerald (father of the former Taoiseach Garret FitzGerald): 'Thus when it is recognised that the Church has been instituted by God himself . . . then it is also clear that the nature of the state and of its authority demands that it should assist rather than hinder the Church in the fulfilment of her mission.' See D. Keogh, 'Catholicism and the Formation of the Modern Irish State', in *Irishness in a Changing Society*, 164. See also, Dermot Keogh, *The Vatican, The Bishops and Irish Politics 1919–1939*, Cambridge: Cambridge University Press 1986, 201.

30. See T. Inglis, 'The Separation of Church and State in Ireland', *Social Studies*, 9.2 (1986), 37–48.
31. See Keogh, in *Irishness in a Changing Society*, 170–7.
32. Whyte, *Church and State*, 363–4.
33. Whyte, *Church and State*, 365. Basil Chubb, *Government and Politics of Ireland*, 2nd edn, London: Longmans 1982, 18.
34. Whyte, *Church and State*, 36, 42.
35. As Keogh points out, the absence of any party conflict on the debate on the draft Constitution and the religious principles which underlay it, indicate how united the two main parties were in their Catholic nationalist view of the relation between Church and state. Keogh, in *Irishness in a Changing Society*, 164.
36. *Constitution of Ireland*, Dublin: Government Publications 1980, 2.
37. Quoted in Whyte, *Church and State*, 312, 313.
38. Ryan, 'Church and Politics', 12–13.
39. *The Irish Times*, 13 February 1985, 30 November 1984.
40. Whyte, *Church and State*, 249, 368.
41. Keogh, in *Irishness in a Changing Society*, 157, 161.
42. *The Irish Independent*, 1 January 1985.
43. Nic Ghiolla Phádraig, 'Religion in Ireland', 126–7.
44. See Max Weber, 'Religious Rejections of the World and Their Directions', in *From Max Weber*, ed. Hans Gerth and C. Wright Mills, Oxford: Oxford University Press 1946, 340–1.
45. *The Irish Times*, 3 September, 16 August, 20 August, 1983. *The Irish Independent*, 23 August 1983.
46. *The Irish Independent*, 26 August 1983. For a detailed description of the referendum and its effects not just on the political parties and professional associations, but on PLAC itself, see Tom Hesketh, *The Second Partioning of Ireland*, Dublin: Brandsma Books, 1990.
47. *The Irish Times*, 17 August 1983; *The Irish Independent*, 19 August 1983; *The Irish Times*, 22 August 1983; *The Irish Independent*, 28 August 1983 & 2 September 1983; *The Irish Times*, 31 August, 2 September 1983; *The Irish Independent*, 3 September 1983.
48. *The Irish Press*, 16 August 1983; *The Irish Independent*, 1 September 1983.
49. *The Irish Independent*, 1 September, 18 August 1983; *The Irish Press*, 19 August 1983; *The Irish Times*, 19 August 1983, 20 August 1983; *The Irish Independent*, 24 August 1983.
50. *The Irish Times*, 5 September 1983.
51. *The Irish Times*, 12 June 1986.
52. *The Irish Times*, 12 June 1986.
53. *The Irish Times*, 20 June 1986.
54. *The Irish Times*, 28 June 1986.
55. Kieran Woodman, *Media Control in Ireland 1923–1983*, Carbondale: Southern Illinois Press 1985, 40.
56. Woodman, *Media Control*, 73. For a detailed account of film censorship from the 1960s, see Carthy, *Confessions of a Sewer Rat*.
57. Michael Adams, *Censorship, the Irish Experience*, Alabama: Alabama University Press 1968, 247ff.

58. Bolster indicates that the Knights of St Columbanus were a major, but, as a secret organisation, also a covert, factor in much of the early social legislation of the Irish State, see Evelyn Bolster, *The Knights of St Columbanus*, Dublin: Gill & Macmillan 1979, 51.

59. Quoted in Woodman, *Media Control*, 33. Indeed, Rome had a similar hope for Irish television when it was being planned in the 1950s. See Robert Savage, *Irish Television: The Political and Social Origins*, Cork: Cork University Press 1996, 154.

60. Savage, *Irish* Television, 213.

61. J. Murphy, 'Censorship and the Moral Community', in *Communications and Community in Ireland*, ed. Brian Farrell, Cork: Mercier Press 1984, 62.

62. *The Irish Times*, 29 September 1984.

Part 2: Origins of the Power of the Catholic Church in Ireland. Introduction.

1. For a discussion of the relation between sociology and history see Theda Skocpol, *Vision and Method in Historical Sociology*, Cambridge: Cambridge University Press 1984; Dennis Smith, *The Rise of Historical Sociology*, Oxford: Polity Press 1991.

2. This was one of Weber's main concerns. He sought to explain how and why modern capitalism developed when it did in Europe from the sixteenth century. See Max Weber, 'Author's Introduction', in *The Protestant Ethic and the Spirit of Capitalism*, London: Allen & Unwin 1956, 13–31. For a discussion of Weber's overall project in relation to history, sociology and a theory of modernity, see G. Roth, 'Rationalization in Max Weber's Developmental History', in *Max Weber, Rationality and Modernity*, ed. S. Whimster and S. Lash, London: Allen & Unwin 1987; T. Fahey, 'Max Weber's *Ancient Judaism*', *American Journal of Sociology* 85, 1982, 62–87. Marx was interested in the same question, although he came up with a different explanation. See, for example, Karl Marx, *The German Ideology*, New York: International Publishers 1974. But others such as Durkheim in relation to education and Elias in relation to civility and Foucault in relation to science have sought similar long term explanations of how Western society developed. See Émile Durkheim, *The Evolution of Educational Thought*, London: Routledge & Kegan Paul 1977; Norbert Elias, *The Civilising Process*, Vol. 1., *The History of Manners*, New York: Urizen 1978; Michel Foucault, *The Order of Things*, New York: Vintage 1973.

3. The notion of characterising history in terms of radical shifts, ruptures and discontinuities follows Foucault's methodology. See Michel Foucault, *The Archaeology of Knowledge*, London: Tavistock 1972.

4. For example, while O'Dwyer basically argues that Ireland has been 'the island of saints and scholars', he also accepts that it was and still is 'the island of sinners and scalliwags'. See Peter O'Dwyer, *Towards a History of Irish Spirituality*, Dublin: Columba Press 1995.

5. See, for example, Mary Condren, *The Serpent and the Goddess*, New York: Harper & Row 1989.

6. Following Bourdieu, we might describe this as a shift within the the field of Irish Catholicism so that there was a closer correspondence or incorporation of religious orthodoxy and the *doxa* or *habitus* of the ordinary lives of Irish Catholics. See P. Bourdieu, 'Legitimation and structured interests in Weber's sociology of religion', in *Max Weber, Rationality and Modernity*, ed. Sam Whimster and Scott Lash, London: Allen & Unwin 1987, 122–4; P. Bourdieu, 'Genesis and structure of the religious field', *Comparative Social Research*, 13, 5–13. For a discussion of Bourdieu's concept of the relation of habitus and the lived histories and lives of ordinary people to symbolic domination by official cultural creators and producers such as bishops and priests see L. Wacquant, 'From Ideology to Symbolic Violence: Culture, Class and Consciousness in Marx and Bourdieu', *International Journal of Contemporary*

Sociology, 30.2. (1993), 125–41; D. Swartz, 'Bridging the Study of Culture and Religion: Pierre Bourdieu's Political Economy of Symbolic Power', in *Sociology of Religion*, 57, 171–85.

7. This notion of symbolic domination is derived from Bourdieu. See Pierre Bourdieu, *Language and Symbolic Power*, Cambridge: Polity Press 1991, 163–70. As Thompson notes, Bourdieu's concepts of symbolic power and violence are based on shared belief among the people in the language and symbols involved and, consequently, an inherent misrecognition of their dominating effects. See John Thompson, Editor's Introduction to *Language and Symbolic Power*, 23. In this regard, the extent of shared belief in the language and symbols of the English State and the Protestant Ascendancy needs to be examined. It may well be that while there was a logical contradiction between the teachings of the Catholic Church and the established Protestant Church in the nineteenth century, many Catholics accepted rather than questioned the symbols and language of the latter and experienced no contradictions.

8. In relation to the close links between the consolidation of the power of the Catholic Church in Ireland and the formation of an independent state see, in particular, the extensive works of Emmet Larkin. For an overview of his argument see E. Larkin, 'Church and State in Ireland in Nineteenth Century', *Church History* 1962, 294–306; 'Church, State and Nation in Modern Ireland', *American Historical Review* 1975, LXXX, 625–52; *The Roman Catholic Church and the Creation of the Modern Irish State*, Philadelphia: American Philosophical Society 1975. See also, David Miller, *Church, State and Nation in Ireland, 1898–1921*, Dublin: Gill & Macmillan 1973. For a more in-depth description of the relation between priests and people, see James O'Shea, *Priests, Politics and Society in Post-famine Ireland*, Dublin: Wolfhound Press 1983. For a more sociological explanation of the relation between being religious and being political, see Tom Garvin, *The Evolution of Irish Nationalist Politics*, Dublin: Gill & Macmillan 1981; Desmond Keenan, *The Catholic Church in Nineteenth Century Ireland*, Dublin: Gill & Macmillan 1983; Séan Connolly, *Religion and Society in Ireland in Nineteenth Century Ireland*, Dundalk: Dundalgan Press 1985.

9. The structure-agency debate is probably the oldest and most problematic issue in sociology. Many sociologists would accept that it is no longer a question of seeing, on the one hand, structures as being determinant of individual action or, on the other hand, emphasing agency as being primary and, that consequently, structures are not permanent soldifications but rather permeable, fragile, ever-evolving entities which are continually created and recreated through the actions of people operating within them. Sociologists now tend to accept that it is a question of mutual conditioning. In other words, structures create the framework within which people say and do things, but what they actually say and do can change the structure. For example, the inherited, accumulated weight of the institutional structure of the Catholic Church, its organisation, teachings, theology and human resources has an impact, or limits, what Irish people think, do and say. But at the same time, it is not completely determining and what Catholics do and say is never completely orthodox and consequently their agency leads to changes in the institutional church. The structure-agency debate relates to many other debates such as how social change takes place and the split between objective or subjective interpretations of social life. These issues are central to the work of Bourdieu. See, for example, Pierre Bourdieu, *Outline of a Theory of Practice*, Cambridge: Cambridge University Press 1977; *The Logic of Practice*, Cambridge: Polity Press 1990. For a good introduction to how Bourdieu deals with the structure-agency debate, see Pierre Bourdieu and Loïc Wacquant, *An Invitation to Reflexive Sociology*, Chicago: University of Chicago Press 1992. For different interpretations of this debate, see

Anthony Giddens, *Central Problems in Social Theory*, London: Macmillan 1979 and *The Constitution of Society*, Cambridge: Polity Press 1984; Zygmunt Bauman, *Culture as Praxis*, London: Routledge & Kegan Paul 1973; Margaret Archer, *Culture and Agency*, Cambridge: Cambridge University Press 1988. For a limited but eminently accessible introduction to the debate see Peter Berger, *An Invitation to Sociology*, Harmondsworth: Penguin 1966.

10. Political interest may also be extended to religious interest. Connolly has argued that the believer and the unbeliever will produce different histories of Irish Catholicism. 'Where the religious historian sees himself as examining the conditions which shaped the development of a religious movement, the secular historian sees himself as examining the conditions to which that movement can be reduced. And sooner or later the difference in approach becomes inescapable. . . .' S. J. Connolly, 'Religion and History', *Irish Economic and Social History*, X, 1983, 67. See also D. W. Miller, 'Irish Catholicism and the Historian', *Irish Economic and Social History*, XIII (1986), 113–16.

11. S.J. Connolly, *Priests and People in Pre-Famine Ireland*, Dublin: Gill & Macmillan 1982, 219.

12. This discussion is derived from Weber. See Max Weber, *The Methodology of the Social Sciences*, Glencoe: Free Press 1949. For a detailed discussion of Weber's theory of concept formation in the natural and cultural science see Thomas Burger, *Max Weber's Theory of Concept Formation* Durham [North Carolina]: Duke University Press 1976.

Chapter 5. The Growth in Power of the Institutional Church in Nineteenth-Century Ireland.

1. Submission from the Irish Privy Council (1719), quoted in William Burke, *The Irish Priests in Penal Times (1660–1760)*, Shannon: Irish University Press 1969, 200–1.

2. Quoted in Jeremiah Newman, *Maynooth and Georgian Ireland*, Galway: Kenny 1979, 33. See also John Healy, *Maynooth College: Its Centenary History*, Dublin: Browne & Nolan 1895, 87–125.

3. William Lecky, *A History of Ireland in the Eighteenth Century*, Vol. 1., London: Longmans, Green & Co. 1916, 146, 151.

4. Patrick Corish, *The Catholic Community in the Seventeenth and Eighteenth Centuries*, Dublin: Helicon 1981, 74.

5. Maureen Wall, *The Penal Laws 1691–1760*, Dundalk: Dundalgan Press 1976, 11–16.

6. Lecky, *History of Ireland*, 160.

7. Corish, *The Catholic Community*, 76.

8. N. Burke, 'A Hidden Church?: the structure of Catholic Dublin in mid-eighteenth century', *Archivum Hibernicum* XXXII (1974), 85.

9. Sidney Smith, *A Fragment on the Irish Roman Catholic Church*, London: Longman 1845, 7.

10. Lecky, *History of Ireland*, 148.

11. The hedge-school is a legend which still needs to be disentangled from romantic myth. Dowling gives an adequate description without analysing their numbers, their curricula, or their relation to the wider community, see Patrick Dowling, *The Hedge-Schools of Ireland*, Dublin: Talbot 1935; see also Phillip O'Connell, *The Schools and Scholars of Breiffne*, Dublin: Browne & Nolan 1942, 52ff., 357ff.; Donal Akenson, *The Irish Education Experiment*, London: Routledge & Kegan Paul 1970, 45–8. The hedge-schools were fundamental to the creation and maintenance of what Foucault has termed a resistant discourse or transgression against the dominant power-knowledge nexus, see Michel Foucault, 'Revolutionary Action: "Until Now"' in *Language, Counter-Memory, Practice: Selected Essays and*

Interviews, Ithaca: Cornell University Press 1977, 208–33. They were crucial to overcoming the symbolic domination of the Protestant ascendancy and to developing an alternative way of reading, interpreting and acting in social life, see Pierre Bourdieu, *Language and Symbolic Power*, Cambridge: Polity Press 1992, 168–70. However, because they remained disorganised, ill-disciplined networks they never became a social movement instigating social change, see Michel Foucault, *Discipline and Punish: The Birth of the Prison*, New York: Pantheon 1977, 172–7.

12. The concept of 'unintended consequences' was originally developed by Max Weber, see Max Weber, *The Methodology of the Social Sciences*, Glencoe: Free Press 1949, 169–89. See also, R. Merton, 'The unanticipated consequences of purposive social action', *American Sociological Review* 1, 1936, 42ff.

13. Corish, *The Catholic Community*, 103.

14. Quoted in Wall, *The Penal Laws*, 9.

15. Lecky, *History of Ireland*, 233.

16. Joseph Robins, *The Lost Children: A Study of Charity Children in Ireland 1700–1900*, Dublin Institute of Public Adminstration 1980, 10–59.

17. Lecky, *History of Ireland*, 235.

18. Wall, *Penal Laws*, 9.

19. Quoted in T. Corcoran, *Education Systems in Ireland from the Middle Ages*, Dublin: University College 1928, 114. Curtis has argued that there was a deliberate attempt among certain Victorians to portray the Irishman, in contrast to the racial superiority of the English, as subhuman and therefore as a candidate for oppression. See Perry Curtis, *Apes and Angels: The Irishman in Victorian Caricature*, Newton Abbot: David & Charles 1971. See also R.F. Foster, *Paddy and Mr Punch*, Harmondsworth: Penguin 1993.

20. Corcoran, *Education Systems*, 113.

21. Commissioners of the Board of Education, 14th Report (1812), 5. As Foucault points out this emphasis on discipline rather than learning was at the heart of the process of producing and maintaining docile, obedient bodies whether it was in schools, prisons, or armies. He traces the origins of this disciplinary society back to the lives of monks and, in the classical era, sees the influence of groups of Religious Brothers, particularly in France, as being crucial in disseminating discipline throughout society. See Michel Foucault, *Discipline and Punish*, New York: Vintage 1979, 161. It is noteworthy that while Elias also makes regular reference to the pioneering work of Jean Baptiste De La Salle in instilling and maintaining discipline, regularity and internalised self-restaint, he, like Foucault, does not discuss the role of religious belief and institutional church life in this process. See Norbert Elias, *The Civilising Process: The History of Manners*, New York: Urizen Books 1978, 127–28. While the move towards a disciplinary society was central to the creation and maintenance of pacified, regulated states, an account of the direct involvement and interest of the state in creating a disciplinary society, as happened with the British state in Ireland, is missing in both Foucault and Elias.

22. As Akenson notes: 'Ireland underwent no industrial revolution, no significant urbanisation, no breakdown in the agrarian order and family structure, and did not experience any other of the forms of social revolution that usually presage the creation of state systems of formal education.' Akenson, *Education Experiment*, 3.

23. Séamus Breathnach, *The Irish Police: From Earliest Times to the Present Day*, Dublin: Anvil Books 1974, 24.

24. Frederick Maitland, *Justice and Police*, London: Macmillan 1885, 105.

25. Breathnach, *Irish Police*, 24.

26. R. B. McDowell, 'Ireland on the Eve of the Famine', in *The Great Famine*, ed. R. Dudley Edwards and T. Desmond Williams, Dublin: Browne & Nolan 1956, 28.

27. Galen Broeker, *Rural Disorder and Police Reform in Ireland 1812–36*, London: Routledge & Kegan Paul 1970, 231.

28. Conor Brady, *Guardians of the Peace*, Dublin: Gill & Macmillan 1974, 3.
29. Breathnach, *Irish Police*, 36–7.
30. Broeker, *Rural Disorder*, 228.
31. Robins, *Lost Children*, 51.
32. John Douglas, *Observations on the necessity of a legal provision for the Irish poor*, Dublin: Wakeman 1828, 4.
33. Douglas, *Legal Provision*, 7–8.
34. McDowell, 'Ireland on the Eve', 33.
35. Maurice Bruce, *The Coming of the Welfare State*, London: Batsford 1968, 97.
36. 18th Report of the Inspectors General on the General State of Prisons in Ireland (1839).
37. Mark Finnane, *Insanity and the Insane in Post-Famine Ireland*, London: Croom Helm 1981, 20.
38. *State of Ireland*, Report from Select Committee, Vol. 8 (1825), 823.
39. *Emigration from the United Kingdom*, Report from Select Committee, Vol.5 (1827), 313.
40. See H.J. Johnson, *British Emigration Policy 1815–1830*, Oxford: Clarendon Press 1972, 71.
41. *Poor Law*. Report from Commissioners, Vol. 34 (1836) Appendix G, 'The State of the Irish Poor in Great Britain, iii, x, xxxvii, xxxix.
42. For an overall impression of the range and extent of these reports, see Arthur and Jean Maltby, *Ireland in the Nineteenth Century*, New York: Pergamon Press 1979.
43. Wall, *Penal Laws*, 58; Lecky, *History of Ireland*, 168.
44. Lecky, *History of Ireland*, 168.
45. See, for example, J. Colquhon, *Ireland: Popery and Priestcraft the Cause of Her Misery and Crime*, Glasgow: 1836.
46. Wall, *Penal Laws*, 66.
47. Quoted in Donal Kerr, *Peel, Priests and Politics*, Oxford: Clarendon Press 1982, 266.
48. Theobald Wolfe Tone, *An Argument on Behalf of the Catholics of Ireland*, Dublin: The United Irishman 1792, 12.
49. This notion of the differentiation of life-spheres is derived from Weber. See M. Weber, 'Theory of the Stages and Directions of Religious Rejections of the World', in *From Max Weber*, ed. Hans Gerth and C. Wright Mills, Oxford: Oxford University Press 1946, 323–62.
50. See John Brady and Patrick Corish, *The Church under the Penal Code*, Vol. 4, *History of Irish Catholicism*, ed. Patrick Corish, Dublin: Gill & Macmillan 1971, 39–43.
51. Wall, *Penal Laws*, 66.
52. See P. Corish, 'Gallicansim at Maynooth: Archbishop Cullen and the Royal Visitation of 1853', *Studies in Irish History*, ed. A. Cosgrove and D. McCartney, Dublin: University College 1979, 176–7. Keenan disagrees with Corish and argues that throughout the nineteenth century Ireland was uniformly Tridentine, and that there was only 'one image of the Church loyal to the Pope'. See Desmond Keenan, *The Catholic Church in Nineteenth Century Ireland*, Dublin: Gill & Macmillan 1983, 240.
53. For a description of the Relief Acts, see Dennis Gwynn, *The Struggle for Catholic Emancipation*, London: Longmans 1928, 8–93.
54. Gwynn, *Catholic Emancipation*, 150.
55. J.F. Broderick, *The Holy See and the Irish Movement for the Repeal of the Union with England 1829–1847*, Rome: Gregorian University Press 1951, 21.
56. J. Murphy, 'The Support of the Catholic Church in Ireland, 1750–1850', *Historical Studies*, V (1965), 118.

57. Quoted in Kerr, *Peel, Priests*, 120. Kerr provides a detailed discussion of Church/State relations during this period, see esp. 141–211.
58. Kerr, *Peel, Priests*, 158–62, 202–8.
59. Desmond Bowen, *Paul Cardinal Cullen*, Dublin: Gill & Macmillan 1983, 254–5, 298.
60. Corish, *The Catholic Community*, 42, 49–51, 57, 67.
61. See John Brady, *Catholics and Catholicism in the Eighteenth Century Press*, Maynooth: Maynooth University 1965.
62. E. Larkin, 'The Devotional Revolution in Ireland, 1850–75', *American Historical Review*, LXXVII (1972), 630.
63. S. J. Connolly, *Priests and People in Pre-Famine Ireland 1780–1845*, Dublin: Gill & Macmillan 1982, 33.
64. Connolly, *Priests and People*, 38.
65. George O'Brien, *Economic History of Ireland from the Union to the Famine*, London: Longmans 1921, 17–19. (£1 = 20 shillings).
66. Kerr, *Peel, Priests*, 238–48.
67. Connolly, *Priests and People*, 48–51.
68. Murphy 'The Support of the Catholic Church', 107.
69. Kerr, *Peel, Priests*, 36.
70. Connolly, *Priests and People*, 204.
71. Murphy, 'The Support of the Catholic Church', 107.
72. Murphy, 'The Support of the Catholic Church', 105.
73. Murphy, 'The Support of the Catholic Church', 114–17, 104.
74. Connolly, *Priests and People*, 53.
75. Murphy 'The Support of the Catholic Church', 104.
76. Kerr, *Peel, Priests*, 19.
77. Quoted in Myles O'Reilly, *Progress of Catholicity in Ireland in the Nineteenth Century*, Dublin: Kelly 1865, 24.
78. O'Reilly, *Progress of Catholicity*, 24.
79. O'Reilly, *Progress of Catholicity*, 25.
80. Tony Fahey, 'Female Asceticism in the Catholic Church: A Case Study of Nuns in Ireland in the Nineteenth Century', PhD dissertation, University of Illinois, 1981, 86.
81. See Martin Brennan, *Schools of Kildare and Leighlin 1775–1835*, Dublin: Gill 1935, 62–3.
82. Corcoran, *Education Systems*, 89–90.
83. Akenson, *Education Experiment*, 52.
84. Dowling, *Hedge-Schools*, 52.
85. Corcoran, *Education Systems*, 115, 125, 129.
86. Corcoran, *Education Systems*, 129.
87. Akenson, *Education Experiment*, 90.
88. Corcoran, *Education Systems*, 151–3.
89. Corcoran, *Education Systems*, 165.
90. Akenson, *Education Experiment*, 384–5.
91. Fahey, 'Female Asceticism', 93.
92. See Brendan Hensey, *The Health Services of Ireland*, Dublin: Institute of Public Administration 1959, 3–7.
93. Sarah Atkinson, *Mary Aikenhead, Her Life, Her Work and Her Friends*, Gill 1879, 238.
94. An Irish Sister of Charity, *The Life and Work of Mary Aikenhead*, London: Longmans 1924, 146, 158.
95. Select Committee on Medical Charities Vol.10 (1843), 198. See Edward Mapother, *The Dublin Hospitals*, Dublin: Fannin 1845.
96. Dublin Hospitals Commission Vol. 35 (1887), xlii.

97. Fanny Taylor, *Irish Homes and Irish Hearts*, London: Longmans 1867, 25–7, 32, 54, 67–9.
98. Robins, *Lost Children*, 294.
99. Quoted in Robins, *Lost Children*, 305.

Chapter 6. The Irish Civilising Process.
1. As Foucault points out, it was the 'juridico-moral codification of acts, moments, and intentions that legitimated an activity' which characterised the ethics of Christian morality and which separated them from the balance of pleasures system devised by the Greeks. See Michel Foucault, *The Use of Pleasure*, Harmondsworth: Penguin 1987, 138.
2. Spear, Linda, 'The Treatment of Sexual Sin in the Irish Latin Penitential Literature', PhD dissertation, University of Toronto, 1979, 42, 36.
3. Spear, 'Treatment of Sexual Sin', 425.
4. Norbert Elias, *The Civilizing Process, I: The History of Manners*, Oxford: Basil Blackwell 1978, xv.
5. Norbert Elias, *The Civilizing Process, II: State Formation and Civilization*, Oxford: Basil Blackwell 1982, 247–50.
6. Elias, *The Civilizing Process, I*, 80.
7. The shift from physical punishment to the confinement of the body is documented by Foucault. In some respects, the shift reaches a peak with the advent of the mass examination system. See Michel Foucault, *Discipline and Punish: The Birth of the Prison*, New York: Pantheon 1977, esp. 136–41.
8. Elias, *History of Manners*, 101.
9. M. Turner, 'The French Connection with Maynooth College 1795–1855', *Studies*, LXX (1981), 78–80.
10. S. J. Connolly, *Priests and People in Pre-Famine Ireland 1780–1845*, Dublin: Gill & Macmillan 1982, 185.
11. Ruth Clark, *Strangers and Sojourners at Port Royal*, Cambridge: Cambridge University Press 1932, 216.
12. Desmond Keenan, *The Catholic Church in Nineteenth Century Ireland*, Dublin: Gill & Macmillan 1983, 22.
13. John Healy, *Maynooth College: Its Centenary History*, Dublin: Browne & Nolan 1895, 274.
14. Desmond Bowen, *Paul Cardinal Cullen*, Dublin: Gill & Macmillan 1983, 44–5.
15. Keenan, *Catholic Church*, 97.
16. Turner, 'The French Connection', 81–2.
17. Healy, *Maynooth College*, 283.
18. Quoted in E. Larkin, 'Church, State and Nation in Modern Ireland', *American Historical Review*, LXXX (1975), 1255.
19. Larkin, 'Church, State and Nation', 1256.
20. Connolly, *Priests and People*, 45.
21. Connolly, *Priests and People*, 47.
22. Turner, 'The French Connection', 81.
23. Connolly, *Priests and People*, 113. This notion of there being cultural residues which lie deep within a habitus, such as the Irish religious habitus, and which are carried forward within practices as normal and legitimate, needs more sociological reflection. It may be accepted that even amongst the most secular of former Irish Catholics, there are residues of Catholic practices which centre on humility and self-denial. However, it is a different matter to argue that these residues were carried over in the religious habitus from the fifth and sixth centuries.
24. It is not that sexuality was repressed in nineteenth century, but that it began to be deployed or invested in bodies in a different manner. There may have been a rigid

control of who could engage in or talk about sex and, outside of official religious discourse, references to sex may have been silenced. However, at the same time, men, women and children became aware, especially through confession, but also within the home, in what was said and not said, in the construction of gendered spaces, that sex was a problem with which they had continually to be aware of, in themselves and others. See Michel Foucault, *The History of Sexuality*, Vol. I, New York: Vintage 1980, 23.

25. Quoted in Connolly, *Priests and People*, 113.
26. L. McRedmond, 'The Church in Ireland', in *The Church Now*, ed. John Cumming and Paul Burns, Dublin: Gill & Macmillan 1980, 30.
27. Connolly, *Priests and People*, 2–3, 143, 162, 189–90, 192–3.
28. Phillipe Ariès, *Centuries of Childhood*, New York: Vintage 1962, 100.
29. Elias, *History of Manners*, 180.
30. K. Nowlan, 'The Catholic Clergy and Irish Politics in the Eighteen Thirties and Forties', *Historical Studies* IX (1974), 121.
31. Connolly, *Priests and People*, 225.
32. Connolly, *Priests and People*, 239–52; see also J. Murphy, 'The Support of the Catholic Church in Ireland, 1750–1850', *Historical Studies*, V (1965), 111.
33. T. Garvin, 'Defenders, Ribbonmen and Others: Underground Political Networks in Pre-Famine Ireland', *Past and Present*, XCVI (1982), 143.
34. Garvin, 'Defenders, Ribbonmen and Others', 151. See also Connolly, *Priests and People*, 238.
35. Bowen, *Cardinal Cullen*, 254–5.
36. Quoted in Connolly, *Priests and People*, 1.
37. Connolly, *Priests and People*, 126.
38. Alphonsus Liguori, *Sermons for all the Sundays*, Dublin: Duffy 1842.
39. Turner, 'The French Connection', 80.
40. Garvin, 'Defenders, Ribbonmen and Others', 148.
41. Quoted in Connolly, *Priests and People*, 132. Weber notes that the magical-animistic-naturalistic type religion associated with agragrian societies became rationalised primarily with the growth of cities; the emergence of urban trades, artisans, a new bourgeoisie and a priesthood which produced a religious symbolic order which matched their needs and interests. But he also notes, however, that '(R)eligious rationalization has its own dynamics, which economic conditions merely channel; above all, it is linked to the emergence of priestly education.' Max Weber, *Economy and Society* 2, Berkeley: University of California Press 1978, 1179. What is interesting in the Irish case is that the while priestly education grew dramatically from the nineteenth century, it was not associated with a radical decline in magical-legalism. On the contrary, despite warnings and promulgations against magical-legalism at an official level, it was continued to be catered for, if not promoted, by priests up to the present day. In other words, the particular form which hierocratic domination took in Ireland meant that the rationalization of religious ethics did not take place with priestly education. Consequently, magical-legalism persisted longer and may have had an inhibiting effect on the rationalization of Irish economics and politics.
42. Weber, *Economy and Society* 2, 54.
43. *Catholic Penny Magazine* (1834–35), 163–4.
44. D. Miller, 'Irish Catholicism and the Great Famine', *Journal of Social History*, IX (1975), 86–7. Corish claims that Miller's figures must be regarded as a minimum. Corish, *Catholic Community*, 107. However, Connolly argues that Corish's claim 'is based on a complete misreading of Miller's text.' Séan Connolly, *Religion and Society in Nineteenth Century Ireland*, Dundalk: Dundalgen Press 1985, 71.
45. Larkin, 'The Devotional Revolution', 636.

46. Larkin, 'The Devotional Revolution', 644–5.
47. Keenan, *Catholic Church*, 148–52.
48. Connolly, *Priests and People*, 90.
49. Dublin Diocesan Archives, Archbishop Murray files.
50. Connolly, *Priests and People*, 121.
51. Alexander Irwin, *Roman Catholic Morality*, Dublin: Miliken 1836, 13.
52. The sermon was a key point in the ongoing reconstitution of the symbolic authority of the priest and his power to morally dominate his parishioners. Through their specialised language, priests developed a strict religious division of labour in which members of the laity were 'dispossessed of the instruments of symbolic production.' Pierre Bourdieu, *Language and Symbolic Power*, Cambridge: Polity Press 1991, 169. As Bourdieu notes: 'There is a rhetoric which characterizes all discourses of institution, that is to say, the official speech of the authorized spokesperson expressing himself in a solemn situation, with an authority whose limits are identical with the extent of the delegation by the institution. The stylistic features which characterize the language of priests, teachers and, more generally, all institutions, like routinization, stereotyping and neutralization, all stem from the position occupied in a competitive field by these persons entrusted with delegated authority.' Bourdieu, *Language and Symbolic Power*, 109.
53. Liguroi, *Sermons*, 245.
54. Murphy, 'The Support of the Catholic Church', 103.
55. Benedict Valvy, *A Guide for Priests*, Dublin: Gill 1879, 78, 303, 307, 308.
56. Valvy, *A Guide for Priests*, 299.
57. Valvy, *A Guide for Priests*, 112.
58. Dublin Diocesan Archives, Murray Papers.
59. Quoted in Connolly, *Priests and People*, 83–4.
60. DDA, Murray Papers, 'Return for Ballymore Eustace', 1833.
61. See, for example, *Rules for the Regulation of the Christian Doctrine Confraternity of St. Patrick*, Waterford: Hanton 1839.
62. *First Report of the Catholic Book Society*, Dublin: Crean 1828, 5, 11–12.
63. T. Wall, 'The Catholic Book Society and the Irish Catholic Magazine', *Irish Ecclesiastical Record*, CI (1964), 294–5.
64. Anon., *The Accomplished Youth: Containing a Familiar View of the True Principles of the Morality and Politeness*, London: Crosby 1811; anon., *Moral Essays in Praise of Virtue*, Dublin: Jones 1821; William Pinnock, *A Catechism of Morality*, London: Whittaker 1827.
65. Elias, *History of Manners*, 140.
66. Quoted in Bowen, *Cardinal Cullen*, 137–8.
67. Quoted in Norman Atkinson, *Irish Education*, Dublin: Figgis 1969, 69.
68. Quoted in J.M. Goldstrom, *The Social Content of Education 1808–1870*, Shannon: Irish University Press 1972, 53–4.
69. *The Schoolmistress or Instructive and Entertaining Conversations between a Teacher and her Scholars*, Dublin: Bentham & Gardiner 1824, 14–15.
70. *The Schoolmistress*, 19.
71. *An Outline of the General Regulations and Methods of Teaching in the Male National Model Schools*, Dublin: John Foulds 1840, 6, 5.
72. Commissioners of National Education, *An Analysis of School Books*, Dublin 1853, 15.
73. Christian Brothers, *Christian Politeness*, Dublin: Powell 1857.
74. Christian Brothers, *Christian Politeness*, 21.
75. Christian Brothers, *Christian Politeness*, 9.
76. Christian Brothers, *Christian Politeness*, 23, 28.
77. These issues have been developed by Cas Wouters. See C. Wouters, 'Formalization and Informalization: Changing Tension Balances in Civilizing Processes', *Theory,*

Culture and Society Vol. 3.2 (1986), 1–18; Cas Wouters,'Changes in the Lust Balance: Love and Sex in the 20th Century'. Paper presented at Theory, Culture and Society Conference, Berlin, August, 1996.

78. Elias, *History of Manners*, 161–91, 162.
79. Henry Tuke, *On Chastity and Temperance*, Dublin: Graisberry & Campbell 1836, 7.
80. Elias, *History of Manners*, 182.

Chapter 7. The Transformation of Irish Society.
 1. Desmond Bowen, *Paul Cardinal Cullen*, Dublin: Gill & Macmillan 1983, 169–75.
 2. Desmond Bowen, *The Protestant Crusade in Ireland 1800–1870*, Dublin: Gill & Macmillan 1978.
 3. W.D. Borrie, *The Growth and Control of World Population*, London: Weidenfeld & Nicolson 1970, 52; Thomas McKeown, *The Modern Rise of Population*, London: Edward Arnold 1976, 1–2, 32.
 4. Ferdinand Braudel, *The Structures of Everyday Life*, I: *Civilization and Capitalism 15th–18th Century*, London: Collins 1981, 32.
 5. P. E. Razzell, 'Population Change in Eighteenth Century England: A Re-Appraisal', in *Population and Industrialization*, ed. Michael Drake, London: Methuen 1969, 131.
 6. K. H. Connell, *The Population of Ireland 1750–1845*, Oxford: Clarendon Press 1950, 25; L.A. Clarkson, 'Irish Population Revisited, 1687–1821', in *Irish Population, Economy and Society*, ed. J.M. Goldstrom and L.A. Clarkson, Oxford: Clarendon Press 1981, 26.
 7. See McKeown, *World Population*, 18–43. Calvin Goldscheider, *Population, Modernization and Social Structure*, Boston: Little Brown 1971, 122–34.
 8. H.J. Habakkuk, *Population Growth and Economic Development since 1750*, Leicester: Leicester University Press 1971, 45; see also K. Gaskin, 'Age at First Marriage in Europe before 1850: A Summary of Family Reconstruction Data', *Journal of Family History* III (1978), 231.
 9. M. Peterson, 'The Demographic Transformation in the Netherlands', *American Sociological Review*, XV (1960), 346.
10. E. Shorter, 'Illegitimacy, Sexual Revolution and Social Change in Modern Europe', *Journal of Interdisciplinary History* II (1971), 256.
11. E. Shorter, 'Female Emancipation, Birth Control, and Fertility in European History', *American Historical Review* LXXVIII (1973), 628.
12. Borrie, *World Population*, 80–1; see also, Michael Anderson, *Approaches to the Study of the Western Family*, London: Macmillan 1980, 18.
13. Liam Cullen, *An Economic History of Ireland since 1660*, London: Batsford 1972, 100.
14. Connell, *Population of Ireland*, 56.
15. Connell, *Population of Ireland*, 90.
16. L.A. Clarkson, 'Marriage and Fertility in Nineteenth-Century Ireland', in *Marriage and Society*, ed. R. B. Outhwaite, London: Europa 1982, 237.
17. L. Cullen, 'Population Growth and Diet 1660–1850', in *Population, Economy and Society*, 93–4.
18. C. Ó Gráda, 'Irish Population Trends 1700–1900', unpublished paper, University College Dublin 1980, 14.
19. Connell, *Population of Ireland*, 156.
20. M. Drake, 'Marriage and Population Growth in Ireland, 1750–1845', *Economic History Review* 2nd series, XVI (1963), 311–12. Ó Gráda indicates that once the 1841 census is corrected for birth underestimation it shows a comparatively high level of marital fertility, i.e. 350 per 1,000 married women aged between 15 and 45

years. This was higher than the reported ratio in England and Wales in the 1850s (281:1000), and Prussia (314) and France (196) in the 1880s. See Ó Gráda, *Population Trends*, 20–1. See also G.S.L. Tucker, 'Irish Fertility Ratios before the Famine', *Economic and History Review*, 2nd series, XXIII (1970) 280.

21. L. Cullen, 'Irish History without the Potato', *Past and Present* XL (1968) 79.
22. J. Mokyr, 'Irish History with the Potato', *Irish Economic and Social History* VIII (1981), 27.
23. Cullen 'Population Growth and Diet', 94.
24. There were widespread famines in 1727–30 and 1740–41. Drake suggests that the latter famine was equally as devastating as the Great Famine. M. Drake, 'The Irish Demographic Crisis of 1740–41', *Historical Studies* VI (1968), 101–24.
25. Clarkson links the decline in famine and disease to improved medical technology and a lower level of urbanisation in Ireland. Clarkson, 'Irish Population Revisited', 30–4.
26. Kennedy estimates that 801,000 emigrated between 1845–49. See Robert Kennedy, *The Irish*, Berkeley: University of California Press 1973, 42. Lee estimates that 800,000 died from hunger and between 1845–1851. Joseph Lee, *The Modernisation of Irish Society*, Dublin: Gill & Macmillan 1973, 1.
27. Clarkson, 'Irish Population Revisited', 28.
28. Clarkson, 'Irish Population Revisited', 26. See also, J. Lee, 'On the Accuracy of the Pre-Famine Irish Censuses', in *Irish Population*, 54.
29. F.J. Carney, 'Pre-Famine Irish Population: The Evidence from the Trinity College Estates', *Irish Economic and Social History* II (1975), 42.
30. For the pioneering discussion of the stem family in Ireland, see Conrad Arensberg and Solon Kimball, *Family and Community in Ireland*, Cambridge [Mass.]: Harvard University Press 1940. For a criticism of this study see P. Gibbon, 'Arensberg and Kimball Revisited', *Economy and Society* II (1974), 479–98; see also, P. Gibbon and C. Curtin, 'The Stem Family in Ireland', *Comparative Studies in Society and History* XXV (1978), 429–47; T. Varley, 'The Stem Family in Ireland Reconsidered', *Comparative Studies in Society and History* XXV (1978), 381–92. In terms of the prevalence of the stem family system in Ireland from 1841, see D. Fitzpatrick, 'Irish Farming Families Before the First World War', *Comparative Studies in Society and History* XXV (1978), 339–74. There is some debate within this research as to what extent the classical stem family, i.e. three-generational household, pertained to Ireland. Gibbon and Curtin conclude that the stem-family system was not the most common form of family in Ireland, even at the time that Arensberg and Kimball did their research. However it was more common than elsewhere, and there was a very large number of extended families, together with a relative scarcity of nuclear and simple families (p. 349). But if the inheriting son postponed marriage not only until the father died but also until after he died, and if one or two brothers or sisters stayed on the farm unmarried, then there would be an extended family constituted basically within stem-family practices.
31. Connell, *Population of Ireland*, 27–8.
32. Kennedy, *The Irish*, 42–3, 212.
33. Walsh notes that during the 120 years following 1841 'Ireland had the highest emigration rate in Europe, and was the only European country in which emigration exceeded natural increase, leading to a persistent decline in population.' B. Walsh, 'A Perspective on Irish Population Trends', *Éire* IV (1969), 8.
34. Kennedy, *The Irish*, 66–109.
35. See D. Hannan, 'Peasant models and the understanding of social and cultural change in rural Ireland', in *Ireland: Land, Politics and People*, ed. P. J. Drudy, Cambridge: Cambridge University Press 1982, 152.
36. Raymond Crotty, *Irish Agricultural Production*, Cork: Mercier Press 1966, 41.

37. M. Drake, 'Marriage and Population Growth in Ireland, 1750–1845', *Economic History Review* 2nd series, XVI (1963), 311.
38. J. Lee, 'Marriage and Population Growth in Ireland, 1750–1845', *Economic and History Review*, 2nd series XXI (1968), 285, 291.
39. Kennedy, *The Irish*, 140–3.
40. Kennedy, *The Irish*, 146, 148.
41. Kennedy, *The Irish*, 152 (emphasis in original).
42. Kennedy, *The Irish*, 159.
43. Kennedy, *The Irish*, 160.
44. For a description of how the limitation and control of marriage was central to social and economic production in the Béarn in France, see P. Bourdieu, 'Marriage Strategies as Strategies of Social Reproduction', in *Family and Society*, ed. E. Foster and P. Ranum, Baltimore: Johns Hopkins University Press 1976. For a discussion of the central role of the family in social reproduction, see P. Bourdieu, 'On the Family as a Realized Category', *Theory, Culture and Society*, 13.3 (1996), 19–26.
45. Bourdieu in *Family and Society*, 154.
46. Bourdieu in *Family and Society*, 147.
47. J. Murphy, 'The Support of the Catholic Church in Ireland, 1750–1850', *Historical Studies*, V (1965), 108–9.
48. K. H. Connell, *Irish Peasant Society*, Oxford: Clarendon Press 1968, 126, 121.
49. P. McNabb 'Social Structure', in *Limerick Rural Survey*, ed. Jeremiah Newman, Tipperary: Muintir na Tíre 1964, 222–3.
50. Richard Stivers, *The Hair of the Dog*, London: Pennsylvania State University Press 1976, 75–100. Edward Shorter, *The Making of the Modern Family*, New York: Basic Books 1975, 209.
51. Stivers, *Hair of Dog*, 73–4.
52. A social history of the Irish pub has yet to be written, which is strange for a society traditionally associated with pub life. Just when, where and how pubs proliferated in Ireland deserves more attention than that brief period of temperance in the 1830s and 1840s which seems to have captured the imagination of some Irish historians.
53. Stivers, *Hair of Dog*, 86.
54. For a discussion of the importance of the gift relationship in attaining social prestige, see Marcell Mauss, *The Gift*, Glencoe: The Free Press 1952, esp. 10–12.
55. Stivers, *Hair of Dog*, 87.
56. M. Peillon, 'Irish Festivities in Comparative Perspective', *Maynooth Review* VI (1982), 39–59.
57. McNabb in *Limerick Rural Survey*, 233.
58. Stivers, *Hair of Dog*, 69, 70–1, 74.
59. For an account of the practices involved in making an Irish match, see Arensberg and Kimball, *Family and Community*, 109.
60. Kennedy, *The Irish*, 175–6.
61. Kennedy, *The Irish*, 193.
62. This argument – that a change in one field or sphere of social life (in this case religion and the Catholic Church) can lead to radical transformations in another field (in this case the economic) – mirrors what Weber analysed to be the greatest unintended consequence in history, that is that ascetic Protestantism gave rise to the necessary spirit which was an essential ingredient in the development of modern capitalism. See Max Weber, *The Protestant Ethic and the Spirit of Capitalism*, London: Unwin 1930. Of course, the modernisation of Irish argriculture within ascetic Catholicism was to produce an economic spirit which was more oriented towards commitment to Church, family and community and less towards risk venture capitalism.
63. As Weber notes: 'The tendency toward affiliation with an ethical, rational, congregational religion is more apt to be found the closer one gets to those strata which

have been the carriers of modern rational enterprise, i.e. strata with middle-class economic characteristics. . . .' M. Weber, *Economy and Society* 1, Berkeley, University of California Press 1978, 480.

64. Weber emphasises the importance of the interaction and collaboration between priests and laity in the rationalisation of religious ethics. Weber, *Economy and Society* 1, 439.

65. For a discussion of the importance of cultural capital in the constitution and reproduction of social class position, see Pierre Bourdieu, *Distinction*, London: Routledge & Kegan Paul 1986, esp. 147–68. It should be noted that although Bourdieu has studied the religious field, when it came to analysing the importance of cultural and symbolic capital in France in the 1960s, he omitted religion as a variable.

66. See, for example, Emmet Larkin, *The Roman Catholic Church in Ireland and the Fall of Parnell 1888–1891*, Chapel Hill: University of North Carolina Press 1979; David Miller, *Church, State and Nation in Ireland 1898–1921*, Dublin: Gill & Macmillan 1973; Dermot Keogh, *The Vatican, The Bishops and Irish Politics 1919–1939*, Cambridge: Cambridge University Press 1986.

67. J. Murphy, 'Priests and People in Modern Irish History', *Christus Rex*, XXIII (1969), 239.

68. James O'Shea, *Priests, Politics and Society in Post-Famine Ireland*, Dublin: Wolfhound Press 1983.

69. O'Shea, *Post-Famine Ireland*, 196, 206, 215.

70. See D. Keogh, 'Catholicism and the Formation of the Modern Irish Society', in *Irishness in a Changing Society*, ed. The Princess Grace Library, Gerrard's Cross: Colin Smythe 1988.

71. Keogh in 'Catholicism and the Formation', 161–9.

Chapter 8. The Irish Mother.

1. 'The Trimming of the Rosary', quoted in Patrick Griffith, *Christian Mothers: Saviours of Society*, Dublin: Browne & Nolan 1926, 62.

2. For an extensive bibliography, see M. Cullinan, 'Irish Women' *Journal of Women's History*, 16.4.(1995), 250–77. For a general discussion of the absence of social historical writing on women, see M. Luddy and C. Murphy, 'Cherchez la Femme: The Elusive Woman in Irish History' in M. Luddy and C. Murphy, ed., *Women Surviving: Studies in Irish Women's History in the Nineteenth and Twentieth Centuries*, Dublin: Poolbeg, 1990.

3. See Mary Kenny, *Goodbye to Catholic Ireland*, London: Sinclair-Stevenson 1997, 274–99.

4. E. Hynes, 'The Great Hunger and Irish Catholicism', *Societas*, VIII (1978), 149.

5. Raymond Crotty, *Irish Agricultural Production*, Cork: Mercier Press 1966, 37–8.

6. J. Lee, 'Women and the Church since the Famine', in *Women in Irish Society*, ed. M. McCurtain and D. Ó Corráin, Dublin: Arlen House 1978, 37.

7. Referred to in J. Goldstrom, 'Irish Agriculture and the Great Famine', in *Irish Population, Economy and Society*, ed. J.M. Goldstrom and L.A. Clarkson, Oxford: Clarendon Press 1981, 162.

8. K. H. Connell, *The Population of Ireland 1750–1845*, Oxford: Clarendon Press 1950, 47–85, esp. 55, 82, 83.

9. Crotty, *Agricultural Production*, 29–30.

10. S. Clark, 'The importance of agrarian classes: agrarian class structure and collective action in nineteenth-century Ireland', *British Journal of Sociology*, XXIX (1978), 25–30.

11. S. J. Connolly, *Priests and People in Pre-Famine Ireland 1780–1845*, Dublin: Gill & Macmillan 1982, 17, 23.

12. E. Larkin, 'Church, State and Nation in Modern Ireland', *American Historical Review*, LXXX (1975), 1245–7.

13. Clarke, 'The importance of agrarian classes', 29, 30.
14. Larkin, 'Church, State and Nation in Modern Ireland', 1248.
15. Quoted in M. Moynihan, ed., *Speeches and Statements by Éamon de Valera*, Dublin: Gill & Macmillan 1980, 466.
16. *Census of Population of Ireland*, 1841. General Report, xiv; *Census of Population*, 1891. General Report, 9.
17. The social history of the transformation of space and time in domestic life in Western society is beginning to receive attention. See Michel Foucault, *Discipline and Punish: The Birth of the Prison*, New York: Pantheon 1977, 159–60. It is not that time and space are not ordered in other societies (see Pierre Bourdieu's classic description of time and space in Kabyle society in *Outline of a Theory of Practice*, Cambridge: Cambridge University Press 1977, 96–109), it is that time and space become more precise, pervasive and predictable. Again it is not that Elias and Foucault might disagree so much about the empirical manifestations of this transformation, but that while Elias would see it as part of the growth in social complexity and social interdependence, Foucault sees it more as part of the new disciplinary power which created docile bodies.
18. Lee in *Women in Irish Society*, 37–8.
19. *Report of Poor Law Commissioners*, 1836 (Vol. 34) Appendix G, 'The State of the Irish Poor in Britain', xiii.
20. G. Rattray Taylor, *Sex in History*, New York: Harper & Row 1970, 81.
21. Alexander Humphreys, *New Dubliners*, New York: Fordham University Press 1966, 139. For similar descriptions of Irish love and marriage see Donald Connery, *The Irish*, New York: Simon and Schiester 1968, 192–213. Richard O'Connor, *The Irish*, New York: Putman 1971, 141–70. Alan Bestic, *The Importance of Being Irish*, New York: William Morrow 1969, 107–19.
22. J. Michelet, *Priest, Women and Families*, London: Longmans 1846, esp. 114–19, 148–9. Horkheimer argued that the mothers' dependence on men, on the family, and on extra-familial institutions such as the Church, restricted their own development and made them a conservative force. It was because of this dependence that mothers became instruments for maintaining existing patriarchal relations. In a social reproductive system, mothers and their daughters become dependent on the security of marriage and the family and this security becomes dependent on the priest. This relationship lasted up until the 1980s and, as we saw, helps explain the defeat of the divorce referendum in that year. See Max Horkheimer, ed., 'Authority and the Family' in *Critical Theory: Selected Essays*, New York: Herder & Herder 1972, 118.
23. R. Stivers, 'The Irish-American Experience with Alcohol', Paper presented at Mid-West Sociological Association Meeting, Chicago 1984, 11.
24. *Catholic Penny Magazine* (1834), 13. This was very similar to the advice being given by contemporary Puritan moralists. See, for example, William Pinnock, *A Catechism of Christian Morality*, London: Whittaker 1827, 57; Henry Tuke, *Temperance and Chastity*, Dublin: Graisberry & Campbell 1815, 7. Tuke's advice was typical in that temperance was put forward, along with economy, industry and honesty, as the virtue to be attained by boys, while chastity was seen as the specific task of girls.
25. As Gibbons notes, not only was sexuality replaced in the Irish narrative by violence and action but, in particular, powerful female figures were systematically written out of stories. See Luke Gibbons, *Transformations in Irish Culture*, Cork: Cork University Press 1996, 118.
26. Quoted in Dominick Murphy, *Sketches of Irish Nunneries*, Dublin: Duff 1865, 64.
27. *Agricultural Class Book*, Dublin: Commissioners of National Education 1854.
28. *The Schoolmistress or Instructive and Entertaining Conversations between a Teacher and her Scholars*, Dublin: Bentham & Gardiner 1824, 17.

29. *Reading Book for the Use of Female Schools*, Dublin: National Commissioners of Education 1845.
30. *Report of Commissioners of National Education in Ireland* (1853), 7.
31. Tony Fahey, 'Female Asceticism in the Catholic Church: A Case Study of Nuns in Ireland in the Nineteenth Century', Ph.D. dissertation, University of Illinois, 1981, 90–2.
32. Katherine Tynan, *Twenty-five Years*, London: Smith Elder 1913, 56.
33. Donal Akenson, *The Irish Education Experiment*, London: Routledge & Kegan Paul 1970, 140, 321, 346.
34. Quoted in Fahey, 'Female Asceticism', 94.
35. Hasia Diner, *Irish Immigrant Women in the Nineteenth Century*, Baltimore: Johns Hopkins University Press 1983, 67.
36. Gibbons notes that the 'virtues of loyalty, fortitude and forbearance, combined with an unlimited capacity to endure suffering, are all too easily reconciled with the domestic ideals of womanhood fostered by the "devotional revolution" in post-Famine Irish Catholicism – ideals which, in effect, helped to disenfranchise women from participating in public affairs.' Following Marina Warner, Gibbons links this model of Irish motherhood to mute stillness of the Virgin at Knock which sets it apart from similar apparitions elsewhere. See Gibbons, *Transformations in Irish Culture*, 108.
37. K. H. Connell, *Irish Peasant Society*, Oxford: Clarendon Press 1968, 113–61.
38. J. Murphy, 'Priests and People in Modern Irish History', *Christus Rex*, XXIII (1969), 258.
39. See Peter O'Dwyer, *Mary: A History of Devotion in Ireland*, Dublin: Four Courts Press 1988; Fr Augustine, *Ireland's Loyalty to Mary*, Tralee, 1952.
40. G. Rattray Taylor, *Sex in History*, New York: Harper & Row 1970, 107.
41. Griffith, *Christian Mothers*, 58.
42. Lockington, *Soul of Ireland*, London: Harding & More 1919, 66.
43. Quoted in Humphreys, *New Dubliners*, 139.
44. N. Walsh, *Woman*, Dublin: Gill 1903, 23.
45. Pope Pius XII, *Woman's Place in the World*, Dublin: Catholic Truth Society of Ireland, 8.
46. Griffith, *Christian Mothers*, 55–6.
47. Hannan and Katsiaouni, *Traditional Families?*, 228.
48. McNabb in *Limerick Rural Survey*, 228.
49. Nancy Scheper-Hughes, *Saints, Scholars and Schizophrenics*, Berekeley: University of California Press 1979, 179–80.
50. Scheper-Hughes, *Saints*, 180–2.
51. Connell, *Peasant Society*, 121.
52. Scheper-Hughes, *Saints*, 184.
53. B. Hutchinson, 'On the Study of Non-Economic Factors in Irish Economic Development', *Economic and Social Review*, I (1970), 525.
54. Scheper-Hughes, *Saints*, 172, 117, 134, 137, 157.
55. Stivers 'Experience with Alcohol', 11.
56. This concept of double-bind which is linked to schizophrenia was developed, among others, by Bateson. See Gregory Bateson, *Steps Toward an Ecology of Mind*, London: Paladin 1973.

Chapter 9. The Decline in the Catholic Church's Monopoly over Irish Morality 1986–1997.
1. L. Ryan, 'Faith Under Survey', *The Furrow*, January 1983, 6.
2. M. Hornsby-Smith and C. Whelan, 'Religious and Moral Values', in *Values and Social Change in Ireland*, ed. Chris Whelan, Dublin: Gill & Macmillan 1994, 7–44.

The authors admit that the interpretation of the evidence 'is dependent on the theoretical perspective that one brings to bear on the data.' Hornsby-Smith and Whelan, 'Religious and Moral Values', 44. They might have added that it can also be dependent on a religious interest or investment in the Church.

3. A. Greeley, 'Are the Irish Really Losing The Faith?', *Doctrine and Life*, 44.3 (1994), 137.

4. M. Hornsby-Smith, 'Social and Religious Transformations in Ireland: A Case of Secularisation?', in *The Development of Industrial Society in Ireland*, ed. John Goldthorpe and Chris Whelan, Oxford: Oxford University Press 1992, 265–90.

5. A. Greeley, 'Why do Catholics Stay in the Church?', *The Furrow*, 45.9 (1994), 495–502. See also A. Greeley, 'Sex and the Married Catholic: The Shadow of St Augustine', *America*, 167.13 (1992), 318–23; and 'Sex and the Single Catholic: The Decline of an Ethic', *America*, 167.14 (1992), 342–59.

6. Greeley, 'Sex and the Married Catholic', 319.

7. For a more detailed account of this argument, see Steve Bruce, *Religion in the Modern World*, Oxford: Oxford University Press 1996, 24–68.

8. Max Weber, *Economy and Society*, Vol.1, Berkeley: University of California Press 1978, 438.

9. Pierre Bourdieu, *Language and Symbolic Power*, Cambridge: Polity Press 1991, 168–70. Bruce sees individualism in spiritual and moral matters as the defining characteristic of religion in the modern world. See Bruce, *Religion in the Modern World*, 5, 230–4.

10. See S. J. Connolly, *Priests and People in Pre-Famine Ireland 1780–1845*, Dublin: Gill & Macmillan 1982, 74–174.

11. Lawrence Taylor, *Occasions of Faith*, Dublin: Lilliput 1995, 242. Taylor's study of a parish in Donegal is a good example of how traditional devotional beliefs and practices permeate Catholic life and how these have been sites of contestation fought out both inside and outside the institutional Church.

12. Desmond Mooney, 'Popular religion and clerical influence in pre-famine Meath', in *Religion, Conflict and Coexistence in Ireland*, ed. R. V. Comerford, J. R. Hill and C. Lennon, Dublin: Gill & Macmillan 1990, 191.

13. This is the goal behind Bourdieu's methodology. See Pierre Bourdieu and Loïc Wacquant, *An Invitation to Reflexive Sociology*, Cambridge: Polity Press 1992, 15–26.

14. This is, of course, recognised by many of the sociologists who take an optimistic view. For example, Hornsby-Smith, following Dobbelaere, identifies three different dimensions to secularisation: (*a*) laicisation, where different institutions take on tasks which used to be performed under the religious umbrella; (*b*) religious involvement, where people's integration within and allegiance to religious bodies such as the Catholic Church, declines; and (*c*) religious change, which refers to internal change in beliefs, morals and rituals within an organisation such as the Catholic Church, as well as the decline of some religious organisations and the emergence and growth of others. See Hornsby-Smith, 'Social and Religious Transformations', 267. See also, K. Dobbelaere, 'Secularisation: A Multi-Dimensional Concept', *Current Sociology*, 29.1 (1981), 3–213.

15. Hornsby-Smith and Whelan, *Values and Social Change*, 33.

16. Hornsby-Smith and Whelan, *Values and Social Change*, 35. The decline since 1974 is even more dramatic. Then 84 per cent of Catholics felt sure that God's love was behind everything that happens and that their prayers were answered. M. Nic Ghiolla Phádraig, 'Religion in Ireland' *Social Studies*, V (1976), 122.

17. See Emile Durkheim, *The Elementary Forms of the Religious Life*, London: George Allen & Unwin 1976, 47.

18. For an analysis of the nation-state as an imagined community, see Benedict Anderson, *Imagined Communities*, London: Verso 1983, esp. 15–16.

19. See Nic Ghiolla Phádraig, 'Religion in Ireland', 120; Council for Research and Devlopment, 'Religious Beliefs, Practice and Moral Attitudes: A comparison of Two Irish Surveys 1974–1984', unpublished report, St. Patrick's College, Maynooth, n.d., 15.
20. Greeley, 'Are the Irish Really Losing The Faith', 137.
21. Irish Marketing Survey, *The Sunday Independent*, 5 November 1995.
22. Market Research Bureau of Ireland Survey, *The Irish Times*, 16 December 1996.
23. See M. Nic Ghiolla Phádraig, 'Trends in Religious Practice in Ireland', *Doctrine and Life*, 42.1. (1992), 5; *The Sunday Independent*, 5 November 1995.
24. Nic Ghiolla Phádraig, 'Trends in Religious Practice', 11.
25. See M. Nic Ghiolla Phádraig, 'Religious Practice and Secularisation', in *Ireland: A Sociological Profile*, ed. P. Clancy, S. Drudy, K. Lynch and L. O'Dowd, Dublin: Institute of Public Administration 1989, 151–3; Hornsby-Smith and Whelan, 'Religious and Moral Values', 28 and 43; Hornsby-Smith 'Social and Religious Transformations', 282. Although these authors conclude that the survey findings tend to provide support for the link between modernisation and secularisation, they argue that the relationship is not unambiguous, pointing to age cohort and life cycle variations, the emergence of new beliefs and practices, and the growth of the Church as a counter-cultural rather than dominant-cultural force. Fahey argues that there is no necessary link to secularisation and modernisation and, as evidence, points to the continuing remarkable success of Christianity in the United States. Indeed, following Kelley, he argues that the more strict the demands of the Church, the more success-ful it has been. T. Fahey, 'Catholicism and Industrial Society in Ireland', in *The Development of Industrial Society in Ireland*, 241–63; T. Fahey, 'The Church and Culture: Growth and Decline of Churchly Religion', *Studies* 83 (1994), 367–75; D.M. Kelley, *Why Conservative Churches are Growing*, New York: Harper & Row 1972.
    Whelan and Fahey go so far as to discount the usefulness of the concept of modernisation in analysing any cultural phenomena, particularly in Ireland. They conclude that 'cultural patterns follow a lurching, unpredictable and changing course, at least some of which appear to have little to do with "modernisation" in any of the usual senses of that term . . . simple schemas of modernisation do not help much. . . .' See C. Whelan and T. Fahey, 'Marriage and the Family', in Hornsby-Smith and Whelan, *Values and Social Change in Ireland*, 81. However, while it is agreed that processes such as modernisation, rationalisation and civilisation are uneven; that they are always culturally conditioned; and that they regularly go into reverse, this does not warrant dismissing them as simple or less than useful concepts, especially when they have always been central to sociological theory and historical sociological research. For a development of this argument, see Bruce, in *Religion in the Modern World*, 25–68. Indeed the debate in the sociology of religion as to whether secularisation is taking place is becoming not just heated, but political. Greeley has claimed that secularisation is 'neither an account of the way things are nor a prediction of the way things are likely to become. Rather, it is a prescription of the way reality should be. . . . "Secularization" is not scholarship; it it the religious faith of the secularized.' A. Greeley, 'The Persistence of Religion', *Cross Currents*, Spring (1995), 39. Bruce, on the other hand, has argued that the argu-ments against secularisation are 'driven by changes in intellectual fashion'; that the debate has been debased by 'the construction and demolition of straw men'; and that they are counter to the sociological arguments of 'such scholars as Weber, Durkheim, Parsons, Berger, Wilson and Martin.' Bruce in *Religion in the Modern World*, 6.
26. See Nic Ghiolla Phádraig, 'Religious Practice and Secularisation', 153. Research and Development Commission, 'A Survey of Religious Practice, Attitudes and Beliefs: (Unpublished) Report No. 2.' Dublin: 1975, 136; Nic Ghiolla Phádraig, 'Religion in Ireland', 126.

27. Hornsby-Smith and Whelan 'Religious and Moral Values', 41.
28. Market Research Bureau of Ireland Survey, *The Irish Times*, 16 December 1996.
29. Although Foucault rectified the fault in his later works on sexuality, one of the main faults of his theory of disciplinary power is that relied too much on external, physical forms of discipline and control, such as panopticism, rather than internalised mechanisms of self-control or restraint. Elias saw this transition as a key moment in the civilising process. See Michel Foucault, *Discipline and Punish: The Birth of the Prison*, New York: Pantheon 1977, 195–228; Norbert Elias, *State Formation and Civilization: Vol. 2. The Civilizing Process*, Oxford: Basil Blackwell 1982, 229–50.
30. Although the Frankfurt School referred to the decline of the authority of the father in relation to the culture industry, it is arguable that the decline initially took place in Ireland through the Catholic Church. See David Held, *Introduction to Critical Theory*, London: Hutchinson 1980, 132.
31. See Research and Development Commission, 'Irish Priests and Religious 1970–1975', unpublished report, Dublin, 1977; Council for Reseach and Development, 'Vocations Returns', unpublished report, Maynooth, 1996.
32. Council for Reseach and Development, 'Irish Priests and Religious', table 10.
33. Tony Flannery, *The Death of Religious Life?* Dublin: Columba Press 1997, 20, 47. In his survey in 1990, MacGréil found that three images of God which gained majority support were the biblical images of 'Father', 'Master' and 'Judge'. However, a majority also agreed that 'there is much goodness in the world which hints at God's goodness'. Micheál MacGréil, *Prejudice in Ireland Revisited*, Maynooth: St Patrick's College, Survey and Research Unit 1996, 197.
34. Flannery, *Death of Religious Life?*, 62.
35. For an account of the 'era of the ego' and the role of ego psychology in its creation and maintenance see Jacques Lacan, 'The function and field of speech and language in psychoanalysis', in *Écrits: A Selection*, London: Tavistock 1953, 30–113. For a description of the culture of narcissism see Christopher Lasch, *The Culture of Narcissism: American Life in an Age of Diminshing Expectations*, New York: Norton 1978.
36. Tony Flannery, *The Death of Religious Life?*, Dublin: Columba Press 1997, 20–1.
37. Jürgen Habermas, 'Three Normative Models of Democracy', *Constellations*, Vol. 1.1, (1994), 7.
38. See *The Irish Times*, 29 June 1995.
39. Lyotard defines postmodernism simply as 'an incredulity toward metanarratives'. See Jean-Francois Lyotard, *The Postmodern Condition: A Report on Knowledge*, Manchester: Manchester University Press 1984, xxiv. For a discussion of the tensions between fundamentalist religion and postmodernism see Ernest Gellner, *Postmodernism, Reason and Religion*, London: Routledge 1992.
40. See Damien Kiberd, 'Have media practitioners a brief to change society', in *Media in Ireland: The Search for Diversity*, Dublin: Open Air 1997, 37.
41. *The Irish Times*, 1 December 1994.
42. For a detailed description of the background and activities of Fr. Brendan Smyth, see Chris Moore, *Betrayal of Trust, The Father Brendan Smyth Affair and the Catholic Church*, Dublin: Marino Books 1995.
43. For an account of these scandals, see Mary Kenny, *Goodbye to Catholic Ireland*, London: Sinclair-Stevenson 1996, 369–84.
44. *The Irish Times*, 2 March 1995.
45. *The Irish Times*, 26 August 1997. Earlier in the year Bishop Walsh apologised for the Church's rule on *Ne Temere* which demanded that children in a mixed marriage be brought up as Catholics. He said that the rule was contrary to the Christian spirit of love and generosity. *The Irish Times*, 27 January 1997. Although Bishop

Walsh is probably the most contrite and radical in his opinions, they have been echoed by other bishops and priests. See, for example, the interview with Bishop John Kirby, *The Irish Times*, 28 November 1994; Bishop Thomas Finnegan's call for the Church to apply the ritual of penance to itself. *The Irish Times*, 5 December 1994; and Fr Kevin Hegarty's review of changes in the Church in 1995, *The Irish Times*, 1 January 1996.

46. *The Irish Times*, 7 June 1994.

47. D. Keogh, 'Catholicism and the Formation of the Modern Irish State', in *Irishness in a Changing Society*, 161–9. Dermot Keogh, *The Vatican, the Bishops and Irish Politics*, Cambridge: Cambridge University Press 1986, 201.

48. See Ryan, 'Faith Under Survey', 14.

49. For a description and analysis of the abortion referendum and related issues, see Ailbhe Smyth, ed., *The Abortion Papers*, Dublin: Attic Press 1992.

50. *Irish Catholic*, 9 November 1995.

51. *The Irish Times*, 13, 18 and 25 November 1995.

52. *The Irish Times*, 23 June 1993. However this type of civil society would not seem to have been acceptable St Patrick's College, Maynooth which in 1994 was still a recognised college of the National University of Ireland, but which was still governed by the Hierarchy. They decided then not to grant recognition to a gay, lesbian and bisexual society. *The Irish Times*, 18 February 1994.

53. 'The Church has abandoned its corporatist positions but no coherent project for society has replaced them. The Church expesses its concern for the most vulnerable groups in society but relies on social assistance to achieve that end. Such problems are solved only within the context of the status quo or, more exactly, independently of it: it is enough that society should wish for it and leave behind its selfishness.' Michel Peillon, *Contemporary Irish Society*, Dublin: Gill & Macmillan 1982, 99.

54. See Máire Nic Ghiolla Phádraig, 'The Power of the Catholic Church in the Republic of Ireland', in P. Clancy, S. Drudy, K. Lynch and L. O'Dowd, ed., *Irish Society: Sociological Perspectives*, Dublin: Institute of Public Administration 1995, 610–11. Seán McDonagh, *To Care for the Earth*, London: Geoffrey Chapman 1986.

55. Hornsby-Smith, 'Social and Religious Transformations', 279.

56. Nic Ghiolla Phádraig, 'Religious Practice and Secularisation', 599, 612–5.

57. Chris Eipper, *The Ruling Trinty: A Community Study of Church, State and Business in Ireland*, Aldershot: Gower 1986, 18, 106.

58. *The Irish Times*, 25 June 1993.

59. *The Irish Times*, 16 November 1996. Archbishop Connell noted that we cannot succeed in reversing the present trend towards lawlessness and crime unless we tackle the weakening of moral convictions. This, he felt, was largely the responsibility of the Church. But, he said, the work of the Church is rendered more difficult by sustained attacks on its moral teaching in so many areas of public discourse.

60. *The Irish Times*, 27 November 1995.

61. Government White Paper, *Charting Our Education Future Together*, Dublin: Government Publications 1995, 149.

62. Government White Paper, *Charting Our Education*, 213–15.

63. *The Irish Times*, 16 May 1997.

64. See Nic Ghiolla Phádraig, 'The Power of the Catholic Church', 606.

65. See Kathleen Lynch, *The Hidden Curriculum: Reproduction in Education*, London: Palmer 1989, 130–1.

66. Nic Ghiolla Phádraig, 'The Power of the Catholic Church', 608.

67. Nic Ghiolla Phádraig, 'The Power of the Catholic Church', 607.

68. *The Irish Times*, 4 and 22 April 1997.

69. *The Irish Times*, 11 April 1997.
70. Transcripts of advertisements for AIDS Prevention Campaign, May 1993, Health Promotion Unit.
71. *The Irish Times*, 13 September 1997
72. *The Irish Times*, 4 September 1993.
73. *The Irish Times*, 10 May 1996.
74. A televison documentary in Australia revealed similar patterns of discipline and punishment. See *The Irish Times*, 2 July 1997.
75. *The Irish Times*, 7 March 1996.
76. *The Irish Times*, 19 March 1996.
77. Mike Milotte, *Banished Babies: The Secret History of Ireland's Baby Export Business*, Dublin: New Island Books 1997. As Milotte points out, the story broke not only within the context of other stories about child sex abuse, but specifically through a series of contributions to talk radio shows. Milotte, *Banished Babies*, 186–90.
78. Milotte, *Banished Babies*, 18.
79. Milotte, *Banished Babies*, 40.
80. Michel Peillon, 'Constructing Irish Welfare as an Object of Social Investigation', paper presented at Sociological Association of Ireland Annual Conference, Dundalk, May 1996, 4.
81. See South Eastern Health Board, 'Kilkenny Incest Investigation', Dublin: Government Publications 1993.
82. This was a report given by two Monsignori sent by the Vatican to contribute to the Commission's hearings, see Robert Savage, *Irish Television: The Political and Social Origins*, Cork: Cork University Press 1996, 154.
83. Quoted in Martin McLoone and John MacMahon, ed., *Television and Irish Society*, Dublin: RTÉ-IFI 1984, 149.
84. For descriptions of the 'bishop and the nightie' episode see Kenny, *Goodbye to Catholic Ireland*, 265–7. See also, Maurice Earls "The Late, Late Show: Controversy and Context", in *Television and Irish Society*, 107–122. Gay Byrne, *To Whom it Concerns*, Dublin: Gill & Macmillan 1972, 75. Joseph Dunn, *No Lions in the Hierarchy*, Dublin: Columba Press 1994, 39. Dunn points out that a major impetus for the whole episode was that the Bishop was not only fond of the programme but also of a drink and that left on his own on a Saturday night he had nobody to assuage his moral indignation. His embodied practice of self, developed from a Catholic *habitus*, was losing its influence on Irish people in general and women in particular.
85. See Flannery, *The Death of Religious Life?*, 20–1.
86. *The Messenger*, as it was commonly known, rose from a circulation of seven thousand in 1870 to nearly three hundred thousand in the 1920s. *The Messenger* was the most successful of a number of religious magazines which also had large circulations see Kenny, *Goodbye to Catholic Ireland*, xxii–xxiii.
87. *The Irish Times*, 18 January 1995.
88. *The Irish Times*, 31 January 1995.
89. Walter Forde, *Church, Communication and Change*, Gorey: Kara Publications 1995, 44.
90. Michael O'Toole, "The Roman Catholic Church and the Media in Ireland" in *The Role of the Media in Irish Society*, ed., T. Fahey and M. Kelly Dublin: Media Association of Ireland n.d., 11.
91. The problem is not confined to Ireland. When the scandalous story of Bishop Wright disappearing from his diocese in Scotland with a female companion reached its peak, the Catholic press and media office closed down. *The Irish Times*, 24 September 1996.
92. Fahey, 'Catholicism and Industrial Society in Ireland', 260.

93. See E. Mahon in *Irish Society: Sociologicial Perspectives*, 684. Central Statistics Office, *Women in the Workforce*, Statistical Release, 22 September 1997.
94. For a detailed discussion and analysis of these changes, see Mahon in *Irish Society: Sociological Perspectives*, 675–708; E. Mahon, 'Women's Rights and Catholicism in Ireland', *New Left Review*, 166 (1987), 52–77; V. Randall and A. Smyth, 'Bishops and Bailiwicks: Obstacles to Women's Participation in Ireland', *Economic and Social Review* 18.3 (1987), 189–214; L. O'Dowd, 'Church, State and Women: The Aftermath of Partition', in *Gender in Irish Society*, ed. C. Curtin, P. Jackson and B. O'Connor, Galway: Galway University Press 1987, 3–36. B. Hilliard, 'Women and Public Life in Ireland', in *Ireland and Poland: Comparative Perspectives*, ed. Patrick Clancy, Mary Kelly, Jerzy Wiatr and Ryszard Zoltanieki, Dublin: Dept. of Sociology, UCD, 1992, 247–60.
95. See Mahon, 'From Democracy to Femocracy: The Women's Movement in the Republic of Ireland', in *Irish Society: Sociologicial Perspectives*, 694–5; Patrick Clancy, *Access to College*, Dublin: Government Publications 1995, 29; T. Inglis, 'Women and the Struggle for Daytime Education in Ireland', *Studies in the Education of Adults*, 26.1. (1994), 50–66.
96. See D. Courtney, 'Demographic Structure and Change in the Republic of Ireland and Northern Ireland', in *Irish Society*, 53–66; P. Clancy, 'Continuity and Change in Irish Demographic Patterns', in *Ireland and Poland*, 165–6.
97. T. Fahey, 'Family and Household in Ireland', in *Irish Society*, 225.
98. L. Ryan, 'The Changing Irish Family', *The Furrow* 45.4 (1994), 213.
99. C. Whelan and T. Fahey, 'Marriage and the Family', 45–81.
100. Fahey, 'Family and Household', 219–23.
101. As Keogh points out, the practice of speaking with one voice emerged with the establishment of the National Episcopal Conference between 1788 and 1882. However, although the procedures of the Conference have been tightened and an executive secretariat established, and although collective statements and pastorals are produced, there have been many occasions, particularly during referenda, when individual bishops have taken different positions to the collective one. In the last ten years, particularly in relation to celibacy and the Church's reaction to the Fr Brendan Smyth affair, there has been a greater number of different [if not] dissenting voices. See Dermot Keogh, 'Episcopal Decision-Making in Ireland' in *Education, Church and State*, ed. M. O'Connell, Dublin: IPA 1992, 1–18.

Chapter 10. The Influence of the Catholic Church on Modern Irish Society.
1. Tony Flannery, *The Death of Religious Life?*, Dublin: Columba Press 1997, 44.
2. Alexander Humphreys, *New Dubliners*, New York: Fordham University Press 1966, 20.
3. For a detailed analysis of this dimension to the development of Irish agricultural production, see D. Hannan and P. Commins, 'The Significance of Small-scale Landholders in Ireland's Socio-economic Transformation', in *The Development of Industrial Society in Ireland*, 79–104; D. Hannan, 'Peasant models and the understanding of social and cultural change in rural Ireland', in *Ireland: Land, Politics and People*, ed. P. J. Drudy, Cambridge: Cambridge University Press 1982, 141–65.
4. See, for example, D. O'Hearn 'The Irish Case of Dependency: An Exception to the Exceptions?', *American Sociological Review*, 54 (1989), 578–96; Raymond Crotty, *Ireland in Crisis: A Study in Capitalist Colonial Underdevelopment*, Dingle: Brandon Books 1986; Eoin O'Malley, *Industry and Economic Development: The Challenge for the Latecomer*, Dublin: Gill & Macmillan 1989.
5. R.D.C. Black, *Economic Thought and the Irish Question 1817–1870*, Cambridge: Cambridge University Press 1960, 157.

6. J. Lee, 'Capital in the Irish Economy', in *The Formation of the Irish Economy*, ed. L.M. Cullen, Cork: Mercier Press 1968, 62.
7. E. Larkin, 'Economic Growth, Capital Investment and the Roman Catholic Church in Nineteenth-Century Ireland', *American Historical Review* LXXII (1967), 874.
8. L. Kennedy, 'The Roman Catholic Church and Economic Growth in Nineteenth Century Ireland', *Economic and Social Review*, X (1978), 52.
9. Kennedy, 'The Roman Catholic Church', 55.
10. Joseph Lee, *Ireland 1912–1985*, Cambridge: Cambridge University Press 1989, 521–2. However, Lee later notes that the relationship between the spiritual and the material is not straightforward and 'requires exploration of surgical delicacy'. Lee, *Ireland 1912–1985*, 650.
11. Lee, *Ireland 1912–1985*, 390ff, 650.
12. T. Tony Fahey, 'Catholicism and Industrial Society in Ireland', in *The Development of Industrial Society in Ireland*, ed. John Goldthorpe and Chris Whelan, Oxford: Oxford University Press 1992, 262.
13. Richard Breen, Damian Hannan, David Rothman and Christopher Whelan, *Understanding Contemporary Ireland*, Dublin: Gill & Macmillan 1990, 108,138.
14. M. Daly, 'The Economic Ideals of Irish Nationalism: Frugal Comfort or Lavish Austerity?', *Éire/Ireland*, XXIX.4 (1994), 79.
15. Flannery, *Death of Religious Life*, 47.
16. Lee, *Ireland 1912–1985*, 522.
17. B. Hutchinson, 'On the Study of Non-Economic Factors in Irish Economic Development', *Economic and Social Review*, I (1970), 528.

Appendix

A comparison of headlines from *The Irish Times* 1987–1996.

Note: Although every attempt was made to make the list of headlines as detailed and accurate as possible, the keywords and search techniques may have caused some omissions and errors.

	1987		1996
		Jan.	
		2	Kevin Hegarty on a year of change and controversy for the Catholic Hierarchy in Ireland.
			State Papers 1965: Lemass asked by the Catholic Bishops to restrict emigration of under 18s.
		3	Bishop Michael Murphy says disenchantment with Church is caused by church administration.
			Church leaders call for careful consideration of report of International Arms Commission.
Peter Barry repeats that Catholics should join RUC.		5	
Seamus Mallon criticises Barry on Catholics and RUC.		6	
		11	Pope appoints Michael Courtney to be Vatican observer to the Council of Europe.
		12	IMS survey shows majority in favour of married priests.
			Dr John Ahern to retire as Archbishop of Cloyne.
Catholic Hierarchy statement on AIDS.		13	Church in Donnycarney robbed of £1,000.
AIDS and the Bishops.		14	
Cardinal Ó Fiaich rejects Brookeborough's prelate remark.		15	
		16	Co. Donegal parish priest charged with child sexual abuse is released on bail.
		17	Forum for Peace and Reconciliation: Catholic Bishops make submission.
			Andy Pollak analyses the Catholic Bishops submission to Forum for Peace and Reconciliation.
		18	High court dismisses legal action seeking to prevent the state from paying the salaries of chaplains.

1987

1996

Bishop criticises Lord's remarks.	20	Cardinal Daly addresses the Forum for Peace and Reconciliation. Saturday Profile: Cardinal Carlo Maria Martini.
Clashes with Hierarchy over request to officiate at funeral.	21	
	23	Bishops Advisory Committee report on clerical child sexual abuse guidelines to be published Jan 30.
	24	Budget: Education – parish school contributions to cease.
	27	Review of *Authority in the Church* edited by Sean MacReamoinn.
Irish Bishops' representative to attend Birmingham Six appeal.	28	
	30	Catholic Bishops' report on clerical child sex abuse due today.
	31	Archbishop Desmond Connell says there is no reason why Church and state cannot co-exist. Recommendations in Bishops Advisory Committee's report on clerical child sexual abuse. Cardinal Daly confident that Bishops' report on clerical child sexual abuse will address Church's problems. Summary of Bishop's Advisory Committee's report on clerical child sexual abuse. Editor of Irish Social Worker welcomes many elements in Bishops' report on clerical child sexual abuse. Analysis of Bishops Advisory Committee's report on how to deal with clerical child sexual abuse.
	Feb.	
	2	Rural depopulation leading to fewer Masses and priests – Bishop Thomas Flynn.
Haughey supporters and media ordered off church grounds.	3	
	5	Rebel Catholic Bishop Jacques Gaillot sets up a 'virtual diocese' on the Internet. John Waters writes that the Catholic
	6	Church is not always right. Dr Hubert Feichtlbauer discusses Austrian petition on reform of Catholic Church.
	7	Dr James Molony awarded papal medal for work with Accord (Catholic Marriage Advisory Council).
	8	Pax Christi calls for Irish government to ban landmines. New Papal Nuncio, Archbishop Luciano Storero, welcomed by Cardinal Daly and Dr Desmond Connell.

1987   1996

Charlie Landsborough was received into
the Catholic Church at White Abbey
Carmelite church, Kildare.

10   Archbishop Derek Worlock of Liverpool
dies.
Alter and crucifix stolen from church in
Tir an Fhia, Lettermore, Co Galway.

12   Dr Donal Murray is appointed new
Catholic Bishop of Limerick.

13   Galway teacher claims there is a crisis in
teaching of Catholic religion in
secondary schools.

14   Church confirms some parental opposition to confirmation by Bishop
Comiskey in his diocese.

15   Archbishop Desmond Connell criticises
attempts to 'politicise' the Catholic
Church.

16   RC Bishops issue statement condemning
London bombing.

Catholic Church committee calls for   17
AIDS hotline.
Pope names new Bishop of Cloyne   18
Bishop of Cloyne.

19   Andy Pollak reports on Bishop
Comiskey's first public appearance in
Enniscorthy.
Nuala O'Faolain discusses the treatment
of Bishop Brendan Comiskey since his
return.

20   Rite and Reason: Implications for the
Catholic Church of the Vatican's ruling
on ordination of women.

21   Meeting between Brendan Comiskey
and delegation of priests is described as
'friendly'.

Preservation group accuses Bishop   26   Theologian suggests methods of Christain
O'Mahony on Rush church.   renewal for Ireland to relieve crises in
church.

Rush church appeal.   27   Priest warns Catholic church may not be
able to make civil registration of marriage.

29   Andy Pollak analyses the performance of
Brendan Comiskey at a press conference
in St Peter's College.
Kevin Hegarty analyses the damage done
to the Catholic Church by Bishop
Comiskey saga.
Brendan Comiskey answers questions on
his dealing with Monageer priest, Jim
Grennan.
Full text of Brendan Comiskey's state-
ment at press conference in St Peter's
College Wexford.

1987		1996
	Mar.	
Rush Church.	3	
Bishop Murray warns of medicine's step into moral realm.	4	Four main churches call for National Day of Prayer for Peace.
Archbishop MacNamara seriously ill.		
	5	High Court to rule on use of surplus funds set up to rebuild church in Tullamore.
		Role of the laity in the Catholic Church.
	8	Fintan O'Toole argues that teachers deal will hand over more control in schools to the Church.
Catholic Church to issue declaration on procreation.	9	
Catholic Hierarchy to consider response to AIDS crisis.		
Rush church dispute.	10	
Dr Steptoe reacts to Vatican.	11	
Vatican on test tube babies.		
Irish clinics react to Vatican statement on IVF.		
Vatican statement on test tube babies.		
The Bishops have no right to be silent.	12	Cahal Daly welcomes media reporting of recent church scandals but warns against anti-church campaign.
AIDS task force to be set up by Hierarchy.		
HEB director and Bishop speak on AIDS.	13	
	14	Catholic Hierarchy welcomes plans to teach religion as exam subject.
Bishops pastoral urges money to be used to create jobs.	16	
Magee says Pope will visit Ireland again.	17	
John Magee ordained Bishop of Cloyne in Rome.	18	John Cooney disputes image of Archbishop MacQuaid as presented by Jim Cantwell.
Co. Wexford curate faces tax judgement.	19	
Rev. Brian Lennon speaks on Northern Ireland.	20	
Inter Church report on marriage.	24	
Encyclical on Virgin Mary issued.	26	John Major meets 4 main NI church leaders at Downing Street.
Extracts from Encyclical on the Virgin Mary.		
Hierarchy launches National task force on AIDS.	27	
The Universe launches leaflet on AIDS.		
Seminar on role of laity.	28	Report by the unemployed urges Catholic Church to address the unemployment problem at parish level.
Throwing open the church doors.		
	29	Fintan O'Toole on the anomaly of Army participation in Church ceremonies and the separation of Church and state.
	30	
Conference on laity concludes.		
Cardinal Ó Fiaich's remarks on women.		

1987   1996

	3	Leaders of 4 main NI churches agree that priority is all-party negotiations. Louis Lentin defends making and screening of *Dear Daughter* TV programme.
Priest shares the suffering of AIDS.	4	
	5	Dr Walsh says voluntary celibacy in Catholic Church will come, but not until well into next century.
Dr Magee installed as Bishop of Cloyne	6	
Marley funeral postponed.	7	
Archbishop of Dublin dies after long illness.	9	
Speculation on McNamara's successor Rush church dispute continues.		
Cahal Daly criticises IRA and RUC over funeral behaviour.	10	
Silence during Marley obsequies helped IRA.	15	Unitas 2000 holds public meeting to organise fundraising for new Catholic TV station; to meet TnG.
Bishop Daly to administer Dublin diocese as caretaker.		
The Church and homosexuality.	16	
Pact badly eroded by funeral riots.		
Bomb scare at Belfast church.	18	Statistics show Catholic parishes in Dublin diocese are more than £2.7 million in debt.
IRA rules out shots at church.		
Widower ordained.	20	Father Maurice Dooley rejects state's marriage laws and says under-age couples should be allowed marry.
St Mary's church for sale.		
Losing 2000 souls every Sunday.		
The search for an Archbishop.	21	
US theologian's clash with Rome.	22	
Sean MacReamoinn addresses conference on church and laity.		
	23	Bishop William Walsh says that the Irish Catholic Church has been 'shattered' by recent sex scandals.
	24	National Conference of Priests told women religious want to be taken seriously and be respected by the Church.
Fr Thomas Norris resigns from Irish Theological Association.	27	Conference of Catholic Primary School Managers Association claims church will cede control on school boards.
Fr Peter McVerry addresses Ogra Fianna Fáil on poverty.		
Bishops' synod to discuss women's' role in the church.	29	Nuala O'Faolain examines why Irish society believes it still needs priests despite recent scandals.
		Good work of nuns should not be ignored in light of recent revelations – Cahal Daly.
The making of Dublin's Archbishop.	30	Frances O'Rourke reports on the growing costs of a child's First Communion.
		Paul Murray believes the future of the Christian church depends on blurring doctrinal distinctions.

1987		1996
	May	
The Realpolitik of Bishop making in the Catholic Church.	1	
Irish celebrate 16th centenary of St Augustine.	4	
Dublin clergy on candidates for Archbishop post.	5	
	6	US nun to support Unitas 2000 in the setting up of religious TV station in Ireland.
	7	The widening gap between consumerism and spirituality. Cardinal Leon-Joseph of Belgium died yesterday aged 91. John Waters believes the 'culture of the time' should not be used as an excuse by the Catholic Church.
Sir John Hermon defends RUC conduct at funerals.	8	
Charlie may have say in choice of Archbishop. Mons. Thomas Finnegan to be Bishop of Killala.	9	
	14	Cathy Molloy argues that women must be involved in theological academic studies.
Priest urges legislation on homosexuality Irish Times debate on Catholic Church.	15	Catholic Church sells some priests' residences.
	17	Four churches represented at 'Peace International' rugby match.
Fr Lavelle says AIDS campaign could be more explicit.	18	
	20	Government to introduce legislation which will copperfasten Churches' control of primary schools.
	21	Niamh Breathnach says churches will not have veto on school boards of management. Excess funding for restoration of church in Tramore can be used for advancement of RC religion. Struggle against poverty and unemployment – Church debate on poverty should continue.
The SEA campaign. Bishop Desmond Williams criticises health cuts.	22	
The changing face of the Church.	28	
Bishop Comiskey urges media awareness in the Church. Dublin diocese debt begins to fall.	29	Mayor of Limerick, Jim Kemmy suggests crematorium at a deconsecrated church
	31	Fr Joseph Steele faces further sex abuse charges.

1987   1996

June

1   Claims by Christina Gallagher to have
    stigmata on her feet are investigated by
    Catholic church.

Planning permission for church in   3   Andy Pollak takes a look at the state of
Loughlinstown granted.   Catholic Church in France.
Priests urge appointment of Archbishop 4
from Auxiliaries.

5   Carmelite Nuns celebrate centenary of
    church mixing with general public and
    family.

Marian year begins on 7th of June.   6
Cooney calls on Hierarchy to urge vote
against Sinn Fein.
Catholic Hierarchy reject Cooney call on 8   Exemption to bias law is criticised by the
Sinn Féin vote.   Campaign to Separate Church and state.
Clergy fear no say in selection of
Archbishop.
SHB cancels Padre Pio statue for Cork 10
regional hospital.
Trusting Rome to choose the Archbishop. 11
Catholic Hierarchy warns on effects of
health cuts.

12   Judge Ronan Keane rules that Catholic
     doctrine is sufficiently adhered to in 2
     reformatory schools.

Dr Daly says Marian Year not an obstacle 15
to ecumenism.
Controversy over commemoration.   18
Silence from Rome over vacancy in
Dublin.

21   Co. Down Church caretaker jailed for 3
     decades of child abuse.
     Policy files on adoptions abroad 1940s
     to 1960s sent to National Archive.
22   1995 report for Catholic Marriage
     Counselling Service, Accord.
     Victim of priest at Monageer, Co
     Wexford, says inquiry should be public –
     angry at Gardai's failure.

Reports on weeping statues in Dublin 23
and Cork.
Church concerned about weeping statues. 24
British and Irish hierarchies cooperation
on North urge .

25   Catholic Church attempts to address
     the problems of male violence against
     women.
     Paul Cullen looks at problems Niamh
     Breathnach faces in legislating for
     Churches' involvement in education.
     Proposed Church veto on teachers is
     dropped but schools to be exempt from
     legislation on equality.

1987		1996

Planning permission for Rush church granted.
When the local church is the great loser. — 26

29 — Alison O'Connor on the background to the jailing of paedophile priest from Kilkenny.

July

1 — Prayer service for peace held in Limerick – response to murders of Veronica Guerin and Jerry MacCabe.

Priests criticise churches' attitude to North.
De Valera sought Papal approval for Constitution.
De Valera's Constitution.
A Catholic Constitution. — 2 — CORI urges government to define its position on EU's future.

4 — Constitution Review Report – political aspects, by Geraldine Kennedy.
Employment Equality Bill – Church-owned schools exempt.
Visit to Achill House of Prayer where local woman claims to be stigmatised.

5 — Conference takes place to discuss the proposals for a Catholic university in Co Mayo.

First guest on the first Late Late Show. — 7

9 — Vandals desecrate ancient remains in vault at St Michan's Church, Dublin.

Norris criticises Waldheim Vatican visit. — 10 — St Michan's Church – public access in doubt after vandalism.
Bodies desecrated at St Michan's Church are reinterred.

Maynooth College organises funds campaign. — 11 — Four main church leaders in NI meet David Trimble to try to broker agreement over Drumcree.
Catholic priest injured in petrol bomb attack on church in Donaghadee, Co Down.

Dr Cunnane resigns as Archbishop of Tuam.
Bishop of Killala ordained.
Rome and the power of public opinion.
Priests want local man for Archbishop of Tuam.
New church in Hartstown.
Padre Pio statue. — 13 — Drumcree parade – 4 main church leaders give their versions.

15

16 — Denis Faul argues in favour of schools run by the Catholic Church.

Padre Pio statue order.
Stained glass window restored at St James' church.
ICABS protest at clergy involvement in bloodsports. — 18

20

1987		1996
Church bias against women.	23	Rite and reason – religion in Irish culture.
	24	Catholic body suggests a new office to deal with the problems of child abuse. Clergy of four denominations call for rejection of divisive action in North.
Medjugorje.	25	
Lay groups attack liberal bishops.	28	
	29	Nuala O'Faolain gives her views on the Church and journalists' reluctance to demystify miracles.
The DeValera papers.	30	Pope John Paul II's pontificate draws to a close but Catholic Church seems unable to plan for future.
The politics of appeasement and DeValera's Constitution. Dermot Clifford favourite for Dublin. Archbishopric.	31	

Aug.

1987		1996
Woman-church in the US.	1	
Rush church appeals.	3	
Churches urged to work for change in society.	5	Catholic secondary school in east Belfast is set on fire – loyalists believed to be responsible.
Pope praises Bishop's stand in divorce.	8	
	9	Catholics in Omagh, Co Tyrone donate £1500 to help repair Methodist church vandalised during recent trouble.
Fr Donal Ó Cuilleanain appointed head of Opus Dei.	11	
Peace groups awarded grants.	14	
Inter church group visits North.		
Pat McCartan attacks Catholic church on Constitution.	19	
	21	International Congress on Child Abuse and Neglect – 50 priests and brothers treated for child abuse.
Irish church group in Russia.	22	
	23	David Emmet is charged with stealing a nun's handbag while she was at church.
Church delegation returns.	25	
	27	Maureen Brazil reports on need to place more emphasis on Mary Magdalene and other Biblical women.
Sean Mac Reamoinn on Ireland and Vatican II.	28	Archbishop of Cashel and Emly tells priests to go ahead with weddings that break Family Law Act.
	29	Church leaders condemn boycotts of Protestant businesses in North.
Reaction to MRBI survey on Irish attitudes.	31	Report on the planned visit to France of the Pope – Some Catholics resign from church in protest.

1987		1996
	Sept.	
Bishop Newman defends Hierarchy in Browne scheme.	1	
Catholic Church is accused on ecumenism.		
Details of MRBI survey on Irish attitudes	2	
MRBI survey on the Catholic church.		
	3	Jim Duffy argues that current liberal agenda is variation of Catholic conservatism.
Dublin diocese; liberals need not apply	4	Archbishop Connell warns that CRG proposals for funding of Catholic hospitals would lead to their destruction.
Dr Joseph Cassidy appointed Archbishop of Tuam.		
	5	Fr Padraig Standún homily warns Catholic Church on women priests.
		Public funding of Catholic hospitals – Dr Connell to speak to Constitution Reform Group.
		Rory O'Hanlon calls on Irish Catholics to mark Popes ordination anniversary.
		Archbishop Connell's criticism of Constitution Group on public funding of hospitals – comment by Gerry Whyte.
70 seminarians enter Maynooth.	7	Birmingham traffic halted for priest's funeral.
Delay in appointing Archbishop to Dublin diocese.		
St Mark's church to be sold.	9	Nuala O'Faolain criticises Archbishop Connell's stance on the sterilisation of women.
	12	Catholic Hierarchy asks for derogation to take action against priests involved in child sexual abuse.
Cardinal Ó Fiaich sees benefit of Anglo-Irish accord.	14	
Would women's role change the priesthood.		
Cardinal Ó Fiaich's speech on the North.	15	
US Catholics spurn the Papal megastars.		
Cardinal Ó Fiaich in Bonn.	16	Politicians condemn loyalist blocades of Catholic churches in Co Antrim, NI.
		Mass-goers in three Co Antrim towns are jeered by loyalist protesters.
	17	DUP and SDLP to discuss loyalist pickets of Catholic churches in Co Antrim.
		National Conference of Priests of Ireland – Dr Brady emphasises opportunities for lay involvement.
Church leaders appeal for research on sectarianism.	18	Cardinal Basil Hume says celibacy rule for priests is not 'divine law'.
	20	Resignation of Bishop Roderick Wright in Scotland renews debate on priestly celibacy.
		Rumours suggest the resignation of Cardinal Cahal Daly as Archbishop of Armagh is imminent.

1987

Woman admits that missing Scottish Bishop Roderick Wright is the father of her 15-year-old son.

21 Scottish Bishop Roderick Wright denied allegations of an affair 3 years ago.

Andy Pollak analyses the divisions in France between the Catholic Church and secular republicans.

Some women involved with Catholic priests speak about their relationships.

Kevin Hegarty calls on the Catholic Church to debate more openly the issue of celibacy of priests.

Priests and Bishops breaking the vows of celibacy is nothing new for the Catholic Church.

Pope John Paul II says Mass in Brittany during his visit to France.

Call for debate on celibacy among priests in the Catholic Church.

National conference of priests of Ireland.

23 Campaign to oppose Bill on Church in education.

Trimble calls for end to Loyalist picketing of Catholic churches.

Topics for Synod of Bishops outlined.
A pyramid or a Penal Law monument.

25 Andy Pollak on the Bishop Wright scandal, the Scottish Catholic Hierarchy and the media.

Maynooth; in debt to its history.
Bord Pleanala hearing on Rush church.
Bishop Cassidy is the right man for Dublin.

26 Article by Fr Jackie Collins says celibacy should be voluntary.

Faith, hope and laity.

30 Dr Martin Mansergh says society moving away from ethos majority dominance.

Some loyalist protests outside Catholic Churches suspended.

Oct.

1 Cardinal Cahal Daly retires as Catholic Primate and Archbishop of Armagh.

Profile of Mgr Sean Brady who succeeds Cardinal Cahal Daly who retires today.

Rite and Reason: sexual misconduct by clergy.

2 Retirement of Cardinal Daly: speech calls for IRA ceasefire/ Sean Brady takes over.

Retirement of Cardinal Daly: Andy Pollak reviews his career.

Retirement of Cardinal Daly: Tributes from politicians and clergy.

Retirement of Cardinal Daly: Sean Mac Reamoinn writes of his personal courage

Retirement of Cardinal Daly: Andy Pollak reviews his life and influence

1987		1996
Bishop Hannon warns of narrow views of history. Cardinal urges Church to speed up canonisation.	3	As Cardinal Cahal Daly retires, Paul Arthur looks back at his contribution to the Church and NI in a time of crisis.
	4	Fintan O'Toole critical of Cardinal Daly
Greater role for women in Catholic church urged. Bishop warns Family Solidarity on social issues.	5	File on sex abuse by Dublin priests sent to DPP. Beatification of Edmund Rice – large number of Irish in Rome. Andy Pollak talks to one of men alleging child abuse by Dublin priest.
Top Vatican posts urged for women at Synod of Bishops. Dr Desmond Williams urges caution on extradition. Speculation on Archbishop post. A long wait.	6	
	7	Report of beatification of Edmund Rice RUC arrest loyalist pickets outside Ballymena Catholic Church.
Bishops told of value of sexual intimacy at Synod.	8	Bishop Jim Moriarty speaks on drugs protests, criminal justice, etc at Mass at start of law term. Rite and Reason: Ann Thurston on priesthood and celibacy.
	9	Comiskey thanks protestants for support during media controversy and absence. Tributes to late Bishop of Cork and Ross, Dr Michael Murphy.
Cardinal Ó Fiaich urges wider role for women.	10	Irish Bishops Conference seeks Vatican permission to change dates of certain holy days.
	12	Andy Pollak reports on how the Vatican feels about the current state of the Catholic Church in Ireland.
New parish priest clashes with parish-ioners.	14	Bishop of Clogher, Dr Joseph Duffy remarks on the drastic drop in vocations for the priesthood.
Bishop of Cork defends decision on parish priest.	15	
Bishop's group criticises health service policy.	16	
	17	Two holy days moved from Thursday to following Sunday, and other changes/ Bishops' autumn meeting.
Dr Cassidy installed Archbishop of Tuam.	19	
	21	INTO Conference: exclusion of religious schools from equality legislation. Archbishop Desmond O'Connell warns of 'new forms of social disorder'.
Lay brothers form association.	22	Rite and reason: Fr Walter Forde on the Catholic Church and the media.
	24	Mary Holland examines 'The Common Good' a pamphlet issued by the Catholic Church in the UK.

1987		1996

Parishioners attempt to save Cratloe 27
church.
Legitimacy of Dr Murphy as Bishop
affirmed in statement.
Plans for Cratloe church are cancelled. 28
Court hearing on Rath parish row. 29
Final list for Dublin's Archbishop. 30 Brother Alphonsus walks free from court
after sex abuse charges dropped.

Temporary agreement in Rath parish 31
row case.
Bishop Daly reaffirms stand on IRA
funerals in church.

Nov.
1 New Catholic Primate Archbishop Sean
Brady stresses need for patience on peace
Fintan O'Toole on state sanctioning of
sectarian education – Employment
Equality Act.
2 Article on Archbishop Sean Brady to be
installed as Primate tomorrow.
Gun used in IRA funerals used in two 4 Dr Sean Brady refers to Northern situa-
Derry murders. tion at his installation as new Catholic
Primate.
Irish Labour History Conference:
Catholic Church's introduction with
trade union education is discussed.
5 Dr Connell says parents have a right for
school ethos to be preserved.
Priest attacks An Taisce protest against 7
pre-fab church.
Dublin clergy support Dr Murray for 9 Andy Pollak on the success of 'Faith of
Archbishop post. Our Fathers' album.
Court case over sale of rare books from 10
St Canice's cathedral.
Aftermath of Enniskillen bombing.
The position of the Catholic Church. 11 Dr Eamonn Walsh warns of changing
bail laws.
Nuala O'Faolain on the success of CD
'Faith of Our Fathers'.
Campaign to separate church and state 12 Rite and reason: Cecil Fitzpatrick defends
launched. the Orange Order re recognition of
Roman Catholics.
Fr O'Donovan agrees to stand as parish 13 Prof Mary McAleese says root of
priest of Rath. sectarianism not school but home.
Dara Ó Maoildhia wants to set up Celtic
Church on Inis Mór.
Inter-church group urges talks on North. 14 Tridentine Bishop Michael Cox launches
phone confession service to help restore
Offaly church.
Bail law changes criticised by Irish
Commission for Justice and Peace.
Bail referendum: intervention of
Catholic Bishops.

1987		1996
	15	Removal of priest from Inis Oirr – Archbishop may have acted too hastily.
	16	Archbishop Dr Connell criticises Quinn for saying Ireland is 'a post-Catholic pluralist republic'.
Alderdice welcomes churches' statement on terrorism.	17	
Religious appeal on budget aid for the poor.		
Irish Franciscan to be beatified.		
British Bishops condemn Enniskillen bombing.	18	Bail referendum – Dr Connell denies he called for 'no' vote.
Catholic Bishops' statement on the cuts in health and education.	19	Canon Sean Durkan persuaded not to resign after row with choir.
Dr Cahal Daly condemns funeral violence.		
Priest drafts reform proposals on illegals in the USA.	20	2 separate cases of Co. Wexford priests sexually assaulting young males – adjourned.
Hierarchy appeals on abolition of NSSB.	21	Bishop calls on Catholics to make more use of Bible.
Irish Franciscan beatified.	23	
St Paul's church closed.		
No politicians invited to Enniskillen ceremony.	24	
	25	Joe Armstrong writes on clerical celibacy
	26	Death of church architect Thomas F. Sheahan.
		Rite and Reason: Tom Hayes on the Catholic Church and the media.
Newborn baby left in Dublin church.	27	Bail referendum: Andy Pollak on the role of the churches in the debate.
	28	Bishops warn politicians of 'pandering to vested interests'.
		Employment equality legislation changes concern Catholic bishops.
	29	INTO rejects new measures for governing primary schools.
	30	Alison O'Connor reports on the horrific case of John Brown, abused as a child and in turn abused young boys himself.
	Dec.	
Recess school dispute continues.	1	
Nuncio urged to defend Dr Murray against allegations.	3	Saturday's violent protest at Catholic Church, Ballymena, blamed on loyalist paramilitaries.
		Arson attack on Catholic Church in north Belfast.
	4	Picketing of churches in NI – Paisley and others try to stop.
Dragging it out for Dublin.	5	4 main church leaders condemn pickets outside North Masses.
		US Catholic parishes donate presents for Irish prisoners.

1987

Emigrant advice office opens.
Former Bishop, Dr Thomas McDonnell dies.
Bishop Patrick Lennon retires.

Gerry Adams invites Bishop to North over GAA RUC ban.

Bishop Desmond Williams urges action on homeless.
The Church, the state and Thomas Bodkin.
Reactions to priests and supergrass claim.

1996

9

10 Harryville church subjected to arson attack.

11

12 C of I concerned at Joe O'Toole's remarks on 'sectarianism' in school enrolment policies.

16 Results of latest MRBI/*Irish Times* opinion poll shows a shift in the country's religious attitudes.
Three people arrested following protests outside Catholic Church in Ballymena at the weekend.

17 Rite and Reason: Canonisation of Matt Talbot.

18 Pope calls for granting of amnesties after armed conflict.

19 St Disen to be erased from church calendars.

21 Seamus Martin speaks to Father Pyotr, a married priest of the Uniate Catholic Church in the Ukraine.

23 60 loyalist protesters gather outside Church in Harryville during Saturday evening Mass.

24 Catholic Church and Church of Ireland unite in condemning 'tit-for-tat' loyalist/republican violence.

28

30 Archbishop Desmond Connell says divorce increases pressures on family life

31 Rite and Reason: Catholics abandoning the Church and damnation no longer being preached.

INDEX

sexual morality, 13, 138–9, 225, 230, 234, 249, 255. *See also* celibacy
  church scandals, 216–19
  control of, 129–30, 156–7
  control of women, 188–90, 200
  control through Confession, 145–6
  drinking groups, 172–3
  role of mother, 179, 193–5
  18th c. Europe, 161–2
Shorter, E., 161
Sisters of Charity, 125, 126, 127, 133, 228
Sisters of Mercy, 122, 125, 127
  Goldenbridge, 228–9
Sisters of Our Lady of Charity, 228
'slagging', 172–3, 197, 254
Smyth, Fr Brendan, 217, 218–19, 260n, 289n
social class, 8, 67, 76, 131–2, 175, 233
  economic changes, 182–3
  and loyalty to Church, 68–9
  of priests, 119–20, 148
  priests and politicians, 222–3
  and religious observance, 69–73
social control, 13, 17, 137–40
  mechanisms of, 140–51
social inequality, 76, 258
social legislation, 78–82, 222
social surveys, 50
social welfare, 61–3, 76, 90, 125, 255
  under British rule, 109–11
  decline in Church influence, 227–31
  state control, 258
Society for Promoting the Education of the Poor in Ireland, 123
Society for the Protection of the Unborn Child (SPUC), 56
sociology, 7, 66, 97
  structure-agency debate, 270n
  study of religion, 9–12, 207, 245–6
Spain, 38, 107, 174
stations, 142
Stay Safe Programme, 224–5
stem-family system, 13, 177, 199, 255
  family relationships, 172–3
  inheritance, 90, 160, 164, 166
  modernisation, 8, 9
  and postponed marriage, 168
  role of mothers, 186–7, 248–9
sterilisation, 226
Stivers, R., 170–3, 189, 198
structuralism, 262n
Studies, 3
superstitions, 25–6
Sweden, 160
symbolic capital, 68, 208

Talbot, Blessed Matt, 132
Taylor, L., 28, 188, 194
teachers, 32, 59, 74
  Catholic training, 123–4
  control of, 59, 60, 224
  declining numbers of religious, 225
  under Penal Laws, 105
television, 92–3

temperance movement, 189, 280n
tenant farmers, 164, 165–6, 167
  civilising process, 150, 157
  emergence of, 119, 137, 175, 182–4, 199
theocracy, 80
time and space, regulation of, 152–3
Treatise on the Decalogue, 145
Trinity College, Dublin, 60, 164
Trocaire, 44, 222
Troy, Dr, Archbishop of Dublin, 102, 114

Ultramontanism, 117, 134, 257
United States of America, 83, 112, 232, 253
  adoptions, 230
  Irish-Americans, 193, 204
  ratio of priests, 46
universities, 60
unmarried mothers, 228, 230, 240
urbanisation, 130–1

Valvy, Benedict, 133, 147, 148
vasectomy clinic, 226
Vatican Council, 1870, 42
Vatican II, 45, 53, 88, 214
  and women, 260n
Vocational Education Committees, 265n
vocationalism, 60, 76
vocations
  decline in, 3, 4, 40, 52–3, 207, 211–14, 225, 227, 257
  role of mothers, 13, 193, 238–9
  19th c. training, 118

wakes, 26, 27, 138
Walsh, Dr William, Bishop of Killaloe, 142, 219, 221, 286–7n
Warner, Marina, 283n
Waterloo, Battle of, 164, 180–1
Weber, Max, 6, 7, 10–11, 82, 205, 244–5, 280n
  on Catholicism, 22, 23
  on celibacy, 42
Whelan, C., 203, 204, 208, 285n
Whiteboys, 108, 139
Whyte, J., 60, 75, 77, 78, 79, 81
Wilde, Sir William, 136
Wolfe Tone, Theobald, 114
women, 12, 63. *See also* mothers
  changing role of, 179–87, 199, 239
  control of sexuality, 5, 145–6, 188–90
  decline in Church influence on, 238–40
  domestic role, 170–1
  emancipation, 162
  employment of, 167–8, 175
  historical role, 178
women priests, 3, 4, 5, 237
women's liberation movement, 239–40
Women's Right to Choose Group, 83
workhouses, 109–10, 110, 126
World Federation of Doctors who Respect Human Life, 83
Wright, Bishop, 216, 288n

'X' case, 220